Praise for

LINCOLN AND CITIZENS' RIGHTS
IN CIVIL WAR MISSOURI

"A thorough and balanced account of Lincoln's relations with his military commanders and their Unionist civilian counterparts in war-torn Missouri. Boman effectively reveals Lincoln's conscientious efforts and skill in dealing with military tribunals, restoring order, and nudging the parties towards the restoration of civilian government."

—PATER KARSTEN,
author of *Between Law and Custom: "High" and "Low" Legal Cultures in the Lands of the British Diaspora, 1600–1900*

"While most studies of civil liberties during the Civil War have surveyed the national landscape, *Lincoln and Citizens' Rights in Civil War Missouri* focuses instead on the nation's most divided state. Even in this cauldron of lawlessness and violence, Lincoln's dealings with both civilian and military leaders showed him to be astonishingly respectful of the rule of law. Boman's deft telling of this story makes a significant contribution to Civil War scholarship."

—TIMOTHY S. HUEBNER,
author of *The Taney Court: Justices, Rulings, and Legacy*

"Civil War Missouri was a state divided against itself. Federal commanders, and some Missourians, believed harsh measures under the laws of war were necessary to control disloyal elements of the population, while their opponents demanded full respect for civil rights under the Constitution. In *Lincoln and Citizens' Rights in Civil War Missouri*, Dennis Boman has produced a well-written, thorough, and balanced account that explains the difficult legal and policy dilemmas state and federal officials faced, while sympathetically capturing the hardships endured by individual Missourians."

—BURRUS M. CARNAHAN,
author of *Act of Justice: Lincoln's Emancipation Proclamation and the Law of War*

"Dennis K. Boman has written the definitive account of the Lincoln administration's controversial efforts to cope with the secession movement in Missouri. His conclusions, measured and fair, are based on years of research in the Missouri legal archives. All Civil War scholars, particularly those with an interest in the continuing debate over Lincoln's handling of civil liberties, are in his debt."

—DAN MONROE,
author of *The Republican Vision of John Tyler*

DURING THE CIVIL WAR, the state of Missouri presented President Abraham Lincoln, United States military commanders, and state officials with an array of complex and difficult problems. Although Missouri did not secede, a large minority of residents owned slaves, sympathized with secession, or favored the Confederacy. Many residents joined a Confederate state militia, became pro-Confederate guerrillas, or helped the cause of the South in some subversive manner. In order to subdue such disloyalty, Lincoln supported Missouri's provisional Unionist government by ordering troops into the state and approving an array of measures that ultimately infringed on the civil liberties of residents. In this thorough investigation of these policies, Dennis K. Boman reveals the difficulties that the president, military officials, and state authorities faced in trying to curb traitorous activity while upholding the spirit of the United States Constitution. Boman explains that despite Lincoln's desire to disentangle himself from Missouri policy matters, he was never able to do so.

Lincoln's challenge in Missouri continued even after the United States Army defeated the state's Confederate militia. Attention quickly turned to preventing Confederate guerrillas from attacking Missouri's railway system and from ruthlessly murdering, pillaging, and terrorizing loyal inhabitants. Eventually military officials established tribunals to prosecute captured insurgents. In his role as commander-in-chief, Lincoln oversaw these tribunals and worked with Missouri governor Hamilton R. Gamble in establishing additional policies to repress acts of subversion while simultaneously protecting constitutional rights—an incredibly difficult balancing act.

For example, while supporting the suppression of disloyal newspapers and the arrest of persons suspected of aiding the enemy, Lincoln repealed orders violating property rights when they conflicted with federal law. While mitigating the severity of sentences handed down by military courts, Boman shows, Lincoln advocated requiring voters and officeholders to take loyalty oaths and countenanced the summary execution of guerrillas captured with weapons in the field.

One of the first books to explore Lincoln's role in dealing with an extensive guerrilla insurgency, *Lincoln and Citizens' Rights in Civil War Missouri* illustrates the difficulty of suppressing dissent while upholding the Constitution, a feat as complicated during the Civil War as it is for the War on Terror.

Cheryl Stockton

Dennis K. Boman is the author of *Lincoln's Resolute Unionist: Hamilton Gamble, Dred Scott Dissenter and Missouri's Civil War Governor* and *Abiel Leonard: Yankee Slaveholder, Eminent Jurist, and Passionate Unionist.* He is an assistant professor of history for Yorktown University.

LINCOLN AND CITIZENS' RIGHTS
IN CIVIL WAR MISSOURI

CONFLICTING WORLDS

New Dimensions of the American Civil War

T. Michael Parrish, Series Editor

LINCOLN AND CITIZENS' RIGHTS IN CIVIL WAR MISSOURI

BALANCING FREEDOM AND SECURITY

Dennis K. Boman

LOUISIANA STATE UNIVERSITY PRESS ⁣)⁣(⁣ BATON ROUGE

Published by Louisiana State University Press
Copyright © 2011 by Louisiana State University Press
All rights reserved
Manufactured in the United States of America
First printing

DESIGNER: Michelle A. Neustrom
TYPEFACES: Minion Pro, text; No. 3 Type, display
TYPESETTER:Thomson Digital, Inc.
PRINTER: McNaughton & Gunn, Inc.
BINDER: John H. Dekker & Sons

Library of Congress Cataloging-in-Publication Data
Boman, Dennis K.
  Lincoln and citizens' rights in Civil War Missouri : balancing security and
freedom / Dennis K. Boman.
      p. cm. — (New dimensions of the American Civil War)
  Includes bibliographical references and index.
  ISBN 978-0-8071-3693-5 (cloth : alk. paper) 1. Lincoln, Abraham,
1809–1865—Views on civil rights. 2. Civil rights—Missouri—History—
19th century. 3. Missouri—History—Civil War, 1861–1865. 4. Military
government—Missouri—History—19th century. 5. Missouri—Politics and
government—1861–1865. 6. Lincoln, Abraham, 1809–1865—Influence.
I. Title.
  E457.2.B67 2010
  973.7092—dc22

                                                            2010009336

The paper in this book meets the guidelines for permanence and durability of
the Committee on Production Guidelines for Book Longevity of the Council
on Library Resources. ∞

For Jillon

Contents

Acknowledgments

I AM DEEPLY GRATEFUL to the Missouri Supreme Court Historical Society for its financial support through its Robert Eldridge Seiler fellowship awarded in 2006. I am also appreciative of the interest and encouragement different members of the Supreme Court of Missouri exhibited in this study, especially Judges Michael A. Wolff and Stephen N. Limbaugh Jr., the latter now serving as a United States district judge in the Eastern District of Missouri.

A number of persons offered useful suggestions, criticism, and support to this project. Among these were Dan Monroe, Griswold Distinguished Professor of History at Millikin University, Silvana Siddali, associate professor of history at Saint Louis University, Burrus Carnahan, professorial lecturer in law at George Washington University Law School, and Missouri state historian James Denny. Their insights and help greatly improved this work.

I would be remiss if I did not recognize and thank those who directed me to interesting and important material for this work. At the Missouri State Archives in Jefferson City, Senior Reference Archivist Patsy Luebbert proved to be an invaluable source of information. In particular, I am indebted to Archivist Steven Mitchell for his guidance to Missouri's militia records. Special appreciation must go to Kenneth Winn, former director of the state archives, under whose leadership were developed finding aids to the files of the Union Provost Marshal Records. Michael Everman, archivist for the local records program, was instrumental in my research of court records. Dennis Northcott, archivist at the Missouri Historical Society, also provided much help in the use of their resources. And finally, one of my former students at Saint Louis University, Brian Fallon, introduced me to some interesting sources on the Catholic Archdiocese of St. Louis.

LINCOLN AND CITIZENS' RIGHTS
IN CIVIL WAR MISSOURI

INTRODUCTION
Lincoln and Civil Liberties in Missouri

Is there, in all republics, this inherent, and fatal weakness? Must a government, of necessity, be too strong for the liberties of its own people, or too weak to maintain its own existence?

—ABRAHAM LINCOLN, special message to Congress, July 4, 1861

THE SUBJECT OF THIS BOOK is Abraham Lincoln's and his administration's management of civil liberties in Missouri. Through this study, much can be learned about the president's decision making as commander in chief, including his reasons for imposing emergency wartime measures. Despite his reluctance, Lincoln found it necessary to become involved in Missouri's tangled affairs during a series of crises, both military and political, which seemed to erupt regularly from the war's beginning. Indeed, many of these difficulties proved to be intractable and were representative of those the president confronted in the rest of the country. One was the threat posed by civilians supporting the South. Some of these supporters, comprising a sizable minority of Missouri's population, provided intelligence to the enemy and organized into irregular units. These guerrilla bands stole and destroyed civilian and public property, ambushed Union forces, murdered civilians, and drove many persons from their homes. Such tactics forced Lincoln to maintain a large force in Missouri. The circumstances precipitated increasingly bitter political infighting among Unionists who disagreed about the wisdom of emancipation, retaliatory measures against insurgents and their supporters, and the competency of military commanders. Unionists soon divided into Conservative and Radical factions. Conservative Unionists believed that security could best be preserved through the establishment of an expanded state militia and a quick restoration of pre-war circumstances, including social and legal protections of slavery. They also thought that northern federal troops often did more harm than good by stealing slaves and insulting slaveholders, thereby pushing neutral and loyal men to support secession. Radical Unionists generally advocated the greater suppression of civil liberties and the employment of more severe measures against guerrillas and their supporters. Both sides frequently appealed to Lincoln to settle policy disputes and lobbied him to appoint departmental commanders they believed would support their policy preferences. After one of these intense disputes, an exasperated Lincoln wrote that "it is very painful to me that you in Missouri can not, or will not, settle your factional quarrel among yourselves. I have been tormented beyond endurance for months by both sides. Neither side pays the least respect to my appeals to your reason."[1]

As president, Lincoln took extraordinary measures to preserve the Union. Citing these, then and now some critics accused him of acting as a military dictator or, at the very least, of having greatly exceeded his constitutional authority. The irony of the accusation of military dictatorship must have been immediately evident to Lincoln, for as a young man, in one of his first public speeches, he had urged his listeners to be vigilant to prevent the usurpation of the United States government by a strong man intent upon subverting our great political system founded upon the classical liberal ideals of the rule of law, representative government, and personal and economic freedom. United States constitutional historian Herman Belz notes that "where real and distinct limitations on the exercise of governmental power exist, in the form of counterbalancing authority and institutions of accountability," there dictatorship cannot exist. In other words, those accusing Lincoln of acting like a dictator must explain how this accusation squares with the operation of an opposition party and press and the holding of state and national elections throughout the war, activities a real dictator would never tolerate. Moreover, a short time before the war Lincoln had demonstrated a genuine commitment to individual civil liberties in his efforts to prevent the further extension of slavery. Lincoln's commitment was founded upon his belief in the natural right of everyone, black as well as white, to "life, liberty, and the pursuit of happiness." Believing as he did that the Union and the Constitution of the United States were built upon this only partially fulfilled ideal, throughout his political life Lincoln worked toward its greater fulfillment, fearing that a retrograde movement would eventually and almost imperceptibly cause the erosion of other liberties. Such idealism and past behavior is difficult to reconcile with some writers' portrayal of Lincoln as someone dismissive of civil liberties and anxious to accumulate as much power to himself as possible.[2]

Likewise, when one considers Lincoln's opposition to slavery it is clear that he found the institution morally abhorrent and objectionable, it being the very embodiment of despotism. These strong antislavery views explain Lincoln's opposition to the 1854 Kansas-Nebraska Act, which repealed the Missouri Compromise's prohibition of slavery in the Kansas territory. He had long hoped that with slavery's confinement to the South the "peculiar institution" would eventually die a painless and unmourned death. When it became clear to him, however, that the Missouri Compromise could only be restored through political action, Lincoln took to the stump and vigorously opposed other attempts to promote slavery. Repeal of the Missouri Compromise, Lincoln believed, was part of the slave states' plan to expand slavery and nationalize the institution. Until the time of his nomination for the presidency in 1860, Lincoln vigorously opposed the proslavery Dred Scott decision, the Lecompton Constitution, and the establishment of a federal slave code. By 1855 the Whig Party, of which he had long been a member, had faded from the political landscape. Lincoln eventually joined the Republican Party, which stood firmly against the further extension of slavery. As president-elect he refused to abandon the Republican principle that slavery should not be permitted to spread further into the territories. As he advised his wavering friend Lyman Trumbull: "Stand firm. The tug has to come, & better now, than any time hereafter."[3]

In considering his performance as commander in chief, one must remember that Lincoln allowed his military commanders to manage their departments independently, preferring to intervene only when necessary. Such restraint was pragmatic and wise, given his inexperience concerning military matters and the great number of difficult questions he confronted daily. Little interested in theory and the abstract formulation of issues, Lincoln sought to understand them from a practical perspective. Unfortunately, this approach occasionally allowed for the unnecessary violation of civil liberties, for in focusing upon the practical, the rights of the individual were sometimes forgotten, or at least subordinated in importance, a circumstance which might have been avoided more often if specific guidelines had been established earlier. Moreover, Lincoln's judgment concerning the character of some political and military leaders was unsound, leading to the unnecessary violation of Missourians' civil liberties. A prime example of this is Lincoln's incredulity concerning reports of depredations and murder committed by Kansas troops under the leadership of United States Senator James Lane. Apparently, Lincoln found it impossible to believe that his friend, whom he knew as a supporter and confidant, could be responsible.[4]

When considering Lincoln's handling of civil liberty issues, it should be remembered that certain principles, which appear obvious today, were unclear at the time. Perhaps this also explains why it was two years into the conflict before a written code for the Union military was issued to guide its commanders, officers, and men on the proper conduct of the war. While some criticism of Lincoln and the military is warranted for this deficiency, one must remember that the issuance of "Lieber's Code," as it came to be known, was the first example of a government establishing written rules of war for its military. The creation of the code was prompted by the realization that because most officers and soldiers, including many general officers, were volunteers unschooled in military tactics, law, and discipline, a manual providing instruction in the conduct of war and the occupation of territory was needed. Named for its principal drafter Francis Lieber, jurist and law professor of Columbia College, Lieber's Code would remain the basis for the rules of war adopted by the United States military to the end of World War One. Later, it also became the starting point for cooperation among various European nations which met in a series of international conventions seeking agreement on the proper conduct of armed forces in the field. These efforts eventuated in the drafting of the Hague Convention on Land Warfare (1899 and 1907), agreements to which the United States and many European governments are still signatories.[5]

When considering Lincoln's decision making, certain questions come naturally to mind. Did Lincoln do everything he could to insure the protection of civil liberties? During a time of war, what types of protections were incompatible with its conduct? Such a question is particularly relevant when considering the circumstances of Missouri, where a bitter guerrilla conflict continued throughout the war. Of course, in evaluating his performance, one must remember that Lincoln's decisions were often made simultaneously while confronting a number of other issues as or more important than those he faced in Missouri. Because of the great complexity of his duties, it must not be forgotten that he relied upon commanders in the field to communicate the true and relevant circumstances in their departments and to be sensitive to citizens' rights, working conscientiously to protect civilians from an overzealous prosecution of the war. However, because of the great threat to the country, Lincoln believed he was justified in taking extraordinary measures to win the war and reunite the country. In the summer of 1863 he wrote a public letter defending his policies and explaining why some measures, which might best be characterized as extraconstitutional, were necessary during times of war. The president noted that at first he was reluctant to violate individual rights, but over time he had adopted "strong measures which by degrees . . . [were] indispensable to the public safety." While the police and judiciary were capable of dealing with individuals, or even small groups of men, they were incapable of confronting a large and well-organized conspiracy to secede from the Union. Thus, this circumstance required the judicious use of his authority as commander in chief.[6]

Many previous studies of civil liberties have invariably covered much of the same ground, focusing on cases like those of Merryman, Milligan, and Vallandigham, whose circumstances, while important, are hardly neglected incidents of the war. A prominent exception is Mark E. Neely Jr.'s book, *The Fate of Liberty: Abraham Lincoln and Civil Liberties,* in which he provided an overview of the issue of civil liberties during the Civil War. Having written a survey, Neely never pretended to have offered a comprehensive and exhaustive history of the subject. In fact, such a study is impossible for anyone to complete, given the great volume of extant materials a scholar would be required to sift through and contemplate. An estimated eighty-five thousand Civil War case records are available to researchers in the Judge-Advocate records alone. Moreover, in addition to the large number of letters written to and by Lincoln, a voluminous amount of material is available in the provost marshal records, in the papers of individual participants, in the *Official Records* of the war, in contemporary newspaper accounts, and in the great volume of soldiers' correspondence and memoirs. For this reason, a more detailed understanding of civil liberty issues during the Civil War can only be gained through the efforts of many.

This study hopes to provide a fuller understanding of this subject by focusing on Missouri and thereby filling in many of the gaps left by Neely's necessarily short treatment of the state's civil liberty issues. Even limiting this study to Missouri hardly makes it a topic of manageable size, for as Neely noted it is clear that the military "arrested far more civilians in Missouri than any other state." Special attention is paid here to many rights generally taken for granted by Americans, but which were curtailed for reasons of military necessity, real or imagined. Some of these concerned freedom of expression, including the traditional rights of speech and the press. Associated with these were freedom of religion, the right to assemble, the election of representatives, and the petition of civil authorities. While the former deal mostly with political rights, other important liberties were personal and included property (of which slaves were a part), protection against arbitrary arrest, and due-process rights, which include the right against self-incrimination, the right to counsel, and protection against improper searches and seizures. However, it should be remembered that "due process of law depends upon circumstances. It varies with the subject matter and the necessities of the situation." Rights sometimes overlooked, which certainly fall under the category of civil liberties, were the freedom to travel and to live where one chooses. Put another way, when attempting to end an insidious and destructive insurgency, how far should the military be allowed to violate civil liberties to put down insurrection, preserve law and government, and protect life? Does it make any difference that the restrictions are intended to be temporary only?[7]

In judging Lincoln's handling of civil liberty issues, one must also place his decision making within the framework of the law of war as it was then understood. Even in 1861, a long history of debate existed among historians, philosophers, jurists, and theologians concerning many issues related to war. This debate, which continues to the present time and has recently intensified, considers questions such as: What constitutes a just war? What strategies and tactics are justifiable and under what circumstances? How should enemy civilians and property be treated? What about the treatment of neutrals? Prisoners? These questions naturally turn to the issues of civil liberties and human rights. How does one balance the need for security and deterrence of one's enemies with proper respect for those self-evident rights to "life, liberty, and the pursuit of happiness"? Much of the answer will depend upon how one views the nature of human rights. Are they absolute rights, that is, rights which are the possession of everyone and cannot be taken away for any reason? Or are these inherent rights forfeited, at least partially, under extreme circumstances—such as the fighting of a war—because of the threat an individual or group presents to others or to society? Most people accept the state's authority to imprison or otherwise punish persons who commit crimes, recognizing that they pose a threat to the property or lives of others. Understanding the need to protect the majority from society's criminal element, the first law codes established lists of offenses and punishments which by today's standards were very severe. It should also be noted that from the start, as is true today, acceptable behavior was different during times of peace and war. Although these rules have changed through the centuries, the major premise underlying all laws of war is the need for special rules allowing government to take extraordinary measures to protect itself. *Salus populi suprema lex esto* ("the safety of the people is the supreme law").[8]

In the seventeenth century, the great Dutch jurist Hugo Grotius wrote *De Jure Belli ac Pacis* ("Concerning the Law of War and Peace") in which he summarized and discussed the status of the law of war as it was then understood in Europe. The great value of the work was in providing the educated elite with a coherent account of the justifications of war, of accepted methods of waging war, and of limitations imposed upon the military's authority and methods. Grotius's investigations considered both ancient and contemporary law and scholarship. His work was inspired by the circumstance of war into which he had been born and the end of which he did not live long enough to observe. In his studies, he sought the discovery of principles to guide Europe in reestablishing the rule of law through the development of an international legal code which, he hoped, might bring and maintain peace. Conceiving man to be a moral and intellectual being, Grotius believed that nature bound humanity together by a common and rational intelligence often referred to as natural law, from which certain universal rights were derived. Grotius argued that these rights were not only universal but eternal, and unlike civil law could not be temporarily suspended, even during time of war. It was in the light of these principles that he considered international law and the conduct of hostilities. Grotius's magnum opus became the foundation upon which others, experts in both legal and military fields, built and revised the law of war. Different scholars and jurists adapted and transmitted many of Grotius's ideas through their own publications. Perhaps the most important of these works was Emmerich de Vattel's eighteenth-century treatise, *The Law of Nations,* which was valued for its clarity and style. This book was translated from French into

many languages and used extensively by statesmen and jurists into the period
of the American Civil War and after. It was this tradition, and the cumula-
tive experience of European and American military campaigns, upon which
Henry W. Halleck and Francis Lieber, two of Lincoln's most important and
influential advisers on military affairs, established a code of military laws as
a guide for the officer and soldier, the vast majority of whom had little or no
military experience before the war. As noted above, this guide was drafted by
Lieber and modified by a committee established by Secretary of War Edwin M.
Stanton. Lincoln approved the code in 1863.[9]

Lieber's Code represents the agreement of the military and civil authorities on what constituted the proper methods of prosecuting the war, providing
both positive and negative directives for dealing with the Confederate army,
guerrilla forces, and enemy noncombatants. Lieber's Code was a practical
guide meant to provide general direction to commanders and soldiers in
the field and was founded upon the premise that even in war men must behave within the bounds of one's duty to humanity and to God. The first article
of the code states that martial law is operative wherever an army is present in
time of war. In other words, civil authority is suspended where necessary and
the inhabitants are subject to the orders of military commanders, who must
exercise their power judiciously. In most cases, according to the code, the civil
courts should remain operative unless determined otherwise by the military
commander. While excesses must be avoided, military necessity, by which
is meant "those measures which are indispensable for securing the ends of
war," must be operative and this includes the destruction of the enemy's life
and property and the deprivation of his liberty. However, cruelty, "wanton
destruction," and poisonings were prohibited, as were "any [other] act of hostility which makes the return to peace unnecessarily difficult." In other words,
war should not be conducted without limitations upon the military's methods
and even the enemy, especially unarmed civilians, were to be spared unnecessary suffering whenever possible.[10]

With our focus upon Missouri, the second and third sections of the
code require no special notice, covering as they do matters which either
were irrelevant to Missouri or were general instructions applicable to the entire military. The fourth and fifth sections, however, instruct troops in the
tactics used against irregular forces, a very important matter for the troops in
Missouri, where throughout the conflict insurgent fighters, often referred to

as guerrillas or jayhawkers, operated in the interior of the state, wreaking a great deal of havoc through their unrelenting destruction of property and life. Those engaged in this type of illegal warfare were described as persons "not entitled to the privileges of prisoners of war, but shall be treated summarily as highway robbers or pirates."[11]

Because of the threat these insurgents' activities represented, and the difficulty in stopping them, very severe methods were employed against unlawful combatants. These irregular fighters often posed as peaceful citizens within a community which supported them, ambushing Union forces and striking against the infrastructure upon which they relied, such as railroads, and forcing many Unionist families to flee areas where the military could not protect them. Moreover, because of this violence, many of the civil courts were closed and local authorities were powerless to enforce the laws. For these reasons, irregular forces were "given no quarter," meaning that they were routinely killed if captured. This part of the code, representing the then accepted method of eradicating irregular forces, is perhaps the most disturbing feature of nineteenth-century warfare to today's sensibilities. Lincoln approved this policy and did not intervene earlier when in December 1861 General Halleck had established the same measures in Missouri through a general order. Apparently, this tactic was meant to deter men from "taking to the brush," as it was sometimes called, thereby tying down large numbers of Union forces, terrorizing peaceful citizens, and plundering property. Another concern was that with success, many more insurgents would rise, undermining the authority of the government and eroding support for the war. In Missouri these concerns sometimes led commanders to employ measures to punish those who supported the insurgents by imposing fines or banishing them from the state altogether. Lincoln intervened in some of these cases, although he was reluctant to interfere with commanders in the field, whom he considered to be "the better judge of the necessity in any particular case." But he added that "of course I must practice a general directory and revisory power in the matter." In the end, the duty of Lincoln and his military commanders was to provide security in a manner which would not unnecessarily delay, indeed should hasten, the return to civilian rule and peace.[12]

It is clear from his actions that Lincoln considered himself bound by the laws of war and the United States Constitution, and although he sought to prosecute the war vigorously, he also reserved for himself the right to mitigate punishments in individual cases, a right some contemporaries believed he indulged profligately. Nevertheless, some of his decisions remain controversial today. Ultimately, one's view of Lincoln's decision making hinges upon one's interpretation of the Constitution (especially in regard to executive authority), the statutory and military law, and ethical considerations relevant to his duties as commander in chief and responsibility to protect civil liberties.[13]

The nature of the war and its dangers must also be factored into one's consideration of his performance, remembering that unlike us Lincoln and his contemporaries struggled in the midst of the conflict without knowledge of how it would turn out. Indeed, Lincoln did not have the advantage of the information available to scholars today, who have open to them the then private papers of many of the conflict's participants and critics. Lincoln often played his cards without any knowledge of the other players' hands. Today, scholars not only know much about Lincoln's hand, but also a good deal concerning that of his opponents. Many times this advantage is forgotten when analyzing the decision making of Lincoln and other presidents, at least those whose papers and contemporaries' papers are now available for study.

Moreover, in considering Lincoln's actions, one must not forget that the Civil War was a struggle to put down an internal peril, a rebellion which threatened to break up the Union of states. If the South had been successful, Lincoln believed that the principle of secession, once established, would tend to erode the cohesion of the remaining states, leading to the further balkanization of the once stable government under the Constitution. The president explained to Congress what he believed was at stake in his message of July 4, 1861.

And this issue embraces more than the fate of these United States. It presents to the whole family of man, the question, whether a constitutional republic, or a democracy—a government of the people, by the same people—can, or cannot, maintain its territorial integrity, against its own domestic foes. It presents the question, whether discontented individuals, too few in numbers to control administration, according to organic law, in any case, can always, upon the pretences made in this case, or on any other pretences, or arbitrarily, without pretence, break up their Government, and thus practically put an end to free government upon the earth. It forces us to ask: "Is there, in all republics, this inherent, and fatal

weakness?" "Must a government, of necessity, be too *strong* for the liberties
of its own people, or too *weak* to maintain its own existence?" So viewing
the issue, no choice was left but to call out the war power of the Government; and so to resist force, employed for its destruction, by force, for its
preservation.[14]

In this scenario, as Lincoln conceived it, the war was for the very survival
of republican government. Under such circumstances the government, and
especially the executive, must employ special powers, many of them extraconstitutional, to preserve the nation.

Later in this same message to Congress, Lincoln forthrightly explained the
basis upon which he had suspended the privilege of the writ of habeas corpus, and by extension the rationale for many of his extraordinary measures in
curtailing or suspending other civil liberties normally enjoyed during peacetime. The suspension of the privilege of the writ of habeas corpus, that is, the
detainment of persons "without resort to the ordinary processes and forms of
law," the president explained, was necessary because the military suspected
those persons, such as John Merryman, to be actively supporting or foment-
ing the rebellion. Moreover, Lincoln argued that it was foolish to maintain a
scrupulous adherence to a law if in so doing great harm or even destruction
of the government could result. "Are all the laws, but one, to go unexecuted,
and the government itself go to pieces, lest that one be violated?" In other
words, the president and Congress must have a good deal of flexibility and
power to preserve the country "when . . . the public safety may require it."
Without such authority, the conspirators could shield themselves from prosecution and use the freedoms provided under the Constitution to destroy it.[15]

Because the Constitution explicitly granted the authority to suspend the
privilege of the writ during times of rebellion, in opposing Lincoln's action in
the Merryman case, pro-southern Chief Justice Roger B. Taney seized upon
a technicality, the fact that the constitutional clause providing the power was
located in article 1, section 9 of the Constitution, which pertained to Congress, not the president. Thus Taney reasoned, as many have after him, that
only Congress had the authority to suspend the privilege of the writ. This argument, however, is very problematic, for if Lincoln had abided by Taney's interpretation and waited to act until he could call a special session of Congress,
which might have been prevented from assembling by men like Merryman,

several months of great mischief against the government would have continued unchecked. What the result of such a circumstance might have been is difficult to say, but the worst-case scenario—one Lincoln would have been foolish to disregard—was that the insurgents could cut the capitol off from military reinforcements and enable a Confederate army to march north and capture the government largely unopposed. Certainly, this circumstance qualified as a danger to "the public safety."[16]

While many northerners agreed that Lincoln was justified in suspending the privilege of the writ, some wished for a fuller constitutional answer to Taney's opinion than that provided by the president in his special message to Congress. Unfortunately, the opinion of Attorney General Edward Bates, to which Lincoln referred in his message to Congress, was disappointing to many. In it Bates argued that as coequal branches of the government, the judiciary by issuing a writ was interfering in the realm of the executive where it had no constitutional authority, especially where the president as commander in chief was responsible for protecting and defending the country. In this way, Bates avoided the entire controversy concerning whom the Framers had intended to exercise the power to suspend the privilege. Whether his assertion was true or not, Bates's argument did not address the main objections to the president's action. A more satisfying answer for many supporters of the president, however, was provided by Horace Binney, a prominent Massachusetts lawyer, who challenged Taney's assertions and provided his own analysis of the constitutional clause. As Binney noted, Taney's argument might be divided broadly into two parts. In the first, the chief justice pointed to the common law roots of our own legal system and to the influence the British constitution had upon it. Noting that only Parliament could suspend the privilege of the writ of habeas corpus in England, Taney argued that it should not surprise us that the Framers of our Constitution would intend for Congress alone to have the same power. Binney, however, found this argument less than compelling, for little could be learned by relying upon lessons derived from the British constitution, which could provide only "a very defective and a very deceptive analogy for the interpretation of the Constitution of the United States."[17]

In the second part of his argument, Taney asserted that the framers had never intended for the president to have the authority to suspend the privilege of the writ, for otherwise they would have placed the clause in article 2 instead of article 1. When one considers how the suspension authority came to be in the first article of the Constitution, however, Taney's argument loses much of its force. In reviewing this history, Binney noted that the Framers had originally adopted the clause "as an amendment to the *fourth* section of the *eleventh* article of the Constitution," which in draft form of the document pertained to the judiciary. Significantly, only later did the committee of style and arrangement place it in the first article of the Constitution and reject the proposal of a member explicitly to give this power solely to Congress. It seems likely that after careful consideration concerning which branch of government should exercise the power to suspend, no firm reason could be ascertained to decide the controversy. This sequence of events demonstrates why in *Federalist 37* James Madison later explained that it was impossible to "discriminate and define with sufficient certainty [government's] three great provinces, the legislative, executive, judiciary; or even the privileges and powers of the different legislative branches." This uncertainty and the unknowable nature of future emergencies, it seems reasonable to conclude, caused the Framers to leave unsettled who should exercise the power to suspend the privilege of the writ. Thus they concluded that in times of great peril posterity should be left to decide how best to meet emergencies without the imposition of restrictions, which might, although well intentioned, prevent the republic's preservation. Moreover, as Binney noted, by far it was more important that the Framers limited the circumstances under which the suspension could be exercised.

> War, generally, was not to be a limitation of the privilege, and ought not to be. War, beyond the limits of a country leaves the courts and the laws of the country in full operation; but invasion by a foreign army or rebellion against the government overthrows or disturbs both the courts and the execution of the laws. In such cases the personal liberty of the freemen of a country becomes secondary to the public liberty of the nation and must yield for the time to a higher interest and a higher principle, the public safety.

If there was a threat to the public safety, Binney believed it mattered not at all who suspended the privilege of the writ, for whether Congress declared the emergency or not, in the end only the president, through his power as commander in chief of the country's military forces, could implement the suspension. Moreover, with the power established in the Constitution, he argued, legislative authority was superfluous. Whether Binney's interpretation is correct or not, it is clear that without the power to suspend the privilege of the writ under the circumstances he faced, and without an opportunity to call Congress to assemble promptly into special session, Lincoln would have been effectively powerless to take any action during the first months of the crisis.[18]

Indeed, this type of threat to the government may have been in the minds of the Framers, many of whom in 1787 had just passed through the crucible of war themselves. During such periods of emergency many measures beyond suspension of the privilege of the writ may be undertaken to preserve the public safety. The framers understood this, but nevertheless, they did not attempt to list these measures and the special circumstances under which they might be employed. Instead, they only designated the privilege of the writ for special notice and this not to prevent its suspension altogether, but to limit when its privilege could be denied. This is often forgotten or obscured in the debate over who has the constitutional authority to suspend the writ.[19]

In judging Lincoln's handling of civil liberties, it is important also to remember that he could not supervise every aspect of the war and had to rely upon his cabinet members to manage their departments and the military authorities to conduct operations in a lawful and ethical manner. As much as possible, Lincoln reserved his strength for monitoring progress of the war, setting policy, and intervening when necessary. For the most part, Lincoln acted prudently and did much to mitigate the severity of the war on civilians in particular. In considering these matters, it is remarkable how little he and his administration wielded their powers for partisan advantage. Indeed, Lincoln recognized from the beginning that he would need the support of Democrats as well as Republicans if the war was to be successfully prosecuted. For this reason, Lincoln appointed a number of Democrats to military command and sometimes felt compelled to support those whose performance, like that of some Republican commanders, was considered to be lackluster or even incompetent. On occasion, however, he erred by allowing military abuses to continue because of his reluctance to intervene in matters about which he believed commanders were better informed. Moreover, because an individual under arrest or severe sentence was a relative or friend of a prominent person, Lincoln sometimes interceded, not allowing strict justice to be meted out and creating an inequity of treatment among those accused of violating civil or military law. Although such inconsistencies were inevitable in the prosecution of a war, by intervening Lincoln sometimes undermined the effectiveness of wartime policies. Perhaps knowing that he could not look into every case, Lincoln felt justified in interfering in special cases because of the importance of maintaining an influential person's fidelity to the Union. Lincoln also prioritized his efforts by limiting himself to the types of cases he felt were most important to review. For this reason, he spent a fair amount of his time reviewing the cases of soldiers and citizens sentenced to long prison terms and never relinquished his authority over the fate of those convicted of capital crimes.[20]

In the end, Lincoln's vigorous prosecution of the war was necessary, for otherwise the country would have remained divided and the institution of slavery left intact in the South. Such an outcome would have been the worst possible from the standpoint of civil liberties. The harshest critics of Lincoln's handling of civil liberty issues and of his caution in ending slavery, then and now, sometimes forget or refuse to consider the many practical and political matters with which he was confronted daily. While they were free to ignore these factors, Lincoln could not. When his decision making is assessed in light of these matters, the president's handling of the slavery issue in Missouri demonstrates an acute understanding of the limitations of his authority, the importance of fostering public support for wartime measures, and his reluctance to exercise more power than necessary to maintain Missouri within the Union. Rather than acting as a despot dictating policy to others, Lincoln sought to remove himself from controlling affairs in Missouri and wished to return the state to civilian control as quickly as possible (see especially chapters 6, 7, and 11, below).[21]

As noted above, in determining to what extent civil liberties should be curtailed, much of Lincoln's wartime decision making was guided by the consideration of military necessity. Such a principle, like most, can be distorted by unscrupulous leaders. Unfortunately, for this reason, the concept of military necessity has been tainted, especially after Hitler's and the German military command's distortion of it into *Kriegsraison*. For them, military necessity justified any measure, including genocide. In contrast, Lincoln and his top military commanders understood that war must be conducted within the bounds of the laws of war (see especially article 14 of Lieber's Code), the violation of which cannot be justified. Moreover, the rule of military necessity as a standard by which measures can be judged, when properly applied, often prevents the military from employing severe measures unnecessary to the achievement of its objectives. Thus, during the first year and a half of the war, Lincoln resisted pressure from many to abolish slavery, although more limited measures, authorized by Congress, permitted the employment of slaves where their labor could benefit the military and freed only those who had aided the enemy. More radical measures at that time would have been counterproductive, perhaps even fatal to the northern war effort. Later, Lincoln issued his preliminary and final emancipation proclamations, after the border states had been secured and it became clear that the southern war cause could be crippled by depriving it of its slave labor.[22]

The concept of military necessity also explains Lincoln's willingness to alter course with changing circumstances, as in his emancipation policy. Another example of this comes from the beginning of the war. At first Lincoln was willing to allow Missouri to remain neutral. However, after it became clear that Governor Claiborne F. Jackson was preparing for war and secession, Lincoln backed more forceful action to prevent this. Eventually, as discussed in chapter 1, conflict broke out between Jackson's supporters, who favored secession, and Federal General Nathaniel Lyon. After the departure of the governor and much of the legislature, Missouri was without a government. In late July 1861 the state convention, which had earlier rejected secession, supplied this deficiency by electing a provisional government headed by Hamilton R. Gamble, who led the state for the next two and a half years. The state convention met occasionally as a provisional legislature. Lincoln supported this action and the establishment of a provost-marshal system and military commissions, which amounted to an additional police and judicial system to punish civilians guilty of violating martial law. These actions became necessary when supporters of Jackson and the South organized into guerrilla bands, who destroyed railroad track and bridges, killed and drove Unionists from their homes, and committed other acts of terrorism. These depredations threatened to plunge Missouri into anarchy and necessitated the establishment of partial military rule.[23]

In presenting Lincoln's and his administration's handling of civil liberties in Missouri, in this book events and issues are placed within the context of the war as it progressed. Thus, the chapters and analysis are organized around the tenures of the military commanders in charge. As one would expect, each of these commanders differed to some degree in method, policy, and competence, although after General Henry W. Halleck's command many military policies remained fixed to the end of the war. Nevertheless, because of the ever evolving political situation in Missouri—especially with the strengthening of the Radical Republicans—Lincoln and his military commanders found it increasingly difficult to satisfy Unionists, some of whom wanted slavery ended immediately, or almost immediately, and others who wanted to preserve it or at least to abolish it only gradually and with compensation. By organizing the narrative in this way, these circumstances, and those of many other civil liberty issues, are preserved, providing the reader with a better understanding of the pressures policy makers in Missouri experienced throughout the war.

From the narrative the reader will also note Lincoln's reluctance to intrude into the daily political, police, and administrative affairs best left to the local civil and military officials most familiar with the complexities and nuances on the ground. However, beginning in late 1862, during the command of Samuel R. Curtis, Lincoln found himself increasingly pulled into the internal affairs of Missouri, prompting him to modify or overturn certain of Curtis's general orders and decisions in specific cases. Eventually, Curtis's radical policies and the opposition they engendered led Lincoln to remove him in May 1863 and again to place John M. Schofield in command. Later that year, this action led to a memorable showdown in the White House between Lincoln and Radicals from Missouri, after which these men, recognizing his independent stance on a number of policies, were much more cautious in their appeals to the president for support in their controversies with state or military officials. What emerges from an analysis of Lincoln's management of the war is that he evolved from an unsure and often reluctant executive cautious about intervening in military affairs to a more confident president willing to order or prohibit action based upon his own judgment. Thus, during the last year and a half of the war, the president became less willing to acquiesce in military commanders' ill-advised or unnecessary measures, especially those restricting civil liberties, some of which led to popular discord and harsh criticism of the administration.[24]

In May and June 1863, the actions of General Ambrose Burnside as military commander of the Department of the Ohio in arresting Clement L. Vallandigham, the infamous antiwar Democratic politician, and the suppression of the *Chicago Times* led to widespread condemnation, even among some who supported the administration's war policies generally. While defending the necessity of suppressing speech and the press as war measures, the president privately regretted Burnside's action, commuting Vallandigham's imprisonment to southern exile and ordering that the *Chicago Times* be allowed to resume its publication. The public protest caused by these events apparently convinced Lincoln that he must intervene in such matters. Later that summer, these episodes probably led to Lincoln advising General Schofield not to close Missouri newspapers, except as a last resort.[25]

Another example of Lincoln's new assertiveness was his repeal of that part of a War Department measure ordering General William S. Rosecrans to ensure that no disloyal ministers served in the Methodist Episcopal Church South, a denomination whose leaders' and lay persons' loyalty was considered especially suspect. The president believed it was unwise for the military to interfere in church affairs except under the most extreme necessity. These decisions demonstrate that while he never completely abandoned measures suppressing civil liberties, Lincoln recognized that the tendency of both military and civil authorities was to restrict freedoms unnecessarily. Moreover, as the war came to a close, the president frequently turned his attention to the task of restoring civil liberties and civilian control when he judged the restrictions no longer indispensable to ensure the public safety. This became Lincoln's pattern to the end of the war: intervening when he felt it necessary but otherwise leaving to the military commanders in the field the proper authority and freedom to prosecute the war and to govern the territory over which they were placed. The account which follows provides and analyzes the context of this decision-making process and the evolution of the president's thought on these matters in Missouri and elsewhere.[26]

1

THE SECESSION CRISIS AND MISSOURI

WHEN ABRAHAM LINCOLN TOOK the oath of office on March 4, 1861, all of the Deep South slave states had seceded from the Union and other slave states were then considering joining the Southern Confederacy. In his inaugural address he sought to reassure the South that he had "no purpose, directly or indirectly, to interfere with the institution of slavery in the States where it exists. I believe I have no lawful right to do so, and I have no inclination to do so." Moreover, he denied the right of any state to leave the Union and declared his purpose, according to the oath he had just taken, to enforce "the laws of the Union" within the limits of his constitutional authority and capabilities. Throughout his inaugural speech, the president frankly related the differences and disputes then existing between the free and slave states, neither diminishing or exaggerating their significance. Lincoln was careful to explain that he intended to pursue a moderate course and contemplated no invasion of the South or war. His desire was to find "a peaceful solution of the national troubles and the restoration of fraternal sympathies and affections." In seeking to avoid war, however, Lincoln was unwilling to recant the policies and principles upon which he had been elected. To do otherwise, he believed, would surrender, or at least undermine, republican government itself. For a victorious political party to be forced to adopt alien policies through threats of force or of secession by the minority would set a dangerous precedent, potentially destroying the important principle of majority rule. As Lincoln asserted to a wavering Republican senator who had written urging him to surrender his stand against the further extension of slavery into the territories: "The tug has to come, & better now, than any time hereafter." By showing weakness or lack of resolve Lincoln believed he would encourage further bullying by Southerners until for all practical purposes they would reverse the election, winning not through persuasion but intimidation.[1]

At the time of the inaugural, the border slave states of the Upper South were at different stages in their consideration of secession. Having lost seven states, Lincoln believed that the loss of many more would make it very difficult, if not impossible, to restore the Union, especially if civil war erupted. For this reason, Lincoln anxiously watched public affairs in the border states and sought advice from congressmen, other politicians, and friends about the policies best calculated to retain the border states in the Union. Given that two of his cabinet members were from Missouri, he was particularly well informed about it. While Montgomery Blair and Edward Bates were both from St. Louis, each man's knowledge and connections throughout the state complemented those of the other. Blair and his brother Frank were active members of the Republican Party in Missouri, which was almost exclusively headquartered in St. Louis. As former Benton Democrats, the Blairs had participated in the intraparty struggles against the proslavery wing of the Missouri Democrats before joining the Republican Party on the eve of the Civil War. Bates, who was appointed attorney general, was a valuable informant because of his ties to the Whig and American parties and his friendship with many Democrats throughout the state whom he knew through his work as a lawyer and judge. Bates provided Lincoln with insight into the more conservative elements of the state, which, while often proslavery in sentiment, were also Unionist to varying degrees.[2]

After the state legislature passed a bill calling an election in February 1861 to choose delegates to a state convention, the results demonstrated that the vast majority of the population supported preserving the Union, although a majority of the delegates elected ran as conditional, rather than unconditional, Unionists. This result must have been heartening to Lincoln, for, with only Unionist candidates elected, he could expect the convention to reject secession when it met later in February. Still, during the deliberations of the convention it became clear that a small number of its members, although they ran as Unionist candidates, really held strong secessionist views. Other delegates, especially among the Conditional Unionists, were very reluctant to be perceived as supporting Lincoln, who had garnered only 17,028 votes throughout the state, the lowest among all the presidential candidates there. The vast majority of Lincoln's support came from St. Louis County, where a substantial community of German immigrants resided and where commerce and industry were centered. Control of St. Louis was very important, for there river and railroad commerce came into the state, making it a very important and strategic part of Missouri.[3]

Offsetting these advantages, however, was the fact that all branches of the state government were under the control of Secessionists. This circumstance was the result of state constitutional provisions which gave greater representation to rural parts of the state where proslavery and secessionist sentiments were strongest. Governor Claiborne F. Jackson had been elected as a Unionist candidate supporting Stephen A. Douglas for the presidency, although in reality he was strongly in favor of secession. In his inaugural address, Jackson declared that Missouri shared common institutions and customs with the South and therefore most naturally sided with the slave states. Although declaring himself devoted to the Union, Jackson also called for a state convention "to determine Missouri's future standing in the union of states as well as asking for legislation to strengthen the state militia." By this means Governor Jackson hoped to bring Missouri out of the Union. Such a crafty and unscrupulous foe could spell future trouble once the crisis fully developed, especially since Jackson held executive authority and was the commander in chief of the state militia.[4]

Fortunately for the Unionist cause in Missouri, Hamilton R. Gamble, former chief justice of the Missouri Supreme Court and brother-in-law of Edward Bates, was elected as a delegate to the state convention. Well respected and popular, he quickly took charge of the convention's deliberations as chairman of the committee on federal relations, crafting the majority report, which declared that no reason then existed for secession and asserted that the South, if any of its constitutional rights had been violated, could seek a remedy through appeal to the federal courts. Although he agreed that Missouri and the South had reason for complaint, mostly resulting from northern criticism of slavery and attempts to prevent the return of fugitive slaves, no valid cause existed to justify secession. Gamble also appealed to the self-interest of the delegates and their constituents when he noted that once out of the Union and finding themselves unable to regain their fugitive slaves from the North, slavery would no longer be a viable institution. Such a circumstance would be quite ironic, he noted, for having seceded to be part of "a slaveholding confederacy" Missourians would soon find themselves without any slaves. The delegates rejected secession.[5]

Despite the decision of the convention, both sides continued to prepare for armed conflict, organizing paramilitary groups to defend themselves. In

St. Louis Secessionists were represented by the Minute Men, who had originally organized as young Democrats supporting Douglas for president. Similarly, the Wide Awakes had been a club for young supporters of Lincoln's
election, who during the spring began to drill for war. The legislature, although disappointed by the decision of the state convention, passed a bill in
late March authorizing the governor "to appoint four commissioners, who,
together with the mayor, should have absolute control of the police, of the local voluntary militia, of the sheriff, and of all other conservators of the peace.
This act virtually threw the whole police force of the city in the hands of the
governor, and seemed also to put under his absolute control not only the ordinary local volunteer militia, but also the Minute Men, and Wide-Awakes
or Home Guards of St. Louis." This was accomplished with the hope that by
controlling St. Louis, secession could be more easily accomplished. Governor
Jackson and other supporters of secession believed that time was on their side
and that popular opinion in Missouri would change as events progressed. In
preparation, Jackson ordered militia commanders to set up camps of instruction and publicly refused to provide troops to the federal government after
the capture of Fort Sumter. Additionally, Jackson began negotiations with
Jefferson Davis, president of the Southern Confederacy, and the governor of
Virginia in the hope of gaining weapons and other aid once hostilities began
in Missouri. He also cautioned others in support of secession to be patient,
allowing time for the state to be properly prepared for war.[6]

Governor Jackson's purchase of arms and the establishment of camps of
instruction caused concern among Unionists throughout Missouri and especially in St. Louis, near to where Camp Jackson was located. Apparently,
Governor Jackson hoped that with a strong military force under Brigadier
General Daniel M. Frost the militia could control Missouri's largest city and
seize the federal arsenal established on a bluff above the Mississippi River.
Having formed a committee of safety to monitor events and take action when
necessary, a group of St. Louis Unionists met to determine what action if
any could be taken. At the meeting was army officer Nathaniel Lyon, who
staunchly supported the government and despised all Secessionists, believing them to be traitors and revolutionaries. Lyon declared Camp Jackson "to
be a nest of secessionists; that its design was to get control of the city and if
possible carry the State out of the Union, and that the only thing which remained to be done was to capture it at once." All except one member of the

safety committee agreed and preparations were made for Lyon's assault upon the militia camp. The committee and Congressman Frank P. Blair Jr. wrote to Lincoln about the serious nature of the threat, requesting that he assign command of the St. Louis Arsenal to Captain Lyon, who immediately upon gaining the assignment worked diligently to secure the defenses and to protect the armaments and ordinance supplied there. Lyon was placed in command over the objections of General William S. Harney, commander of the department, and although loyal, he was slow to act and was considered by many Unionists to be a liability, especially because he had tried to prevent Lyon from taking vigorous action during the crisis. For this reason, Blair had asked the administration to replace Harney with Lyon as department commander. Unwilling to take this step without consulting him, Lincoln called Harney to Washington D.C. On his way, the Confederates captured and held him as prisoner. After the authorities in Richmond determined that he would not join their cause, Harney was released, whereupon he continued his journey, eventually convincing the president that he should be returned to his command.[7]

After learning that arms from the Confederate government had arrived there, upon approval of the committee, Lyon moved with his command to capture Camp Jackson on May 10. Surrounding the encampment, General Frost was left with no choice but to surrender. While Lyon and his men marched their prisoners through town, many residents of St. Louis began throwing stones at the soldiers and were fired upon, killing approximately twenty-five people, some of whom were probably innocent bystanders. When this occurred, the state legislature, having been called into special session, was deliberating on a militia bill which was quickly passed. In it all state treasury funds were diverted to provide revenue for defense of the state. Moreover, property taxes were raised and Governor Jackson was authorized to contract a $500,000 loan and to put down any insurrections.[8]

With the refusal of Governor Jackson to provide troops for national service after the hostilities at Fort Sumter and the legislature's passage of the militia bill, Lincoln consulted with different visitors and his cabinet over the fallout from the Camp Jackson Affair, as it came to be known. James E. Yeatman, Hamilton R. Gamble, and Charles Gibson, fearing that Lyon's actions could cause some neutrals to support Jackson's efforts to secede, traveled to Washington D.C. to inform the president of the circumstances in Missouri and the need for caution. They represented those moderates who feared that precipitous action could strengthen Governor Jackson's position and cause a change in popular opinion in favor of secession. During their discussions Yeatman, Gamble, and Gibson, enlisting the aid of Attorney General Bates, argued that it would be a mistake to remove Harney at that time, trusting his judgment over Lyon's, whom they considered to be without any understanding of the culture and the politics of Missouri. While this was true, it was also a relief that Lyon's forceful action had removed the military threat against the arsenal.[9]

Undoubtedly remembering the reaction of Marylanders when troops from Massachusetts marched through their state, Lincoln assured the Missourians that he would do all he could to avert a crisis, pledging, according to Gibson, that he would not send "troops through Missouri, as over a bridge, for the purpose of operating in any other place, & anticipates none." Lincoln was willing to allow the state to remain neutral in the conflict and promised to do nothing to inflame the populace. However, he also warned Missourians that if they chose to secede, their "utter destruction" would be their own fault. However, while making these conditional pledges, Lincoln also sent an order to Frank Blair for the removal of General Harney from command in Missouri if, in Blair's opinion, he was not vigorous enough in defending the interests of the government and opposing secession. Others, including Franklin A. Dick and Dr. Charles L. Bernays, editor of *Anzeiger des Westens* in St. Louis and a friend of Lincoln, also came to Washington D.C. supporting a more vigorous policy and seeking assurances that Lyon would not be removed, requests which Lincoln quickly granted. These decisions of Lincoln probably pleased and disappointed each group at the same time by adopting portions of their requests while allowing for a change of course whenever such a contingency seemed necessary. While hoping to avoid violence if possible, Lincoln prepared for hostilities if they should be forced upon him. In this his policy in Missouri was similar to that employed during the Fort Sumter crisis. Such decision making would be typical of Lincoln throughout his presidency, and very much characterized his willingness to listen and demonstrated his independence of mind.[10]

Upon his return to St. Louis, General Harney sought to quiet the anxiety and panic of some who regarded the capture of Camp Jackson as a prelude to violence against anyone favoring secession. On May 12, panic gripped many Secessionists in St. Louis causing them to flee the city or to barricade themselves within their homes in preparation for an imagined attack. According to one account, the streets were crowded with carriages and other conveyances hastily filled with peoples' property as they fled to various parts of the globe from an attack they believed would come from the Germans who had enthusiastically supported the Union. Recognizing that he was expected to assert vigorously the rights and authority of the federal government, Harney published a proclamation informing the people of Missouri that the military act recently passed by the legislature was unconstitutional and "an indirect secession ordinance," and therefore not to be obeyed. While having no desire to interfere with the legal functions of the state government, he clearly warned of his intention to protect the prerogatives of the national government and approved of the capture of Camp Jackson, which had been established in preparation for secession.[11]

Working with the federal court, which issued warrants to search the tobacco warehouse and the police station on Chestnut Street, where it was suspected that Secessionists were storing weapons, Harney ordered troops to accompany the United States marshal to enforce the warrants. At the warehouse the marshal and troops seized several hundred rifles and pistols with assorted accoutrements and ammunition; at the police station were found two cannon and a large number of rifles. In dispatches to the War Department, Harney also called for authority to raise a regiment "of Irishmen" to offset the prejudice of many against United States troops in St. Louis who were mostly German. Noting that "loyal men are now being driven from the State by the secessionists," Harney requested "10,000 stand of arms" be sent to distribute among Union men who could protect themselves and proposed that regiments be raised in Iowa and Minnesota for operations in Missouri if necessary.[12]

Harney also was given the opportunity to demonstrate his trustworthiness to Unionists in Missouri in his reply to a writ of habeas corpus issued by Samuel Treat, the federal judge of the eastern district of Missouri. The judge ordered Harney to produce Emmett MacDonald, an officer captured at Camp Jackson and the only remaining prisoner to refuse to give his parole of honor. Harney explained that his authority did not extend to the military prison in Illinois where MacDonald was being held. However, the department commander made it clear that under the circumstances he would have been reluctant to release MacDonald but promised to refer the matter to the administration. Apparently, MacDonald was successful in gaining his eventual release through the courts, or perhaps he was later exchanged, for by early July he was serving as a voluntary aide with the Missouri State Guard, the state militia organized by Governor Jackson. In that same month, after John C. Frémont was appointed commander of the Department of the West but before he had arrived in St. Louis to assume his duties, at least two more writs of habeas corpus were issued to the military, but this time by the St. Louis Criminal Court. Assistant Adjutant General Chester Harding Jr. complied with the order and appeared before the court. The judge ruled that both John Griggs Jr. and Bartholomew Barth had been detained illegally and ordered the men to be released. Perhaps he considered it prudent to avoid a controversy, for Harding released both men, apparently not believing them to present an imminent danger to the community.[13]

Unfortunately, on May 21 Harney concluded an ill-advised agreement with Sterling Price, former governor of Missouri and commander of the state guard, to keep the peace, which eventually led to his dismissal. Price, who became a determined Secessionist from the time of the attack on Camp Jackson, promised to maintain the peace in Missouri in return for Harney's assurance that he would "make [no] military movements" to avoid causing any unnecessary "excitements and jealousies" among the people. Frank Blair, who was not deceived by Price's conciliatory actions and cooperation with Harney, soon complained to Lincoln that the agreement was foolish, for it allowed Price and Jackson time to prepare for secession and war. It was also clear that throughout the state Secessionists continued to kill and drive Unionists from their homes. These depredations not only represented transgressions against the rules of war, but also the violation of many Missourians' civil liberties and the creation of a humanitarian crisis. This situation prompted Lincoln to intervene, ordering Harney to take action to protect the innocent. The president noted that despite their pledge to maintain the peace, "loyal citizens in great numbers continue to be driven from their homes. It is immaterial whether these outrages continue from inability or indisposition on the part of the State authorities to prevent them." Moreover, Harney was to act swiftly to protect the people and uphold "the authority of the United States."[14]

Lincoln's judgment that Harney was being deceived by Price is verified by their correspondence. Receiving reports from various sources that volun-

teers for Confederate service were organizing as state militia, that ammunition was coming surreptitiously into Missouri, and that Unionists were being driven from their homes, Harney transmitted this information to Price,
who at first denied the reports and then discounted some of the violence as
the acts of individuals, not representatives of the state government. Harney's
dismissal may have come, however, before he had a chance to take action, for
he was superseded in command by Nathaniel Lyon on May 31, only four days
after Lincoln's warning was written. According to one account, when he met
with Price, the members of the St. Louis safety committee were led to believe
that Harney intended to accept Governor Jackson's and Lieutenant Governor
Thomas C. Reynold's resignations and exile from Missouri. This understanding explains Frank Blair's expression of "the great disgust and dissatisfaction
to the Union men" upon learning of the Harney-Price agreement and why
Blair delivered the order for Harney's removal soon thereafter. While this discretion was given to Blair, Lincoln had warned him to use it only if "in your
judgement the necessity . . . is very urgent."[15]

In early June 1861, with Nathaniel Lyon in command of troops in Missouri,
secessionist leaders could not mistake the Lincoln administration's intention
to take more vigorous action against the state authorities' preparations for war
and secession. Secretly, Governor Jackson and Lieutenant Governor Reynolds
sought aid from Jefferson Davis, sending envoys and letters representing their
circumstances as dire, but retrievable, if provided adequate military assistance. Reynolds assured Davis that if the people of Missouri were then allowed to vote they would overwhelmingly support secession and that with the
proper organization of their troops and a supply of arms and other provisions
Missouri could field a substantial force to drive federal troops out of the state.
Reynolds cited the suspension of the privilege of the writ of habeas corpus
and the Camp Jackson affair as evidence of the grave danger with which the
state government was faced by "a military dictator" and the necessity for a
Confederate army to intervene.[16]

While the state authorities sought aid from Richmond, Lyon requested
from the Lincoln administration reinforcements from Iowa, Illinois, and
Kansas, noting the position of Confederate armies within easy striking distance of Missouri in Memphis and northern Arkansas. Lyon believed these
forces were preparing to act in concert with Secessionists in Missouri to gain
control of the state. Secretary of War Simon Cameron soon authorized Lyon

to recruit loyal Missourians for service and sent weapons to him. Moreover, Lincoln appointed John Pope and Stephen Hurlbut as general officers of volunteer forces who soon brought regiments from Illinois into northern Missouri after hostilities began. On June 11, Lyon provided Governor Jackson and General Price safe conduct to St. Louis to meet with him and Blair. The conference lasted several hours and ended when Lyon declared that he would never "consent that the State should dictate to 'his Government' as to the movement of its troops within her limits. 'This,' said he, 'means war.'" Jackson and Price immediately fled to Jefferson City, where they hastily called for troops and organized what forces they had available. They also ordered the destruction of telegraph lines and the Gasconade bridge near Jefferson City. Lyon soon pursued Jackson and the forces with him, including many state officials and legislators who supported him, confronting and routing them at Boonville. Lyon had sent troops to cut off the southern retreat of Jackson and Price, although this force turned out to be too small, being outnumbered four to one at the Battle of Carthage.[17]

Shortly after Harney's dismissal, some concern apparently existed about Lyon's capacity to command the Department of the West, for the administration added Missouri to General George B. McClellan's command and moved the headquarters of the Department of the West to Fort Leavenworth, Kansas. Soon it was decided to make Missouri part of the Department of the West and to place John C. Frémont in command, with his headquarters in St. Louis. Both Montgomery and Frank Blair had recommended Frémont, and Lincoln, perhaps recognizing that McClellan could not oversee operations in western Virginia, Kentucky, and Missouri, made the change. At the time Frémont seemed a very good choice, for he was a celebrated explorer of the West, had very strong ties to Missouri through his wife Jessie, the daughter of longtime United States Senator Thomas H. Benton, and had conducted a successful campaign to conquer California during the Mexican War.[18]

In his July 4, 1861, address to Congress, Lincoln stated that the seceding states had rejected his efforts at conciliation and war had commenced. Similarly, he noted that his efforts to avoid war in the border states, of which Missouri was a part, had failed and hostilities had begun there as well. Governor Jackson and his supporters, as did administrations in other border states, professed neutrality while arming and otherwise organizing themselves for secession, a policy meant only to delay war until they had prepared and coordinated their efforts with Richmond. Confronted by these circumstances, Lincoln established a naval blockade of southern ports and called for seventy-five thousand militia to meet the emergency of an armed insurrection. Responding to Lincoln's call for militia in Missouri, Governor Jackson stated that such a request was "illegal, unconstitutional, and revolutionary in its object, inhuman and diabolical," and that he intended never to provide troops for "such an unholy crusade."[19]

In his address, Lincoln also explained his suspension of the privilege of the writ of habeas corpus, allowing for the arrest and holding of those persons considered dangerous to the republic "when in Cases of Rebellion or Invasion the public Safety may require it." While assuring Congress that he intended to use "this authority . . . very sparingly," he nevertheless believed that these measures were absolutely necessary in light of the very real and serious threat that the Confederates then posed to the federal government and against whom the civil authority was powerless. In suspending the privilege of the writ and declaring martial law in limited areas, Lincoln believed his action was proportionate to the emergency with which he was confronted, and to his critics he asked the now often-quoted question: "Are all the laws but one to go unexecuted and the Government itself to go to pieces lest that one be violated?" In this way, Lincoln justified his decision to support General Cadwalader in defying Chief Justice Roger B. Taney's order to release John Merryman, who had been arrested for recruiting and training soldiers for the Confederate army in Maryland. If Taney's opinion in the case had prevailed, Lincoln and the military authorities would have found it very difficult, if not impossible, to stop sabotage and other insurrectionary civilian activities detrimental to the Union war effort from continuing. Moreover, as demonstrated in the cases mentioned above, without the suspension of the privilege of the writ, prisoners of war could challenge their imprisonment in civil courts. As seen below, the suspension of the writ was expanded to prevent civilians from using it to avoid the draft. Of course, those then actively trying to undermine federal authority in Missouri, most notably Lieutenant Governor Reynolds, complained loudest concerning these measures. Remarkably, he argued that military conspirators at war against the government should be shielded from imprisonment by the protections of judicial proceedings just as in peacetime.[20]

In considering Lincoln's exercise of special wartime powers, one must examine how these powers accrued to the administration and the military and whether they were truly necessary to fight the war effectively. What is evident in many cases is that Lincoln and the military and civil authorities of his administration often took unusual action in reaction to a threat, real or imagined, with which they were confronted. If their policies were reasonable and necessary in light of the threat, only then were their actions justified. Furthermore, policy should be conformable to the Constitution and the laws of war. If, however, Lincoln and his administration took extraordinary measures for partisan or other purposes, then such action should be condemned as unnecessary and illegal. It should be remembered as well that Lincoln had to rely upon his subordinates, beginning with his secretary of war and other military leaders, to respect as far as possible the constitutional and human rights of citizens. That Lincoln felt uncomfortable suspending the privilege of the writ and establishing martial law is evident from a memo in which he stated that "unless the *necessity* for these arbitrary arrests is *manifest*, and *urgent*, I prefer they should *cease*." Missouri presented a particularly difficult set of circumstances, however, for no civilian government was then in authority and a large part of the population supported secession to varying degrees; and of this group many had joined the state guard in response to Governor Jackson's call. These troops would soon combine under General Sterling Price's command and threaten to drive out the federal forces from Missouri.[21]

In response to these threats, General Lyon instituted wartime measures designed to punish Secessionists and to protect the state. That Lyon took these actions without consulting Lincoln or anyone else within the administration is clear from the fact that he considered it necessary to justify them in a letter to Secretary of War Simon Cameron. Lyon explained that he had seized the steamboat *The Swan* because its owners had conspired with Governor Jackson to smuggle into Missouri weapons captured from the United States arsenal at Baton Rouge. These weapons, captured at Camp Jackson in crates labeled as marble, consisted of howitzers, mortars, muskets, and ammunition. Lyon believed that these circumstances justified him in seizing the steamboat and thought the matter should eventually be adjudicated in the courts, although he noted that the St. Louis district judge, whom he believed had "well-known proclivities in favor of secession," might not be the best person to preside over the case. In a special order, Lyon also stationed a regiment in central Missouri to consolidate federal control there and to patrol the Missouri River from Kansas City to St. Louis. Armed boats were to patrol the river above and below Boonville to maintain "a strict surveillance" over river traffic, insuring that enemy forces could not transport troops and supplies in this way. Lyon authorized the seizure of vessels to enforce this measure and ordered the crews of the armed boat to "make frequent landings" to scout the territory, break up enemy camps, and protect "loyal citizens."[22]

In perhaps his most controversial action, on July 12 Lyon ordered the suppression of the St. Louis *Missouri State Journal,* edited by Joseph W. Tucker, who had close ties to Governor Jackson and other leaders of secession in Missouri. Tucker, a native South Carolinian who had moved to St. Louis only recently, was a staunch Secessionist and sometimes wrote in an inflammatory and insulting style against Unionists. One of the objects of these diatribes was Galusha Anderson, a Baptist minister and supporter of the Union. Perhaps Tucker's ire was inflamed further because Anderson was a northerner. Whatever the reason, Tucker wrote an editorial in which he referred to Anderson as "the devil [who] preaches at the corner of Sixth and Locust streets, and he is just the same sort of a being that he was more than eighteen hundred years ago; he wants everybody to bow down and worship him." To insure his insult did not go unnoticed, Tucker sent the editorial by special express to Anderson, who, instead of issuing the expected challenge to a duel, found the ludicrous insult uproariously funny. After his arrest, the United States Attorney James O. Broadhead searched Tucker's office, in which was found an April 28 letter from Governor Jackson explaining the delay in his efforts to bring Missouri out of the Union and requesting Tucker to support his efforts to prepare for war. This discovery led to charges of treason against Tucker, who was arrested but later fled, forfeiting a $10,000 bond he had posted for his release. Two days after the seizure of Tucker's press, Lyon ordered the suppression of three other papers considered disloyal.[23]

Without a civilian government, some concern existed that Missouri could easily slip into anarchy and that the normal functions of state government would be suspended indefinitely. Perhaps sensitive to the charge of military dictatorship, and really without a military organization able at the time to govern Missouri, the Lincoln administration privately advised Unionist leaders to reconvene the state convention and establish a provisional government. The call to reconvene was made easier by the convention's resolution adopted at the end of its first session to provide three of its leading members with the authority to recall the convention whenever they believed it necessary. This measure was possible because the legislation establishing the convention had placed no limits upon its authority, excepting only that it could not bring Missouri out of the Union without a majority vote of the people, nor was a time limit imposed upon it. Meeting in July, a committee of seven was formed to decide whether to oust the state government and replace it with another. James O. Broadhead, John B. Henderson, William A. Hall, Willard P. Hall, William Douglass, Littlebury Hendrick, and Joseph Bogy were appointed to the committee.[24]

During deliberations, a small number of the convention proposed that the state government be left as it was and that Missouri's independence be recognized in Washington D.C. Moreover, they recommended that the border states be allowed to hold elections to determine whether or not they should remain in the Union. The majority of the convention, however, believed that the Jackson administration had committed treason in openly opposing federal forces, and by fleeing the state they had vacated their duties and offices in the midst of an emergency of their own making. In its majority resolution, the committee of seven declared that it was the convention's duty to restore peace and government to Missouri, recommending that the state offices be declared vacant; that the offices of governor, lieutenant governor, and secretary of state be filled provisionally by the convention; that an election to fill these offices be held in August 1862; and that four new judges be appointed to the Missouri Supreme Court. The committee also recommended the repeal of the military act passed recently by the legislature.[25]

Arriving late to the convention, Gamble was added to the committee of seven. As happened before, because of his prestige and influence he was able to make important revisions to the document. Working quickly, he revised the committee's report, excising any mention of the Supreme Court and moving up the election to November 1861. He also required voters to take a loyalty oath and recommended the convention's work be submitted to the people. Uriel Wright, who later left Missouri for Virginia where he supported the Confederacy, led the opposition to Gamble's revised report, claiming that the convention was unconstitutionally deposing a state government elected by the people. Wright argued that only through impeachment proceedings, as provided by the state constitution, could officials be removed from office. Gamble countered that the convention derived its power from the people and was representing their interests in much the same manner as had the 1820 constitutional convention when it had created Missouri's first state government. Some members of the convention, who either did not wish to take vigorous action or were secretly Secessionists, argued against the committee report in different ways. E. K. Sayre wanted the convention to convince the Jackson administration to return and work peacefully with federal authorities. P. L. Hudgins declared that the only constitutional means to oust state officials was through impeachment, requiring the House to impeach and the Senate to convict officeholders of the indictments brought against them. The constitution further provided that vacancies be filled by election. If this advice had been adopted, the convention could not have taken any action at all, and instead could only await the reconvening of the legislature, most of whose members were then scattered throughout Missouri and the adjoining southern states and whose loyalties remained predominately with the governor and secession.[26]

The vote to vacate the offices of governor, lieutenant governor, and secretary of state was 56 to 25 and to depose the General Assembly was 52 to 28. Opposition to this came mostly from members representing counties along the Missouri River and in the southeastern corner of the state. The convention then declared itself the people's representative with the power to fill the vacated offices 54 to 27 and voted to repeal the Military Act of 1861. The delegates also agreed unanimously to submit their work to the people. Several members of the convention declined to vote to fill the vacated offices of governor, lieutenant governor, and secretary of state, believing this action to be illegal. Excusing these members from voting, the other delegates unanimously elected Gamble as governor, Willard P. Hall as lieutenant governor, and Mordecai Oliver as secretary of state. In a proclamation to the people, the convention justified its work, stating that

> it is one of the fundamental principles of our government that all political power resides in the people, and it is established beyond question, that a Convention of delegates of the people, when regularly called and assembled, possesses all the political power which the people themselves possess, and stands in the place of the assemblage of all the people in one vast mass. If there be no limitation upon the power of the Convention, made in the call of the body, then the body is possessed of unlimited political power.[27]

Now, in time, just as it was then, the convention's action was considered by some to be unconstitutional, or in the very least unwise. Historian William E. Parrish has written that of all the arguments presented at the convention, Hudgins's "opposing the convention's power of impeachment was probably the soundest," although he does not explain why he believes this to be so. However, Parrish did concede that the circumstances of Missouri were "deplorable" and that "it became necessary to set up a state administration which could work with the federal authorities in restoring peaceful conditions in Missouri. In such circumstances expediency won out." Here, Parrish mischaracterizes the convention's action, for it never impeached any officers of the state executive or legislative branches; instead it declared the offices vacant and moved to fill them. The convention did more than act in an expedient manner, it acted out of necessity, for otherwise Missouri would have been left without a civil government during a very critical time when delay could have been disastrous. Moreover, Parrish was incorrect in stating that the convention's action was "illegal," for article 13 of the state constitution provided "that the people of this State have the inherent, sole, and exclusive right . . . of altering and abolishing their Constitution and form of Government, whenever it may be necessary to their safety and happiness." If the convention had the power to abolish the constitution and the government, it also had the lesser authority to oust its officers. Jackson, after much arm twisting, had gained passage of the bill creating the convention, in the expectation that its delegates would follow the lead of many other slave states and pass a resolution calling for secession. Unionist members of the legislature had gained the reluctant concession that only a vote of the people could bring Missouri out of the Union. The Secessionists in the legislature also blundered in placing no other limits upon the convention and allowing its members to take action unintended by its creators. However, it should be remembered that the work of the convention was no more remarkable than that of former conventions held to revise state law, the law code, and the constitution. In fact precedent for ousting even lifetime-appointed officers of the state was readily available in the work of the 1849 constitutional convention, which had ended the terms of the judges then serving on the Missouri Supreme Court and made their offices elective. Whether in the end the convention's action in July 1861 was proper must be judged by the circumstances then confronting the members and by the traditions of republican government. Instead of creating a military dictatorship as an emergency measure, the convention provided the people with a Unionist provisional government in the traditional form established by Missouri's constitution. Moreover, it should not be forgotten that Governor Jackson and his allies had continued planning and preparing for secession despite the clear majority opinion of the voters against secession and the convention's rejection of it. Having failed to gain ratification of secession through the convention, the rump legislature was called into secret session, during which it passed measures giving Governor Jackson extraordinary powers to enable him to prepare for war. Therefore, it was Jackson and other state officials who precipitated the crisis to which the convention was forced to respond. Having observed many slave states secede and the efforts of Jackson surreptitiously to accomplish the same, it was necessary to act immediately. Delay was to the advantage of those favoring secession.[28]

Undoubtedly, the convention's work pleased Lincoln very much, for it had placed control of the state government into responsible Unionist hands, insuring that Missouri would not secede. Moreover, he could expect Provisional Governor Gamble to cooperate with the new military commander Frémont to establish Unionist control and secure the state militarily. Perhaps believing that many young men who had rallied to Jackson's call now realized their error, Lincoln agreed to support Governor Gamble's proclamation of pardon for anyone willing to return home and remain loyal to the government. Unfortunately, the expectation of peace would be dashed by unforeseeable events, leading to the need for even more vigorous action by the state convention, which would soon meet as an extraconstitutional legislature, and by the military in confronting a dangerous insurgency. In all of this, the Lincoln administration would be pulled along by events and struggle to balance the need to meet the very real emergencies it confronted, while at the same time, to the extent possible, trying to respect the civil liberties of the people.[29]

2

THE COMMAND OF JOHN C. FRÉMONT

JUST AFTER THE DEFEAT at the First Battle of Bull Run in the latter part of July 1861, President Abraham Lincoln and his administration were faced with a number of daunting and pressing tasks. Making a list, he noted the importance of perfecting an effective naval blockade of Confederate shipping, of training and equipping military forces for duty at different strategic points, of holding Baltimore "with a gentle, but firm, and certain hand," and of General John C. Frémont organizing his command to prepare for operations "in the West as rapidly as possible, giving rather special attention to Missouri." Although a loyal provisional state government under Governor Hamilton R. Gamble had been established, the danger still existed that combined Confederate forces in Missouri, Arkansas, Kentucky, and Tennessee might push north toward St. Louis, where a hub of strategic railroad and river communications were situated. After General Nathaniel Lyon's defeat at the Battle of Wilson's Creek on August 10, the reestablishment of Claiborne F. Jackson's secessionist administration seemed very real, especially with General Sterling Price's army then operating in southern Missouri without opposition and with other forces under Generals Gideon Pillow, William J. Hardee, and M. Jeff Thompson threatening to push through the boot-heel portion of southeastern Missouri toward St. Louis.[1]

For some time after his appointment to the command of the Department of the West, Frémont remained in New York City arranging for the procurement of weapons and supplies for his troops and preparing for his move to St. Louis where his headquarters would be established. Learning that railroad lines had been destroyed and the mails disrupted in northern Missouri, he ordered General John Pope to take command there with three regiments. On July 19, Pope issued a proclamation warning the inhabitants of the consequences of guerrilla activities. Apparently, he had delayed moving into the region earlier because of assurances from Missourians that they would maintain order on their own. Pope promised that as soon as he could be sure that guerrillas would commit no more depredations among them, he would withdraw his troops. However, he also pledged to those under arms against the federal government that he would deal with them "in the most summary manner without awaiting civil process." The presence of federal troops was necessary to protect the railroads and other communications strategically important to the region.[2]

Despite Pope's warnings and the disposition of troops along the Hannibal and St. Joseph Railroad, guerrilla forces continued operating in small bands, destroying railroad property and terrorizing supporters of the Union. Apparently, because it was owned by Bostonians, a strong prejudice existed against the Hannibal and St. Joseph Railroad, the locals sometimes referring to it as an "abolition road." To a lesser extent attacks were made against the North Missouri Railroad as well. Recognizing that great numbers of troops would be needed along the railroads to prevent further depredations, Pope coordinated the use of regiments from Iowa with the state's governor and issued a notice to the region's communities that they would be held responsible for what happened in their vicinity. The citizens of each town were informed that they would be made to pay for any damages upon the railroad for five miles on either side of their community, unless they could show that they had tried to prevent the destruction and had informed military authorities of those responsible. Failing this, an amount equal to the value of the damages would be levied immediately from the community to pay the cost of repairs. Moreover, Pope sent troops to all the county seats north of the Missouri River to organize committees of public safety, the members of which were given personal responsibility to organize and call out citizens as militia whenever guerrillas in their area threatened the public peace or property. In choosing the committees, he wanted selected "men of substance and property, preferring those of secessionist proclivities," thereby placing the burden of keeping the peace as much on them as upon Unionists. These measures were important to the war effort, Pope believed, for the railroads were necessary to bring supplies, arms, and more troops into the region. Local law enforcement, whether through inability or support for the insurgency, had done little to restore order. Hoping to further constrict the locals' ability to resist, Pope also ordered commanders to prevent "illegal assemblages," by which he probably meant to stop any

meetings where speakers sought to incite others to violence through "inflammatory words or publications." However, he also ordered that no one be arrested "for opinion's sake" alone. In his memoirs written many years after the
war, Pope argued that all of these measures were preferable to the continuance
of guerrilla warfare and the establishment of martial law. His purpose was
to drive those who wished to take part in the fighting to Price's army, leaving "those who did *not* wish to take personal part in the war to live quietly at
home, attending to their usual vocations without troops or provost marshals
to keep them in constant terror and unhappiness."[3]

In the region north of the Missouri River, despite the absence of a Confederate army, other circumstances tended to undermine Pope's and other
commanders' efforts and to create animosity between federal soldiers and
the people. One of the problems with which the Lincoln administration and
the military authorities would contend throughout the war was the misbehavior of volunteer troops in the field. Part of the difficulty was that young
men, accustomed to independent action, perceived no reason to conduct
military service differently. In the opening months of the war, politicians and
other prominent locals raised regiments by making promises to potential recruits as they would to constituents during a political canvass. Given this circumstance, it is not surprising that recently recruited volunteers believed it
no impropriety to consider the orders of their officers before obeying, many
of whom they had elected from among their ranks. Moreover, northern soldiers enlisted for various reasons, primary of which for many was the opportunity to punish Secessionists and free the slaves. Whatever the reasons, in
mid- July 1861, only a short time after troops under his command had been
ordered there, General Stephen A. Hurlbut found it necessary to warn the
commanders of volunteer regiments sent into northeastern Missouri to tolerate "no violence or robbery, no insults to women and children, no wanton
destruction of property." He also issued a general order to guide officers and
enlisted men in their duties to protect the property of law-abiding citizens
and to prevent the destruction of the railroads. They were also to stop citizens from providing the Confederacy with any material assistance. Such orders were not unique to Hurlbut's command but would be issued to soldiers
in every region where the military of both sides operated.[4]

As the new commander at Jefferson City, General Ulysses S. Grant documented many of the same problems in central Missouri. On August 22 he

reported to Frémont the condition of affairs there and in the surrounding territory. The regiments, Grant noted, were disorganized and without the supplies and weapons necessary for service in the field. From his investigations Grant concluded that "the whole of this country is in a state of ferment. They are driving out the Union men and appropriating their property." Having fitted out an expedition of 350 men, Grant was confident he could arrest many of the culprits. Other reports from the western region along the Kansas-Missouri border depicted a similar situation of lawlessness and the commission of atrocities. In a private letter to President Lincoln, Frémont reported that "nearly every county [is] in an insurrectionary condition, and the enemy advancing in force, by different points of the southern frontier." Moreover, he had reinforced strategic locations and held the railroads in the south.[5]

These circumstances sometimes led to the abuse of military power directed at those considered to be instigators or prominent supporters of the insurrection. This abuse manifested itself in different ways. During the period following Governor Jackson's flight from Jefferson City and Boonville, soldiers, apparently without orders, arrested ministers whom they considered to be disloyal. As seen below, Lincoln discouraged interference with churches, although in rare cases he acquiesced in the removal of clergy from the pulpit if their influence upon the community was deemed especially dangerous. The ministers D. J. Marquis and J. B. H. Wooldridge of the Methodist-Episcopal Church South, and George W. Johnson of the Baptist Church, were arrested at Tipton and sent to Jefferson City where Colonel Henry Boernstein, who was temporarily in command, confined them in the basement of the state capitol building for twenty-four hours without food. According to their own accounts after the war, they were "abused" by military officers there, by which they probably meant that profanities and scorn were heaped upon them. Taken out of confinement, Boernstein sent them to Boonville where they were detained for ten days in the fairgrounds and then sent to St. Louis and kept two days in the guardhouse of the St. Louis Arsenal. On their behalf William M. McPherson, a prominent St. Louis lawyer and businessman, intervened with General Frémont to gain their release. Frémont also promised soon to "put a stop to this indiscriminate arrest of citizens unless guilty of an overt act[;] men will be undisturbed and allowed to enjoy their opinions."[6]

While these arrests of ministers were unjustified, it is perhaps under-standable that some excesses occurred, especially given the often inaccu-rate information upon which the military felt compelled to act and the great anxiety people experienced on both sides in the midst of a conflict about which no one could know when it would conclude or how it would turn out. Cer-tainly, this circumstance and the short period of the ministers' incarcerations tended to mitigate the offenses committed by officers and provost marshals in their cases. However, it should be remembered that some ministers were a real threat to the peace because of their influence upon their congregations and communities. Such an individual was J. B. Fuqua, a Baptist minister in Chillicothe who, according to many of his fellow townsmen, in a secessionist meeting advocated putting a committee together to burn bridges and depots and tear up the track of the Hannibal and St. Joseph Railroad. Afterward, it was alleged that Fuqua commanded a party of forty men to watch a railroad depot "for the purpose of firing into the train, tearing up the track & imped-ing the progress of U.S. troops." To avoid taking the oath of allegiance, Fuqua fled to the town of Glasgow where he accused federal troops of brutality and claimed that they had driven him away, an account denied by Fuqua's former townsmen. It was not until January 1862 that Fuqua was arrested and placed in a military prison in St. Louis. He denied the charges and referred to his having taken the oath of allegiance "about three months since." The final dis-position of his case is not in his file and it is unclear how long he was incarcer-ated, although in all probability he was released soon thereafter.[7]

During this time, communications from private individuals to Lincoln and his cabinet brought complaints about Frémont's lack of energy, his inac-cessibility to important military and political leaders, and his reliance upon foreign military aides. Lincoln relayed some of these concerns to Frémont and urged him to pacify Missouri quickly. Some military leaders, citing his failure to reinforce Lyon prior to the Battle of Wilson's Creek, had already begun to question Frémont's capacity and competence to command the large department with which he had been entrusted. In a letter to the president, Frémont promised that he would take the field as soon as he had completed the organizing, arming, and outfitting of the troops under him. Moreover, he detailed his preparations, which included the construction of fortifica-tions at St. Louis, Jefferson City, Cape Girardeau, and Ironton, and the line of his proposed movement to begin "in a few days." If reassured by Frémont's preparations and plans, Lincoln nevertheless relayed to him the advice of others, which he considered sensible. He also established a force of one cavalry and five infantry regiments in southwestern Missouri under the command of Congressman John S. Phelps from Springfield, Missouri.[8]

Occasionally, Frémont's task was complicated by the overzealous actions of federal commanders and troops. Throughout the war, all efforts to quiet guerrilla activities in Missouri were unsuccessful, although the degrees of failure varied from region to region. Much depended on maintaining an adequate force to deter attacks. Another important factor determining failure or success was the appointment of officers who understood the people of the region and could command both respect and fear. Unfortunately, such men were not in great supply but were in great demand, often leading to the reassignment of successful commanders to other battlefields. The loss of effective commanders in Missouri would be a problem throughout the war. Moreover, because Confederate forces were no match for federal troops on the battlefield, they often operated as guerrilla forces, compelling Union commanders to rely primarily upon intelligence gathered from the loyal civilian population and the advice and help of local political leaders. An instance of misbehavior by federal troops occurred in early August 1861, of which John T. K. Hayward, the superintendent of the Hannibal and St. Joseph Railroad, complained that federal troops had "repeatedly fired from trains at quiet, peaceable citizens." Apparently, the soldiers, who previously had been fired upon numerous times while traveling by train, were either nervous, vengeful, or both toward the people of northern Missouri. Hayward reported that the animosity of the people had increased markedly after many individuals had "been arrested without any cause, except that they were reported secessionists, and not only this, but indignities have been put upon them, such as requiring them to 'mark time,' dig ditches, and sink holes for filth." One of the men, Hayward mentioned, was John McAfee, former speaker of the state house, "no doubt a very bad and dangerous man." Hurlbut personally ordered McAfee to dig ditches in the hot sun all day long. Soon thereafter, in transferring him from Macon to Palmyra, Hurlbut ordered McAfee "to be tied on top of the cab on the engine." However, this indignity was prevented when the train's engineer, who objected strongly to this, signaled their departure while McAfee's escort was marching him to the front of the train, "giving them barely time to get on the cars." Hayward feared that wily agitators would soon use these incidents to provoke others to join guerrilla bands or enlist in Price's army. Moreover, he believed that Pope's proclamation was harming the Union cause in northern Missouri, although he later admitted that "leading secessionists manifest a desire of late to have a stop put to this irregular warfare." Despite Hayward's appeal to him, Frémont approved of Hurlbut's arrest of McAfee, but he did suspend temporarily an order to confiscate the property of the residents in Marion County, a small part of the region commanded by Pope, where recent guerrilla depredations had occurred.[9]

Pope's system of assessments and community responsibility for guerrilla activity produced a number of complaints, the most powerful being that in many of the safety committees prominent Secessionists often used their new authority to harm personal enemies and Unionists. Moreover, many loyal citizens found themselves punished monetarily for the actions of others. In establishing safety committees, Pope had hoped to provide a strong enough incentive to all property holders of the region to exert maximum pressure to stop insurgent activities. However, many loyal persons like Hayward feared that such tactics would backfire, increasing the number of guerrillas and their activities.[10]

One of those concerned about the effect of Pope's methods was Governor Hamilton R. Gamble. Recognizing that the war was as much a political contest as it was a military conflict, he promised in his inaugural speech not to interfere with slavery in Missouri and appealed to Missourians to return home to their civil pursuits. He also disbanded the militia units called into service by ousted governor Claiborne F. Jackson. In the wake of the capture of Camp Jackson, the General Assembly in secret session had provided Jackson with unprecedented military authority, which the state convention had promptly repealed during its July session. Hoping that guerrilla warfare would soon subside and quickly become only an unhappy memory, Gamble ordered all sheriffs and other civil officers to restore order in their jurisdictions. Those officers in regions where anarchy prevailed were to seek aid from the state. Finally, he ordered all white men of military age to enroll in the state militia. A few days later on August 13, Gamble published a proclamation offering pardon to those who had enlisted in Price's army. Those willing to put down their weapons, return home, and take an oath of allegiance to the state and national governments would receive amnesty, excepting only those who had committed crimes while in the field. This offer of pardon was made after consulting with Lincoln and Secretary of War Cameron, who was directed by the president to promise "security to citizens in arms who voluntarily return to their allegiance and become peaceable and loyal." Unfortunately the offer came just a few days after Lyon's defeat, explaining perhaps why initially few of Price's soldiers accepted it.[11]

Governor Gamble next turned his attention to Pope's system of confiscation and abuses committed by Union troops. He had received reports from reliable Union men complaining about Pope's order and what they considered to be unwarranted searches in private homes and of persons' belongings. Apparently, home guard units, most of whom had been recruited from among German immigrants in St. Louis, and out-of-state federal troops had sometimes treated the people of northern Missouri roughly. While he understood that war meant the ruin of property and lives, Gamble also believed that it must be waged intelligently and with discrimination between friend and foe. Unfortunately, since the introduction of the home guard units and out-of-state troops, many Unionists had been arrested along with Secessionists in the military's dragnet, the assumption being that everyone living in a slaveholding region was disloyal. Such military oppression, Gamble asserted in a letter to Lincoln, was injurious to the restoration of peace in Missouri.

> I very little hope that peace can be restored while the friends of the Constitution are unable to defend the acts of the military officers of the government. Those friends are first silent and then lukewarm. I am not ignorant of the fact that in all wars there are violations of private rights, but it is seldom in modern times that such abuses have the express sanction of officers high in command. I leave this subject to your consideration merely remarking that I am continually embarrassed by the complaints of real union men against the action of the military whose conduct I can neither excuse nor control. While I have become hardened against complaints of secessionists I have a deep interest in the protection of real union men. If it were possible to subject the military in acting upon unarmed citizens to any control of a civil officer or of a body of civilians much of the cause of present complaint would be removed.

Although no record exists of Lincoln's response to Gamble's letter, in just a few days Pope repealed his General Orders No. 3, announcing on August 30 that this was done in deference to Governor Gamble, Congressman Frank P. Blair Jr., and other prominent civil authorities. Pope warned that resumption of the former policy, or one even more severe, would occur if necessary. This intervention demonstrates the uncertainty of policy makers then prevalent at all levels. It is clear, however, that the goals of these early efforts were to restore peace and allow for the restoration of civil control in Missouri. Moreover, it shows the difficulty, which was never completely solved, in coordinating efforts between the Lincoln administration, the Gamble government, and the different military commanders.[12]

No better example of this lack of coordination between the military and civilian authorities is demonstrated than in Frémont's decision to issue his proclamation on August 30 without consulting Lincoln or anyone else. In it Frémont promised to shoot all persons captured in arms against the United States government and to confiscate the property of anyone aiding the rebellion. He also declared the emancipation of disloyal persons' slaves. Thus, all in the same month Governor Gamble offered pardon to soldiers of Price's army, Pope issued a special order revoking assessments in northern Missouri, and Frémont proclaimed a much more harsh method of dealing with the enemy. Thus the civilian and military authorities published contradictory signals of severity and leniency to the public and may have caused many to wonder who was really in charge. This impression probably did not improve after the president intervened.[13]

Perhaps remembering his own missteps earlier, Lincoln demonstrated a good measure of patience in a letter written just days after Frémont's proclamation. In it he explained that the policy of shooting prisoners was inhumane and unwise and would undoubtedly provoke retaliation by the enemy. Before the execution of anyone, Lincoln insisted that he must approve it first. Moreover, as a matter of policy, he believed that the confiscation of property and the emancipation of all slaves of disloyal persons would probably turn their southern friends against the Union. As a matter of law, Lincoln believed that it violated the act passed by Congress on August 6, a copy of which he enclosed with his letter. In the first and fourth sections of the bill, Congress made clear that only that property, including slaves, used to aid the rebellion could be confiscated. A slave could not be freed just because his master was disloyal. Frémont's proclamation omitted this distinction and therefore went too far. The confiscation law also provided for a regular procedure to insure due process to those being deprived of their property. Lincoln requested that Frémont modify the proclamation to conform it to the law. In reply, Frémont complained that his circumstance was tenuous given the dangers he faced from "the rebel armies, the Provisional Government, and home traitors" in his department. His belief that Governor Gamble was an enemy on par with the Confederate armies and those secretly plotting against the government is remarkable and probably resulted from the counsel he received from his advisers. These were mostly foreign aides and abolitionists from the German population in St. Louis, men who were naturally suspicious of Gamble's pro-slavery stance and perhaps considered him a natural rival. If Frémont's perspective was the same as many abolitionist Republicans, men who later referred to themselves as Radical Republicans, then he considered anyone who was proslavery to be disloyal also. Not wishing to repeal his proclamation, and thereby disappoint and possibly anger his friends, Frémont asked that Lincoln order it rescinded, which he did immediately.[14]

The part of Frémont's proclamation which Lincoln did not repeal was his declaration of martial law over all of Missouri. Such action had precedent before the Civil War in the Continental Congress's grant of special authority upon the principle of "self-preservation," Andrew Jackson's imposition of martial law in New Orleans during the War of 1812, and the Rhode Island government's quelling of an insurrection commonly called the Dorr Rebellion. In *Luther v. Borden* (1849), the establishment of martial law was recognized by the United States Supreme Court as a necessary expedient to restore order where civil and judicial rule were ineffective.[15]

Frémont's proclamation of martial law was not the first time that he had given extraordinary police powers to the military. On July 28, not long after his arrival there, he had appointed Colonel John McNeil the "military commandant of St. Louis." McNeil was ordered to insure the "safety of St. Louis . . . to dissolve secret associations and meetings," to station troops where needed, to keep in contact with "the secret police . . . to collect daily reports concerning the different Home Guard regiments, and to submit daily a general report to the commanding general." Also he was "to repress insurrection or sudden attack" and to arrange "infantry and cavalry patrols throughout the city." Previous to this in May, General William S. Harney, during his brief tenure as commander of the Department of the West, had ordered that all commerce coming in or out of St. Louis be carefully examined to prevent "contraband of war" from falling into the hands of the enemy. Presumably, this policy had continued through the summer. On August 14, just after the defeat of Lyon, Frémont declared martial law in St. Louis County where it was believed that approximately eight thousand Secessionists stood ready to revolt violently. Provost Marshal Justus McKinstry promised not to "interfere with the operation of the civil law, except in cases where that law was found inadequate to the maintenance of the public peace and safety." He also prohibited the carrying of concealed arms and the sale of weapons to civilians except by special permit. A week after sending out this "manifesto," McKinstry ordered the release of "Mr. Brownlee" from prison if he agreed to "resign his commission as president of the board of police commissioners" and leave St. Louis to the free states, not to return except with permission from the military authorities. McKinstry also issued order no. 107 stating that satisfactory evidence showed that persons were coming and going from the city to provide aid and comfort to the enemy. To prevent this from continuing, he ordered all persons traveling in or out of the city to acquire passes from the provost marshal's office. He also ordered all public conveyances not to issue tickets for any destination outside of St. Louis County to persons without these passes. McKinstry's actions, whether considered necessary or not, demonstrate the vast authority he wielded and the danger of abuse possible under such a system.[16]

Under martial law, commanders in the field wielded extraordinary powers as well. Ideally, their actions were guided by the laws of war and the military code of justice. However, because every circumstance was unique, military commanders and their troops were guided by the orders of their superiors and military necessity. They also were expected to use their common sense and mete out punishment proportionate to the offense committed. When encountering enemies in combat, they had the power to kill or capture those they confronted. With others, such as "a dangerous and subtle enemy" like John McAfee (see above), the proper treatment of persons who did not take up arms themselves, but who encouraged and advised others to do so, was more problematic, especially given the traditional freedoms of speech and the press guaranteed in the First Amendment of the United States Constitution. Much depended upon the judgment of the military and the Lincoln administration about the consequences of allowing subversive statements to go unchecked. While it was agreed by almost every supporter of the Union that some speech, like that recruiting troops for the Confederacy, or publishing important military secrets, was properly suppressed, what was to be done, if anything, about many other types of dissent and opposition was less clear and caused much uneasiness and confusion among the authorities and the public.[17]

As noted in chapter 1, before Frémont took command in Missouri the military had already suppressed the *Missouri State Journal* and arrested its editor Joseph W. Tucker. He and other editors supporting Governor Jackson and secession were considered especially dangerous because of their influence upon their readers. Without the law of seditious libel, as in England, the American tradition provides wide latitude to critics of the government. While no congressional acts were passed concerning First Amendment rights during the Civil War, the Lincoln administration suppressed some newspapers, premising its actions on the belief that these suppressions were militarily necessary. Lincoln assumed this power as part of the powers the president wields during time of war as commander in chief. At first no coherent policy was established and military commanders were given wide latitude in dealing with most civil liberties and constitutional rights. In the North, while many instances of abuse of power have been documented to show the unnecessary suppression of newspapers and the intimidation of editors, nevertheless, many other opposition papers, some of them harsh in their criticisms of the administration, continued to be published unhindered throughout the war. This circumstance demonstrates the inconsistent and haphazard manner in which decisions were made early in the war and after.[18]

In Missouri, where armed conflict made the stakes much higher than in the North, Lincoln permitted his commanders considerable latitude in establishing policy. For this reason Frémont and other commanders were often able to influence how the war was covered or prevent the publication or distribution of newspapers which had fallen out of favor. In August the *War Bulletin* and the *Missourian* gained the unenviable distinction of being the first newspapers suppressed by Frémont for being "shamelessly devoted to the publication of transparently false statements respecting military movements in Missouri." In a strange twist, if true, it was claimed in an article from St. Louis that the editor of the *St. Louis Morning Herald,* James L. Fawcett, had purposely published items favoring secession to escape creditors through military seizure of his press. Moreover, Frémont prohibited the distribution in Missouri of five New York newspapers which Postmaster General Montgomery Blair had ordered excluded from the mails. Additionally, Frémont suppressed the

Louisville Courier. Apparently Frémont's favorite, the *St. Louis Democrat,* received police protection. The editor of the *St. Louis Daily Evening News,* Charles G. Ramsay, who had argued for Missouri to remain neutral after the attack on Fort Sumter but later had supported the Union cause, was arrested in September for criticizing Frémont's less than speedy efforts to relieve the besieged garrison at Lexington, Missouri. The military also "seized and destroyed" the offending edition of the paper. Upon agreeing no longer to publish anything "injurious to the government," Ramsay was released, but nevertheless his treatment is an example of an egregious misuse and overreach of military power. Despite the possible danger posed by southern armies at the time, such attempts to squash loyal criticism in the press were completely unjustified, especially when one considers the innocuous nature of the violations the military accused the newspapers of committing, whether real or imagined. Unfortunately, Frémont and his subordinates erred in the manner sometimes manifest among persons in authority who equate criticism with disloyalty.[19]

Perhaps the best documented and most revealing example of the military's relations with the press concerns the case of a prominent member of the clergy, David R. McAnally, editor of the *St. Louis Christian Advocate,* whose activities came under close scrutiny during the first months of the war. As a member of the Methodist-Episcopal Church South, he represented the perspectives of the proslavery wing of that denomination after the split with what became the Methodist-Episcopal Church North. Religious newspapers were published by both branches of the denomination throughout the country and McAnally had participated in an ongoing dispute with Charles Elliott, the editor of the *Western Christian Advocate,* a member of the northern branch of his denomination. In his columns, McAnally regularly mentioned or reprinted items from Elliott's paper. According to McAnally, Elliott and others from the northern church had wrongly accused him of being a Secessionist and publishing prosouthern items in his newspaper. For his part, McAnally argued that it was wrong for religious papers such as the *Western Christian Advocate* to support the Union war effort and to take sides in any political dispute. During the first months of 1861, his own efforts to present a neutral position about secession and the political controversies were well executed, consistently arguing for peace and against measures that could provoke hostilities. Similarly, in his reporting about different events, he presented the facts and both sides' analysis of them. During the Fort Sumter crisis, McAnally, perhaps for the first time revealing his prosouthern bias, argued that it would be futile to attempt to coerce the seceding states back into the Union. Moreover, in an article about the "facts" concerning the early founding of the United States government and the ratification of the Constitution, he presented a decidedly one-sided, states-rights account. Apparently, in reply to this long article, Elliott in the *Western Christian Advocate* accused McAnally of favoring secessionist ideas. During the summer, McAnally's reporting demonstrated his bias in favor of Confederate forces under the command of Sterling Price and tended to emphasize the misbehavior of federal troops. In his account of the Battle of Boonville, McAnally discounted the reliability of those reports asserting a decisive victory under Nathaniel Lyon's command, while presenting without comment a description of a defeat of federal forces elsewhere. In his next issue, McAnally complained about the inaccuracy of war reports in other papers, perhaps realizing that the accounts he had published favoring the state forces, which had been partisan and inaccurate, had revealed his own bias. Articles and letters written for publication about the violation of private citizens' civil liberties by home guard units or federal troops were regular features as well. Just prior to the establishment of martial law and McKinstry's tenure as provost marshal, McAnally had expressed himself freely, stating that the present troubles were the result of electing a sectional president. He had also criticized the syntax of Lincoln's July 4, 1861, message to Congress. Moreover, commenting on Missouri's affairs, McAnally argued that the state convention had no authority to oust Governor Jackson and the legislature and elect in their place a provisional government, a common assertion made by many who were either Secessionists or opposed to "coercion."[20]

While his reporting certainly did not achieve the neutrality he had argued for earlier, McAnally did not support the state forces openly. When in August newspapers were suppressed and some editors were arrested, McAnally was allowed to continue publishing the *Christian Advocate,* although some readers and friends expressed anxiety that he might become a target of McKinstry next. Confronting the possibility directly, McAnally told his readers that he did not intend to publish anything which would end in his newspaper's suppression, but, of course, he could not say that the military authorities would not suppress it. He also published a letter to the provost marshal in which he asked whether the paper was to be suppressed.

In the letter, McAnally offered to send to McKinstry each issue of the paper to see that nothing in it warranted concern. McKinstry replied that it would be wise to omit all mention of political or secular matters, only publishing religious material as befitted a religious newspaper. This suggestion the *Christian Advocate's* editor ignored, for he continued to publish features about the war and politics. In response to the offer to send any previous and all current issues of the paper to him, McKinstry said that he had already perused the paper and was familiar with it, indicating to McAnally that his paper was being watched closely.[21]

Some of the above events were written about after the war in two volumes compiled by another minister of the Methodist Episcopal Church South, William M. Leftwich, composed of accounts solicited from ministers in the *St. Louis Christian Advocate.* In this, Leftwich claimed that during the war they were persecuted "for no other cause than that they were ministers of the gospel." Throughout the book, much like in the pages of McAnally's paper, were accusations against the press of the northern branch of the Methodist-Episcopal Church and against "abolitionists" who, it was claimed, sought to destroy their southern counterparts. These accounts, often written as indictments in a lurid style, are mostly unconfirmable today and present only one perspective, perhaps demonstrating that history is not always exclusively written by the victors. In the book, McAnally provided his personal story, including the claim that in July 1861 "a mob of Home Guards" surrounded his house and church because he "had publicly baptized a child whose parents chose to name it Harry Beauregard." This conspiracy against him was thwarted only after a leader of the mob was told by one of McAnally's friends that "thirty or forty men" would avenge him. McAnally also alleged that "a company of armed men, forty-four in number, wearing the uniform of United States soldiers, and acting professedly under orders from headquarters, surrounded my house and ransacked it from cellar to garret. What they expected to find, or were looking for, I never asked—I never knew." Whether these incidents actually happened is impossible to know with any certainty, although it is significant that McAnally wrote nothing about these outrages in his newspaper at the time, when he often included accounts of similar episodes allegedly happening to others. Moreover, at times he had included other "personal" items demonstrating that he had no policy against publishing news about himself.[22]

The final incident of which McAnally wrote, occurring during the period of Frémont's tenure as commander of the Department of the West, concerned his summons to the provost marshal's office in October. McAnally provided two very different accounts of the same event. In an article published in his newspaper on November 7, 1861, he explained that he had been seriously ill when the military authorities summoned him. However, not wishing to appear to be in hiding, he went to his office at the newspaper and soon accompanied an officer sent for him. The provost marshal John McNeil, whose name is not given in the article, asked him a question concerning an item McAnally published recently about Lyon's capture of Camp Jackson. In it he had sarcastically compared the victory to military successes of the past like Thermopylae, the great Greek stand against a Persian invasion in the fifth century B.C. As before, he characterized those militia at Camp Jackson as loyal men and boys doing their duty and said that most of the casualties of the day were civilian men, women, and children, who as onlookers were fired upon by Lyon's troops without cause. Apparently responding to his critics, McAnally did not exactly deny that he was arrested, instead writing that if he was under arrest he did not know it. Nor was he aware, he claimed, that his friends had intervened for him, stating that he was too ill to be jailed. Of course, one presumes that McAnally could have easily discovered the truth by simply asking them.[23]

The later account of the same incident published in Leftwich's book was different from the first in what McAnally omitted and included. In it he asserted that he was arrested "not on a charge of any thing having been done, but on a suspicion that something might be done." While it is true that he undoubtedly was brought to the provost marshal's office to be warned against publishing articles like his parody on the capture of Camp Jackson, McAnally did not include this information, thus potentially giving the reader a false impression about the motives of the military. Moreover, he added details to his former account, some of which were more believable than others, asserting that he was

> carried before the Provost-Marshal, where, defenseless and surrounded by armed men, I was coarsely harangued, vilified, abused and lectured as to my editorial and ministerial duties, during a half hour or more, which was at length terminated by my plainly informing the Provost-Marshal that, as

I was in their power, the military could do with me as they chose; that they
had the power, and could suppress my paper when they chose, but until
it was suppressed it should contain just what I might think fit to put into
it—neither more nor less.

McAnally's bravado in his account after the war appears to be a later embel-
lishment, for during the war in the pages of the *St. Louis Christian Advocate*
he never openly challenged the authority of the provost marshal, although he
demonstrated a great facility in the use of language in slanting his reporting
favorable to Jackson's government and to the detriment of the Lincoln administration. Nevertheless, little justification existed for the military's threats
against papers like McAnally's, in which little more than mild criticisms of the
policies of the military and the administrations of Gamble and Lincoln were
published. Moreover, much of what McAnally published during the early days
of the secession crisis certainly supported Lincoln's policy of seeking to calm
the political waters by discouraging young men from enlisting in either side
of the conflict. Of course, it is only fair to note that no settled legal doctrine
then existed concerning free speech and press questions to guide the military
and the Lincoln administration, like the cases litigated during World War One
and afterward, eventually greatly limiting the United States government's authority to exercise power over the press. And yet, even if Lincoln had today's
settled precedent on free speech cases, it must be remembered that the danger
to the republic was far greater then, than has been confronted before or since,
excepting perhaps only the circumstances experienced during the American
Revolution. While much of the North was relatively safe militarily, some border states, and especially Missouri, did not enjoy the same security, thus making more drastic measures justifiable in limited cases.[24]

Another controversial wartime measure instituted under martial law was
the use of military commissions. These tribunals not only tried soldiers who
had committed offenses not triable before a court-martial proceeding, but
more importantly, military commissions had jurisdiction over civilian defendants wherever the civil courts were inoperative or some military offense
had been committed. These proceedings, if not properly monitored by commanders, could easily be misused to intimidate the public or to settle personal
scores. Whenever a regional commander decided that it was necessary to adjudicate cases before a military commission, he appointed military officers to

serve, designating one of them to be judge advocate of the court. In particular, two factors influenced their effectiveness and fairness: the integrity and
character of the members of the court and the quality of the evidence provided for their deliberations. As seen above, volunteer regiments sometimes
took questionable action against civilians, like arresting a number of persons
they believed were disloyal or perhaps behind guerrilla attacks made in their
community. In an incident which may have been typical, General Grant sent
troops to capture men who had fired into a train. After examining the prisoners, Grant concluded that "from all the evidence they were the most innocent
men in the county." In this way many innocent, as well as guilty, individuals
were ensnared in military dragnets and were quickly released by higher authority, although others found themselves transported to stand before military commissions.[25]

Having received little guidance, coupled with the difficulty of their task,
it is not surprising that the hodgepodge of volunteer regiments garrisoning
Missouri towns made mistakes and sometimes used heavy-handed tactics, including the arrest of persons for no other reason than that the troops considered them dangerous or otherwise suspicious. Evidence of such irregularities
was uncovered when a military commission convened in September at the
St. Louis Arsenal to consider the charges and evidence presented in the cases
of a number of prisoners. The commission found more than twenty prisoners, against whom no charges or evidence, or only "trivial charges," were presented. Unable to find witnesses to present the necessary evidence to hold
these prisoners, the court released them after they had taken an oath of allegiance. Moreover, a large number of other prisoners were held in the arsenal
accused of "being spies and traitors," but no evidence or witnesses' names
were available to enable the court to proceed against them. For this reason,
most were released, although a small number were "retained" because of their
own statements "and suspicious appearance and behavior." The commission
believed that some men had been arrested for the purpose of stealing their
property and suggested that Frémont issue orders forbidding the confinement
of anyone without "some strong circumstantial proof of facts" upon which the
commission could adjudicate their cases. Frémont agreed, issuing the commission's report in the form of a general order.[26]

Other prisoners, however, against whom charges and evidence were
brought, were tried before military commissions throughout Missouri. Some

of these men had surrendered to gain the benefit of Governor Gamble's proclamation of amnesty to anyone willing to return home to live in peace and swear
an oath of loyalty to the state and federal governments. One of these prisoners
was Joseph Aubuchon, who apparently had left his home at Ironton around
July 1 to buy and sell cattle to the southern army. While in the Van Buren,
Arkansas, area he was "induced to act as clerk or Agent of Major Pander," a
Confederate officer, for "three or four weeks," after which he made his way
home. Aubuchon was captured around August 20 at Charleston, Missouri,
and imprisoned at the St. Louis Arsenal. While acting as a clerk, he was ordered to requisition "a wagon and provisions" from a Union man to whom he
supplied a receipt. Aubuchon claimed that this was the only instance in which
he had acted in such a manner and stated his desire to gain a pardon through
Governor Gamble's proclamation. Convicted of treason and sentenced to be
imprisoned during the war at hard labor and to have his property confiscated,
the commission recommended to General Frémont that he be released and
returned to his home. Factors working in his favor were the testimony of his
father, who was a Union man, and his relatively minor role in the rebellion.
For these reasons, Aubuchon's sentence was rescinded and he was released.[27]

During the same month, another military commission at Ironton convicted a pair of men for treason and sentenced them to imprisonment at hard
labor for the war. One man's property was ordered to be confiscated and sent
to the quartermaster to help support the war effort. These commissions appear to have observed the basic principles of due process in requiring charges
and evidence to be presented against the accused in very much the same manner followed in civil courts. The accused had the right to representation and
to confront his accusers and present evidence or circumstances to exoner-
ate himself, or at least to explain mitigating circumstances for why he had
committed the offense. Moreover, the proceedings of the commissions were
reviewed by the commander of the department, or a designated subordinate,
within which the trial was held. Very early in the war, Lincoln prohibited
the execution of anyone before he could review the defendant's case personally. These types of safeguards helped to assure fair trials and provided oversight to prevent abuses from being practiced without fear of discovery.[28]

One of the greatest and most controversial problems with which Lincoln
was confronted during the war was what to do about slavery. When out-of-state
troops came into Missouri, many of whom had never encountered slavery

before and held strong prejudices against it, it is not surprising to learn that members of some of these regiments helped slaves to escape from their masters. These incidents, along with the rest, made difficult the reestablishment of peace in Missouri and the other border states. Lincoln, who had always made clear as a candidate and then as president that he would not interfere with slavery where it then existed, had rescinded that part of Frémont's August 30 proclamation declaring free all slaves of disloyal persons. Although he hated slavery, believing it a violation of slaves' natural rights guaranteed in the Declaration of Independence and the very embodiment of tyranny, Lincoln nevertheless was unwilling to violate the Constitution or the law to abolish "the peculiar institution." On September 22, 1861, in a private letter to United States Senator Orville H. Browning, the president explained his order countermanding Frémont's emancipation proclamation of all slaves of disloyal masters within his command, which, Lincoln believed, violated the legal and constitutional rights of slave owners. He did not object if a military commander seized property out of "military necessity," but under the laws of war once the property was no longer "needed for military purposes" then it must be returned. "And the same is true of slaves. If the General needs them, he can seize them, and use them, but when the need is past, it is not for him to fix their permanent future condition. That must be settled according to laws made by law-makers, and not be military proclamations. The proclamation in the point in question is simply 'dictatorship.'" Lincoln conceded to Browning that in all probability Frémont's action was more popular than his in rescinding it, but that as president he could "not assume this reckless position; nor allow others to assume it on my responsibility." Ironically, this principle of "military necessity" later became the basis of Lincoln's decision to publish his own emancipation proclamation, but even it would be carefully constructed to protect the property rights of slave owners in regions, including Missouri, not in rebellion to the United States. To emancipate the slaves of loyal persons was unnecessary militarily and therefore without justification even under the laws of war.[29]

As with all military policy, the ideal was to win with the minimal amount of damage and expense to the country and to enable a reunification of the country as quickly as possible after hostilities had ended. Moreover, it was necessary to calculate the effect policies would have upon one's supporters as well as the enemy. The issue of slavery, like none other, demonstrates the delicate balance Lincoln sought to maintain in determining how best to win the war while simultaneously seeking to prevent the alienation of the slave-holding border states. The importance of his close supervision of slavery policy was evident immediately after Frémont's proclamation was published, for it had produced a tumult of protest and scorn from the border states. Before the proclamation was modified, the president learned that the legislature in Kentucky had refused to support the North and that some Union troops, in one instance "a whole company of our Volunteers," declared their intention not to serve. Indeed, some danger existed that Kentucky troops might use the weapons provided to them against the government. If this happened, Lincoln believed that "to lose Kentucky is nearly the same as to lose the whole game. Kentucky gone, we can not hold Missouri, nor, as I think, Maryland. These all against us, and the job on our hands is too large for us."[30]

It is not surprising then, with so much at stake, that Lincoln expended a good deal of time and energy in the establishment of his slavery policy. Because many circumstances could not be anticipated, commanders often found themselves confronted with difficult questions of policy, which they presented to the administration for resolution. Before the passage of the Confiscation Act of August 6, 1861, the first question regarded what was to be done with fugitive slaves coming into the lines of federal troops. The administration adopted the shrewd policy of General Benjamin F. Butler, who employed runaways as laborers for the military, providing a receipt to their owners for the value of the services of their slaves. Butler refused to return the slaves as required under the fugitive slave law, noting that the act did not apply to "a foreign country which Virginia claimed to be and that she must reckon it one of the infelicities of her position that in so far at least she was taken at her word." Also, because many of the slaves were employed by the enemy to erect fortifications and for other military purposes, Butler thought it useful militarily to deprive the Confederates of their labor. After passage of the Confiscation Act, Secretary of War Simon Cameron wrote to Butler stating that the policy toward slaves in areas of insurrection had not changed and that he should continue to employ fugitives for military purposes, noting, however, that those slaves used to aid the rebellion would gain their freedom, but only through the procedures delineated in the law.[31]

As the reaction in Kentucky demonstrated, the federal government's policy toward slavery in Missouri had important ramifications for the border states and possibly for the war's outcome. Evidently, after Butler's use of fugitive slaves became known, other commanders began employing them similarly in Missouri and elsewhere. With slaves streaming into the camps of federal troops in Missouri, commanders were confronted with the difficult task of finding suitable employment for the slaves and determining who among them were entitled to freedom because their masters had employed them to aid the insurrection. Others were given protection from masters who were angry at their slaves for helping federal troops in some way. Not only was this humane, but it also encouraged slaves to continue providing help to the North. Moreover, when conducting raids, federal troops sought to free any slaves deserving their freedom under the confiscation act as a means of punishing disloyal persons, especially the families whose men were serving in the Confederate military. These policies developed under Frémont's command would be refined by his successor, providing greater security for troops in Missouri but often to the detriment of runaway slaves.[32]

During the period following Frémont's establishment of martial law and the revocation of his emancipation proclamation, the military situation degenerated in Missouri. Unfortunately for the Union cause, Frémont lacked energy and seemed unable to take forceful action. During this period, without opposition Price's army moved deliberately through Missouri gathering new recruits and encouraging guerrilla attacks. In northern Missouri where General Pope commanded, federal troops were dispersed to capture small bands of guerrilla forces terrorizing communities and attacking the railroads. One of the atrocities committed by guerrillas during this time occurred near St. Joseph where the railroad crossed over the Little Platte River. On September 3, bushwhackers from the area burned a railroad bridge and destroyed it "a short time before the regular passenger train was due," killing or wounding thirty men, women, and children. Many of the survivors could not be rescued until the next day, spending a horrifying night among the wreckage and dying fellow passengers. Such acts of sabotage remained a problem throughout the war.[33]

At this time, Price's movement proceeded toward Lexington, a town located along the Missouri River in northwestern Missouri. His cautious approach provided Frémont ample time to prepare an expedition to rescue a garrison of troops there. Despite the evident danger, Frémont took no effective action to relieve the garrison, allowing it to be captured on September 20.

Later, he claimed not to have sufficient transport for troops to relieve the garrison, an excuse that is difficult to credit given Lexington's location along the Missouri River, which federal troops controlled, and the passage nearby of the Hannibal and St. Joseph Railroad, along which General Pope had sent troops to St. Joseph just days before. Coming so soon after the defeat at the Battle of Wilson's Creek on August 10, the capture of Lexington demoralized Unionists in Missouri and outraged those who had futilely warned Frémont of the impending disaster. Aware that Lincoln had sent Secretary of War Simon Cameron and Adjutant General Lorenzo Thomas to investigate his competence as a commander, and especially the circumstances leading to the capture of Lexington, Frémont began a tortuously slow pursuit of Price's army, eventually preparing to attack it at Springfield. Whether these preparations were intended to prevent Frémont's imminent sacking, or were based upon a genuine misunderstanding of the location of Price's army, probably can never be known definitively, although it became clear that the enemy was some distance away at Neosho and Cassville at the time. While holding a council of war in Springfield, Frémont was relieved of his command by General David Hunter, who followed Lincoln's suggestion to pull part of the army back to Rolla, the southern terminus of the railroad, and the rest to Sedalia. This move was prudent because Frémont had begun his expedition without the wagons and supplies necessary for a cross-country trek in the wake of an enemy foraging upon the country. Thus ended Frémont's command in Missouri.[34]

In October, while this drama unfolded, the state convention convened to pass legislation necessary for the state to provide better support to the war effort. The convention's members organized committees to consider matters concerning the militia, finances, civil officers, and elections. The most pressing matter concerned reforming the militia. The committee reported out a bill giving to Governor Gamble more authority as commander in chief, removing any state legal barriers to the recruitment, organization, and subsistence of the militia. The bill also made all men from eighteen to forty-five years of age liable for service in the Missouri State Militia, as it came to be known, and made the militia subject to the same rules as the United States military. After the dismal response to Governor Gamble's first call for volunteers in August, the convention agreed to increase militia pay to parity with that of volunteer federal forces, allowing state recruiters to compete more successfully with their federal counterparts. Recognizing the need to surround himself with people he could trust, Governor Gamble was given the power to appoint his staff and aides, as well as all officers down to the rank of major, only subject to state senate approval. Moreover, the convention's trust in the governor's judgment was further confirmed in the members' decision to commission him to establish state court-martial procedure and to modify the United States Army regulations to conform them to the special circumstances of Missouri and its militia. Finally, the convention passed a resolution requesting the governor to travel to Washington D.C. to coordinate state efforts with the federal government.[35]

Another pressing matter to which the convention turned concerned the holding of state elections that fall. Many of the delegates doubted that an election could be held with Price's army then occupying central Missouri and with bands of guerrillas operating throughout the state, often intimidating and even driving out the loyal population. Under such conditions, coupled with many local election officials supporting the rebellion, the probability of holding a fair election was low and the danger of disloyal persons being elected to office seemed quite high. Governor Gamble, before his election by the convention to the provisional gubernatorial office, had optimistically expected the turmoil in Missouri to have ended quickly and it to be possible to hold elections later that year. However, with the military situation becoming worse rather than better, he and most of the delegates reluctantly concluded that the elections must be postponed and that the portion of the electorate who had taken up arms against the United States government must be disqualified from the right to vote and to run for office. One of the major concerns of Governor Gamble and the convention during its summer session was the issue of the provisional government's legitimacy. All were agreed that a provisional government should only be temporary and should last no longer than the emergency that had required its institution. For this reason, the convention had followed Gamble's advice in agreeing to hold elections to accept or reject their actions and to elect state executive officers. Moreover, having accepted the office with reluctance, Gamble, in his message calling the convention to assemble, had indicated that a new governor should be chosen during the session.[36]

Nevertheless, a small minority of the delegates argued vigorously for the elections to be held as planned. Uriel Wright, proving himself to be as resourceful an advocate for his positions as he had been during the convention's earlier sessions, once again gave prolix speeches in which he argued that the state convention, in its ouster of the Jackson administration and the state legislature, was responsible for the outbreak of hostilities in Missouri. Wright also asserted that the real reason for the postponement of the election was to avoid the people's rejection of the convention's work. More than anything, Wright sought to prevent the convention from taking action to strengthen the state militarily and financially. The vast majority of the members of the state convention, however, in a vote of forty-nine to one rejected Wright's arguments, deciding to follow Gamble's advice to postpone the election because of "the disturbed condition of the State," but at the same time rejecting Gamble's call for the appointment of a new governor.[37]

In late October, Governor Gamble traveled to Washington D.C. to confer with the president as requested by the convention. One of the major obstacles to the establishment of the militia as a viable and formidable military force was the lack of funds in the state's treasury, the result of ousted Governor Jackson's pillaging of it. This circumstance had also prevented the state from staying current in the payment of outstanding loans, thereby harming Missouri's credit. Because of the ongoing conflict and the resignation of a large number of civil officers, some of whom were responsible for the collection of taxes and fees upon which the state normally derived its revenue, little prospect then existed that the financial situation in Missouri would change soon. Gamble, a former chief justice of the Missouri Supreme Court and state legislator, presented to Lincoln a well-conceived plan for the coordination of state and federal forces in Missouri. Gamble reminded the president that the Constitution (article 4, section 4) guaranteed to the states the federal government's protection in case of invasion. He had already prepared the way for his visit and proposal by writing letters to both of Lincoln's cabinet members from Missouri, Montgomery Blair and Edward Bates, seeking a commitment either to fund the state militia or to provide sufficient federal troops to protect the state. By this time, after three months as Missouri's executive, Gamble had already met with Lincoln on three occasions in Washington D.C. and communicated with him through surrogates and letters. Agreeing in principle to Gamble's plan to establish a federally funded militia operating exclusively in Missouri, Lincoln requested that he compose a memorandum setting out his plan. This memorandum was circulated at the War Department and its advice was gained. Eventually, Gamble met with General George B. McClellan to discuss his plan.[38]

In his memorandum, Gamble noted the military circumstance and the suffering of Unionists in Missouri. One of the advantages to funding the militia, he argued, would be the presence of troops with knowledge of the geography and the people. Gamble also believed that more men would enlist, especially those with families to support, when told that they were not to serve anywhere outside of Missouri. Recognizing that Lincoln and the military might be concerned about the loss of federal recruitment to the militia, Gamble promised to permit any militia unit which so desired to become a volunteer federal regiment. Moreover, wishing to prevent from the start any possibility of even an appearance of impropriety, he proposed that federal funds pass through regular military channels.[39]

During these negotiations, an important question arose concerning the practicability of maintaining two separate military forces in Missouri under different commanders. General McClellan, however, who had worked with a similar arrangement as commander of the Department of the Ohio, perceived no problem so long as the militia was subject to the orders of the commander of the department. Lincoln, who routinely deferred to the military experts, agreed to Gamble's plan asking him to draw up a military order in conformity with United States volunteer laws and departing from them only where the change was indispensable. In the agreement, the Missouri State Militia would serve exclusively in Missouri, would be subject to military law, and would be paid, armed, and subsisted by the United States government, but only when the militia was in active service. In his request for funding, Lincoln sought sufficient money to maintain forty thousand militiamen, but Congress allocated enough for ten thousand only.[40]

After several months of hostilities in Missouri, the situation could be characterized as stabilized politically with the provisional government firmly in control in the civil sphere. The military situation, however, was more complex. Although Price's army had retreated before federal forces, General Hunter did not pursue the Confederate army and they were allowed to establish themselves in southern Missouri. While a plan for the organization of an effective militia force was ready, it would take several months for the state to recruit troops, gather supplies and uniforms, and train the men to operate effectively. In the meantime, guerrilla activities continued including the destruction of railroads and the property and lives of Missourians, many of whom wished merely to remain at home in peace. Many difficult battles and skirmishes remained to be fought and Lincoln was soon to appoint a new commander for the Department of the Missouri, Henry W. Halleck, a West Pointer and lawyer best known to his contemporaries for a treatise he had written on international and military law. He would prove to be a very effective administrator and organizer, insisting that his subordinates follow correct procedure in acquiring supplies and money, and in recruiting and mustering in soldiers. Of particular importance were his reforms to the procedures of the military justice system in the department, correcting the form and practice of courts-martial and military commissions. He would also institute a much more severe policy against guerrillas and other irregular bands operating behind the front lines in Missouri.

3

GENERAL HENRY W. HALLECK
AND THE LAW OF WAR

WITH GENERAL HENRY W. HALLECK's appointment to the command in Missouri Abraham Lincoln obtained a brief period of respite from the burdensome task of navigating through the often tumultuous sea of Missouri politics. During this time, the president was less involved in shaping policy and mediating disputes in Missouri than during any other period of the war, although it should be remembered that he continued to monitor and supervise events. Halleck's performance as commander was largely responsible for this circumstance. His reputation as an expert in military tactics and law and the favorable impressions he had made in Washington D.C. upon Attorney General Edward Bates and Charles Gibson, a federal judge and agent for Missouri, raised expectations among Missourians that Halleck could quickly correct the disastrous condition of the department, which had suffered under General John C. Frémont's mismanagement. For the most part, Halleck met these expectations, establishing policies which his successors largely left unmodified throughout the war.[1]

General George B. McClellan, overall commander of the United States military, instructed Halleck to reduce Frémont's bloated staff, many of whom were incompetent or were illegally appointed, and to end "a system of reckless expenditure and fraud" established through the granting of irregular contracts for supplies and arms. Halleck took command of the Department of the Missouri on November 19, 1861, and reported to McClellan that a large number of Union refugees had been driven out of southwestern Missouri, that about half the state was under the control of the enemy, and that a large part of the population was secessionist. This assessment of the circumstances in Missouri turned out to be excessively pessimistic, but Halleck did not overstate the difficulties of the task before him. Moreover, the military in the department was "utterly disorganized, clamorous for pay, but refusing to be regularly mustered in," and, he thought, some regiments were mutinous. He also complained that his officers were insubordinate, refusing to send him regular reports by telegraph and making it impossible for him to coordinate military operations for maximum effectiveness. Of particular concern was the circumstance that approximately thirty thousand men had no weapons and many of the troops were without clothing and blankets.[2]

Ever the bureaucrat, Halleck repeated in reports to McClellan the difficulties under which he was operating. In imposing discipline and dismissing many of Frémont's staff and partisans, he warned that he would naturally make enemies and that he must not be interfered with unnecessarily "in this chaos of incendiary elements." In particular, Halleck had in mind "the injudicious orders of the War Department and the jealousies of the Governors of the States." Before much progress could be expected, he must reorganize and supply his forces, for which he sought patience, although he allowed that "the administration and the machinery for the supply of the army is rapidly getting into working order." He was also happy to report that his troops had been successful in a series of small engagements throughout central and northwestern Missouri, that the situation of Confederate General Sterling Price was desperate, and that "another retreat would effectually ruin his cause in this State." Whether his circumstances were as desperate as Halleck portrayed them, it is clear that Price then had little chance of capturing St. Louis, the goal of his expedition, and indeed, it was doubtful that he could hold his army together, which was more poorly supplied than were federal troops.[3]

Soon after his arrival in St. Louis, Halleck quickly established his authority. First, he seized the secessionist headquarters in St. Louis and incarcerated those driving carriages with a Rebel flag, confiscating their carriages as well. Nor did he show deference to anyone, ordering the arrest of both men and women displaying a Rebel flag and expelling from the state a woman caught spying for the enemy. Halleck also reviewed Frémont's policies and began to enforce measures passed by the state convention in October. Under Frémont a number of provost marshals had required passports to travel through their districts. Appointed by Halleck to supervise their efforts, Provost Marshal General Bernard G. Farrar ordered the provost marshals to explain "the special object, and purpose of the passport system under your control; what [is] its general plan and special management; and means for attaining the end proposed; and [provide a] statement in detail, of expenses, logistics with such reasons as you may have for continuing such system." After this investigation, Halleck determined that no military necessity existed for passports throughout most of Missouri, only maintaining the requirement in those regions where one was passing through military lines from territory occupied by the enemy. Moreover, Halleck nullified all financial agreements and arrangements which any institution had made with officials of the Confederacy. He also enforced the regulation passed by the state convention requiring all state and city officials and lawyers and other officers of the courts, including jurors, to take the oath of allegiance. Some of these officials refused and were forced to resign, enabling Governor Hamilton R. Gamble to appoint loyal men in their place. Those most obstinate in aiding the rebellion were arrested and in special cases banished to the Confederacy.[4]

In late November 1861, Dr. John R. Moore, who hoped to bring peace to Missouri, sought permission, first through Governor Gamble and then through the military, to offer to General Price and his army an opportunity to lay down their arms, take the oath of allegiance, and return home where they would remain in peace and receive a pardon for having taken up arms against the United States government. For his part, Governor Gamble was skeptical about Moore's plan, believing "that those in arms will not appreciate the kindness which is still felt for them by those who conduct the General and State Governments. I fear that they will regard all offers of amnesty as indicating rather imbecility than kindness." However, Gamble observed that Moore's plan was very much in harmony with President Lincoln's desire to reconcile to the government anyone willing again to become loyal citizens. Upon this basis, therefore, Gamble pledged that "the past will be forgotten" for anyone, including General Price, willing to put down their arms. Apparently, instead of consulting with Halleck also, Moore traveled to Syracuse in central Missouri and requested to be passed through the lines to present his offer to Price. As General John Pope reported to Halleck, Moore possessed a letter from Gamble defining the terms upon which Price and his force could receive "immunity for past offenses as defined to him by the President." Apparently, Price was uninterested in such a deal, for when a St. Louis lawyer later asserted that Price and most of his army would gladly lay down their arms and return home peacefully, if only given an opportunity, Halleck replied that in fact Price was adamantly opposed to reconciliation to the government and despite "the fairest offers" had vowed to "fight the Federal Government to the bitter end." And so, it would be upon this basis that Halleck would implement a very severe policy in Missouri, understanding as he did that "nothing but the military power can now put down the rebellion and save Union men in this state."[5]

Amid his efforts to reorganize the federal regiments under his command, Halleck began to pinpoint problems to which he gave special attention. Because of the arrangement between the president and Governor Gamble, Halleck was also the commander of Missouri's militia, which was then more a potential force than real. As commander in chief, Gamble issued an order detailing the terms of the arrangement, explaining that the Missouri State Militia was created to prevent invasion and insurrection within the state and that the discipline, organization, and pay would be the same as that of federal troops. The militia, however, could not be ordered to serve beyond the limits of Missouri, unlike other states' militia forces, a guarantee that insured that more Missourians, many of whom were unenthusiastic about fighting against their southern compatriots, would enlist to protect their homes and communities. This measure seemed necessary given the lackluster response to his first call for militia in August 1861. Gamble had asked the federal government to fund forty thousand militia, with which he intended to supplant the out-of-state volunteer forces then stationed in Missouri, but Congress had allocated enough funds for only ten thousand. The governor believed that northern troops, having arrived from free states, did not understand Missouri culture and were inclined to interfere with slavery, causing much animosity and a multitude of problems, especially since the vast majority of Unionists in Missouri were also proslavery.[6]

Because of these special circumstances, Halleck and Gamble recognized the need for the coordination of their efforts. Gamble, in announcing that persons could then enlist in the state militia, was careful to remind everyone that they could also join the federal service. Halleck, realizing that he could not personally oversee the Missouri State Militia, ordered General John M. Schofield to the overall command, an appointment welcomed by Gamble, who had great confidence in him. Schofield, who after the war would serve as secretary of war and commander of the army, demonstrated bureaucratic skill and good common sense in the organization of the militia. In appointing regional commanders, for instance, he made clear the extent and limitations of their commands and the necessity of cooperating well with the commander of federal forces within their area. Another area of difficulty was the competition for supplies and weapons between the state and federal forces. This rivalry caused some tension for a short time when Halleck took clothing and blankets intended for the militia and transferred them to federal troops, thereby disappointing Gamble. Soon, however, the matter was resolved to Gamble's satisfaction. For his part, Halleck complained about a militia recruiter urging federal troops to join the state service. Gamble replied that he would forward to the individual responsible the orders "prohibiting all intermeddling with home guards and reserve corps." If he persisted, Gamble urged Halleck to court-martial and shoot him. Soon both understood and trusted the other, each developing a respect and appreciation for the other's judgment and abilities.[7]

Another concern to Halleck, one he would find difficult to solve, was the imposition of proper discipline upon troops under his command. The most troublesome group with whom he dealt were German troops, who apparently contemplated revolting. These soldiers were deeply devoted to Frémont, were adamantly committed to abolition as a war goal, and were influenced by the German press in St. Louis. Halleck, who had undercover police investigating the matter, learned that German leaders had held secret meetings conspiring to oust and replace him with General Franz Sigel. Apparently, Lincoln learned of Halleck's concerns and intervened by sending to him Illinois Lieutenant Governor Gustave P. Koerner, who was sent to help Halleck straighten out what Lincoln considered to be no more serious than a "misunderstanding." In reply to the letter from Lincoln delivered by Koerner personally, Halleck explained that he believed the Germans were disgruntled because their troops had not been paid regularly and had been stirred up by the German press, especially in the notion that Sigel had somehow been mistreated. The controversy had escalated when Sigel had resigned after his command was reorganized and Governor Gamble had appointed "unpopular officers" to serve under him. It is evident from Koerner's report to Lincoln that Sigel believed he should be in command of federal troops in southwestern Missouri instead of General Samuel R. Curtis, whom Halleck had appointed. Of course, such second guessing and complaining could not be allowed to influence or pressure the authorities, and so Halleck believed only "a firm and decided course" would cause an end to these types of tactics by the Germans. Lincoln, confronted with the need to mollify the predominately Unionist Germans, but

reluctant to interfere with Halleck's command and undermine his authority, decided to promote Sigel and remove him from the Department of the
Missouri. In this way, Lincoln avoided a confrontation with an ethnic group
and its leaders who, although volatile, were vital to the war effort.[8]

While the problem of insubordinate German leadership was a matter of
some concern for Halleck and Lincoln, the behavior of some of the German
military units operating in the field proved to be a more insidious problem for
them. Halleck found these "foreign troops" deficient in discipline and led by
"adventurers" and "perhaps refugees from justice." He also learned that "political partisans" had sought to foment insurrection among these regiments,
many of whom had not been paid or provided with clothing. To prevent
trouble, Halleck paid these troops and began to muster out those regiments
he could replace. Others he had disarmed. Halleck had learned of a German
battalion, part of the Reserve Corps Cavalry under the command of Major
Hugo Hollan, which was responsible for murdering Union men and indis-
criminately stealing and destroying the property of Unionists and Secessionists alike. General Schofield described the battalion as "utterly worthless" and
had requested them to be replaced. Upon his arrival at Warrenton, Schofield
had found that Hollan's command, which had been there only a brief time,

> had already murdered one of the few Union men in that vicinity and com-
> mitted numerous depredations upon the property of peaceful citizens.
> Since that time their behavior has been absolutely barbarous—a burning
> disgrace to the army and to the Union cause. In spite of all my efforts to the
> contrary they have plundered and destroyed the property of citizens (many
> of them the best Union men in the State) to the amount of thousands of
> dollars. Their officers either connive at it or else have no power to restrain
> their men. I cannot trust them out of my sight for a moment, and of course
> are of no use to me as cavalry so long as this is the case. I have succeeded in
> detecting five of the robbers and have them in irons and have arrested the
> major and one of the captains and placed them in close confinement.

Such behavior did great harm to the Union cause in Missouri. Many persons,
who had remained neutral in the conflict so far, after having their property,
or that of a neighbor, plundered or destroyed, fled to General Price's army for
protection and to gain revenge against their oppressors. Many of these men

were Secessionists but had little enthusiasm for participating in the war until Unionist forces had treated them roughly. One of those fleeing such treatment was Clay Taylor. Hollan's command had entered Taylor's home, searched it, and "destroyed part of the furniture." However, in their search evidence was found of Taylor's "disloyalty." In fact some of the documents indicated that he had been posing as a Unionist while supporting the insurgency. This only confirmed the suspicions of General Halleck, who had ordered Schofield on December 31, 1861, just days before Hollan's command had gone on its rampage, to investigate Taylor's probable involvement in the destruction of the North Missouri Railroad in mid-December. By March 1862, apparently believing that he could remain there no longer, Taylor joined Price's army, first serving as aide-de-camp and later as chief of artillery and ordnance.[9]

Despite his determined efforts to instill proper discipline among his troops, Halleck never resolved the problem during his tenure as commander of the Department of the Missouri. It is clear from his correspondence that while the German troops represented the worst difficulty, some out-of-state regiments also continued to loot, murder, and interfere with slavery despite his best efforts to stop their crimes. These instances of troop indiscipline, Halleck explained, were due to a failure of officers, who apparently condoned their subordinates' behavior. For this reason, he dismissed from service those officers whose troops had been particularly troublesome and ordered the enlisted men to work at fortifications and other hard-labor details. Moreover, he disbanded some of the worst regiments, believing that they were more of a liability than a benefit to the Union war effort. In late February, Halleck even resorted to sending out a general order to his officers in which he explained to them in a heart-to-heart manner the importance of maintaining discipline, especially as it would do much to further the Union cause. He reminded them that it was not the duty of the military to decide issues properly settled by the civil government and he exhorted them to respect the lives and property of noncombatants.[10]

Upon taking command of the Department of the Missouri, General Halleck also scrutinized Frémont's provost-marshal system for irregularities and ordered the investigation of charges against prisoners, especially civilians. In obedience to Halleck's order, George E. Leighton, provost marshal at St. Louis, provided information relating to the departments under his authority, the number of forces in his employ, and the expense. In the provost marshal's office, Leighton employed three clerks where most of the "general business" was conducted. While the police department was under the supervision of a senior officer, morning reports were submitted to Leighton, who gave daily instructions of duties to be accomplished, directing, in particular, the activities of detectives from the department. Moreover, Leighton explained that he employed three detectives unknown to the chief of police for "special cases under my own immediate instructions."[11]

Perhaps the most important duties of Leighton as provost marshal were the maintenance of security and supervision of the military prison in St. Louis, where were imprisoned up to 140 men, most of whom were federal soldiers charged with violating civil law, but including some prisoners of war and "political prisoners." Only two keepers were employed to maintain order and attend to the other needs of the prisoners. Having capacity for only ninety men, Leighton recommended that the prison be moved to a location with better security and more space. Of those civilians arrested and held at both St. Louis and Alton, Illinois, in the first few days of Halleck's command, the vast majority were accused of "aiding and abetting the enemy." These prisoners were typically held for a short time and released. Other offenses for which civilians were arrested included spying, attempting to travel to the South, carrying mail to and from the South, using "treasonable language," and disloyalty. Most of these prisoners were released after a few days as well. Furthermore, Leighton reported to Halleck his confidence in the mayor's and the police department's full cooperation, making it unnecessary for closer supervision of them. Finally, Leighton assured Halleck that St. Louis was reasonably secure and therefore thought that he could then "disentangle [the provost-marshal's office] from all connection with civil matters except in cases of absolute necessity."[12]

On November 20, 1861, Halleck wrote to General McClellan requesting written orders to establish martial law in his command, explaining that no such authority could be found. Upon this telegraphic dispatch, Lincoln, who sometimes monitored the communications of the military, authorized "martial law at Saint Louis" if both men "deem[ed] it necessary." When Halleck sent his request he was aware that Frémont before him had imposed martial law, but he was not one to assume powers not officially granted to him in writing. Perhaps his caution was a manifestation of the lawyer in him, an instinct to insure everything he did was scrupulously legal, or a recognition of the political minefield within which he found himself. For his part, McClellan replied to Halleck's request by asking him to explain why the need for martial law in his command was necessary, showing a caution that may have resulted from the controversy left in the aftermath of Frémont's ouster. In his reply, Halleck outlined the difficult military situation with which he was confronted. Guerrilla forces were operating in small groups in many counties, stealing supplies and kidnapping Union men. Such forces tended to melt away upon the approach of federal forces, but civil authorities found them too formidable to confront. Only martial law could reimpose order and provide protection to loyal citizens. Unaware that the president had already authorized it, Halleck stated that, although it had been "exercised by his predecessors," he would not impose martial law until he had received written authority. Moreover, without martial law, Halleck preferred to be relieved from command, for he was certain that he could not be successful otherwise. This letter brought a swift response in which Lincoln gave Halleck authority to suspend the privilege of the writ of habeas corpus and to impose martial law within the bounds of his military command.[13]

Although he did not immediately declare martial law, on December 4 General Halleck circulated General Orders No. 13, in which he explained what constituted violations of the laws of war and that persons involved in such crimes were "liable to capital punishment." Insurgents robbing and stealing property and killing their fellow citizens behind Union lines could expect severe punishment without mercy. The insurgents themselves were responsible for their treatment, he explained, for "they have forfeited their civil rights as citizens by making war against the Government, and upon their own heads must fall the consequences." All persons in arms or aiding the rebellion were to be arrested and the evidence against them reduced to writing in sworn affidavits to be forwarded to Provost Marshal General Farrar. Moreover, Halleck authorized the seizure of property useful to the federal war effort from persons aiding the rebellion and announced that military commissions would be established to try those civilians accused of violating the laws of war. All of these measures and more, he asserted, "may by some be regarded as severe, but they are certainly justified by the laws of war, and it is believed that they are not only right but necessary, it is therefore expected that all loyal citizens in this department will assist the military authorities in strictly enforcing them." On December 26, after an increase of insurgent activity against the railroads in northern Missouri, Halleck finally imposed martial law in St. Louis and along

Missouri's railroads. However, he made clear that in taking such action he did not intend to replace the loyal civil courts, which he expected to support the military.[14]

In February 1862, Halleck found it necessary to remind the civil authorities and courts in St. Louis that they must continue to operate as usual except in cases where military jurisdiction or necessity prevented them. In other parts of Missouri, where strong secessionist opinion prevailed, disloyal persons employed the judicial system to punish local militia for performing their military duties. In one instance, after an indictment was brought against a lieutenant in the Missouri State Militia for horse stealing, James Totten, commander in central Missouri, wrote to the deputy sheriff and the grand jury of Moniteau County warning against using the courts to interfere with the militia. In this instance, the officer had taken the horse in the conduct of his official duties. Totten observed that two-thirds of the grand jury "were secessionists, known and avowed," and according to official reports had sought to use their position to persecute Unionists. According to the information he had received, the grand jury had brought other indictments against Unionists while ignoring many examples of lawlessness committed by Secessionists. Totten reminded the deputy sheriff and grand jury that civilian control had been "partially suspended" and martial law was in force along the railroads and telegraph lines. He warned that their actions would be "closely observed, and will be, if persisted in, further investigated and they held accountable."[15]

As he sought to reestablish peace in Missouri, Halleck had the benefit of his experience during the Mexican War and his studies of military history and law. Nevertheless, such preparation must have seemed inadequate, especially given the complexity and the number of problems with which he was faced. Perhaps the most difficult of all the matters confronting him was how to protect Unionist families driven from their homes by Price's army and guerrilla bands. From the start Halleck received reports about Unionist refugees, especially those from southwestern Missouri, whose arrival in St. Louis presented a great humanitarian problem. Many of the refugees were in need of food, clothing, and shelter, having lost almost everything due to the cruelty of Secessionists, who had vowed to punish anyone in the region supporting the federal government. Halleck summarized the reports he received in this way: "Men, women, and children have alike been stripped and plundered. Thousands of such persons are finding their way to this city barefooted, half clad, and in a destitute and starving condition." To meet this emergency, Halleck decided to impose assessments against persons "known to be hostile to the Union" in St. Louis for a total of $10,000. Unionists had already donated aid to the first refugees and Halleck decided that the supporters of the rebellion should make contributions as well. Moreover, Halleck probably intended this policy to deter both Price's army and guerrilla forces from committing any more atrocities against loyal citizens. The levy was to be paid in supplies, clothing, housing, or money "in proportion to the guilt and property of each individual." The largest contributions were to be assessed against the property of those in arms against the federal government. Persons who had furnished money or other aid to the Rebels were to be assessed amounts next in value. Finally, others who had provided only verbal or written support to the rebellion were to contribute the least. Halleck next established "a board of assessors" to determine how much to assess each person, in part, by consulting the municipal tax records. Those failing to pay their assessments were to have property equal to the amount plus a penalty of 25 percent sold at auction. Persons contending by affidavit that they had been wrongly assessed were required to provide evidence of their loyalty within a week or pay a 10 percent penalty. Provost Marshal General Farrar was ordered to direct the distribution of the money and provisions collected with advice from the Sanitary Commission. Halleck also ordered that an accurate account of the money and provisions be kept and that any money collected in excess of $10,000 was to be turned over to the Sanitary Commission to benefit sick soldiers. Anyone resisting the collection of the assessment against them was to be arrested and tried by a military commission.[16]

This collection was different from General John Pope's assessment earlier in the war (see chapter 2), for those from whom Halleck's levy was collected were not either directly or indirectly culpable for the depredations for which they were paying. Apparently, Halleck believed military necessity required that Price and other Secessionists be deterred in some way from again driving thousands of noncombatant Unionists from their homes. On December 26, 1861, a group of citizens, who were the unfortunate objects of Halleck's levy, sent a petition of protest complaining that the assessment against them was unconstitutional and unfair and refused to cooperate or pay. Their refusal to pay the levy only allowed the board of assessors to penalize the petitioners 25 percent in addition to the assessments against them. Another protester, merchant Samuel Engler, went even further, making the mistake of challenging Halleck's authority in the St. Louis Common Pleas Court. Engler's lawyer sought to recover eighty boxes of star candles valued at $460 through a writ of replevin. On January 22, 1862, Engler gave a sworn statement and the next day the court ordered Sheriff John H. Andrews to recover Engler's property. Despite Andrew's attempt to carry out the court's order, he found it impossible because of "an armed body of men purporting to act under the authority of the United States which force it was not possible for me to resist or overcome." Furthermore, Engler discovered not only that the civil courts could not recover his property, but in return for his challenge to General Halleck's authority, he was arrested and banished from the Department of the Missouri. Halleck explained that

> Martial Law having been declared in this city by the authority of the President of the United States, all civil authorities, of whatsoever name or office, are hereby notified that any attempt on their part to interfere with the execution of any order issued from these Headquarters, or to impede, molest, or trouble, any officer duly appointed to carry such order into effect, will be regarded as a military offence, and punished accordingly.

Halleck's action against Engler was calculated to deter others from resorting to the civil courts to challenge his authority. The deterrence worked, for others did not repeat Engler's mistake, apparently even spooking two former prisoners from the Camp Jackson affair to drop their suits before the St. Louis Common Pleas Court as well.[17]

In implementing his confiscation policy, General Halleck instituted clear policies to insure that those persons most responsible for secession should support those persons hurt most by their activities. In doing so, he did not intend for his subordinates independently to institute their own confiscation policies. And so, when Colonel L. F. Ross, in command at Cape Girardeau, ordered assessments for destitute refugees in his district, Halleck countermanded the order and commanded Ross to provide information concerning the need. Orders from headquarters at St. Louis, he was told, would be sent to alleviate the suffering. One of the persons punished for his part in secession was former United States Senator Trusten Polk, who traveled to the South and in October 1862 was appointed presiding judge over a Confederate military court. Halleck ordered Polk's home in St. Louis seized, where women soon met thereafter to sew clothes for Union soldiers. However, implementation of Halleck's assessment order was delayed initially for a short time and the first board did not complete its work. A second board, composed of civilians wishing to do their work in secret, was dismissed, Halleck wanting his policy implemented publicly. This decision, and that to disband the first board of assessors, may have been in response to the petitioners' complaints that they had a right to an impartial jury and a public trial. These delays concerned Congressman Frank P. Blair Jr., brother of Postmaster General Montgomery Blair, who wrote to Halleck encouraging him to enforce his confiscation order. Halleck reassured him that "the growl of secessionists don't trouble us a particle." And true to his word, a new board of assessors soon completed the work, collecting assessments to aid Union refugees. The final report of the board revealed that upon appeal the board had rescinded assessments amounting to $3,715 against persons who were able to prove their loyalty. Another $2,000 in assessments against disloyal persons were not collected because they had no means to pay. The total of the assessments came to $11,887.50, less the penalties of $1,262.50 imposed on those refusing to cooperate.[18]

And finally, to meet the housing needs of the refugees coming to St. Louis, Halleck ordered that they be quartered in the homes of disloyal persons. A contemporary later estimated that forty thousand refugees came to St. Louis during the war. At first, many were ill and filled with despair, some having just seen their husbands and fathers murdered and themselves driven from their homes. During this time, about half of the refugees arriving were hospitalized until they were well enough to care for themselves. Having received aid when they first arrived, and considering work the duty of slaves, some of the refugees did not become self-sufficient as soon as possible. Moreover, white refugees residing at the Virginia Hotel, where some freedmen and freedwomen were allowed to stay also, objected to their integrated housing situation. For their part, black refugees had no objection to this arrangement and willingly worked to provide for themselves as soon as they were able. Those white refugees from the South who supported the Confederacy were left to fend for themselves.[19]

Halleck's implementation of assessments in St. Louis County was a formal type of property confiscation. The creation of assessment boards to confiscate the property of disloyal persons was an impractical system for troops in the field in pursuit of the enemy. To meet their immediate needs under nineteenth-century international law, the military could simply seize whatever supplies they needed. Moreover, commanders had the authority to use land and buildings to establish forts and other posts necessary to maintain control over a conquered region. The military routinely paid rent to loyal property owners, often contracting with them other terms to insure that their property when returned would be in its original condition. The real estate of disloyal persons was taken without compensation or contract. Despite these rules, some commanders and their soldiers still pillaged the homes and other property of peaceful citizens. Soon after taking command, Halleck, recognizing the need to confine the action of troops in the field, established rules to guide the military in making such seizures, warning of dire consequences for those violating his order. He noted that "numerous cases have been brought to the attention of the commanding general of alleged seizure and destruction of private property in this department, showing an outrageous abuse of power and a violation of the laws of war." To correct this circumstance he ordered that property was only to be seized when it was needed in the field or when held by armed persons and those helping the enemy. In those instances when subsistence or transportation was taken, an officer must keep a detailed account and provide the owner with a receipt. Once the property was no longer needed it must be returned to the owner. "Any unauthorized and unnecessary seizure or destruction of private property will be punished with the extreme penalty imposed by the laws of war, which is death." Even the seizure of enemy property was not to occur "except by the orders of the officer highest in command, who will be held accountable for the exercise of this power."[20]

As a warning to other leaders of the community and those with substantial wealth, the valuable property of Secessionists could be seized for military use. This power was sometimes exercised arbitrarily and imprudently, or even as a means to punish those who were admitted "southern sympathizers." Such was the case when in June 1861 Charlotte A. Armstrong's and her husband's land, which was adjacent to the fairgrounds in Boonville, was seized by General Nathaniel A. Lyon and used for various purposes including as a place to bury soldiers. While seizure of the land did not violate Halleck's military order, many irregularities occurred during its occupation. Union soldiers apparently destroyed much of the Armstrongs' fencing, trees, and a crop they had planted and generally harassed the family. After enduring this for several months, in

March 1862 Armstrong wrote to Halleck asking him to permit her and her family to remove to Kentucky. Gaining no satisfaction from Halleck, in May she traveled to Washington D.C. and gained an order requiring the restoration of her land unless it was absolutely necessary for the military to occupy it. Apparently, even this did not cause the removal of the troops, for in the end Armstrong complained that it was unreasonable for her and her family to move to the free states where they would be unable to gain assistance from family or friends. In refusing to allow the Armstrongs to travel to Kentucky, the military authorities probably were concerned that they could in some way do harm to the Union cause there.[21]

A similar case to that of the Armstrongs was that of Samuel B. Churchill, a state legislator and editor of the *St. Louis Bulletin*. As a member of the state legislature, Churchill had supported Governor Jackson in his attempt to make Missouri a member of the Southern Confederacy and in the fall of 1861 was arrested for "aiding and abetting the enemy" and was held for seventeen days before he was released on his parole in early November. Churchill's arrest appears to have been in retaliation for having complained about Union troop activities on property he had rented outside of St. Louis. According to him, he had "been already annoyed & suffered more than almost any man in the County of St. Louis." In September he had moved his family onto the Wash place, which he had rented wishing to take care of his family in quiet. However, "a regiment of German Cavalry was ordered out there, and although there was nearly a hundred acres of land unenclosed immediately in front of me, yet the officers selected the grounds inside of my enclosure on which to build stables for some six or seven hundred horses and had their stables within thirty or forty yards of my front door." The soldiers destroyed fencing and damaged his yard and much of a cornfield. He was able to harvest only a small part of the apple crop and had lost all of his poultry, peaches, pears, and melons "as if by magic." Despite his complaints to the commanding officer nothing changed, either because the officer could not or would not prevent the thefts. During his imprisonment, some of Churchill's friends concluded that it was unsafe for his family to remain at the house and moved them into St. Louis at an expense of between $300 and $400. Moreover, as a disloyal person Churchill was assessed $400 and in January 1862 Provost Marshal General Farrar prepared to sell some of his property, when Churchill paid the assessment. All of this and the destruction of ninety-five acres of wooded land, Churchill estimated, cost him $4,000, adding that this had happened while he was still "a prisoner upon parole . . . violating neither its letter or its spirit." Unfortunately for Churchill and his family, this was not the end of his troubles with Union military authorities.[22]

Another instance of valuable property being confiscated was McDowell Medical College in St. Louis. Its founder, Joseph N. McDowell, was a fine surgeon and teacher, but also an enthusiastic and outspoken supporter of the South. With the outbreak of hostilities, he offered his services as a physician and surgeon to the Confederate military and served in that capacity throughout the war. In his absence, the authorities converted the college into a military prison, which came to be known as the Gratiot Street Prison. Because of his disloyalty, no compensation was paid to McDowell and when he returned to St. Louis after the war he found the college in disrepair. Moreover, much to his chagrin and despair, he discovered that the medical equipment and extensive library he had supplied to the college at considerable expense was gone. Through the help of friends, however, in a short time he was able to restore the buildings and supplies and reopen the institution, which came to be known afterward as the Missouri Medical College.[23]

In mid-December 1861, just a few days before Halleck established martial law, a large number of insurgents combined to attack the railroads in northern Missouri, destroying track, bridges, and other property. The North Missouri Railroad had been "torn up and otherwise destroyed to such an extent as to stop the running of the cars from Hudson to Warrenton, a distance of over one hundred miles." Because this type of destruction was accomplished easily, and could not be prevented except by guarding every foot of track, these activities represented a substantial threat to the supplying of troops and their transportation, not to mention the danger to lives of military and civilian riders. From the extent and coordination of the attacks, it seemed almost certain that they had been ordered and organized by Confederate military authority, although only later would Halleck learn of General Price's complicity. As noted in chapter 2, these types of attacks were very difficult, if not impossible, to prevent. On December 22, Halleck issued General Orders No. 32, demonstrating the seriousness with which he took the destruction of railroad track and bridges, his main line of communications into the interior of the state. Halleck declared that anyone caught in the act of destroying the railroads or burning bridges were liable to immediate and summary execution by federal or state troops. Those persons convicted of this "highest crime known to the code of war" could expect capital punishment or some other severe penalty. Moreover, in the regions where these attacks occurred, the slaves of Secessionists, and when needed, the Secessionists themselves were to be employed in repairing the damage. Those "pretended" Unionists who had not done all they could either to prevent or to capture those responsible were to be treated as accomplices. Finally, in a policy very similar to General John Pope's General Orders No. 3, July 31, 1861, Halleck made the communities monetarily responsible for the expense of all repairs unless it could be proved that the local residents were unable to stop the attacks.[24]

In the aftermath of these raids, Halleck vigorously pursued those responsible, coordinating by telegraph the efforts of the federal and state troops in northern Missouri. He believed that the harm to the railroads amounted to $150,000 in damages but could be quickly repaired, and that only "severe punishment" would prevent such activities from continuing. The difficulty in guarding the extensive railroad and telegraphic system in northern Missouri became painfully clear, despite the presence of ten thousand soldiers stationed along the railroads to prevent just such attacks. However, the coordinated efforts by which the bridge burners and guerrilla bands were pursued aggressively soon resulted in the killing or capturing of a significant number of the culprits. Because their activities represented a serious threat to the peace of Missouri and support for the provisional government and the Union, Halleck ordered the establishment of military commissions to try captured guerrillas. These commissions were necessary, for the regular military judicial system restricted the types of cases which could be tried by courts-martial and the civilian authorities were powerless to deal with such a vast uprising. In fact, it was clear that in many places throughout Missouri the courts were either inoperative or were located in regions where judges and juries held very strong secessionist opinions and could not be relied upon to convict guerrillas for their crimes. Without a significant military presence and the institution of emergency measures under martial law, including the establishment of the military-commission system to meet the crisis then confronting the state, little if any prospect existed for the return of peace. Recognizing that some might object to the use of military commissions, arguing that the civilian courts certainly had laws against the destruction of property and murder, Halleck explained that where courts were operative those persons violating state or municipal law could still be brought before them. However, those committing such crimes, which were also perpetrated to provide support to the enemy, came under the jurisdiction of military authority and must be prosecuted under martial law. Halleck directed the local provost marshals to gather evidence against these prisoners in the form of written affidavits, to the truthfulness of which the witnesses were to swear under oath. The originals of this testimony were then sent to the provost marshal general. After reviewing the evidence, Farrar decided whether the prisoner should be held over for trial or be released.[25]

These "tribunals of necessity," as Halleck referred to them, were employed during wartime to try persons warring unlawfully, not being part of a regularly organized military force, and who were "no more nor less than murderers, robbers, and thieves." Because of the seriousness of the threat they posed to society and military operations, these "insurgents" or "guerrillas" were not accorded the status and rights of prisoners of war. However, Halleck made it clear that only he as overall commander could convene military commissions and that under no circumstance was "a soldier duly enrolled and mustered into the enemy's service by proper authority" to be prosecuted "for taking life in battle or according to the rules of modern warfare." A commander's authority to convene military commissions proceeded "directly from the fact of the existence of war and of the hostile occupation," that is, powers derived from international law to confront a military emergency. Moreover, as Halleck explained later, a military commander's authority was still subject to federal and state constitutions, to the president in his role as commander in chief, and to laws passed by Congress. As a military measure, commanders or the president determined whether military commissions were justified and when it was safe to terminate their operations. These commissions followed the same rules of evidence and procedure used in courts-martial, but operated apart from them to punish military offenses not falling under their jurisdiction. The role of Congress would normally be a secondary one, for while it could pass legislation to regulate or terminate the operation of these commissions, such would be subject to a presidential veto, which, of course, could be overridden. Usually during wartime this would be unlikely, given the normal expansion of the president's power and influence in his function as commander in chief and the general reluctance of legislators to interfere in military matters. This attitude seems appropriate and wise given that the conduct of war was primarily an executive function. Nevertheless, congressional oversight is also necessary to serve as a proper check upon abuses of presidential power which might otherwise occur. In extreme cases, Congress could impeach and try a president who sought to use the circumstances of war to accrue to himself inappropriate powers.[26]

After instituting his policy, Halleck received a written protest from General Sterling Price, who argued that the policy was contrary to the rules of war, asserting that military commissions were improper and Halleck's summary execution of the bridge burners was uncivilized. One purpose of his letter was to establish the idea that Price's written commissions to destroy railroad bridges provided protection to persons going behind Union lines disguised as discharged Confederate soldiers. While communications and transportation were lawful military targets, Price's methods, rather than Halleck's retaliation, were outside the accepted modes of warfare of his day. As Halleck explained in his reply, more in the tone of an instructor correcting an errant student than of a general to an opposing general, the attack upon his communications was proper so long as the men Price sent were properly uniformed and organized to fight in open warfare. Halleck promised to engage such forces as lawful combatants and to treat those he captured humanely as prisoners of war. However, Halleck rejected Price's assertion as ludicrous that his commissions provided immunity to those acting as "spies, marauders, robbers, incendiaries," and guerrillas. Halleck challenged Price to "refer me to a single authority on the laws of war which recognizes such a claim."[27]

The second purpose of Price's letter was to gain Halleck's agreement to disband his military commissions and to turn over the bridge burners to be tried in the civil courts. To Price, the matter was less a concern over the constitutional rights of Missourians than it was an effort to gain military advantage by eliminating an effective deterrent to the guerrilla activities of his supporters. Without such support, Price could not expect to tie down so many federal troops in Missouri. That Halleck found Price's demand preposterous is evident, for he did not even address it in his reply. However, in his pre- and post–Civil War writings, Halleck explained the historical basis and pragmatic reasons for instituting military commissions. As a lawyer, Halleck sought precedent, like that provided in the actions of a predecessor such as General Winfield Scott, to follow in making his own policy decisions. As commander of United States forces during the Mexican War, General Scott had instituted military tribunals to govern captured Mexican territory and to adjudicate civil and criminal cases between citizens of Mexico and United States troops. This was necessary, for otherwise General Scott either would have left the Mexican civil courts in operation or allowed chaos to ensue in the wake of the American army. While Scott's circumstance was not exactly analogous to Halleck's as commander of the Department of the Missouri, in both instances the military operated where the civilian courts were inoperative or were hostile to their forces and where, without military rule, many law-abiding civilians would have been left to the not-so-tender mercies of unscrupulous war criminals. In Civil War Missouri, during this period of great turmoil and lawlessness, the civil authorities and courts could do little to try persons committing military offenses, lacking the necessary force to deal with most of the marauders. Therefore, Halleck deemed military commissions necessary in the interest of reimposing order and insuring fair trials with due process for defendants. Moreover, the use of military commissions was considered far preferable to military officers or their subordinates deciding the fate of persons summarily, excepting only those cases in which individuals were captured in the act of committing serious violations of the law of war and no question of the individual's guilt existed. While military commissions today are still very controversial, especially in trying the cases of United States citizens, the federal courts in the nineteenth century held them to be constitutional so long as their use was defined narrowly. Even in *ex parte Milligan* (1866), a case often cited by opponents of military commissions, the United States Supreme Court did not find military commissions unconstitutional, instead ruling that such tribunals could be convened and operate only during times of military emergency.

> If, in foreign invasion or civil war, the courts are actually closed, and it is impossible to administer criminal justice according to law, then, on the theatre of active military operations, where war really prevails, there is a necessity to furnish a substitute for the civil authority, thus overthrown, to preserve the safety of the army and society; and as no power is left but the military, it is allowed to govern by martial rule until the laws can have their free course. As necessity creates the rule, so it limits its duration; for, if this government is continued after the courts are reinstated, it is a gross usurpation of power. Martial rule can never exist where the courts are open,

and in the proper and unobstructed exercise of their jurisdiction. It is also confined to the locality of actual war.[28]

In his implementation of military commissions, as with many other policies, Halleck tried to anticipate different problems he would face and shaped his policy to achieve particular ends. His policies bore none of the ad hoc characteristics which Frémont's efforts often revealed. Still, Halleck received advice from others, some of which he found useful. During the early period of his command when he was faced with a crisis of widespread guerrilla activity, Halleck communicated with many prominent individuals, some of whom provided advice about how best to quell the insurrection, especially after Halleck had issued his general orders. Because a large part of the population was involved in some manner with the insurrection, some providing intelligence and others participating in armed conflict, Halleck knew it was impractical, if not impossible, to imprison everyone implicated and instead, must employ some other means of persuasion or deterrence. Some of his correspondents suggested treating severely those guerrillas committing the most heinous crimes, such as the destruction of the Little Platte River Bridge, and offering conditional leniency to young men who were easily influenced by leaders and their peers. The wisdom of using a carrot and stick approach was verified when commanders in the field reported that influential members of communities, observing the consequences of rebellion to themselves and their towns, promised to discourage the organization of insurgents and to provide intelligence of any enemy movements in their regions. Moreover, believing that only the threat of imprisonment or worse would deter some of the worst offenders, Halleck ordered that "notoriously bad and dangerous men though no specific act of disloyalty can be proven against them will be kept in custody and their cases referred to the commanding general." At the same time, military commissions were organized and began their work in different locations.[29]

Halleck strictly supervised the proceedings of the military commissions, even going so far as to nullify every judgment of a commission held in Tipton, Missouri, because the commander had not received authority to order the organization of a military commission there. Halleck also ended the practice under Frémont's command of trying persons for treason, for it "is an offense technically defined by the Constitution, and is not triable by a military commission." Moreover, he insisted that in so far as was possible, the military commissions would follow the same procedures as courts-martial and maintain an accurate record of the charges and testimony in each case. From these trial records, one learns a good deal about how the attacks on the bridges and railroad track were organized and how some of the men became involved. People from all walks of life were witnesses and often were very well-acquainted with the persons on trial. Sometimes during their testimony long-held animosities surfaced, the result of differences in religious or political belief or some other disagreement or misunderstanding. Another disturbing aspect of guerrilla attacks was that now and then the targets were selected to satisfy some personal vendetta or jealousy. Furthermore, it is evident that in some parts of Missouri, especially in southwestern Missouri, in the counties along the Missouri River, and in the Missouri-Kansas border region, crime and violence were widespread and so prevalent that large numbers of people abandoned their homes and communities. In establishing military commissions, Halleck intended to reestablish order and hoped to return power to the civil authorities as the majority of his command moved against and defeated the enemy along the Mississippi River.[30]

From the proceedings and decisions of the military commissions, it is clear that the results were not foregone conclusions. In many instances, defendants were acquitted of some or all of the charges, even when it was evident that the individual was part of a group which committed murder or some other heinous crime but did not personally commit the offense. In the trial of Joseph W. Bollinger, testimony demonstrated that he was a willing and enthusiastic member of a band of guerrillas who murdered John Crowder, a loyal man whom Bollinger referred to as "a Black Republican," a term of derision Democrats often used to indicate the antislavery position of Republicans. Witnesses testified that Bollinger had helped to arrest Crowder and bragged about hanging him. Another witness, Christopher Tippet, testified that Bollinger threatened to hang James Utley, another Republican. Moreover, Bollinger was heard to exclaim that "Utley had a black spot in him and he said he allowed to hang him or something of that kind." Tippet thought this happened in May or June of 1861, sometime before Crowder's murder in late August or early September of the same year. While much of the testimony tended to implicate Bollinger, other witnesses stated that Bollinger was not with the group who killed Crowder, a fact which apparently accounted for his acquittal. However,

Bollinger was convicted by the military commission of being part of a guerrilla band in violation of the laws of war and of threatening to hang or kill a Union man, although they found him not guilty of the specification of the charge. For this reason, Halleck overturned this part of the commission's ruling but approved the rest. In the end, Halleck ordered Bollinger to be held in the Alton Military Prison until he took the oath of allegiance and paid a $1,000 bond.[31]

Further evidence of the ability of military commissions to try even prominent secessionists fairly, or at least find them not guilty, is demonstrated in the trial of Jefferson F. Jones, who during a brief period of the early part of the war was the leader of guerrilla forces in Callaway County. A prominent lawyer, Jones had organized men from the area in preparation for an anticipated "invasion" of militia troops led by General John B. Henderson, who later served in the United States Senate and was instrumental in guiding the Thirteenth Amendment of the Constitution to ratification. In his agreement with Henderson, before any battles were fought, Jones promised to disband his forces and remain peacefully at home if Henderson agreed to respect the constitutional rights of the people of Callaway County. On November 1, 1861, Jones published a letter in the *Fulton Telegraph* advising the community of the agreement. However, not long after this, guerrilla activity increased there and federal troops were sent into the region. From the testimony in his trial, prior to the concerted attacks against the railroads in northern Missouri, different guerrilla bands and soldiers from Price's army posing as impressed Union men began to organize for guerrilla activities. Some of these men, along with others who joined the bridge burners, were captured soon after the raids of December 20 and testified at Jones's trial.[32]

For his part, Jones denied that he had in any way aided or encouraged the destruction of the railroad in his area. While he did not deny that armed bands of men, many of whom were the bridge burners, came onto his property and were fed, Jones explained that since his agreement with Henderson he had discouraged guerrilla activity and especially had tried to keep armed men from coming to his home, fearing that he would be accused of aiding and abetting the insurrection. As a wealthy man, if his testimony was true, Jones may have been concerned that his property might be seized, especially after Halleck's general order threatening the confiscation of the property of supporters of the rebellion. Some of the guerrillas' testimony corroborated

Jones's story, although it is difficult to know whether these witnesses were telling the truth or were just protecting a co-conspirator. Certainly some of the testimony implicated Jones, especially that of Isaac McIntyre, one of the captured guerrillas, who recalled that Jones stated he did not like so many men to be at his place in the daytime and thought it best that they come only at night. Jones also provided feed for their horses. Another guerrilla, Robert Hughes, a boy of sixteen years of age, corroborated part of McIntyre's testimony when he recalled that upon their arrival at his house Jones was angry they had come, for "they might implicate him and his property." Other witnesses, including Walter Scott, a member of the Eighty-first Ohio Regiment and held prisoner by the guerrillas, provided other details stating that two to three hundred men, along with the guerrilla leaders Cobb and Dorsey, were at Jones's house.[33]

Jones called a number of witnesses to testify for him, to support his version of events, and to explain why he had a large amount of shot and powder at his home. Two of the witnesses were officers in the Confederate army and another was a leader of a guerrilla band. Each stated that Jones had discouraged their activities and would not participate in the rebellion after his agreement with Henderson. The merchant from whom Jones had purchased the large amount of shot and powder stated that he supposed the large order was made because Jones didn't want "to be piddling so often with the stores." One of the judges on the commission was able in cross-examination of Major Thomas Breckinridge to gain the admission that he considered Jones friendly to his guerrilla activities but for "prudential reasons" did not want himself and his men to stay on Jones's place, fearing he would be arrested. While Breckinridge and his men did not obtain forage for their horses from Jones, he thought Johnson's men had. In his closing statement to the commission, Jones admitted that in October 1861 he "was elected to the command of a large body of citizens, who took up arms to repel as they thought a threatened invasion of their most sacred constitutional rights & guarantees." After his agreement with Henderson, however, Jones asserted that he had maintained his part of the bargain and was not involved in any way with the rebellion. Jones also claimed that all the troubles in Callaway County had come from outsiders. The commission then found Jones not guilty on all charges against him, although in their report to General Halleck they recommended that he impose a security bond upon Jones, considering him "an influential and dangerous person." Apparently, the commission believed that Jones was possibly guilty but also thought that the evidence did not support the charges against him. Halleck approved the proceedings and ordered Jones released only after he had taken the oath of allegiance and posted a bond of $10,000 guaranteeing his future good behavior.[34]

In most of the cases tried before military commissions during this chaotic period, those suspected of burning bridges and other military crimes were convicted and sentenced to death, or at least imprisonment during the war. Halleck, and later President Lincoln, reduced some of these sentences. These commutations were sometimes conditional, as in the case of eight men, who were to remain in "close confinement" at the Alton Military Prison. However, Halleck also promised to carry out the men's original sentences of death, "if rebel spies again destroy railroads and telegraph lines." While he premised his leniency upon recent federal victories, it was most probably a calculated measure to demoralize the insurgency where the men lived. In essence, Halleck was holding the eight men hostage with a threat of death if the former depredations resumed. Moreover, he might have been seeking an opportunity to show clemency to men whom he and other federal generals believed were "misguided dupes" influenced by unscrupulous men. That this was Halleck's motive is verified for at least two of the men, Stephen Stott and John Patton, about whom he had received information from Union men demonstrating that both were young men who knew not "a word of the alphabet" and upon whom an aged mother and siblings depended. According to Halleck's correspondents, both had been deceived by others and never would have participated in the depredations for which they were convicted had they known the severe penalties for their crimes. Because of their situation it was argued that executing such men would harm the Union cause and tend to foment, rather than deter, insurrection.[35]

While Halleck was willing to treat such men mercifully, he also sought to insure that no one could continue to be ignorant of the consequences of guerrilla activity. On March 13, 1862, on the same day he received the expanded command of the Department of the Mississippi, Halleck promised that as soon as the rebellion was over in Missouri, "the partial and temporary military restraint exercised in particular places may be entirely withdrawn." However, until then he intended to punish those responsible for military offenses, especially guerrilla warfare, to the severest rigors of the law of war. Furthermore, no one operating in guerrilla bands could expect to be treated as prisoners of war, whether he possessed a commission from General Sterling Price or not, but instead, could expect to be "hung as robbers and murderers." Halleck also noted that Price should have known, if he did not, that under the rules of "civilized warfare" he had no authority to issue commissions to men to burn bridges and otherwise wage war unlawfully. Halleck's point, undoubtedly shocking to those men already convicted of or about to be tried for guerrilla activities, was that Price had misled and betrayed them.[36]

General Halleck's policies punishing civilians operating as bridge burners and destroyers of railroad property and telegraph lines were very successful, ending such activities except for sporadic and militarily insignificant incidents occurring to the end of the war. Less successful, however, were his efforts to stop the depredations of guerrilla fighters operating throughout Missouri, sometimes in cooperation with Confederate forces and other times independently as armed thugs robbing, murdering, and terrorizing the population, often without distinction to their loyalties. Operating in the brush on horseback behind Union lines, guerrilla bands were very difficult to find and even more difficult to capture or bring to battle. Their main weapon was swiftness of movement, surprise, and ruthlessness. Usually when attacked, these groups scattered in various directions to rendezvous later at predesignated locations. They specialized in terrorizing civilians, not fighting organized troops in battle. Because they wore civilian dress, guerrillas were able easily, especially where they had support from the locals, to pose as residents and avoid detection. One historian, in describing guerrilla warfare in Missouri, wrote that it "produced the most widespread, longest-lived, and most destructive guerrilla war in the Civil War. Missouri provides a horrendous example of the nature of guerrilla war in the American heartland." When Halleck took command in Missouri, guerrillas had already committed a number of atrocities, but the worst was still to come.[37]

As noted above, on December 4, 1861, Halleck issued General Orders No. 13, commanding insurgents to be shot if captured in the act of destroying the railroads or telegraph lines. Others suspected of such crimes were held for trial. Because, like other insurgents, guerrillas were fighting in an irregular and illegal manner, Halleck ordered that they be treated similarly. Such a policy continued during his command in Missouri, providing severe treatment for guerrillas and their supporters, while offering protection to those persons remaining at home in peace. Halleck justified this policy as necessary, for leniency had "only served to increase crimes of this character." Initially, commanders and officers in the field sought clarification, probably fearing to take such severe action without direct orders. For this reason, in private letters and orders Halleck explained the policy and made clear that captured lawful combatants were to be treated as prisoners of war but irregular forces were not to be accorded such status. Soon everyone down to the private soldier understood that no quarter was to be given to those caught in arms "in the brush" and that those suspected of guerrilla activity were to be arrested and tried by military commission. A fairly typical incident, recorded in an Ohio cavalryman's diary, demonstrates the summary manner with which armed guerrillas were often treated.

> Co D took two prisoners (who had killed a union man) disarm'd [sic] them told them to run for life one was making good his escape when one of the officers took after him and killed him with his revolver, the other was shot down almost instantly with several balls—(This in Mo)[.] A great deal of bushwhacking now going on in Mo. Soon as leaves are out, they boast that they will have a fine harvest picking off Feds[.][38]

Later, this policy gained greater authority when, at Halleck's request, Francis Lieber, law professor at Columbia College in New York City, wrote a scholarly essay explaining that guerrillas were not part of an organized armed force and were illegal according to the laws of war. They operated "chiefly by raids, extortion, destruction, and massacre." Because they must remain constantly on the run, guerrillas "cannot encumber themselves with many prisoners, and will therefore generally give no quarter." For this reason, guerrilla forces "are peculiarly dangerous," are difficult to capture, and typically "degenerate into simple robbers or brigands." Moreover, Halleck did not allow guerrilla bands from Kansas to operate with impunity in Missouri. To Secretary of War Edwin M. Stanton, Halleck complained that some of the depredations in Missouri were being committed by "Kansas jayhawkers," regiments organized by United States Senator James Lane, a controversial figure of the war. These Union regiments were responsible for many depredations in Missouri, as were some of the out-of-state volunteer troops. Halleck ordered the Kansas regiments out of Missouri and dismissed from the service those officers he believed were participants with their men in these marauding activities.[39]

The response of General Price to Halleck's measures to prevent insurgency and guerrilla activities again was to commission officers and men to organize and operate as guerrillas behind federal lines in a region where he had no control. This guerrilla force was to operate "in the Sixth and Seventh Military Districts" under the command of J. C. Campbell, a justice of the peace in Wright County. During time of war, such measures were considered illegal, for according to military law a commander cannot give orders or commissions to persons outside his own lines. Having already covered these issues in his correspondence with Price over the matter of commissions to bridge burners, in a general order Halleck commented that Price "ought to know that such a course is contrary to the rules of civilized warfare" and warned anyone presuming to act under Price's commission that they would be hung "for the barbarity of their general."[40]

Soon after Halleck had reiterated his tough policy against guerrilla forces, General James Totten, commander of the district of central Missouri, concentrated his forces and sent a sizable expedition against guerrilla bands operating in Moniteau and Boone counties along the Missouri River. Although the main force of guerrillas could not be brought to battle, the federal troops from Missouri and Indiana captured and killed a small number of the band and scattered the rest, preventing them, at least temporarily, from concentrating and operating with impunity in the region. Because of this military pressure and Halleck's policy, which "has caused some stir among the guerrilla bands," one of their local leaders, apparently feeling the pressure, sent a messenger to a state militia recruiter to determine if he and his men might be permitted to return to their homes based "upon reasonable terms." Failing that, the messenger warned that the guerrillas intended to destroy property and murder the region's inhabitants in retaliation. Fortunately for the people of central Missouri, only three days later the guerrilla leader was killed and his force defeated. However, despite this victory, the circumstance illustrated how Halleck's policy was a double-edged sword. While it certainly deterred anyone considering taking up arms as an irregular combatant, it also provided no incentive for those already operating as guerrillas to end their criminal activities. How much the policy was responsible for the later intensification of guerrilla warfare in Missouri is difficult to measure, although one can point to strong circumstantial evidence, especially in the spring of 1862, that at least some of the activity was retaliatory. In considering the overall guerrilla activity in Missouri as the war progressed, however, the evidence tends to point to other factors contributing as well, including the bitterness of many over the atrocities committed by some federal and state militia troops and as a reaction to the increasing control the federal and state forces imposed upon those Missourians whose loyalties were considered suspect. Ironically, perhaps the most significant and contributory reason for the increased guerrilla warfare in Missouri, especially after northern victories in the West, was the increasing weakness of regular Confederate forces from which many soldiers deserted and returned home, some of whom later became guerrillas.[41]

Today, Halleck's policy of soldiers in the field summarily executing irregular forces is shocking, in part because of its brutality, and partly for the lack of contemporary protest to it. Even at this early stage of the war, it is probable that both Lincoln and his new secretary of war Edwin M. Stanton were well aware of Halleck's severe policies, including that concerning insurgents and guerrillas. With guerrilla bands operating extensively in Missouri and reconciliation with the South unlikely, Lincoln probably believed such severity was necessary to protect the lives of peaceful citizens. Certainly, a short time later in a letter he expressed his exasperation with those who continued to counsel inaction for fear that some Union men's lives and livelihoods might be harmed and vowed his determination to "do *all* I can to save the government." Later, no doubt can exist that Lincoln approved the summary execution of guerrillas and insurgents captured in arms, for General Halleck, who by then was general in chief, commissioned eminent jurist and educator Francis Lieber and other committee members to draft General Orders No. 100, also known as Lieber's Code, which in 1863 provided to the Union army's officers and men the principles and policies for fighting the war, including that against irregular fighters. Lincoln approved this document before its promulgation.[42]

But why did Lincoln accept a policy of summary execution for insurgents and guerrillas captured in the field with weapons? Well known among his contemporaries and today as a compassionate man, Lincoln was unwilling to allow the execution of persons condemned to death by military commission or court-martial without his review of the case first. So why under these circumstances did his compassion not extend to guerrillas and insurgents? It seems likely that military necessity, as he perceived it, influenced his thinking.

The ease with which a small group of ruthless men could terrorize a region, coupled with the great destruction of property and the murder of noncombatants, probably convinced Lincoln, especially as he read military dispatches and his military advisors explained the realities of guerrilla warfare, that he should not interfere with these summary executions. Moreover, it seems apparent that he accepted this measure despite knowing that inevitably some innocent persons would be killed mistakenly. Lincoln may have concluded that if he stopped the practice of summarily executing guerrillas and insurgents, he would be making many persons even more vulnerable to guerrilla attacks. It is also evident that another factor in his decision was his desire to protect women and children, who were the most common victims of guerrilla outrages, from the brutalities associated with it. Finally, it should be remembered that this policy was consistent with his notion that during wartime extraordinary measures are justified when they can stop the suffering of innocent persons. Certainly, Lincoln demonstrated such a willingness in his suspension of the privilege of the writ of habeas corpus, realizing that the courts and law enforcement were unable to put down widespread insurrection. Lincoln had also warned that he might execute Confederate prisoners of war in retaliation for the Confederates' sale or execution of black prisoners of war. Only such a demonstration of his determination, although unjust to the individuals executed, could protect black soldiers from such treatment. Undoubtedly, Lincoln calculated that many more innocent lives would be saved than lost through his policy. While strictly unjust, like the loss of life on the battlefield, these policies were probably necessary to prevent the much greater calamity of unchecked guerrilla activity. Another reason for Lincoln's acquiescence in this policy may have been his recognition that an order prohibiting the summary execution of guerrillas would be ignored and without effect in the field. However, it should also be noted that once guerrillas and insurgents were captured and tried by military commissions, Lincoln no longer believed himself constrained from reviewing and interfering in cases whenever he deemed it proper. This leniency was judged by some, it will be seen below, to be counterproductive to the vigorous prosecution of the war.[43]

4

MILITARY GOVERNMENT
AND CIVIL LIBERTIES

ONE OF THE STRIKING FEATURES of General Henry W. Halleck's command of the Department of the Missouri was the extent to which his military government controlled many aspects of Missourians' lives. As observed in chapter 3, he took extraordinary measures to stop guerrilla activity and to punish those aiding them and the regular Confederate army under General Sterling Price. To gather intelligence and enforce his general orders, Halleck had expanded the provost-marshal system established under Frémont and placed Bernard G. Farrar in charge as provost marshal general. While he did not want them interfering with the civil authority except when militarily necessary, Halleck ordered the provost marshals to enforce a state convention ordinance requiring all officeholders to take an oath of allegiance to the governments of Missouri and the United States. This requirement had the effect of causing many disloyal persons to resign their positions. Similarly, the convention required everyone to take an oath before voting in local and state elections, a policy intended as another safeguard against disloyal persons holding political office. Halleck supported these and other policies, coordinating his efforts with the state authorities. This cooperation was very important given the unusual circumstance of civil and military government operating together simultaneously. However, the military's involvement in determining who was eligible to vote and hold political office was a remarkable intrusion into civil affairs.[1]

Like his predecessor (see chapter 2), Halleck ordered provost marshals to monitor newspapers and other literature published in Missouri. To expedite this, in January 1862 Halleck ordered all newspapers published outside of St. Louis to provide his headquarters with copies of their publications. Those failing to do so would be "liable to suppression." Of course, while not exerting prior restraint, such oversight could coerce some editors into omitting items critical of Halleck or the Lincoln administration. If such intimidation of editors was intended, however, it was largely ineffective, for press criticism of the military and civil authorities continued throughout the war. Policy debates, especially concerning emancipation and security, were regular features as well. Halleck's foremost concern was to prevent the publication of military movements and other intelligence helpful to the enemy. This policy was in harmony with Lincoln's later direction to General John M. Schofield not to interfere with the press "where no evil could result." Moreover, it is important to remember that no attempt was ever made to establish specific censorship rules, although it is also clear that secessionist publications were not tolerated and were summarily suppressed. By the time Halleck took command, however, few secessionist papers if any remained in Missouri and his overall record was largely one of restraint, although military authorities suppressed publications they considered supportive of the enemy. Only after his departure from Missouri would Halleck demonstrate a peevish disdain for the press and issue orders making it difficult for reporters to gather wartime information.[2]

In response to the publication of military movements, however, Halleck took vigorous action ordering all copies of the offending publication destroyed. He warned officers and their men that they would be held responsible according to "the law and Army Regulations" for the publication of any military intelligence they provided to the press. Moreover, recognizing the importance of public opinion, he rescinded General E. A. Paine's order to "hang one of the rebel cavalry for each Union man murdered, and after this two for each." Halleck noted that such a policy was "contrary to the rules of civilized war, and if its spirit should be adopted the whole country would be covered with blood. Retaliation has its limits, and the innocent should not be made to suffer for the acts of others over whom they have no control."[3]

Halleck delegated the authority to enforce his restrictions upon the press to Provost Marshal General Farrar, who enjoyed a good deal of latitude in such matters. In addition to the problem of important military intelligence being published in newspapers, Farrar and his provost marshals sought to prevent the publication of literature which would inspire resistance to the state provisional government under Governor Gamble and the military. Perhaps Farrar and his provost marshals feared another destructive uprising like the one which had occurred just a short time before in late December. One of those prosecuted at the time was George J. Jones, who had published pamphlets and reprints from English articles which Farrar considered "treasonable and libelous." Jones was a British subject and upon his arrest appealed to the British consulate in Chicago for help. According to depositions taken of his customers and an employee, Jones owned a shop selling newspapers and books and strongly supported the South. According to one of the witnesses, Jones was especially angry about the confiscation policy instituted to aid Union refugees. The British Consul at Chicago, J. Edward Wilkins, investigated Jones's case and told George E. Leighton, the provost marshal at St. Louis, that Jones denied having violated any laws or military orders and claimed to have scrupulously complied with the "Queen's Proclamation" enjoining all British subjects to maintain a strict neutrality during the conflict between the North and the South. While he was unable to determine the truth or falseness of the charges, Wilkins asked that Jones either be released or tried as soon as possible.[4]

In his reply, Leighton explained that he had arrested Jones "for rendering aid and assistance to the enemies of the Government." Concerning the reprinted articles, Leighton did not claim that their content was "strictly *treasonable*." However, he believed the articles had been written to heap scorn upon the government and its officers and "to sustain the failing hopes of rebels in our midst; to defend the cause of the rebellion as just and right; and to disseminate as facts the most gross fabrications." Leighton also observed that during wartime actions permitted in other parts of the country far from military operations could not be allowed in St. Louis, where "many disloyal citizens [were] easily inflamed, excited and encouraged in their disloyalty by such articles as" Jones had published. Despite this, three days later Leighton wrote Wilkins to inform him they had released Jones, who was allowed to return to his business, at which he continued unhindered until a new commander of the department was appointed.[5]

In another instance of the military's supervision of the press, David McAnally, editor of the *St. Louis Christian Advocate,* provided an account of his arrest on April 21, 1862, and monthlong imprisonment in the Myrtle Street Prison. According to McAnally, the arrest was part of a campaign to discredit him and other members of the Methodist Episcopal Church South and to silence his newspaper. Later he was released upon his own recognizance while awaiting trial before a military commission. The charge was violating the laws of war, but after a short trial he was released, having taken an oath not to help the enemy and to remain in St. Louis County. McAnally also claimed he was never advised of the military commission's verdict and remained under parole until November 1865. However, it is difficult to render any judgment about McAnally's account, for apparently no records exist for his trial before a military commission and the accuracy of his testimony concerning previous events is questionable (see chapter 2). Critics circulated these types of accounts to undermine support for the provisional government under Governor Hamilton R. Gamble and the military's efforts to secure Missouri for the Union. After the war these stories, some of which were undoubtedly true, were politically advantageous in attacking Missouri's Radical Republican government. As one might expect, the Radical Republicans also had their own version of events beneficial to themselves.[6]

Another arrest demonstrated the differences of opinion which existed even between Unionists concerning what constituted material worthy of suppression. United States Congressman Thomas L. Price, a staunch proslavery Unionist, interceded on behalf of C. P. Anderson, the editor of the California, Missouri, *News*, arguing that nothing had been published warranting his arrest. Although he agreed to release him on humanitarian grounds, Farrar promised to arrest the editor again if he published "articles of a like import as those contained in his paper for several months past." It is apparent also that Farrar believed he should prosecute not only those editors who provided details concerning military movements, but those who wrote "disloyal articles" as well. These measures were taken against those who might otherwise be considered loyal by most Unionists in Missouri. However, most of the military's resources were directed at papers considered disloyal, while newspapers supporting the Union were allowed to be critical of the policies of the military and government to some degree. When an editor's opinions were considered questionable, while not considered prosecutable, a provost marshal sometimes required him to take an oath of allegiance, thereby placing him on record as loyal. Of course, an editor might take the oath unfaithfully, but the exercise had the effect of putting him on notice that he might be prosecuted for publishing disloyal articles.[7]

Soon after Provost Marshal General Farrar began receiving copies of newspapers from across Missouri, Edmund J. Ellis, the editor of Columbia's *Boone County Standard,* came under scrutiny for an article he had published on February 7, 1862, entitled, "News from General Price." According to the charge brought against Ellis, the article provided intelligence "to the enemies of the Government" and encouraged "resistance to the Government and laws of the United States." Further investigation by the military authorities uncovered more articles in earlier editions of Ellis's paper, with titles such as "Letters from Our Army," which referred to the Confederate army under Price's command, and "Root, Abe, or Die." Ellis also published a pamphlet, "To the Patriot Army of Missouri," and communications from General Sterling Price to Missourians encouraging guerrilla warfare. Moreover, in his paper Ellis included letters from some of Missouri's secessionist leaders and even a proclamation by Confederate President Jefferson Davis. Perhaps wishing to make an example of him, the military convicted Ellis and sentenced him to be banished from Missouri for the duration of the war and ordered confiscated the press and other property of the newspaper for sale. General Halleck approved the court's findings and sentence, directing that the property of the *Boone County Standard* be delivered to the quartermaster's department, and further ordered that if Ellis returned to Missouri before the end of the war without permission he would be imprisoned in the Alton Military Prison. Secretary of War Stanton "heartily approved" of Ellis's treatment and all military departments were ordered to follow the same measures in similar cases. Without the publication of military intelligence or movements, the military necessity of such a policy is questionable, although it demonstrates the level of frustration and anger felt among the Union military in the context of Missouri's bitter guerrilla war, in which often one could not identify or bring to battle an elusive enemy.[8]

Another civil liberty restricted in Missouri under General Halleck's command was freedom of speech. Under Provost Marshal General Farrar and his subordinates, extensive efforts were made to collect information about civilians and to arrest dissenters whose speech was often referred to in the records as "disloyal." While it is difficult to imagine a similar suppression of dissent today during wartime, one must remember that the possibility of a general uprising among Secessionists in Missouri was strong, especially if Confederate General Price was again able to invade Missouri. Unionists feared that with the help of guerrilla bands Price would attempt to drive out Union troops, seize St. Louis, and return ousted Governor Claiborne F. Jackson and the state legislature to office. Moreover, Unionists had already witnessed the extensive destruction of railroad track and bridges, causing much property damage and loss of life, as in the September 1861 Little Platte River Bridge disaster, and the murder of persons whose sole crime was support of the United States government. Under such circumstances, the large number of men sympathetic with the Confederacy posed a significant security threat, and the collection of information on such persons was certainly prudent. Among this group probably only a minority was willing to engage in guerrilla warfare and this often only sporadically. Still, this minority numbered in the thousands scattered throughout the state ready to attack federal and militia troops, murder Unionists, and steal and destroy property. More Confederate sympathizers, both men and women, were willing to help local guerrilla fighters by providing supplies and intelligence so long as they believed they could do so without detection by the authorities. Moreover, Confederate General Price had provided substantial aid and organization to these efforts by issuing officers' commissions to guerrilla leaders. The severe punishment of guerrillas had deterred many from becoming involved with the insurgency, but the danger always existed that with success those then not participating would conclude that it was safe to join or help the guerrillas. For this reason, the authorities worked diligently to identify the insurgents and their supporters. Almost inevitably, in the collection of this intelligence and the arrest of those who had "violated the laws and customs of war," abuses of power sometimes occurred. Given the dangers and the zeal with which many provost marshals and soldiers pursued those they considered to be traitors, it is not surprising that dissent was sometimes suppressed unnecessarily.[9]

Because of their numbers, it was impossible to incarcerate all disloyal persons as "political prisoners," nevertheless, some method of dealing with them was necessary to confront the threat they posed. The method which emerged was probably the unintended consequence of a policy established when President Lincoln promulgated his executive order regarding political prisoners on February 14, 1862, ordering the parole of those prisoners willing to swear an oath "to render no aid or comfort to the enemies in hostility to the United States." On the same day, Halleck issued his own order intended to insure compliance with the president's, but also adding details to safeguard against the release of certain dangerous persons and to prevent many of those receiving amnesty from later violating their oath. In this circular, Halleck ordered persons involved in the rebellion to be arrested, thereby making it clear that such arrests would not cease. Persons involved in violence or destruction of the railroads and bridges or other property were not under any circumstances to be released. Others could be freed, but Halleck ordered that along with an oath of allegiance the parolees must post a bond securing their good behavior. Typically this bond would be set at a minimum of $1,000. Persons with considerable financial means were made to post a larger bond. These rules led to more arrests, but also to less long-term imprisonment of persons who had not committed violence or some other egregious act like destroying property.[10]

Farrar and his subordinate provost marshals stationed throughout the state gathered their intelligence through a number of sources. Detectives collected information through undercover operations, and soldiers and civilians reported on persons who had expressed themselves in favor of the South. The majority of persons arrested for making disloyal statements were common, working-class people, some of whom had spoken under the influence of alcohol. In many of these cases, the persons arrested had only expressed themselves passionately in the heat of a dispute or voiced support for the South to annoy a roommate or neighbor. This, of course, could only be determined through questioning of the accused and further investigation. Apparently, this was the circumstance which led to the arrest of Mrs. Gazzolo. Her neighbor Anne Whitehead had accused her of being "in the habit of having her children hurrah for Jeff Davis," singing secession songs in her parlor, and referring to the American flag as an "old rag." Such behavior was annoying perhaps, but hardly worthy of notice by the provost marshal's office. Some like Ambrose McFaul had not only spoken with "treasonable language," but also had done so "publicly and in presence of soldiers." If a law existed to punish stupidity and imprudence, perhaps McFaul and many others like him should have been arrested, but certainly not for expressing their support for the South. These type of dissenters, of whom there appear to have been a fair number, were typically held for a short time and then released after a brief hearing and their taking the oath of allegiance and posting a bond as security for their future silence. Occasionally, individuals bore false witness against others with whom they had a dispute. This apparently happened in the case of Alick Henry, who was the barkeep at the Cleveland Beer Saloon in St. Louis. His two accusers had come into his establishment and played cards with "one of the beer girls." The men afterward went to the bar claiming to have won a free drink there, which Henry refused to provide. This led to a fight between Henry, who was aided by a patron of the bar, and the two men, who were thrown out and arrested. While awaiting trial the two brought charges against Henry and accused him of disloyalty. An investigation soon demonstrated that he was a loyal man.[11]

Others, whose expressions were regarded as more serious, sometimes were given a short prison sentence before being paroled. Such was the case of William Turton, who had claimed that the federal army then besieging Corinth, Mississippi, had suffered a major defeat and that General Halleck had been wounded. Turton also stated that Lincoln wanted "to make slaves equal to white men." Such false reports were probably considered demoralizing to Union supporters, thus provoking a slightly more vigorous response from the provost marshal, who sentenced Turton to twenty days in prison and imposed a bond of $3,000 upon him.[12]

The circumstances of a few of the persons arrested, however, such as former Supreme Court of Missouri Judge James H. Birch, were more complicated, indicating divisions among supporters of the United States government. Birch's attitudes are representative of many Missourians who often referred to themselves as conditional Unionists. This group, which comprised a majority of Unionists in Missouri, was not prepared to support the Lincoln administration and its war effort without reservation. Many of these Unionists, like the Virginia-born Birch, identified more with the South than the North and were strongly opposed to any effort to abolish slavery either gradually or immediately. On the other hand, unconditional Unionists were often, although not exclusively, in favor of emancipating the slaves and were suspicious of Unionists who only wanted to fight the war to maintain the Union. As the war progressed, these policy disputes would become bitter and, as discussed below, led to greater conflict and undermined the war effort. The provost marshal records of Birch's arrest demonstrate the animosity of some unconditional Unionists toward their conditional counterparts for not embracing a more vigorous prosecution of the war. At a political meeting held in Rolla, while campaigning for the governorship in late May 1862, Birch was reported to have criticized Lincoln for posing the possibility that if circumstances necessitated it he might yet free slaves as a war measure. "Judge Birch thought the President had no such power under any circumstances and that he should not have intimated any probability or possibility of such power ever being exercised by him." Birch also promised if elected governor that he would never furnish soldiers if Lincoln intended to free the slaves. Birch asserted that Halleck would resign and many soldiers would also if the president sought to emancipate the slaves. For these remarks Birch was arrested but soon after released, although later in the fall while running for a congressional seat he alerted Governor Gamble that he might be arrested again.[13]

While the majority of arrests for dissent were only temporary and some unjustified, other persons arrested represented a more genuine and imminent threat to the civil and military government in Missouri. These persons not only expressed their disdain for the Union and the "Black Republicans" and their policies, but also advocated specific actions to support the South. Some, like Joseph B. Hussey, William Chappell, and Robert D. Irvine, advocated resistance to federal troops and violence. Hussey, who was charged with a violation of his oath of allegiance, had threatened to cut the throats of Unionists. Despite having a number of witnesses for his defense claiming that he was actually a Unionist involved in raising a company of federal troops named Birge's Sharpshooters, the military commission found him guilty and sentenced him to death. However, the commission recommended that Hussey be shown mercy and receive a commutation of his sentence. Even one of the witnesses, who was a personal enemy of Hussey, wrote a letter to President Lincoln requesting the commutation of his sentence. Before Lincoln could intervene, Halleck commuted Hussey's sentence to imprisonment during the war. William Chappell's case was similar to Hussey's in that he was charged with threatening to kill men loyal to the United States government and ordering John Francisco, a Unionist, to leave the state. Chappell was ordered imprisoned in the Alton Military Prison. Robert D. Irvine, who like Chappell lived in Callaway County, one of the most active regions for guerrilla warfare, was arrested for arguing that those fighting as insurgents should be treated like those fighting as regular troops. No record exists for how Irvine's case was handled by the provost marshal.[14]

The case of Isaac N. Shambaugh is an example of the type of dissent that went beyond expressing disagreement with the authorities and their policies, demonstrating the mischief possible if a leader within a community advocated violence. During peacetime, and without the instigation of violence, Shambaugh's remarks should not have caused any response from the police and judicial authorities. However, in the midst of civil war, the instigation of

violence and resistance to the national government was a more serious matter indeed. It is unclear why Shambaugh was not prosecuted earlier for the
remarks he had made in June 1861, but the most probable reason was that
he had been absent from Missouri until the time of his arrest in February
1862. Shambaugh had been a member of the Missouri General Assembly
and had supported Governor Jackson's secret military bill, which was passed
in the aftermath of the Camp Jackson affair in May 1861, and probably he
was one of the legislators who had fled the state with General Price's army.
Shambaugh's speech was made in northwestern Missouri at Maysville in
reply to the speeches of James H. Birch and Willard P. Hall, former congressman and later governor in 1864, both of whom had argued before a
meeting of the town against secession. Afterward, a group of the residents
marched to the courthouse and raised an American flag. Shambaugh declined to reply to the speeches of Birch and Hall, but after their departure he
went to McPherson's Tavern and spoke in favor of secession. According to
Shambaugh, "Hall and Birch had been telling the people a parcel of lies in
their speeches, that the soldiers at St. Louis had shot women and children,
and waved his hat over his head, at which the people commenced shooting
at the flag. He said in his speech that the people would be compelled to take
the oath to support Lincoln's government or be dragged out and shot, and
if they wanted to escape they must do it quickly." While from the file it is
unclear what happened to him, Shambaugh most probably was held for a
period of time before being released upon taking the oath of allegiance and
posting a bond to secure his future good behavior.[15]

A form of civil liberty related to freedom of speech was that of religion,
particularly in respect to the right of ministers to preach and administer to
their congregations. As already noted in chapter 2, under General John C.
Frémont's command a small number of ministers were arrested for statements
considered disloyal and in one instance for participating in guerrilla warfare.
After some complaints concerning his policy, Frémont promised to stop arrests of persons for expressing their opinions alone. While at first he followed
the same policy of nonintervention, General Halleck's decision to order ministers to take the same oath of allegiance as that required of state officials led
to much military interference within the churches. Apparently, Halleck never
provided a justification for this policy. Certainly, no military necessity existed for preventing ministers from preaching so long as they did not advocate

violence or resistance to the war effort. Nevertheless, in the first months of Halleck's command, ministers suspected of continuing to preach without having taken the oath of allegiance were arrested and brought before the local provost marshal's office and questioned. One of these was Catholic priest W. Hennessey, who was accused of advocating secession from the pulpit at St. Vincent's in St. Louis. This charge was denied by the priest, who perhaps violated one of the Ten Commandments in claiming that his sermon topic was not secession, but rather the ascension, and that he had been misunderstood. Many of the ministers arrested undoubtedly harbored strong southern sympathies, but otherwise had remained silent, or at least had made no overtly secessionist statements from the pulpit to call attention to themselves. Some ministers remained silent believing that their calling set them apart from and above politics; others recognized that their congregations were divided on the war and understood the turmoil they would introduce by taking a position; and still other ministers remained silent out of fear of arrest.[16]

One of the unintended consequences of Halleck's policy was that ministers' refusal to take the oath of allegiance was sometimes used as a pretext by local provost marshals to arrest them. In one instance, a provost marshal in central Missouri, where a large part of the population favored the South, surrounded an association meeting of Baptist ministers in Saline County and forced them into three lines. The first was reserved for supporters of the Union. In the second line were Southerners who had taken the oath and posted a bond. The final line was for those supporters of the South who had not taken the oath. This final group was then notified that they were under arrest and marched a distance of fifteen miles from Rehobath to Marshall where they were paroled. Moreover, some ministers were apparently targeted because they were members of denominations like the Methodist-Episcopal Church South, whose members and preachers were considered to be predominately disloyal. The publications of this denomination after the war claimed that they had been singled out particularly for persecution by the military authorities often through the agency of the northern branch of its denomination, the two branches having split over slavery. This was the claim of James M. Proctor, who was arrested in July 1862 near Cape Girardeau and paroled until he was arrested again in late September by Lieutenant Colonel James Peckham of the Twenty-ninth Missouri Volunteers. In early October, in compliance with orders from General John W. Davidson, commander of the St. Louis District, to arrest "bad and dangerous men," Proctor was sent to the Gratiot Street Prison in St. Louis but was released later that month after his case was dismissed for lack of evidence by a military commission assembled in St. Louis. Moreover, he claimed he had been imprisoned with "several worthy ministers of different denominations," which if true indicates that perhaps the persecution of ministers was more widespread than previously known. After the war, Proctor asserted that he had never taken the oath and continued to preach despite continuing harassment during the war and after. Other ministers were also arrested ostensibly for preaching without having taken the oath, but actually they had been incarcerated as disloyal men and were considered potential threats to their communities.[17]

On rare occasions, commanders not only prohibited preachers from administering to their congregations, but went so far as to close the church. Such a case occurred in St. Joseph, a town in northwestern Missouri where much bitter warfare continued throughout the war. William M. Rush, understanding that his congregation was bitterly split over the war, took extraordinary precautions to prevent conflict within his church, including devising an innocuous and neutral prayer calling for God so to direct events to insure that He might be glorified and mankind benefited. Rush purposely refrained from asking for God's blessing to either side. It appears, however, that he may have devised his prayers as much to avoid praying for the president of the United States and his administration as to avoid controversy. Nevertheless, this tactic had the merit of avoiding conflict until one Sunday Rush called upon another minister, W. C. Toole, to give the closing prayer. Being a strong supporter of the Union, in his prayer he complained bitterly about the rebellion, thereby exciting the very type of controversy Rush had taken pains not to ignite, for persons with "opposite views thought it much out of place." For this reason, Rush, after consulting with some of the leading members of his congregation, decided it best to give the closing prayer himself to avoid any further controversy. Nevertheless, a short time later military commander General Benjamin F. Loan notified Rush that his church was being closed for disloyalty, citing as proof that prayers could not be offered for the United States government without offending the congregation. Rush then explained his policy of neutrality to General Loan, who still refused to allow the church to remain open. Soon afterward, Loan prohibited Rush from preaching in the military district, an order which ultimately forced his return to Chillicothe, Missouri, where he had resided before moving to St. Joseph. Having gained a reputation as a disloyal man, attempts upon Rush's life by anonymous persons eventually forced him to remove to St. Louis, where he ministered to a congregation until the end of the war.[18]

Not all arrests of ministers, however, were unjustified, and in fact it was the unfortunate misbehavior of a few which brought suspicion on the rest. Early in the war some ministers spoke out against federal troops sent to Missouri and prayed for the expulsion of "the invaders." In one instance, a minister organized and participated in guerrilla warfare, although this was probably an exceptional case. Others encouraged members of their congregations to join the Confederate army and some joined themselves.[19]

Of those ministers joining the Confederate army, William G. Caples was perhaps one of the first, serving as a chaplain in General Price's army for a company of Confederate troops recruited in Chariton County. Caples was captured on December 18, 1861, at Blackwater Creek near Milford. Imprisoned for several months in McDowell's College, which was seized and used as a military prison in St. Louis, the military authorities eventually released him on parole. Caples was well-known as an outspoken Democrat and defender of slavery. Provost Marshal General Farrar prevented him from accepting an appointment to preach in Glasgow in March 1862, writing to the commander there that Caples had caused "much trouble" and should be prohibited from "exercising in any manner the functions of a preacher or public speaker in the counties of Saline, Chariton and Howard until further orders." Farrar justified this order by stating that he had an "abundance of evidence that the peace and well-being of that section of country requires this course toward Mr. Caples." Despite this warning and the requirement that he make a monthly report, Caples continued to advocate secession among friends and acquaintances, eventually leading to more trouble for him during Price's raid into Missouri in 1864.[20]

Another minister who also enlisted as a chaplain in Price's army was Marcus Arrington, who claimed after the war that early during the conflict he had tried to remain neutral, but soon after was labeled a Secessionist and forced to take the oath of allegiance. After the Battle of Wilson's Creek on August 10, 1861, Arrington administered to the needs of Confederate soldiers, for which he learned he was persona non grata among Union authorities. When Frémont pushed into Springfield, Arrington fled to Arkansas. In December 1861

Caples, who was then still serving in Price's army, told Arrington that he was no longer bound by his loyalty oath because of an agreement recently concluded between Generals John C. Frémont and Sterling Price, which announced the end of arrests of persons for expressing political opinions. Caple's interpretation of this agreement is odd, for it said nothing about the abrogation of oaths. Nevertheless, for this reason, Arrington decided to enlist in the Seventh Brigade of the Missouri State Guard as a chaplain, which function he filled until captured on the battlefield of Pea Ridge in early March 1862. Arrington and other prisoners were marched eighty miles to Springfield and then a short time after to Rolla, where they were sent by train to St. Louis. He was imprisoned at the Alton Military Prison until August and exiled to the South for the remainder of the war.[21]

The case of William Cleaveland was another instance of a minister whose imprudence led to his arrest. As an itinerant preacher for the Missionary Baptists, in 1862 Cleaveland was sent to preach to the regiment of Confederate Colonel Martin Green on a Sunday. For this, Cleaveland was placed in the guardhouse in Hannibal in northeastern Missouri and claimed that the soldiers stationed there had treated him with disrespect and ridicule. However, from Cleaveland's own account one gains the impression that he might have instigated some of this "abuse" by his own provocative remarks in which he maintained stubbornly his devotion to the South and its institutions. The commander in charge, Colonel David Moore, was not amused by Cleaveland's haughty manner and ordered him to remain in the guardhouse for nine days, during which a time was appointed each day for him to pray for Lincoln and his administration in public. Cleaveland claimed, in what might be described a fanciful account, that his first prayer reduced to tears Colonel Moore and others among the officers and men present, many of whom left his presence in shame. Whatever the reality, Cleaveland complained of continued persecution for having stood up to the military authorities in Hannibal.[22]

To understand Civil War Missouri and why the misbehavior of some out-of-state troops was so detrimental to the Union cause, one must recognize the majority's desire to preserve both the Union and slavery. Most Missourians were conditional Unionists, a designation reflecting a wide range of views to include persons strongly for the Union and others who supported the Union only a shade more than they did secession. Another, much smaller group was often referred to as unconditional Unionists, who were composed mostly of persons opposed to slavery, although a minority of them were proslavery. For this reason, and to counter the rhetoric of those persons who warned that slavery could be preserved only by seceding from the Union, Gamble in his first major address to the people of Missouri in August 1861 promised to preserve slavery along with the Union. Federal troops, who were flooding into Missouri from the free states, were unaware of these distinctions, and many regiments, considering the possession of slaves a proof of disloyalty, sometimes stole slaves from their masters or helped them escape. These incidents led to many difficulties and sometimes transformed friend into foe. Moreover, the proclamation of General Frémont declaring free the slaves of all disloyal persons tended to reinforce such behavior. President Lincoln, whose political skills and understanding of the circumstances in Missouri were far superior to Frémont's, repealed the proclamation and sought to quiet the controversies then beginning to grow between conditional and unconditional Unionists. Despite his own animosity for the "peculiar institution," Lincoln was unwilling to violate prevailing law, which he believed prevented him from interfering with slavery. He also recognized that such a policy would have the devastating effect of losing the support of many slaveholders in Missouri and other border states so essential to success.[23]

While it is evident that the war in Missouri would have been a long and hard fought war without it, the misbehavior of federal troops in the field contributed greatly to these circumstances. In particular, many members of German and out-of-state regiments were guilty of treating Missourians roughly. These troops, many of whom encountered slavery for the first time, carried with them partisan and sectional prejudices which led to misunderstandings and misdeeds. In particular, the German and Kansas regiments stole property and slaves, often simplistically equating slave ownership with disloyalty and secession. Missouri congressman John S. Phelps wrote to Lincoln about this behavior, complaining of federal troops' illegal seizure of his and his neighbors' property in southwestern Missouri, especially the removal of his slaves, for whom he claimed a strong attachment. While Lincoln's reply to Phelps is not extant, he probably reiterated his policy of noninterference with slavery and communicated these incidents to Halleck.[24]

At the same time, Halleck received from Governor Gamble independent corroboration of the "outrages perpetrated by troops of the United States stationed at different points and wholly without discipline who range over the country plundering inhabitants who have no connection with the rebellion." Not wishing to belabor the point, and making it clear he understood that Halleck did not condone such behavior, Gamble provided an example of the types of misdeeds being committed by out-of-state regiments. "A crippled inoffensive farmer," Spencer Coleman, who lived a short distance "from the post at Franklin," was treated menacingly by a group of soldiers who came to his home and accused "him of not affording proper food to his negroes and obliging him and his son to eat of it in the presence of the negroes telling them that the negroes had more sense than their master—exciting the negroes to insubordination, breaking open his cellar and helping themselves to what they wanted, taking his guns and ammunition, and robbing him of the money he had in the house." In reply, Halleck promised to do what he could to prevent such behavior in the future, although he also noted the difficulty of disciplining volunteer troops, especially when their officers were involved in their crimes. In this Halleck was correct, for a short time later Gamble and others informed him of more incidents involving out-of-state regiments preventing slave owners from recovering their slaves.[25]

In November 1861, when General Halleck took command in Missouri, the only law providing for the freeing of slaves was the Confiscation Act of 1861, becoming law on August 6. It provided for the seizure of slaves and other property used to support the Confederacy. Other slaves, even those of disloyal persons, could not be taken from their masters. One of the oversights of the legislation, or perhaps a matter Congress purposely ignored, was that it did not determine whether the confiscated slaves would be permanently free or not. Despite the shortcomings of the Confiscation Act, the duty of Halleck and the rest of the military was not to criticize the law, but to ensure that it was fairly interpreted and strictly enforced. To this purpose on November 20, 1861, Halleck issued General Orders No. 3 directing the troops under his command not to allow fugitive slaves and other persons to come within their lines without good reason. Apparently, to prevent any interference with slavery, Halleck prohibited all slaves from army camps. This, he no doubt thought, was in accord with congressional intentions, especially that expressed in a resolution of the House of Representatives on July 9, 1861, which prohibited Union forces from capturing fugitive slaves. Nevertheless, within three weeks of issuing General Orders No. 3, a resolution was introduced in the House rebuking Halleck for ordering a policy which was "cruel and inhuman and in the judgment of this House based upon no military necessity." However, this resolution did not pass, demonstrating that divisions existed in the Congress as they did in Missouri.[26]

Because of the resolution critical of Halleck, which had substantial support in Congress, some of his subordinates worried that enforcement of General Orders No. 3 might lead to problems for them in the future. Moreover, certain practical considerations made implementation of Halleck's order difficult. As would be true throughout the war, whenever Union troops came into a region, slaves, perceiving an opportunity to obtain their freedom, fled to the military and sought protection from their masters. Some of these runaways also found employment as servants to officers. Faced with this problem, General Alexander S. Asboth forwarded to headquarters a letter he had received from Major George E. Waring explaining the hardships occasioned in strictly enforcing Halleck's order. Waring, in detailing these difficulties, also wisely expressed his desire to comply fully with Halleck's order. In that spirit, Waring had ordered his troops to question all blacks to determine whether they were fugitive slaves or not. Unsurprisingly, all claimed to be free. Waring reported that he had handed over only one black person from his camp, a woman who had been working as a cook, after an officer identified her as a runaway owned by his father-in-law. Waring was reluctant to expel any of the others because he had no proof they were fugitives and, to that time, no one had come to claim them. Another consideration, he believed important, was that many were employed as servants, teamsters, and hospital attendants, thereby providing useful services to the military. However, Waring worried that if made to leave, the "servants," for whom he and his men had gained an attachment and concern for their welfare, would have nowhere to go and therefore would be without any means of providing for themselves. Given these circumstances, Waring requested that Asboth clarify the policy and instruct him what to do. Thus the matter came to Halleck's attention.[27]

In reply Halleck explained the Confiscation Act and his policy, noting that Waring should never have handed over the slave as it was not the military's job to act "in the capacity of a negro-stealer or negro-catcher." However, in the cases of those black persons working as servants in the military camps, Halleck had no objection to that arrangement so long as they were not fugitives. He also encouraged Waring to provide "food and clothing" to any destitute persons outside of camp. Despite Halleck's orders, some federal troops continued to harbor and aid fugitive slaves, often with the active participation or acquiescence of their officers. This problem, coupled with the general disorder of troops on the march, who sometimes plundered and outraged the local people, was a serious breach of military discipline. John Pope, who was then in command of a district in Missouri, took the drastic action of ordering "patrols on the flanks and rear" of columns "to shoot" any soldier caught in the act of stealing or committing any other unmilitary conduct. Pope also found it necessary to provide a civilian with a special order allowing him to bring his slaves through the state without interference from the military. In February 1862, various reports of troop misbehavior also prompted Halleck to send out an order to commanders of troops throughout Missouri "to have an immediate inspection of all their troops, for the discovery of stolen and contraband property and fugitive slaves. . . . Any officer who has permitted [General Orders No. 3] to be violated by his command will be arrested and tried for neglect of duty and disobedience of orders."[28]

The practical application of Halleck's orders concerning slavery and all other matters of military law in Missouri ultimately fell to the judgment and discretion of the provost marshals, whose duty it was to direct the military and civilians how best to comply with regulations. As noted above, Provost Marshal General Bernard G. Farrar enforced military law in the Department of the Missouri and exercised authority over the provost marshals in the department. Moreover, Farrar ordered officers and men not to violate Missouri law, except when it conflicted with federal or military law. One of the duties of police officers in St. Louis was to arrest fugitive slaves. Under Missouri law, the state authorities presumed that all black people were slaves, unless they could demonstrate otherwise, and a reward was provided to anyone capturing a suspected fugitive. The authorities were required to incarcerate them in their jails, advertise their names and descriptions in the newspapers, and after three months, if they were not claimed, to sell them at auction. However, in an eleven-page report to Halleck, Farrar explained that a number of black people then held in jail were from southwestern Missouri and apparently had been employed in various ways to support the Confederacy. Because no one had claimed them, Farrar believed that their owners were likely involved in the rebellion. Upon these facts, state law dictated their sale at auction, while federal law made them free. In his reply, Halleck agreed with Farrar's analysis and stated that until the Confiscation Act of Congress was declared unconstitutional by the United States Supreme Court it superseded the state statute. Therefore, Farrar should release the black prisoners to the quartermaster's department for whom they would work until they had paid for the clothing and other things given to them in their necessity. Then they were free to go wherever they desired, so long as no one claimed them. This action was very controversial and, according to one contemporary, excited a good deal of discussion generating a "very bitter war, waged by tongues on the street, in the marts of trade and in the parlor, as well as with Minie balls, solid shot and shell in the field."[29]

The statute requiring Missouri's civil authorities to detain all suspected runaways also created a problem when the police attempted to detain blacks working as camp servants and in other important duties for the military. Farrar advised the city's police commission that officers would be required to hand over their servants only if a civilian court had issued the proper writ. This was necessary, Farrar explained, because many regiments were under marching orders and officers should not be deprived of their servants while in the field unless there was good reason to believe them to be fugitives. While this ruling may have helped some fugitives escape with regiments heading for the front, state law still protected the rights of slaveholders. Farrar deferred to state action whenever military necessity did not require his intervention. For this reason, he did not release slaves from McDowell Prison in St. Louis, despite his personal sympathy for their plight, without proof that they had been employed by their masters to labor for the Confederate army as they claimed. He also was unwilling to prevent whites from leaving the state with black people whom they claimed were their property. Upon this basis, he ordered the Wiggins Ferry Company to allow whites with their slaves to cross over to Illinois unless a court issued a writ to prevent it, or when it was clear that an individual was seeking to bring slaves for sale from Missouri to the Confederacy, a clear violation of the Non-Intercourse Act passed by Congress. Moreover, Farrar refused to interfere in disputes of title to slaves between individuals.[30]

In March 1862 Lincoln, after much deliberation, proposed that Congress pass legislation offering to compensate slaveholders in the border states who voluntarily emancipated their slaves. One of the reasons for Lincoln's decision was his judgment that the border states were then firmly under the control of federal forces and were unlikely to be retaken by the South. Another was his perception that northern public opinion, having concluded that slavery was the cause of the war and a prop of the Confederacy, had begun to favor that more vigorous action be taken against slavery. Moreover, Lincoln believed that once slavery was abolished in the border states no incentive would remain for the South to conquer them. In presenting his plan, Lincoln promised just compensation to slaveholders for the forfeiture of their slaves. Despite this, most of the border state congressmen, including Missouri's, opposed the legislation and some used their time in the floor debate to criticize those whose opposition to slavery, they argued, had brought on the conflict. These congressmen, probably reflecting the attitudes of a majority of their constituents, demonstrated that they retained a strong attachment to the institution of slavery, making the same proslavery arguments typically used before the war. They also noted that no provision to guarantee the welfare of large numbers of new freedmen and their families had been made and the question of their political and social status had not been determined. Opposition also came from unlikely sources; many of the congressmen opposed to slavery objected to using public funds to purchase slaves and others opposed the legislation because emancipation was only voluntary and gradual. Nevertheless, enough congressmen supported the measure for it to pass, although later attempts to pass a funding bill were unsuccessful.[31]

Even with it passing both houses, without support from the border state congressmen, Lincoln's plan had little chance of being implemented. Of Missouri's congressional delegation, initially only Congressman Frank P. Blair Jr. and Senator John B. Henderson supported Lincoln's effort. Although by the summer of 1862 Missourians had already suffered significant losses in life, property, and the authority to govern themselves, the majority were still opposed to emancipation. Some opponents noted that the state constitution prohibited any emancipation scheme without full compensation to slaveholders and safeguarded the right of immigrants to bring slaves into Missouri. Other opponents warned that the newly freed slaves would gain equality with whites and that some of the freedmen, out of resentment for their unrequited toils, would join forces with Kansas Jayhawkers and do great harm to their former owners and others. Still others opposed to the plan concluded simply that slavery was just too important and integral a part of the economy to be prohibited.[32]

These attitudes were reflected in the Missouri State Convention, a body that had rejected secession and, after the flight of Governor Claiborne F. Jackson and the legislature, had established a provisional government with the convention acting as an extraconstitutional legislature. In this capacity the convention had convened in October 1861 and again in June 1862. During the latter session, Senator Henderson, who happened also to be a member of the convention, along with Samuel M. Breckinridge, a delegate from St. Louis, led the effort to pass "an ordinance to provide for submitting to a vote of the people of Missouri certain amendments to the constitution, and a scheme for the gradual emancipation of slaves." Much of the support for emancipation was centered in St. Louis among the German population, although these supporters were divided between those who believed that it was necessary to amend the state constitution and others who considered the provisions protecting slavery to be void as a violation of natural law. Breckinridge argued that the war had reduced substantially the number of slaves in the state and that the institution was no longer viable. For this reason, he believed that they should accept Lincoln's proposition as a means of recovering for slave owners at least a part of their investment and making a smooth transition from a slave- to a free-labor system. If for no other reason, the convention should take up the measure because of its fairness, which at the very least ought to be given a respectful hearing. Breckinridge agreed with Lincoln that the effect of emancipation would be to end the efforts of the South to conquer Missouri. Breckinridge also advocated the expulsion from Missouri of all emancipated slaves, for he considered free blacks "a pest upon her bosom—a class necessarily inferior and depraved."[33]

Of the opponents of the emancipation measure, James H. Birch was probably the most ardent, arguing that the right to own slaves was constitutionally protected and that the plan would cost too much. He also threatened to side with the South if the convention passed the ordinance. Others asserted that after their emancipation Missouri would be controlled "by brutal negroes alone." In the end, the convention rejected the ordinance by a vote of 52 to 19. After this, Governor Gamble intervened, asking that a resolution at least be passed thanking Lincoln for his proposal, if for no other reason than to demonstrate that his efforts in providing arms and men to the Union cause in Missouri was not unappreciated. Eventually, after much deliberation, the delegates passed a resolution by a vote of 37 to 23 expressing the convention's "profound appreciation" to Lincoln for "the liberality" of his proposal.[34]

Despite these setbacks, Lincoln later that summer again sought to persuade the border state congressmen of the propriety of his emancipation plan and the advantages it would provide to their constituents. Meeting at the White House with the congressmen, Lincoln argued that if slavery was abolished in their states the South's hope to make them a part of the Confederacy would end. He also noted that slavery could not long survive during times of war as it would eventually "be extinguished by mere friction and abrasion—by the mere incidents of war. It will be gone, and you will have nothing valuable in lieu of it. Much it's [sic] value is gone already." Thus the president argued that the interests of their constituents, and those of the nation, would best be served by the border state congressmen persuading slaveholders to accept compensation for their slaves in return for their emancipation. Despite his efforts, a majority of the border state congressmen rejected Lincoln's appeal, asserting that the president and Congress had no constitutional authority to emancipate the slaves in their states and that the expense of compensating slaveholders for their loss would be too great to fund. They also believed that Lincoln's emancipation plan, if implemented, would not quickly bring about the collapse of the rebellion, a conclusion time proved correct.[35]

Nevertheless, even after its rejection, Senator Henderson did not give up on the idea completely. After the meeting of the convention, he traveled to northeastern Missouri and held a series of meetings in which he argued for acceptance of the president's emancipation plan, claiming that his efforts, along with the recent upheavals in Missouri, had convinced many that the institution of slavery could not long survive during wartime. For this reason, Henderson urged Lincoln not to abandon the plan. "Good men will soon acknowledge its justice and consent to its acceptance. I am very certain that I will be in a condition by the meeting of Congress, in December to propose acceptance by Missouri." In this Henderson was mistaken, but not long after, Governor Gamble introduced an emancipation proposal of his own to the state legislature, of which more is considered below.[36]

5

THE STRUGGLE FOR MISSOURI
AND MARTIAL LAW

IN APRIL 1862, SOON AFTER the Battle of Shiloh, General Henry W. Halleck left St. Louis to take personal command of Union forces there and direct the movement toward Corinth, Mississippi. Halleck retained command over federal forces in Missouri and his subordinate, General John M. Schofield, continued as commander of the state militia forces, whose organization would not be completed until the middle of April. In accord with the agreement between Governor Hamilton R. Gamble and President Abraham Lincoln, the militia cooperated with federal forces and, because of their close association with experienced troops in the field, "rapidly acquired . . . the discipline and instruction necessary to efficiency, so that by the time the organization was completed this body of troops was an efficient and valuable force." The Missouri State Militia, the first of multiple militia organizations created in Missouri during the Civil War, numbered 13,800 men, most of whom were organized into cavalry units.[1]

Halleck also left in place his provost-marshal system under the direction of Provost Marshal General Bernard G. Farrar. Halleck believed the work of the provost marshals to be important, but nevertheless he was careful to establish firm control and direction over them through his general orders. Moreover, Provost Marshal General Farrar oversaw the work of his subordinates to prevent abuses of power and especially any encroachments into civil and judicial matters not justified by military necessity. Indeed, because the military was so successful in establishing control over some regions, Halleck found it necessary occasionally to remind police authorities and judges that they were expected to continue the performance of their duties to the extent that they did not interfere with the proper functions of the military.[2]

To understand better just how far the activities and authority of these provost marshals extended, it is useful to look at the daily affairs of Arnold

Krekel, provost marshal for the counties of St. Charles, Lincoln, and Warren. As provost marshal, Krekel had the authority to arrest those suspected of disloyalty, regulate business activities, gather intelligence of enemy activities, and seize property for military purposes. Despite his strong views against slavery, it appears that he carefully followed Halleck's strict orders prohibiting any interference with the peculiar institution. Krekel's records indicate that one of his major activities was the questioning of persons suspected of disloyalty and compelling them to take an oath ensuring their good behavior. Others required to take the oath were state officials. For this reason, Farrar ordered Krekel to arrest the marshal at St. Charles for conducting his duties as an officer of the city without having taken the oath. Persons suspected of being disloyal, in addition to taking the oath, were required to post a bond, the amount of which varied according to the wealth and property owned by the person placed under its obligation. This policy was especially effective with persons who owned a substantial amount of property. Those persons with little wealth to lose were required to have others with property secure their bonds before their release. The loss of bond could occur if the individual aided the Confederate cause in any way or even failed to provide information to Union authorities concerning guerrilla activities. Those persons against whom strong evidence of disloyalty was discovered were not released until their activities had been investigated. Moreover, those persons captured as combatants after taking the oath were liable to execution.[3]

Another effort of major concern to Krekel and the military forces in his district concerned the confiscation of weapons from disloyal persons. Sometimes these weapons were surrendered voluntarily, but often Union soldiers seized the weapons during a search of the home of someone suspected of disloyalty. These latter incidents naturally led to complaints of soldiers stealing, some of which were undoubtedly true, especially when it became evident that some of the weapons and other valuables were not reported to Krekel as required. This was in clear violation of Halleck's order to provide certificates to owners of all property seized and was a serious violation of military law. Krekel's concern about weapons and ammunition led him to issue an order prohibiting "the sale, giving away, bartering or exchanging of powder and lead" in St. Charles, unless provided special permission from the provost marshal's office. Moreover, he ordered all persons and merchants not to sell, give away, or barter powder and lead to anyone suspected of disloyalty in the district. Apparently, this order caused some protest from merchants and led to Krekel ordering all persons wishing to sell powder and lead to notify the provost marshal immediately and to keep complete records detailing the amounts and to whom these were sold. All merchants were required to make reports of their transactions on the first and fifteenth of each month and it was further ordered that only small amounts could be sold at a time. This policy continued until all sales of powder and lead were prohibited throughout Missouri in July.[4]

Perhaps the most important responsibility of provost marshals was to protect the lives and property of peaceful citizens from attacks, including those occasionally committed by federal and militia forces. The level of guerrilla activity in Krekel's district was not great, although troops under Major Hugo Hollan did manage to capture, wound, and kill a small number of guerrillas. In comparison to enemy activity in other parts of the state, the level of property damage and loss of life had been minimal, and yet, even this threat could be serious if a small group of determined men were provided with an opportunity for mischief. Concerned that guerrillas would destroy railroad track and bridges, federal troops were posted along this valuable communication line to protect it. At the same time, Krekel received reports of the misbehavior and crimes committed by Hollan's command. According to civilians, the soldiers were stealing and destroying the property of persons they considered disloyal. Other credible reports indicated that Hollan's force was helping slaves escape from their masters and a prisoner had been killed while in the custody of some of these troops. Krekel ordered the troops to return the slaves to their masters and reported these and other incidents to General Schofield, who believed their misconduct was so serious that he sought authority "to dismount and disarm Major Hollan's battalion and send it to Saint Louis," requesting another battalion be sent to replace them. After this report was written, several more incidents occurred, which Krekel did his best to investigate. Most of them were minor incidents concerning the theft of weapons or other property of small value and some harassment of civilians who complained to him. In the end, the decision was made to break up Hollan's command and place the men into two different federal regiments, the 4th and 5th Cavalry of Missouri Volunteers. Apparently, Hollan was stripped of his command but was allowed to resign and later gained an appointment as a captain in the 119th Illinois Infantry Volunteers, a regiment which participated in various campaigns in the West including the pursuit of Price's army through Missouri into Kansas in 1864. Shortly after this action was taken, Krekel's district quieted down significantly.[5]

Krekel's experience as provost marshal was probably typical to that of others. As with most military positions during wartime, extraordinary power was exercised over both soldiers and civilians. The extent of this authority reached into almost every aspect of people's lives in Missouri. As noted in chapter 4, through his provost marshals Halleck did not hesitate to deny to citizens certain constitutional rights if he believed military necessity justified his action. These provost marshals restricted many other rights in one way or another. Many of these, such as the freedom to travel, were then as today generally taken for granted. However, with the threat of extensive guerrilla activity throughout the state, many commanders and provost marshals established a passport system placing restrictions upon the movements of people. In January 1862, Halleck ordered these passport systems discontinued except where persons needed to pass through military lines. Still, he did not prohibit provost marshals from arresting persons suspected of disloyalty or some other crime and placing them under a restriction to stay within a specified region, usually consisting of a county or some other area.[6]

By April 15, 1862, General Schofield as major general of the Missouri State Militia was in substantial control of most of Missouri as state troops replaced federal regiments who were then being sent south in large numbers. Not long after, Halleck ordered Schofield to send as many federal infantry forces as he could possibly spare to help in the investment of Corinth, Mississippi. This left much of southern and western Missouri with almost no federal troops. On June 4, 1862, in Halleck's absence Schofield officially took command of the District of Missouri, which comprised the entire state excepting only three southeastern counties. The following day Halleck ordered Schofield to remove troops from northern Missouri to the southeastern part of the state to protect lines of communication upon which General Samuel R. Curtis was dependent as he moved his forces against Little Rock, Arkansas. Schofield's shift of troops left forces dangerously overextended throughout much of the state, which had been divided up geographically into six districts and placed under the command of militia officers. The entire force, including both militia and federal troops, numbered approximately 17,360.[7]

The problem of a lack of Union troops in Missouri was exacerbated by the success of the forces under Halleck and Curtis. Many Confederate soldiers captured at Shiloh, Corinth, and in Arkansas were paroled and allowed to return to Missouri. Some of these men, as it turned out, were not particular about adhering carefully to their paroles in which they promised not to take up arms against the United States without being properly exchanged. Under these circumstances, Schofield recommended to Curtis that he require all paroled prisoners also to provide a bond, for "we find that the bond proves to be much the most binding of the two." A short time later, Schofield wrote a letter to Halleck's assistant adjutant general requesting a change in the provost-marshal system. As Schofield explained, he and other military commanders, who were responsible for defeating enemy forces and protecting law-abiding citizens, were without any control over the actions of provost marshals within their districts. The provost marshal general had absolute authority over these provost marshals who implemented policy independently from local and district commanders, who were ultimately responsible for the success or failure of the regions they commanded. Most important, these provost marshals, who were often low-ranking officers or even civilians, together with the provost marshal general decided the disposition of prisoners, a decision which, if wrongly determined, could undermine the region's peace. For these reasons, Schofield proposed that provost marshals be placed under the authority of district commanders (thereafter referred to as division commanders), who could then direct their activities within their military divisions. Schofield also believed that he and his division commanders should have the authority to appoint their own provost marshal generals and through them make policy best conformable to circumstances which sometimes changed rapidly.[8]

Soon after this request was made, Schofield gained the authority he sought, issuing a general order allowing division commanders to appoint their own provost marshal generals, recommending that they be members of their personal staff. Schofield also ordered the division commanders to appoint provost marshals "for all important points occupied by troops, and will have jurisdiction over definite portions of the State." These local provost marshals, Schofield directed, should normally be officers of the Missouri State Militia permanently detached from their regiments to prevent the frequent turnover of personnel in their important duties. One of the advantages to this system was its flexibility. Through experience Schofield also learned of the impracticality of some of Halleck's rules pertaining to prisoners and sought their modification. The main problem was that under Halleck significant numbers of persons were being tried by military commission. Under such circumstances Schofield believed it was "useless to attempt to try all the prisoners captured and who are technically guilty of violation of the laws of war." Most of the prisoners, Schofield observed, received at most sentences of imprisonment for the duration of the war, a punishment which could be meted out just "as properly in most cases without a trial as with." Clearly, Schofield had in mind mostly civilian prisoners here, for normally all lawful prisoners of war were imprisoned automatically for the war unless they were exchanged or paroled. Thus, Schofield's assertion that civilians could be held for the war without a trial, civil or military, was a remarkable assertion of military power and certainly increased the likelihood of innocent civilians being wrongly incarcerated. Moreover, Schofield directed that military commission trials should be convened exclusively to try persons charged with capital crimes against whom the evidence was overwhelming. His decision to reduce the number of military commission trials, however, was sound, for when one peruses the proceedings of these trials from this period in Missouri, it is evident that many defendants were charged with minor crimes and often the evidence against them was very weak, resulting in their acquittal. Given the amount of time and labor expended in gathering evidence, interviewing witnesses, and formulating charges and specifications against the defendants, it made sense to narrow the types of crimes tried by military commission. This decision allowed officers, otherwise serving on military commissions, to devote more time to military operations.[9]

One of the most controversial topics to emerge during the war concerned the condition of northern and southern military prisons and the treatment of prisoners. A consideration of this subject is difficult given the widely divergent accounts about prisoners' circumstances after their capture, even among the prisoners themselves. This is true also for prisoners in Missouri and at Alton, Illinois, where many of Missouri's prisoners were incarcerated. These divergent accounts can be explained in a number of ways. First of all, the accuracy of the testimony varied according to the trustworthiness of the witnesses and their purpose in communicating their experiences. In light of the scandal concerning the treatment of Union soldiers at Andersonville, Georgia prisoner accounts after the war about their treatment must be judged in the context of the desire of some to prove that their treatment as Confederate prisoners of war was just as bad as that experienced by northern prisoners of war. As is almost always the case, contemporary accounts are the most reliable, although these can seem contradictory as well unless one remembers that the circumstances in Missouri's military prisons changed over time. Much of this change was the result of overcrowding, a problem that continues in state and federal prison systems to this day. Another explanation for the different accounts may simply be that in any institution the experience of each prisoner was different and the worst circumstances could be explained as factors of luck or of purposeful mistreatment. Thus, in attempting to make sense of the evidence, one must make judgments in light of all these factors.[10]

To facilitate the secure holding and processing of captured Confederates, Halleck ordered that immediately after battles enemy officers and enlisted men should be separated and each prisoner listed on a roll detailing the "name, rank, regiment, and corps of each individual" before being sent to a prisoner depot in preparation for transport to a military prison. Confederate medical officers, however, were allowed to attend to the sick and wounded. Prisoners received the same care and rations as Union soldiers and a board of officers, including a surgeon, determined what clothing and other personal items were necessary for their general good health. While in the depot or camp, the commander in charge was responsible to ensure that prisoners policed the grounds and maintained sanitary conditions to prevent the spread of disease. Commanders of the camps were to permit the distribution of letters and other articles from friends and family, although only after having examined their contents. Halleck also directed the commanders of these depots to allow enemy chaplains to administer to the religious needs of the prisoners and provide decent burial for those succumbing to their wounds or disease.[11]

When he arrived in St. Louis in late November 1861 to take command of the Department of the Missouri, General Halleck discovered that the provisions and facilities were inadequate for the proper maintenance and holding of prisoners. As with so many other matters, he found it necessary to improvise the establishment of military prisons. One of the first of these in Missouri was located in St. Louis at McDowell's College, a medical school then empty because its founder, Joseph N. McDowell, was serving as a surgeon in the Confederate army. After his departure the military first used the college as a barracks, only later converting it into the Gratiot Street Prison.

To prepare for its use, General Halleck first ordered subordinates to report on the condition of the buildings and grounds. Once he was satisfied that the location was suitable, Halleck adopted the recommendations and placed officers in charge to oversee the preparations and the confinement of the first prisoners. To the commanders of the prisons, he ordered that the facilities be cleaned and repaired to provide adequate shelter and that the prisoners receive sufficient food and exercise. Halleck also required that prisoners have the opportunity to wash themselves regularly. This measure and the institution of proper sanitation regulations helped to prevent the development of disease. Fortunately, Halleck had some time to prepare before large numbers of prisoners began to arrive in St. Louis. Another prison was located on the grounds of Lynch's Slave Pen and came to be called the Myrtle Street Prison. These facilities were not large and together could hold less than a thousand prisoners without overcrowding. Fortunately, a state penitentiary, which had been closed just prior to the war, was located across the Mississippi River in Alton, Illinois. This facility was refurbished and had a capacity to hold 1,750 prisoners without overcrowding.[12]

At first, these facilities were adequate to the needs of the department, but this soon changed with the taking of approximately twelve thousand prisoners after the first major Union victories at Forts Henry and Donelson. Of these prisoners, about one thousand were wounded and were taken care of in military hospitals in St. Louis. Of those prisoners of war well enough to be transported, many were sent to Alton, Chicago, and other prisons located throughout the North. Further waves of prisoners followed Union victories at Pea Ridge, Shiloh, Corinth, and Little Rock, and from Missouri smaller numbers of prisoners of war and civilians, who were designated "political prisoners," joined the stream of prisoners sent to St. Louis before being sent on to larger military prisons. Unfortunately, because of a lack of transport and the difficulties associated with caring for large numbers of men in the field, some prisoners waited at prisoner depots for several months and often suffered a good deal until they arrived at a military prison.[13]

Upon their arrival at a military prison, prisoners probably adapted easily to the rules, for they were little different from those of the prisoner depots. Each of the prisons was under the command of officers, who were made responsible for the security, health, and safety of the prisoners. At first, Halleck allowed enemy officers to be released from prison during the day, and under special circumstances some were permitted to reside outside of the prison. This privilege, however, was rescinded after it was reported that at Alton "all the secesh officers here have received new and elegant uniforms since General Hamilton paroled them. They were manufactured in Saint Louis by M. J. Murphy. They are making quite a swell here." This policy, instead of reducing the bitterness of Secessionists against the United States government, was raising their morale and allowing them more easily to plot new trouble. Recognizing this danger, Halleck ordered the officers sent to the military prison in Columbus, Ohio.[14]

As the largest and primary prisons, it was befitting that Halleck and later Schofield focused most upon perfecting the arrangements and facilities in St. Louis and Alton. Periodically, both men received reports about prison conditions from prisoners and their family and friends, prison commanders, grand jurors, committees, and the Western Sanitary Commission. Fortunately, throughout most of 1862 prison overcrowding was not a problem. Occasionally, minor problems concerning a lack of supplies or complaints of the quantity or quality of food were reported. Other, more serious problems such as an outbreak of measles or smallpox, it should be remembered, were not maladies occurring exclusively in the prisons and caused the death of many soldiers in both armies. Most important, the reports of both civilians and military personnel demonstrate that prison conditions overall were good, although the need for certain improvements was noted. In June 1862, after an inspection of the Gratiot Street Prison, Assistant Provost Marshal General H. L. McConnel reported the need for stricter discipline over the guards and the separation of various classes of prisoners from one another, but he also found that "the culinary and sanitary arrangements of the prison are in most admirable condition. The method adopted whereby a thorough police of the prison is secured is perfect." Undoubtedly, this success was in no little measure due to the work of the Western Sanitary Commission, a charitable organization established during the war, which had been given a supervisory role over the Gratiot Street Prison.[15]

Of all the military prisons in Missouri, perhaps the one in the worst condition was that located in Springfield. The facilities were nothing more than wooden buildings without a stockade or fence to hinder the escape of prisoners. These buildings were described as "low, illy-ventilated buildings" into which prisoners had been crowded and thus they were "living in filth," leading to a good deal of disease. The guards were detailed from various regiments stationed there and lacked the proper discipline and vigilance necessary to prevent escapes, the opportunity for which large numbers of prisoners had already availed themselves. Fortunately, General E. B. Brown in June 1862 recognized these problems and began converting a college building into a more suitable and healthy prison, around which he had ordered a fence be built. Instead of using a haphazard method of acquiring prison guards, Brown designated the 37th Illinois to serve in that capacity. A military commission was also instituted to consider the cases of the prisoners, many of whom it was expected could be released or sent elsewhere, greatly reducing the numbers there.[16]

Jefferson City had no military prison, many prisoners being held in the basement of the capitol building or in the state penitentiary. By the summer of 1862, General James Totten, commander of the central division, also hoped to reduce the number of prisoners by convening military commissions to consider their cases, but he found few soldiers with the requisite education to serve. General Schofield suggested that Totten find "a suitable building . . . for a prison in Jefferson City large enough to hold all the prisoners of your division. If this cannot be done they will have to be sent to Saint Louis and Alton." Schofield also recommended that those regular Confederate soldiers voluntarily surrendering should be released upon taking the oath and posting a bond, but he warned that care must be taken not to release "bad men in this manner."[17]

To meet the medical needs of the military department, the Western Sanitary Commission established hospitals throughout the St. Louis area. Philanthropists had founded this organization to prevent the kinds of calamities, especially high rates of mortality through disease, that had befallen European soldiers just a few years earlier during the Crimean War. These hospitals provided care to both Union soldiers and prisoners of war. In St. Louis, just a few weeks after the Battle of Wilson's Creek in July 1861, four general hospitals were established with two thousand beds. By May 1862, when General Schofield had placed the military prisons under the supervision of the Western Sanitary Commission, fifteen military hospitals and four "floating hospitals" were operating in or near St. Louis. From the start, both General John C. Frémont and General Halleck cooperated with the Western Sanitary Commission, providing most of the resources necessary for the good health of prisoners. Here Halleck, whose administrative and organizational skills were excellent, placed medical officers in charge of the prisoners' health and ordered the commanders of the prisons to allow representatives of the commission access to sick prisoners. Halleck also ordered the authorities to supply the medical officer with adequate medicine and other medical supplies to treat their patients. Not all of the military hospitals in Missouri were as well situated as those in and around St. Louis, such as the hospital in Springfield. Located in a hotel too hot for convalescing patients during the summer, it also had the disadvantage of providing no exercise grounds for ambulatory men. As with the prison there, too much of the effort was makeshift, demonstrating the importance of effective leadership and organization to prevent circumstances from deteriorating rapidly. Because of this situation, some of the patients with less serious ailments or wounds were allowed to stay at private residences among their friends, and the most serious cases were transferred to St. Louis.[18]

After having expended considerable oversight during Frémont's brief tenure in command, Lincoln was relieved that Halleck exercised sufficient good judgment and self-reliance that little intervention in the affairs of the Department of the Mississippi—of which Missouri was a part—was required. Indeed, Lincoln's inclination was to leave the details of war to the generals and their subordinates as much as possible. This was partly due, no doubt, to a recognition that he lacked sufficient understanding of military law, tactics, and strategy to interfere intelligently. From the start, however, Lincoln questioned military men and read military treatises to educate himself so as to fulfill his role as commander in chief competently. While he was willing to accept very harsh measures in the prosecution of war, most notably the summary execution of armed guerrillas captured in the field, Lincoln nevertheless retained supervision and control over the disposition of prisoners and required his approval before the execution of a sentence of death against anyone. Moreover, he sometimes intervened in the cases of prisoners of war who were prominent or related to persons whose support for the Union was very important.

Perhaps no better example of Lincoln intervening can be found than in the case of Ebenezer Magoffin, a Missourian whose brother Beriah Magoffin happened to be the governor of Kentucky. Governor Magoffin, while sympathetic to secession, ultimately thought that the bluegrass state's rights would best be protected within the Union. Believing that Kentucky's retention in the Union was absolutely necessary for the North to win the war, Lincoln intervened in the case of Magoffin after a military commission found him guilty of having violated his parole and sentenced him to death. Lincoln suspended the sentence and ordered the trial transcript sent to him for review. Apparently, in early December 1861 Magoffin, who was a colonel in the Confederate state guard, was granted a temporary safe conduct to allow him to visit his wife who was near death. After her death, Magoffin, despite receiving an offer of pardon from the military if he remained at home, decided to return to the Confederate army under General Sterling Price and was recaptured just a few days later. The transcript of Magoffin's trial and the report of Judge Advocate John F. Lee cast considerable doubt upon the correctness of the military commission's guilty verdict. In addition to suspending the sentence, Lincoln wrote to Halleck that "if the rigor of the confinement of Magoffin at Alton is endangering his life or materially impairing his health I wish it mitigated so far as it can be consistently with his safe detention." What is surprising is that in July Magoffin's case was still unresolved and would never receive a final determination, for he and thirty-five other prisoners, two of whom were his sons, escaped from the Alton Military Prison. These men had dug a fifty- or sixty-foot tunnel under the outer wall of the prison and through it made their escape.[19]

Another prominent individual whose case came to the attention of Lincoln was that of Nathaniel W. Watkins, a half-brother of Henry Clay. As a longtime admirer of Clay, Lincoln naturally desired to aid Watkins if in so doing he would not harm the Union cause in Missouri. In March and April 1861, Watkins had served as a conditional Unionist delegate to the state convention, voting against secession. He served as a general of the state guard, responding to Governor Claiborne F. Jackson's mobilization, but soon resigned when he concluded that war between Missouri troops and United States forces was inevitable. In December 1861, Watkins, who was then with Confederate General M. Jeff Thompson, negotiated with the Union commander at Cape Girardeau to return home. Earlier that year some of Watkins's property had been destroyed and one of his sons, Richard Watkins, had already returned home and taken the oath of allegiance. As commander of the small force there stationed at Cape Girardeau, Colonel Leonard F. Ross promised to allow Watkins to return home and live in peace. Watkins, however, wanted assurances that he could recover his slaves who had run away, and he wished to avoid taking an oath of allegiance, which he regarded as a tacit admission of disloyalty. Halleck insisted, nevertheless, that upon Watkins's return he either take the oath of allegiance or as a prisoner of war gain a parole upon his honor. Either way, he could return home without loss of his freedom.[20]

While negotiating with Ross and Halleck, Watkins wrote to Attorney General Edward Bates, who knew him quite well, complaining about the military's confiscation of some of his stock and the loss of his slaves. Watkins may have purposely misrepresented his circumstance, for Bates had the impression that he might be under some kind of indictment and asked U.S. District Attorney James O. Broadhead to inquire about Watkins's case for him. Although he entertained "a very friendly feeling for General Watkins" and hoped "that he may be dealt with as leniently as the state of his case will permit," Bates was unwilling to commit any impropriety, even for an old friend. Evidently, negotiations between the military and Watkins were at an impasse, and for that reason Lincoln stepped in and granted Watkins a pardon, leading to his return home in July 1862. In late November, however, Colonel Albert Jackson, commander of a regiment stationed near Cape Girardeau, seized Watkins's home, giving him and his family three hours to leave. Once again Watkins requested that Lincoln intercede on his behalf. The president ordered an investigation and Watkins's home returned to him unless in so doing the Union cause would be harmed. Jackson explained that he could not "give up his house without injury to the service." He also asserted that Watkins had two sons in the Confederate army, that Watkins had another and better home to use, and that he had been given three days (not three hours) to move out of the house then being used by the military. Here apparently the matter remained for some time.[21]

His handling of the cases of Magoffin, Watkins, and others encountered little opposition, but Lincoln's order to stay the execution of all death sentences until he had reviewed the military trial proceedings was opposed by Governor Gamble, who believed that only the certainty and immediacy of punishment could deter men and women from violating the laws of war. This law had developed as part of international law and was founded upon natural law, treaty obligations, and custom. Apparently, except for Judge Advocate Lee, no one questioned the propriety of military commissions, an innovation General Winfield Scott had instituted as commander of American forces to deter the outbreak of guerrilla warfare and the violation of parole by enemy soldiers in the Mexican War. As noted in chapter 3, Halleck cited Scott's action as justification for the establishment of these commissions to adjudicate cases not falling under the jurisdiction of courts-martial, especially in determining the fate of persons against whom evidence indicated their involvement in guerrilla warfare. Lee argued that military commissions had "no validity," for no statute, state or federal, provided for their establishment nor was there provision for authority to sentence persons to death. How much consideration was given to Lee's views by Lincoln and other decision makers is unclear, although in the end his opinions, while expressing valid concerns, were probably considered impractical and legalistic in the context of Missouri, where martial law was necessary and anarchy existed in many places. Moreover, another consideration was the likelihood that guerrilla activity would increase with the departure of federal troops to join the commands of Halleck and Curtis, reducing the number of troops in Missouri to only seventeen thousand. When the vast majority of this force was ordered along the southeastern border of Missouri to support Curtis's operations in Arkansas, many areas in Missouri were left with few troops to protect citizens from guerrilla activity. Through reports from various regions, it became evident that guerrilla bands were then organizing into larger military forces to aid regular Confederate forces in preparation for an invasion of Missouri. In the midst of this crisis, Governor Gamble wrote to Attorney General Bates to seek a change in the president's policy concerning the execution of persons convicted of committing war crimes. Gamble did not want to eliminate the review of capital sentences, but instead he argued that examination of the record by the commander of the District of Missouri or the governor was sufficient, especially given the need "for prompt punishment" to demonstrate to "these bands of robbers that their villainies are dangerous to themselves." Nevertheless, Gamble conceded in his letter that he thought it improbable that "our good, kindhearted, President will . . . [ever] comprehend that severity in such cases is real humanity." Other observers like John Hay, one of Lincoln's personal secretaries, had come to the same conclusion independently, noting the almost desperate manner in which Lincoln, when reviewing court-martial cases, sought plausible—and some implausible—pretexts to commute death sentences to lesser punishments.[22]

A few days later, Gamble's recommendation was considered during a cabinet meeting in which Bates argued that Lincoln's leniency was counterproductive by lessening the deterrent effect of military law. Bates asserted that the approval of a commanding general or the governor of a state should be "sufficient" review and "was more than is allowed a prisoner in cases of common conviction, in civil courts." When it became clear that Lincoln remained unpersuaded, Bates pointedly observed that the likely unintended consequence of the president's decision would be "that few or no Courts Martial would sit for that purpose in Mo [sic]; but that the guerrillas would hereafter, for the most part, disappear 'without specification.'" Bates meant by this that soldiers in Missouri, recognizing that many of the guerrillas might be released later, to prevent this would summarily kill those persons only suspected of being guerrillas rather than face the possible prospect of meeting them again on the battlefield. In fact, Bates believed that many of the best officers in Missouri were "already acting upon that idea." This, he believed, was probably the best outcome, for such punishment would deter others from joining or helping guerrilla bands. Indeed, as seen below, during the next few weeks Bates's prediction was confirmed, as many prisoners, who before had been imprisoned and tried before a military tribunal, instead were executed in a summary fashion.[23]

During the late spring and summer of 1862, General Sterling Price sent soldiers with passes and commissions to encourage southern sympathizers to join guerrilla forces in a general uprising throughout Missouri. These men traveled through regions where they could count on aid from the majority of the population and brought letters to persuade civilians to participate in the guerrilla insurrection. After preparations were completed, on July 20 the guerrilla leaders Porter, Poindexter, and Cobb began attacking Union supporters and driving many from their homes.[24]

To meet this crisis, on July 22 Schofield and Gamble ordered the enrollment of military-age men into the Missouri militia, forming what came to be known as the Enrolled Missouri Militia to distinguish it from the Missouri State Militia. Members of the enrolled militia served only during times of crisis and were then promptly returned to their regular pursuits as civilians. Some of those persons unwilling to serve either left the state or joined guerrilla forces "to resist the State enrollment by a kind of State mutiny." Eventually, Schofield decided it was better to exempt disloyal persons from serving to avoid putting in the field enrolled militia units with a majority of members being southern sympathizers. Because the militia elected their own officers, it was all but inevitable that the leadership of such militia units would be disloyal too. Within a week "about 20,000 men had been organized, armed, and called into active service."

The enrolled militia received most of its weapons from the St. Louis Arsenal, which were poor quality, having been refused by other units. Because Missouri had no money in its treasury, Schofield also instituted an assessment of $500,000 upon disloyal persons to fund the enrolled militia. Many of these troops were ordered to take over guard duty at railroads, bridges, posts, and other strategic points, allowing the Missouri State Militia forces to take the field against the guerrilla bands, most of which had concentrated in northeastern Missouri. Part of this region was led by Colonel John McNeil, commander of the Northeastern Division, and part by Colonel Lewis Merrill, commander of the St. Louis Division. To insure proper cooperation, that portion of the St. Louis Division north of the Missouri River was added to the Northeastern Division, and Colonel Merrill was placed in command. This force traveled lightly, subsisting upon the country, especially the disloyal elements in it, and pursued the guerrilla forces relentlessly, finally cornering the largest force under Porter in Kirksville on August 6. Porter expelled the town's inhabitants and used its buildings as cover. Although outnumbered, the Union forces stormed the town, fighting from house to house and completely routing Porter. Another Union force under General Odon Guitar, after a long chase on August 10, attacked a force under Poindexter while crossing the Chariton River, resulting in another significant defeat of the guerrillas. Although Porter and Poindexter tried desperately to combine their forces and retrieve their situation, they were unsuccessful, leading to their entire commands being either "killed, captured, or dispersed," and Poindexter taken prisoner. The guerrilla leader Cobb dispersed his forces to avoid a similar fate.[25]

During this campaign, Union forces captured 560 prisoners. At Kirksville a number of prisoners were seized, and among these were fifteen men who were found to have taken an oath of allegiance. From the early part of 1862, General Halleck, his subordinates, and Governor Gamble and other Union leaders in Missouri had observed that many Confederate soldiers and irregular forces had surrendered to local commanders and later violated their parole by gathering intelligence for the enemy and participating in guerrilla raids. As noted in chapter 3, these persons were ordered summarily executed if captured in the field with arms. Moreover, in a general order Halleck warned that anyone accepting a commission to operate behind the Union lines as a guerrilla would, along with the men serving under them, be subject to the same treatment. In his report of the Battle of Kirksville, Colonel McNeil explained his decision to execute the fifteen prisoners found in violation of their parole. Confirming that they had violated their parole, the prisoners themselves having admitted that they "had been discharged on their solemn oath and parole of honor not again to take arms against their country under penalty of death, I enforced the penalty of the bond by ordering them shot." Many of these guerrillas, he discovered, carried paroles from provost marshals and post commanders. McNeil also released the remaining prisoners on parole to demonstrate "clemency and mercy" to the rest. Soon after this, while McNeil's forces rested in Kirksville, more prisoners were captured, among whom was the guerrilla leader Frisby H. McCullough. After another "drum-head court-martial," an on-the-spot proceeding to determine the fate of a known violator of the laws of war, it was decided to shoot him by firing squad. McCullough, although protesting the injustice of the decision, bravely accepted his fate and requested the right to give the order to fire himself. This was granted, and in so doing, McCullough varied from the regular commands, causing one soldier to shoot before the others. As a result, McCullough was only wounded and thus it was necessary to shoot him again. Throughout the ordeal McCullough demonstrated remarkable calm and courage.[26]

Inevitably, even with clear orders distinguishing between regular and irregular combatants and detailing how those captured were to be treated, some confusion remained concerning the matter among officers and men. An example of this occurred in late August 1862 when the Thirteenth Missouri State Militia Cavalry captured John M. Meadows and G. B. Blakely. According to Provost Marshal Joseph B. Reavis, instead of executing both men on the spot as guerrillas, they were delivered to him and imprisoned in the guardhouse. As he understood departmental policy, troops were ordered to shoot all guerrillas when caught in the field with arms, but otherwise all combatants taken prisoner, regardless of their status, could not be executed without a trial. Soon afterward, Colonel Albert Sigel, who was then in command at the post in Waynesville, may have ordered Lieutenant William C. Kerr to retrieve the prisoners from the guardhouse and "to finish his job," words interpreted, or misinterpreted as Colonel Sigel later claimed, to mean that Meadows and Blakely were to be taken out and shot. Believing that the killings were contrary to the department's policy, Provost Marshal Reavis reported the matter to Schofield, who ordered Major H. A. Gallup to investigate the incident. The officers under Sigel's command claimed that they did not want to kill the prisoners but did so only after ordered to do so. While it is possible that his version of these events was accurate, it seems more likely that Sigel, angry that Lieutenant Kerr had not immediately shot both men, ordered him to do so, despite such action being a clear violation of departmental policy.[27]

After Lincoln's refusal to change his policy of reviewing all cases of persons under sentence of death, it is surprising that a short time later a pair of commanders in northern Missouri executed prisoners before firing squads without presidential review. To the officer chosen to command the firing squad, General Merrill directed the executions to "be done publicly and with due form and solemnity, inasmuch as I wish the necessary effects produced without being compelled again to order an execution." One of the three condemned men, however, was to be reprieved, but only after he had been marched to the place of execution in full expectation of suffering the same fate as the others. The man received this reprieve, it was to be announced, out of consideration for his older brother's service in the Missouri State Militia.

Despite his desire to avoid it, later that same month Merrill ordered the execution of ten more men at Huntsville. Merrill commanded the officer in charge to choose by lot six men for each of the firing squads. He also directed that their weapons were to be loaded by persons other than those serving as executioners and that one of the six muskets was to be loaded with a blank to insure "that no individual of the firing party may know to a certainty that his piece contained a ball. The prisoners [were] then blindfolded and made to kneel before the firing parties, and the commanding officer [gave] the order, 'Ready! Aim! fire!'" Each of the men were guerrillas and had been captured a third time despite having taken the oath of allegiance at least twice. The evening before their execution, Reverend R. W. Landis ministered to their spiritual needs and found each of the men greatly troubled and penitent for having "wronged the Government, wronged the State, wronged their neighbors, and wronged themselves, yet, as partial relief to their smarting consciences, they declared themselves not wholly responsible for their own acts," believing that they had been misled by their leaders. All of the men were executed together publicly and the entire spectacle was meant to deter others from joining or aiding guerrilla bands.[28]

Before the executions at Huntsville, Merrill and Schofield had hoped to make an example of the notorious guerrilla James A. Poindexter, who had been captured recently. Initially, Merrill had intended to shoot him without trial before a military commission, but Schofield decided that it was best to try him, noting that he was confident he could "secure the execution of a sentence." By this he evidently meant that he was certain, given the nature and number of Poindexter's crimes, of securing Lincoln's approval of a death sentence. Soon after this, however, Poindexter was wounded seriously in an escape attempt and was not expected to survive. This circumstance prevented his being tried immediately and eventuated in his being imprisoned for the rest of the war. Responding to the initial report that Poindexter was to be shot as a spy without trial, Confederate General T. C. Hindman wrote from Arkansas to southwestern division commander General James Totten protesting this decision. Totten replied that he had been told that Poindexter had been "in citizen's garb, at a private house, and within our lines. If so, he is by the laws of war a spy and should be treated accordingly." Totten also defended the policy of not according to guerrillas prisoner-of-war status, for they were "but robbers, horse-thieves, and assassins, men innocent of any honorable impulses, and their acts cannot be regarded as even the least excusable form of partisanship." He pointedly observed that the Confederate senate "had [also] refused to accord to guerrillas the rights of honorable warfare." Under such circumstances the policy seemed reasonable and necessary to Totten, although really his opinion mattered little because he had no authority in the matter, and he suggested that Hindman write to General in Chief Henry W. Halleck concerning Poindexter.[29]

As noted above, besides Hindman, General Sterling Price had protested the summary punishment of guerrillas, maintaining that their activities were lawful because he had commissioned them to sabotage the infrastructure behind Union lines in Missouri. Such a claim was ludicrous, for if Price's assertion was accepted, any activity, no matter how heinous or contrary to the laws of war, could be made legal simply by issuing commissions to the individuals committing them. Apparently, this was a claim unique to Price, for his superiors regarded such activities as punishable by death, although they insisted that before executing anyone, even guerrillas, spies, and saboteurs, they should receive a trial.

To press their case and force a change in Union policy, Confederate Secretary of War George W. Randolph ordered General Robert E. Lee to inquire into the killing of Colonel John L. Owen, who had been captured at his home and executed without trial. In his letter to General George B. McClellan, Lee noted, as Randolph instructed him, that Owen had a commission in the Missouri State Guard and asserted that his killing was unjustified if he had been captured in uniform. Lee also argued that even if Owen had participated in guerrilla warfare, he should not have been executed without a trial. McClellan sent Lee's letter to Secretary of War Edwin M. Stanton notifying Lee of his action. After almost a month without a reply, Confederate President Jefferson Davis intervened, ordering General Lee to inquire again about the killing of Owen and others and to learn whether or not the United States government endorsed what its military officers had done. Davis also commanded Lee to warn the United States authorities "that in the event of our failure to receive a reply to these inquiries within fifteen days from the delivery of your letter we shall assume that the alleged facts are true and are sanctioned by the Government of the United States. In such event on that Government will rest the responsibility of the retributive or retaliatory measures which we shall adopt to put an end to the merciless atrocities which now characterize the war waged against us." A short time afterward, General Halleck, who had been elevated to general in chief, answered Lee's letter, reasserting as lawful under international law the execution of guerrillas without trial, referring Lee to his letter to Confederate General Sterling Price on the same subject. Moreover, Halleck noted that "retaliation by taking the lives of innocent persons" was against international law, except, however, when one's enemy had instituted such a policy first. Two days after this reply, perhaps after having consulted with Secretary of War Stanton or President Lincoln, Halleck wrote a terse note informing Lee that because his communications were "couched in language exceedingly insulting to the Government of the United States I must respectfully decline to receive them. They are returned herewith." It is unfortunate that this is where the matter apparently ended, for before Davis had accused the United States military of committing "merciless atrocities," some chance remained for negotiation concerning the treatment of guerrillas. This might have provided an opportunity for the North to draw back from its severe policy and grant the reasonable concession of trying guerrillas before executing them. Halleck's reply in repudiating Davis's threat of retaliation ended communication over the incident, although another event soon brought another protest from the Confederate government.[30]

This incident was the killing of ten prisoners in retaliation for the murder of Union supporter Andrew Allsman, a longtime resident of Palmyra, Missouri. Initially, Allsman had enlisted in the 3rd Missouri Cavalry, but because of his age, he was unable to endure the hardships of military service. However, the military authorities soon discovered that Allsman could provide useful information about the location and sentiments of local residents. These services led to the arrest of a number of Rebels and incurred the wrath and hatred of those supporting the Confederate cause. Thus, when guerrilla leader Joseph C. Porter captured Allsman in early October 1862, Union residents feared that he would be harmed. General John C. McNeil, commander of the northeast Missouri military division, gave Porter ten days to return Allsman home unharmed. If Porter did not comply, McNeil promised to execute ten prisoners then held at Palmyra. With the expiration of the deadline on October 18, these men were executed at the fairgrounds near town. Apparently, this matter was brought to Confederate President Davis's attention by a resolution adopted by members of the 1st Missouri Brigade who were then in Mississippi and had probably learned of the killing of the ten "authorized Partisan Rangers" through newspaper accounts. Davis again caused one of his generals, T. H. Holmes, to communicate with federal forces about the execution of guerrillas. In this instance, however, Davis directed Holmes first to ascertain the facts before protesting the action of McNeil, recognizing that the communication would go nowhere if it were begun with accusations of atrocities.[31]

In his letter to Samuel R. Curtis, who by then was in command of Missouri, General Holmes referred to an account in the *Memphis Daily Appeal* of the execution of ten prisoners in Palmyra as "the murder of ten confederate citizens of Missouri." In his reply, Curtis disputed Holmes's claim that the prisoners were Confederate citizens, noting that the Confederacy had no military or civil authority whatsoever in Missouri. Moreover, because these men were members of a guerrilla force raised to avoid being drafted into the enrolled militia, their action amounted to "a kind of State mutiny," and therefore, they were subject to Missouri law. As a federal officer, Curtis had no jurisdiction over the internal affairs of Missouri, whose authorities were competent to protect the lives of their citizens. Apparently, Curtis's states' rights reply convinced Confederate President Davis that the matter should be dropped, and no more official inquiries were made. Many supporters of the Confederacy, however, criticized Davis's inaction as a display of weakness at a time when bold measures were needed, especially after various northern and southern newspapers had published accounts of the "Palmyra massacre" excoriating McNeil's execution of the men.[32]

While this controversy was debated in newspapers, even gaining the notice of a publication in London, some prominent Missourians, including United States Senator John B. Henderson, a longtime resident of northeastern Missouri, worked behind the scenes to inform Lincoln about the circumstances in Missouri and to defend McNeil. Henderson sent to Lincoln correspondence he had received about the matter and personally vouched for McNeil. This correspondence explained more fully the circumstances leading to McNeil's decision to execute the prisoners, including the crimes of Porter and the men who were executed, information omitted from the account published in the *New York Times* in an apparent intent unfairly to portray McNeil as "an arbitrary tyrant." A petition to Lincoln from several hundred residents in northern Missouri supported McNeil's action and his overall performance as commander, arguing that he was responsible for the decrease in violence they had recently experienced. Another factor preventing Lincoln's interference was that the guerrillas had been captured by the enrolled militia, a force raised to meet an emergency for which he probably felt partly responsible, since he had approved the removal from Missouri of most of the federal regiments earlier that summer. At the time, the enrolled militia was under the exclusive authority of Governor Gamble and received no funding from the United States government. Moreover, the president understood well Gamble's position regarding the need for swift retribution against irregular forces and probably was wise not to intervene, especially given the support McNeil had among the public, although not all Unionists agreed with McNeil's methods.[33]

In judging whether Halleck's and Schofield's actions were warranted in supplanting civil authority and establishing security policies that inevitably restricted people's liberties, one must consider the circumstances and emergencies they confronted. One test of the justifiability of these policies is to determine if their restrictions were absolutely required to insure the security of the troops and the people in Missouri. Just as important—and often overlooked—was these officers' duty to use their powers to prevent the violation of other people's civil liberties. A failure to protect citizens' lives whenever possible was very serious indeed, especially where a bitter internecine conflict had continued for some time. Because of guerrilla activity, many Unionists without military protection were a helpless minority, particularly in the regions along the Missouri River, the Missouri-Kansas border, and other parts of the state where support for slavery and the South were strongest. For this reason, significant numbers of federal troops remained in Missouri longer than anticipated by Lincoln, Halleck, and Schofield. Moreover, it was necessary to declare martial law and confront a number of unexpected problems, many of them caused by the resourcefulness of the supporters of the Confederacy, leading to an unforeseen expansion of state and federal military power.

Nevertheless, having noted the emergency, another test of the prudence of Halleck's measures must be some judgment regarding how well they were devised to achieve their ends and limited in their scope so as not to overreach their legitimate object. This was important to prevent unwarranted bitterness and to accomplish the enemy's reconciliation to the government as soon as possible. Thus, even in the midst of civil war and irregular warfare, a military commander's responsibility was to prevent the forces under him from abusing their power and to remain subordinate to civil authority. In this Halleck and Schofield were only partly successful, although it should be remembered that many of their failures should be tallied properly upon the accounts of subordinates who failed, either willfully or through incompetence, to enforce their general orders. While insubordination cannot be discounted as a major contributing factor to much of the chaos and bloodshed expended in Missouri in 1862, responsibility for the military policies, including that of summarily executing guerrillas captured in the field, must be shared by Halleck, Schofield, and ultimately Lincoln, although it is unclear exactly when the president agreed to them. These extraordinary policies did much to cause the further downward and deadly spiral of the war in Missouri. In noting this failure, one must remember that ultimately the guerrillas themselves and their supporters bear the greatest responsibility for the destruction of property, lives, and civil liberties in Missouri, for if they had not deviated from the recognized and lawful methods of warfare, federal commanders would not have needed to resort to more brutal methods. Lincoln's next appointee to command the Department of the Missouri would encounter the same difficulties as his predecessors, but he at least had the advantage of having served in Missouri from the war's outset.

At the time of General Samuel R. Curtis's assumption of command of the Department of the Missouri, a considerable amount of guerrilla warfare and other violence remained a problem during the fall campaign of 1862. Of course, debate concerning the proper conduct and goals of the war became an important issue and exposed disagreements among supporters of the Union. On the stump, many Radical Republican candidates criticized Governor Gamble and military leaders for not fighting the war vigorously enough. In particular, the Radicals charged that the Gamble administration's and many military officers' reluctance, especially among conservatives, to interfere with slavery was a sure sign that they were unserious about winning, instead preferring a stalemate to preserve slavery. In June 1862 these Radicals held an abolition convention at which B. Gratz Brown, who would become a prominent leader within their movement, pushed through resolutions criticizing Governor Gamble and the state convention. Brown, a journalist and politician with close ties to his cousins Frank and Montgomery Blair, called for the employment of harsher military measures to break the rebellion in Missouri. Moreover, a delegation of Radicals traveled to Washington D.C. in August to undermine Lincoln's confidence in Gamble's leadership and cause his removal, apparently not considering whether it was proper or constitutional for the president of the United States to decide who should fill the political offices of a state, hoping thereby to clear the way for Curtis to govern Missouri without interference. The president rejected this request, no doubt considering such action justifiable under only the most extreme circumstances and otherwise an unwarranted violation of the federalist principle, which divided power between the states and national government, and the equally important principle of military subordination to civil rule.[34]

While the state convention had decided not to hold elections for state executive offices, the need for a state legislature and representatives to Congress required an election be held in the fall of 1862. Of primary importance was the question of who should be allowed to vote. Some members of the convention sought to prevent Missouri's state militia and volunteer soldiers from voting. The debate that developed centered on the proper role of the military in society. One member of the convention asserted that the military must be subordinate to and separate from the civil authority and therefore soldiers should not be allowed to vote. Moreover, he pointed to the provision of the Missouri constitution prohibiting regular United States troops from voting in state and local elections. It was pointed out, however, that militia and volunteer United States troops were not regular soldiers and could not be prohibited upon that basis, especially when one remembered that Missouri's voluntary forces who served during the Mexican War were allowed to vote then. Another member of the convention also noted the unfairness of expecting soldiers to endure the hardships and dangers of the battlefield while simultaneously disenfranchising them. In the end, the convention passed an ordinance granting to Missouri's militia and volunteer forces in the United States service the right to vote.[35]

Another matter generating considerable debate concerned the issue of a loyalty oath. The purpose of the oath was to disqualify disloyal persons from voting and holding office. During the October 1861 session, members of the convention had passed an ordinance requiring all officeholders to take an oath of loyalty to the governments of the United States and Missouri. With the offices of governor, lieutenant governor, and state legislature already vacated by their occupants' flight from the capitol in July 1861, significantly more state offices became vacant after the state convention had passed an ordinance requiring all persons holding elective or appointive office to take an oath of allegiance to the governments of the United States and Missouri. The convention also granted to Governor Gamble the authority to appoint replacements. The removal of supporters of the Southern Confederacy during the summer and fall of 1861, a critical period in the struggle between Secessionists and Unionists, seemed prudent, for some officeholders were well placed, such as Missouri Supreme Court Judge William Scott, to cause much mischief in opposing the provisional government's efforts to put down the rebellion in Missouri. Recognizing that the new state legislature would soon be making very important decisions about war funding, policy, and the appointment of military officers, the members of the June 1862 convention debated the wording of an ordinance to protect against the election of disloyal persons.[36]

The debate over the oath focused on who should be disenfranchised and the affect different proposed versions of the oath would have upon the war effort. Some of the members wanted to prohibit from voting all persons who had ever taken up arms against the state and national government or had supported them in any way. Others, who advocated wider participation in the franchise, argued that it was unfair to exclude those who had forsaken the cause of the Southern Confederacy and were again loyal citizens. Moreover, a member asserted that denying the vote to men for their participation in the rebellion amounted to an ex post facto law and, therefore, was unconstitutional. The majority rejected this argument, a member noting that the Supreme Court of the United States had ruled that the prohibition against ex post facto laws did not include the denial of civil liberties. This interpretation of article 1, section 9 of the Constitution of the United States, which prohibits the passage of retrospective laws, distinguishes between legislative acts meant to punish and those meant to regulate a profession or restrict the exercise of a civil right. If this test is applied in the case of voting rights in Civil War Missouri, one must consider the intent of the members of the state convention to determine whether their decision to disenfranchise disloyal persons was penal or civil in nature. From the record of the debate, it seems clear that the majority believed it was dangerous to allow persons to vote who had recently supported the rebellion. One of the members noted that "it is contrary to the dictates of common sense to invite men who have come back here, and are yet hardly rested from their armed effort against the Government— to invite them to use against it the still more potent weapon of the ballot." In the end, however, the convention recognized that a blanket prohibition on all persons who had fought for or supported the South was imprudent. Instead, the majority decided to allow the vote only to those who had set aside their weapons before December 17, 1861, and returned to their allegiance to the United States government. On the other hand, without exception the convention disqualified for political office anyone who had ever fought for or aided the rebellion.[37]

In his Special Order No. 45, Governor Gamble ordered the Enrolled Missouri Militia to prevent any disorder or intimidation at the voting polls and members to refrain from such behavior themselves. Despite these orders, some irregularities were reported during the canvass and on the day of the election. For the most part, however, these seem to have been minor and isolated events, although it is difficult to say with complete certainty how widespread such problems were and whether they affected the outcome of the election. After Lincoln promulgated his preliminary emancipation proclamation in September 1862, the survival of the institution of slavery became an important election issue and may account for some instances of soldiers seeking to interfere with the election. Another reason for some violence and possible intimidation of persons at the polls was the belief that some were there to vote illegally. The convention's ordinance designated the election officers at the polls as judges of voter qualifications and directed that all voters take the loyalty oath, but these provisions apparently did not allay the fears of many that disloyal persons might vote, or even worse, might be elected to an important position.[38]

The circumstances of James H. Birch, former judge of the Missouri Supreme Court and a member of the state convention, demonstrate the sometimes rough-and-tumble nature of Civil War Missouri politics. In late May 1862, while campaigning then for the gubernatorial office (before it became known that Governor Gamble did not intend to resign), Birch was arrested by the provost marshal for threatening to provide no more soldiers for the Union war effort if Lincoln emancipated the slaves. Birch was placed in a St. Louis hotel on parole and was soon thereafter released, enabling him to attend the state convention. Undaunted, Birch was soon again on the campaign trail running for Congress. In early September, he wrote to Governor Gamble complaining that newspaper editorials were attempting to foment anger among the militia against him and that he feared he might again be arrested. Having traveled through several counties making speeches, Birch complained that some militia "could not have . . . treated [him] with greater discourtesy, or with more vulgar menace." Moreover, at Carrollton, "[he] was suddenly interrupted by the entrance of a captain of a militia company (quartered in the town) and compelled to desist from longer 'abusing the *government*,' as he chose to interpret and denounce my line of remark." As commanding officer of the post, Captain Wakefield Standley ordered Birch not "to address or interfere with the citizens of this county with your 'secesh' doctrines." Birch also claimed that some of his supporters had been threatened with having to post a bond if they voted for him. He admonished Gamble to take action to ensure that "the first election which is to be held under his administration shall be *unmenaced, full and free.*" This type of interference in the campaign was probably unusual, for Birch from his own testimony did not claim that he was unable to campaign in the sixth congressional district of Missouri. Moreover, after having written to Gamble in early September, Birch continued to canvass the district opposing emancipation and criticizing President Lincoln. Birch also instructed his supporters that the oath requirement should not discourage them from voting. Nevertheless, after the returns came in and he had lost to former governor Austin A. King, Birch renewed his complaints and challenged the election results to Congress.[39]

Another case of the military's interference in the election was more serious. Sample Orr was arrested after giving a speech a few days before the election on November 3 in Jefferson City. Although Governor Gamble intervened to gain his release, Orr still faced trial before a military commission in June 1863. In 1860, Orr had run a very vigorous and exciting independent campaign for governor as a strong supporter of the Union and the Constitution. Perhaps taking a page from President Lincoln's campaign strategy book when he opposed Stephen A. Douglas for the United States Senate in 1858, Orr followed the Democratic nominee Claiborne F. Jackson on the campaign trail and debated him on several occasions. Orr turned out to be a very effective stump speaker and debater, transforming a dull and one-sided campaign into a close and exciting race. After the election Orr, as a legislator and a delegate to the state convention, again opposed Jackson, but this time in his efforts to bring Missouri out of the Union. From the proceedings of Orr's trial, it is clear that District Commander Benjamin F. Loan had arrested him for opposing the abolition of slavery, for criticizing the military's assumption of powers normally exercised by the civil authorities, for the confiscation of property, and for the widespread use of arbitrary arrests. Indeed, at that time Loan was then energetically rounding up persons he considered disloyal, banishing some and imprisoning some two hundred more. Moreover, Loan's arrests of "disloyal" persons was almost certainly an effort to silence his critics and political opponents, chief among whom was Orr, well known to be a persuasive and popular orator. Fortunately, in the end he was acquitted before a military commission that apparently recognized that his views and criticisms were not calculated to undermine the Unionist cause in Missouri, but instead these were the types of dissent, whether wise or misguided, intended to quicken a return to normalcy and the restoration of constitutional rights. Loan's reaction to Orr's criticisms was typical of Radicals, who then and afterward could not or would not understand that the criticisms of Conservatives expressed their genuine concerns that some of the military policies then being employed were unnecessary and were even detrimental to a restoration of federal control in Missouri. In their zeal for the abolition of slavery, in particular, the Radicals would increasingly consider those Unionists who did not share their views as persons whose loyalty was *counterfeit*

and therefore was even more insidious and dangerous than the *honest* disloyalty of secessionists.[40]

Inevitably, Radical ascendancy under the command of General Curtis led
to controversy and accusations by some that the election was conducted unfairly. One such instance concerned the congressional seventh district, then
located in the northwestern part of the state, in which Conservative candidate John P. Bruce contested the election of Loan. Bruce presented his case
to a special congressional committee, offering as evidence depositions from
persons who claimed that either they had sought to vote and were unsuccessful or had seen others turned away at eight of the 150 polling precincts
in the district. According to Bruce's witnesses, "many qualified voters were
forcibly prevented from voting; others were so much intimidated by the force
used, and the threats made on and prior to the day of the election, that they
refrained from attending the polls; and in numerous instances persons refrained from voting after they reached the place of holding the elections from
well-grounded apprehension of personal injury." In the published report of
the committee, portions of the testimony given in deposition revealed that
much of the evidence was based on hearsay and often speculative. Moreover,
the witnesses provided few names of persons actually deprived of the franchise, or other details of what had happened. During cross examination, it
also became clear that most of these witnesses were supporters of Bruce and
some supported the Southern Confederacy. A complaint made again and
again concerned the gathering of members of the Enrolled Missouri Militia at the polling stations and how their presence unnerved and intimidated
Bruce's supporters from voting. However, Bruce's counsel failed to explain
that most of Missouri's men of military age were then in the militia, including Bruce's supporters, so that their presence on election day was unavoidable. In fact, only a small number of on-duty personnel were there, and the
evidence demonstrated that their purpose was to maintain order and ensure
the integrity of the process. Nevertheless, there were aspects of the testimony
which indicated that some intimidation of voters occurred, although the nature of the evidence makes it impossible to know whether these persons were
supporters of Bruce or were even qualified to vote. However, it is clear that
many of the militia were absolutely opposed to allowing to vote those persons
who had avoided militia service by enrolling as disloyal persons. How could
persons, they asked, swear allegiance to the governments of the United States

and Missouri and claim to be disloyal at the same time? If these persons were prevented from voting, such action, whatever else one might think about it, would have been in accord with the convention's election ordinance. Only at one polling station was there irrefutable proof of the militia's misbehavior. In St. Joseph, a crowd of "German soldiers" rushed into the courthouse and seized and destroyed the poll books in which were tallied the decisions of voters. While this egregious misconduct deserved condemnation, it is obvious that it had little impact upon the election, for five other polling stations remained open in the town and Bruce offered little evidence of a significant effort to prevent voting elsewhere. While it was clear that the vote totals for the election revealed fewer votes tallied than in previous years, the majority of such a deficit was best explained by the large numbers of Southern sympathizers who were either then serving in the Confederate military elsewhere or were disqualified from voting because of their refusal to swear to the loyalty oath. Moreover, Loan received 2,028 more votes than did Bruce, a margin of victory which could not be overcome even if every claim of voter suppression was allowed and factored into the final tally. In the end, the House of Representatives rejected Bruce's challenge, allowing Loan to retain his seat. This decision apparently convinced other challengers, including Birch, to abandon their efforts to overturn the official results.[41]

Of course, misconduct occurred elsewhere, but these incidents were apparently isolated and not part of a conspiracy to prevent a fair and free election. One case involved Alexander S. Hughes, a private of the 65th Regiment of the enrolled militia, who printed a counterfeit special order stating that no disloyal man should vote in Chillicothe and ordering the militia to determine the qualifications of voters, in place of the local judges of the election. Hughes also personally challenged the right of some who had taken the oath to vote, claiming that they were disloyal, and encouraged fellow soldiers to follow his example. For these flagrant violations of the convention's election ordinance, Hughes was arrested and tried less than two weeks after the election before a court-martial. Other fallout from the election included military commanders forcing men into the enrolled militia who, despite having claimed disloyalty status to avoid military service, had taken the loyalty oath so they could vote. In the end, despite some irregularities, the election proceeded remarkably well, leading General Curtis to remark afterward that "the election in Missouri last fall was the most quiet and free and fair ever had in this region, and I have rejoiced to see the propriety of our troops during the canvass and on the day of election." He also believed that the election demonstrated the loyalty of the people of Missouri in electing candidates who took "the boldest stand in favor of the Government." The results probably pleased Lincoln as well, for five Republicans, one "Emancipationist Democrat," two unconditional Unionists, and two proslavery (but Unionist) Democrats were elected to the United States House of Representatives. With the election of a state legislature in both houses favorable to Lincoln's plan for compensated emancipation, the prospects were excellent that whoever was elected to the United States Senate would be supportive of the administration.[42]

6

CIVIL LIBERTIES UNDER
GENERAL SAMUEL R. CURTIS

EARLY IN GENERAL SAMUEL R. CURTIS's command, Abraham Lincoln considered reducing the federal presence in Missouri and allowing the state government to accept greater responsibility for civil and military matters there. On December 17, 1862, in a telegraphic communication to Curtis, Lincoln asked simply: "Could the civil authority be reintroduced into Missouri in lieu of the military to any extent, with advantage and safety?" This question was premised upon the idea that, even during time of war, Missouri should be returned to civilian control as soon as circumstances permitted. Certainly, in surveying the military situation in late 1862, there seemed little chance that the Confederates could ever gain military or political control over Missouri. Moreover, Lincoln's willingness to return to the *status quo ante bellum* demonstrates his desire to abandon the exercise of extraordinary wartime powers whenever they were no longer necessary. Nevertheless, Lincoln was unwilling to decide the matter without a full debate over the viability and safety of ending martial law, or even diminishing it substantially, in Missouri. His policies throughout the war were best characterized as cautious, in keeping with his naturally conservative outlook. Therefore, he inquired of General Curtis, Governor Hamilton R. Gamble, members of Congress, and others who were knowledgeable about the situation there. If he had hoped that a consensus would develop on this question, Lincoln, as in so many other matters, was disappointed, discovering that the question again broke along the Radical-Conservative fault line of Missouri's wartime politics.[1]

In judging the varying answers to Lincoln's question, one must remember the distrust, as already chronicled in chapter 5, which was growing between the factions led by Gamble and Curtis. The fall election of 1862 had exacerbated these mutual suspicions as Radical and Conservative candidates assailed each other and defined their differences. While each shared the ultimate goal of maintaining Missouri in the Union and reestablishing peace, nevertheless, a substantive policy difference developed because of each faction's differing understanding of the circumstances there. The calculations and policies of the Radicals were premised upon the notion that slavery was the cause of the war and that it could not be won without removing its cause. Therefore, anyone still supporting the institution of slavery, according to the Radicals' point of view, was either secretly disloyal or at least unwilling to do what was necessary to win the war. Additionally, the Radicals' efforts were often tainted by political opportunism, demagoguery, and an unwillingness to compromise, often sacrificing the possible on the altar of the ideal. An example of this failing was evident during the 1863 session of the legislature at which, despite having a majority in both houses, the Radicals were unable to pass a bill emancipating Missouri's slaves. On the other hand, the Conservatives' policies, founded as they were upon a much clearer and realistic comprehension of the values and character of the people of Missouri, were calculated to encourage cooperation with the military and an expectation of a soon return to normalcy. Moreover, unlike the rigid and unbending formulations of the Radicals, conservative policy evolved with the changing circumstances of the war. Thus Governor Gamble, who at the outset of his administration had promised Missourians that he would protect the institution of slavery, found this position no longer viable by the end of 1862 and in his message to the legislature proposed a plan for the gradual emancipation of Missouri's slaves. In his plan he provided for the eventual emancipation of children born to slaves after its passage, thereby holding out the possibility, which became increasingly more remote as the war continued, that the institution might be preserved for some time to come. Gamble, very much like Lincoln, moved with public opinion and circumstances, bowing to the exigencies of the times. As seen below, however, the Radicals were never satisfied with his movement—nor with its speed—and whenever he met one of their demands they simply moved the bar again.[2]

Another important factor in understanding the difference of opinion between both factions regarding the propriety of reducing emergency military powers was that the civilian executive was controlled by Conservatives under Gamble, while Curtis and his primary subordinates administering the Department of the Missouri were largely Radical. Thus, the Conservatives welcomed the return to civilian control, or at least its substantial increase, as an excellent opportunity to reduce a considerable part of the Radical influence in Missouri. The Radicals, because they believed that the vast majority of Conservatives were disloyal, viewed the military situation as remaining very dangerous. To entrust the security of the state to the Conservatives, from the Radicals' perspective, was tantamount to surrendering Missouri to the Rebels. No doubt, both factions' attitudes would have been different if the Radicals had controlled the civil government and the Conservatives the military department. Provost Marshal General Franklin A. Dick, in representing the Radical position, argued that as the state courts and juries were disloyal, maintaining the peace and protecting supporters of the Union was difficult at best, and that only the provost-marshal system could prevent great injustice from occurring. "Missouri is disloyal, deeply so from end to end, and the arm of military power alone has kept up a show of quiet. In view of this, I believe that some military system of Government, is absolutely necessary to be kept up." The Conservatives understood more precisely, as already noted, the character of the people and their attitudes, and did not fear leaving the protection of Unionists and their property to Missouri's judicial system, although most did not want the immediate and complete withdrawal of military power. For his part, Governor Gamble knew all too well that pockets of strong support for the rebellion remained in Missouri and some mischief, whether because armed bands were too strong for the civil authorities to subdue them or their acts were not judicable under state law, required military power and law to punish wrongdoers. He also recognized that new bands of guerrillas could form and there was still the danger of General Sterling Price invading Missouri again. Nevertheless, he believed that the Missouri State Militia and enrolled militia could defend the state from most'threats, diminishing the need for federal troops. In the end Lincoln, unable to gain a consensus, and probably uncertain about the true conditions in Missouri, left intact the military department and provost-marshal system, although in the early months of 1863 he allowed the withdrawal of most federal regiments, leaving the security of Missouri largely to its militia. By far, the largest number of troops, the Enrolled Missouri Militia, were under Gamble's control, leaving to Curtis a smaller force, amounting to just over ten thousand officers and men, but also the most efficient and experienced, the Missouri State Militia.[3]

In the latter part of 1862, perhaps emboldened by the strong showing of the Radicals in Missouri's election and the president's decision to publish his preliminary emancipation proclamation, General Curtis promulgated orders to institute a more stringent enforcement of martial law—with the unfortunate consequence of further restricting civil liberties—soon forcing Lincoln to intervene in Missouri's affairs to an extent that he had hoped to avoid. During the military administrations of Henry W. Halleck and John M. Schofield, the president only found it necessary to turn his attention to affairs in Missouri occasionally. Lincoln preferred that his commanders run the daily affairs of their departments, leaving him more time to spend on devising and supervising the implementation of northern war policy. Curtis, who was a Republican congressman from Iowa when the war began, had resigned his office and rallied to the flag serving in both Missouri and Arkansas until appointed by Lincoln for command of the Department of the Missouri. Like his predecessors, Curtis established his headquarters in St. Louis. There he associated freely, as he had before, with Radical Republicans who were abolitionists and advocates for a severe war policy against the South and southern sympathizers. By this time, the differences of opinion between Conservative and Radical supporters of the Union had festered to the point that both regarded the policies of the other with disdain and their opposition to one another grew very bitter, so much so that despite Lincoln's repeated appeals for cooperation Unionists in Missouri remained "split into two factions."[4]

One of Curtis's first acts was to prohibit disloyal persons from engaging in trade, a sensible and necessary measure to prevent the diversion of resources and aid to the Confederacy. While this order was in keeping with the spirit of his predecessors' policy regarding trade, Curtis went a step further by establishing guidelines whereby officers and men of the Department of the Missouri could determine whether or not a person was loyal. He also provided justification for the military's restriction of certain civil liberties. "In time of war," Curtis explained, "disloyal persons are dangerous to the State, because they exert a pernicious opposition when every fibre of the Government should be devoted to the cause of the country." In this statement, Curtis expressed the concern of many that "disloyal persons" could undermine the war effort by forcing the military to divert resources to protect against sabotage and espionage behind Union lines that otherwise might have been used against the enemy's military forces. For this reason, he asserted, "disloyal persons may . . . in time of war be confined, banished, or restrained in their pursuits, as a security against their destructive influence." The problem, of course, was to determine who represented a real danger to the war effort and who did not. Curtis advised his subordinates to consider persons' actions and statements when judging their loyalty. Taking the loyalty oath and keeping its obligations was good evidence that a person was loyal. A good indicator of one's disloyalty, Curtis counseled, was the expression of sympathy for the South or association with those who held such views. In the end, he warned against hasty decisions.

> It may be difficult to obtain positive proof of disloyalty, but a cautious, candid scrutiny of acts, expressions and influences will most generally discover whether or not an applicant is loyal. In time of war, crimes against the State are ascertained by a summary process, yet we must avoid hasty or inconsiderate action against those who profess loyalty, and where it is honestly espoused it should be kindly encouraged.

Curtis's advice, while providing help in identifying who was disloyal, however, did not resolve all questions regarding the proper policy toward Rebel sympathizers. Later under Curtis's command a more severe treatment of disloyal persons would be established.[5]

Interestingly, while Curtis considered how he could strengthen military rule in Missouri, others, who were concerned about the policies, politics, and capacity of the new department commander, sought to reduce the federal army's role there. This opposition from Conservatives, especially that of Governor Gamble and his supporters, stemmed largely from their lack of confidence in Curtis's capacity to administer the department competently and their concern over his radical politics. As a result of this opposition to the new commander and some of his policies, a remarkable number of disputes arose early in Curtis's administration and led to a greater polarization of the conservative and radical wings of the Unionist movement. In broad terms, these divisive issues concerned civil liberties, control of the militia, martial law, and emancipation and the treatment of African Americans. Lincoln, who had no desire to become involved in Missouri's disputes, soon found himself entangled in controversies between Conservatives and Radicals and between the state government and the military. Because of the animosity and rancor of these disputes, which continued unabated for several months, the president was forced to assert his authority in two separate showdowns during the summer of 1863, one with Governor Gamble and the other with a large delegation of Radicals as antagonists over policy matters.

During the first months of Curtis's command, a controversy developed between the Department of War and Gamble concerning his authority to dismiss officers from the Missouri State Militia. This question foreshadowed a number of issues which soon arose in Missouri straining relations between the provisional state government and federal military authorities. In November 1861, Gamble had traveled to Washington D.C. to negotiate with the administration to establish this special military force. According to the agreement, the militia was not to serve outside of the state. The Missouri State Militia, as it came to be known, was advantageous from Lincoln's perspective, for its organization allowed federal troops, then operating as garrison troops throughout the state, to leave Missouri and to campaign elsewhere in the western theater of the war. While in Missouri, these volunteer troops from free states had often interfered with slavery, many of them assuming that all slaveholders were Secessionists. Many of these regiments were not well disciplined and violated orders meant to protect the property and lives of civilians. Because of these violations of military order and discipline, these regiments may very well have provoked more guerrilla attacks than they prevented. Militia troops from Missouri, on the other hand, were familiar with the people and culture of the state and, therefore, were less likely by their presence to provoke animosity and retaliation among southern sympathizers. Moreover, the establishment of this new militia force had the advantage of enlisting those who for various reasons were otherwise unwilling to serve further from home. Under normal circumstances, Gamble could have established this militia force without the aid of the federal government—as he did later when he created the Enrolled Missouri Militia—but he had found this impossible without any funds, these having been stolen by the secessionist governor and legislature when they fled the state.[6]

The issue of Governor Gamble's authority to revoke the commission of an officer of the Missouri State Militia, normally a matter of little apparent significance, took on much importance when Colonel Albert Jackson of the 12th Cavalry, Missouri State Militia, appealed his discharge from the service to the Department of War. This appeal was made at a time when coincidentally a group of northern governors had asserted their authority over state militias, which had been "received into the service of the United States." Apparently, the War Department viewed Jackson's appeal as an opportunity to respond to these governors' demands. The problem with the department's response was that the Missouri State Militia had never been nationalized like the militias of other states. Therefore, in making his case to Gamble, Halleck, who was by then general in chief of the Union military, argued a case largely irrelevant to the issues of Jackson's dismissal. Halleck must have known this, but nevertheless composed his argument in the manner of a lawyer who must do the best he can with a bad cause. In his public letter, he asserted that once the militia had been nationalized, under the law governors could no longer exercise authority, including the dismissal of officers, over them.[7]

In his reply to Halleck, Gamble did not disagree with the premise or conclusion of his letter regarding militia forces *in the United States service*, focusing instead on the central issue by demonstrating that the Missouri State Militia was unique, having been established through negotiation among himself, the president, and the Department of War. Thus, it was "a special corps of Militia raised under a special agreement with the President." Moreover, Gamble cited various passages from the agreement to show that both he and Lincoln understood the special nature of the Missouri State Militia. The fact that Lincoln had agreed that this new militia force would never leave Missouri set it apart from other states' militias. If the Missouri State Militia was like all the rest, why then, Gamble asked, was it necessary to stipulate that the United States government would supply and pay the militia? Why did Gamble promise to cooperate with United States troops when this new force served in the field with United States troops? If the militia was nationalized, why was it stipulated that the Missouri State Militia would "be held in the camp and in the field, drilled disciplined and governed according to the Army Regulations, and subject to the articles of War"? All of these stipulations were unnecessary except in the case of a special arrangement. Indeed, the most difficult task in negotiating the agreement was ensuring that no command problems would present themselves because the Missouri State Militia had not been nationalized. General George B. McClellan, who was consulted concerning the matter, offered the solution of making the departmental commander the major general of the state militia. Of course, again, this command arrangement would not have been necessary if the state militia had been nationalized.[8]

Concerning the matter of Colonel Jackson's dismissal, Gamble noted that an examination of the muster rolls for all of the Missouri State Militia regiments demonstrated that they were enrolled into the state service, which, indeed, even Jackson himself understood for, as a mustering officer, he had also enrolled regiments as state rather than United States forces. As with other volunteer forces, some of the officers once in the field were found wanting in ability, and review boards were established to determine who should be dismissed and to make recommendations to Gamble. As governor and commander in chief of the militia, his duty was to dismiss those found to be incompetent, as in Jackson's case, or otherwise unfit for their positions. Finally, Gamble asserted that he had acted in good faith and in accord with the agreement concluded in November of the previous year and cared little about how the matter was resolved, excepting only as it influenced the effectiveness of the Missouri State Militia. In reply to Gamble's letter and defense of his interpretation of the agreement, Halleck admitted that "I must confess there was some doubt in my mind in regard to the proper construction to be given to the 'agreement' referred to," although he claimed that this was because the agreement had been constructed "expressly to dodge the question." It is clear from this that Halleck was unaware that Gamble had drafted the document himself. Whatever Gamble thought of this criticism he did not say, although he probably concluded that Halleck found it difficult to admit his mistake in interpreting the document. In the end, both men felt no animosity toward the other, and Halleck asserted his willingness, regardless of how the matter was resolved, to ratify all of Gamble's decisions, "for I know that you will do nothing which is not right and just." Gamble replied in kind, expressing his hope that he would be able to see Halleck when he traveled to Washington D.C., where he would confer with the president in a few days.[9]

Despite the correspondence over the agreement, the question concerning Gamble's authority to remove officers from the Missouri State Militia remained unresolved. For this reason, Gamble, after consulting with Attorney General Edward Bates, decided that the question could only be settled by Lincoln. The president was very reluctant, however, to become entangled in the controversy and employed convenient dodges to avoid it for some time. Therefore, on November 17 Gamble was still in Washington D.C. and, unable to speak personally with him, wrote to Lincoln explaining the importance of resolving the issue soon. The regiments of the Missouri State Militia needed to be consolidated and this could not occur before the question of their status was settled. Moreover, as he had exercised various powers over these regiments upon the premise that they were state forces, Gamble was anxious for the president to support his actions by settling this matter in his favor.[10]

Apparently, the controversy put Lincoln somewhat out of temper, probably because he felt pressure from Secretary of War Edwin M. Stanton and Attorney General Bates, who took opposite positions in the controversy. In the end, instead of satisfying one member of his cabinet—and consequently disappointing the other—Lincoln sought to split the difference by not addressing the question at all, but instead he recognized Gamble's authority to dismiss officers on condition that he notify the War Department of his action. Lincoln claimed that this solution, after gaining Stanton's assent to it, would avoid the "hatching" of numerous other disputes which, he asserted, would arise if he himself determined the status of the Missouri State Militia. This dodge, while providing the president a temporary reprieve from the controversy, only postponed resolution of the dispute and ironically fostered many more disagreements. As one might expect, Gamble was very disappointed with Lincoln's decision, but he did not complain at the time and, although he must have felt betrayed that the president had not upheld his part of the bargain, he let the matter drop, probably recognizing the great burden under which Lincoln labored. Later in 1864, the question of the Missouri State Militia's status would arise again in determining its eligibility to receive bounties provided by Congress for United States troops. William Whiting, Solicitor of the War Department, after reviewing the order establishing the Missouri State Militia, concluded that Governor Gamble had been correct in his argument that the force was state militia. Therefore, they were not entitled to these bounties.[11]

Other disputes, Lincoln soon discovered, were not so easily evaded, especially those between the Conservative and Radical Unionists. While the controversy over the status of the Missouri State Militia continued, Lincoln learned from a member of Congress that it might be possible to remove a good number of the federal troops then in Missouri by employing the enrolled militia in northern Missouri to relieve them. This appealed to Lincoln, for it would permit the reassignment of these federal troops to the command of General Grant, who was then in the midst of his Vicksburg campaign. To determine the expediency of such a change, Lincoln wrote to Governor Gamble, General Curtis, members of Congress, and others. The varied nature of the answers he received once again highlighted the divisions among Unionists in Missouri. Governor Gamble replied that he was confident that members of the Enrolled Missouri Militia were capable of maintaining security so long as they were supplied and funded by the federal government. Other Conservative Unionists held the same view. The Radicals, however, were suspicious of this plan. General Curtis and Provost Marshal General Franklin A. Dick asserted that Missouri was not completely secure, warning that the enrolled militia was somehow unreliable because many members, both officers and men, were proslavery. Moreover, Curtis complained that Governor Gamble was then attempting to exert complete control over the enrolled militia and partial authority over the Missouri State Militia. Curtis hoped to avoid trouble with the state authorities but was apprehensive about it. "So far, I have got along without much difficulty with mixed forces, but I have required of my officers and acted myself with great caution and courtesy toward State troops for fear of trouble." Despite these warnings about the enrolled militia, Lincoln did not abandon the idea of their taking over control of northern Missouri and requested that Gamble and Curtis discuss the matter and see if they could not come to some mutual understanding over this and other issues.[12]

To his credit, Curtis, although staunchly radical in his views, carefully attempted to avoid trouble between himself and Gamble. For his part, the governor, who had observed a considerable amount of mischief on the part of free-state regiments in Missouri, understandably wanted them removed and replaced by Missourians serving in the enrolled militia. And although he did not trust General Curtis, Gamble was willing to work with him where he could. Still, he also decided, especially given his difficulties over the dismissal of officers in the Missouri State Militia, to exercise as much control as possible over the enrolled militia, much to Curtis's chagrin and concern. In this Gamble was very successful largely because Curtis eventually backed down from a confrontation despite maintaining that as department commander his authority extended over all military forces in Missouri, including the enrolled militia. Understanding as he did that his tenure as commander of the department depended very much on his ability to work harmoniously with the governor and other state officials, Curtis was reluctant to press the matter further. Nevertheless, with state and federal district commanders exercising authority over the same regions, collisions between commanders were bound to occur, especially whenever their orders conflicted.[13]

Such a circumstance led to controversy between the commander of the 53rd Enrolled Missouri Militia, Colonel Orwin C. Tinker, when the state authorities ordered him to move his headquarters to Hannibal in northeastern Missouri. Colonel J. T. K. Hayward, commander of the 38th Enrolled Missouri Militia, refused to relinquish command there, where he was then headquartered, on the premise that he had been placed in command by General Lewis Merrill, federal commander of the Northeast Missouri District. Hayward claimed that Merrill's authority was superior to that of all the state forces within the district. In reply Tinker pointed to the correspondence between Governor Gamble and General Halleck, which had been published in the newspapers, concerning the governor's dismissal powers in which Halleck admitted that the command of United States officers did not include the enrolled militia. At this point an impasse developed in which neither man was willing to budge. Tinker acknowledged the situation and suggested that because little hope existed for them to resolve the matter between themselves, Hayward should refer his concerns to headquarters. Soon after this, Hayward ordered the provost marshal at Hannibal to arrest Tinker, who was released on his own recognizance pending trial by court-martial.[14]

The source of the dispute and reason the state authorities had sought to replace Hayward was the operation of an underground railroad, its terminus at Hannibal, through which fugitive slaves were making their way to freedom. As a Radical, Hayward was apparently doing little to hinder the escape of runaways and it was alleged that some of the federal troops there were facilitating the flight of slaves owned by loyal persons. One of Hayward's critics summed up the situation in Hannibal thus: "Negroes are flowing in from all directions constantly & then disappear. . . . The question for immediate decision here at this time is whether the citizens' rights, the Civil law, and good order shall be maintained, or that the higher law doctrines shall usurp their place." Knowing that Hayward was permitting slaves to escape into the free states, Curtis wrote to him that state law protected slavery and that the enrolled militia must be allowed to "act as negro-catchers" so long as they "do not interfere with the freedom of the slaves of rebels." Unlike its federal counterpart, as a state force, the enrolled militia did not fall under the congressional restrictions against their use to capture fugitive slaves. Hayward, for his part, argued in a letter to Governor Gamble that the enrolled militia was filled with disloyal men, no doubt meaning in particular Colonel Tinker, and that it was important for

General Lewis Merrill to have command over the enrolled militia in northeastern Missouri. Nevertheless, Tinker, who was later acquitted by a court-martial, soon took command at Hannibal. Learning of the controversy and concerned about the diminution of his authority, Merrill wrote to Gamble arguing that he must have command over the enrolled militia, for, having just been ordered to send five regiments of federal troops to Curtis, he was left with only one regiment to control one-fourth of the state. He asserted, however, that "if I can control the enrolled militia, I do not fear the result; but if they are to set my authority at defiance I am powerless." Merrill's appeal was apparently rejected, for Gamble soon formulated his own plan to maintain order using state troops. Meeting with General Curtis, he proposed designating four regiments of the enrolled militia for special, temporary duty, choosing them from the best regiments and commanders available. These regiments would be posted throughout Missouri, where they were most needed and could do the best service. Despite Curtis's objections to this plan, who recognized that its implementation would diminish his authority, Gamble proceeded with it and informed Lincoln that he expected his support, explaining that he "could not wait for any negotiation with you or Gen'l [sic] Curtis." Undoubtedly, given Lincoln's failure to abide by his former agreement, the governor was reluctant to negotiate another. These forces came to be known as the Provisional Missouri Militia.[15]

During this period of controversy and struggle between Unionists, two of General Curtis's most trusted subordinates, Provost Marshal General Dick and General Merrill, considered departmental policy regarding the treatment of disloyal persons. Merrill, who advocated a tough policy against all supporters of the rebellion, explained why he was especially dissatisfied with allowing influential Secessionists to remain at home.

> The disloyal of Missouri are composed mainly of two classes: One the designing, unscrupulous, shrewd, and unprincipled leaders, and the other (by far the largest) of their poor deluded dupes—men who, but for the poisonous talk and influence of these men, would have remained, at worst, neutral, and who, under better influences, would have been thoroughly loyal. These leaders have, in almost every instance, confined themselves to the secret exertion of their influence and the spreading of mischievous lying reports, while their cat's-paws have done the work in which they were too cowardly and too shrewd to be implicated directly.

Moreover, Merrill noted that the vast majority of disloyal persons who had taken the oath of allegiance had not kept it. To support this claim, he pointed to the thousands of bonds already forfeited by disloyal persons who had violated their oaths, amounting to, he estimated, a "million dollars." For a time, he had "summarily" banished a number of troublemakers but had discontinued this practice because, invariably, such persons had influential friends who interceded for them and gained their recall. Apparently, Merrill's argument convinced Dick of the need for a change in policy. More important, Curtis agreed with Merrill, leading to his publication of an important general order on Christmas Eve 1862.[16]

In General Orders No. 35, Curtis instituted a policy to provide more guidance and power to the military in dealing with those troublemakers about whom Merrill was most concerned. In the context of wartime Missouri, these powers were not extraordinary, although they were established at a time of relative calm. As noted in preceding chapters, under the commands of Halleck and Schofield guerrillas were shot, disloyal persons were arrested and, depending upon the circumstances, were released, imprisoned, or banished. Other controversial policies included the confiscation of property, including weapons and ammunition, and restrictions upon travel and trade. Curtis extended and refined these policies while simultaneously expanding and reorganizing the provost-marshal system throughout the state and regularizing its operations. One of the measures of General Orders No. 35 provided provost marshals and district commanders with the authority to arrest "notoriously bad and dangerous men, where peace and safety require it, though no specific act of disloyalty can be proven against them; and such may be put under bonds, imprisoned, or required to leave the State." Previous to this, provost marshals were ordered to release anyone against whom no evidence of wrongdoing was available. Moreover, Curtis designated "disloyal preachers" for special scrutiny and punishment, for they "have disgraced their profession by encouraging others to rebel, while they may have committed no other kind of disloyal act." Because of the liberality with which they had been treated previously and the great amount of influence they wielded within the community, Curtis felt justified in ordering the banishment of these disloyal preachers.[17]

In considering General Curtis's policy regarding "disloyal preachers," one must remember that in his General Orders No. 35 the policy was not much different than that of his predecessors. Those preaching or publishing disloyal statements were subject to arrest, imprisonment, and banishment, depending upon the facts of their case. What was different, as noted above, was the summary manner in which they were treated. This, of course, increased the possibility that innocent persons could be punished. In northeast Missouri as district commander, and apparently without authority to do so, General Merrill had banished a large number of persons without even a military commission trial. Curtis adopted this policy for the entire department, thereby removing an important check upon officers and commanders who might be inclined to indulge in bigotry or personal animus against others. No evidence exists that Curtis, in doing so, wished to restrict the freedom of religion—or freedom of speech and the press, of which more later—or to persecute anyone in particular. Nevertheless, the policy could hardly have had a different consequence. This potential for injustice, once realized in individual cases, quickly came to the attention of state authorities and of Lincoln.[18]

Even before this new summary power was exercised, persons considered disloyal were sometimes persecuted despite having remained neutral throughout the war. This appears to have been the circumstance of Bartlett Anderson, a Baptist minister, who along with six other men was taken hostage by an enrolled militia unit on September 6, 1862, after "ten or twelve horses" had been stolen. Anderson acknowledged that he had "a reputation of being a Southern Sympathizer but" he explained, "I have refused to participate in our troubles. I was in favor of the Union Convention in Missouri." After refusing to take the oath of allegiance Anderson was sent to St. Louis. A board of officers, still operating under the previous policy requiring a consideration of charges and evidence against civilian prisoners, reviewed his case and released him unconditionally from the Gratiot Street Military Prison on December 6. From the record it is clear that despite having no evidence against him, Anderson waited, along with fifteen hundred other prisoners, for three months before his case was reviewed. While such a wait must have been frustrating, the process protected prisoners from summary punishment, the procedure which was soon to be implemented. Despite his release, General Merrill ordered Anderson banished on December 24 (notably the same day as the publication of General Orders No. 35), to "reside east of the State of Illinois and north of Indianapolis, Indiana." Anderson was ordered to leave Missouri within ten days of receiving the banishment order and to report by letter monthly to

Merrill's headquarters at Warrenton. Nevertheless, in March 1863 Anderson was able somehow to gain a review of his case and trial by military commission. The evidence presented against Anderson consisted of sworn testimony of acquaintances concerning various statements they had heard him make favorable to the South and critical of various actions of the military and of the provisional government which, the witnesses said, Anderson regarded as illegitimate. A witness claimed he had heard Anderson threaten to become a guerrilla if the military came after him. However, no one accused him of preaching treason from the pulpit. While the record is unclear concerning the final determination of his case, it appears that while Dick was unwilling for Anderson to return to his home, he agreed to permit him to reside in St. Louis.[19]

Another minister arrested at this time was Robert P. Farris. Earlier in the war in late July 1861, Farris, who was the pastor of a Presbyterian church in St. Charles, was accused of misconduct from the pulpit. One of his accusers was Mary Easton Sibley who, along with her husband George Sibley, had founded Lindenwood Female College. In a letter to the provost marshal she stated that "when a large number of troops under General [John] Pope camped in St. Charles," Farris had prayed "that the invaders be driven out of Missouri and called for resistence [sic] to 'oppression.'" Such a prayer, if made, hardly met the standards of the Thornwell theory, upon which Farris and other Presbyterian ministers later refused to take an oath of allegiance, declaring their duties to extend only to spiritual matters. Thus Farris's situation remained until September 1862 when Provost Marshal Edward Harding arrested him. General Merrill interrogated Farris and concluded that he was disloyal and ordered him confined in prison for the war. After some six weeks in the Gratiot Street Military Prison in St. Louis, Provost Marshal General Dick decided to release Farris upon condition that he leave Missouri. For the next six weeks Farris sought to arrange his affairs before his departure for Chicago, where he intended to remain during his exile. During this time, Farris was able to procure the aid of Justice David Davis of the Supreme Court of the United States, who was a good friend of Lincoln, having been the presiding judge of the circuit courts in Illinois before which the president had practiced. Farris had his friends send "testimonials from 'Union' men" who vouched for him. Hearing of this effort, on December 12 Dick wrote to the president that Farris is one of the most impudent, persistent and ingenious Rebels in the State, and as a Minister, has wielded a powerful influence in aid of the rebellion. Undoubtedly he ought to be removed from this State during the War. I understand, that he has a strong hope, of procuring an order from Your Excellency, rescinding the sentence against him, and therefore I send this statement, that it may be known that such action would encourage a dangerous and influential class of cunning aiders of the rebellion in Missouri.

Dick also included a short note from Barton Bates, the son of Attorney General Bates, strongly requesting that Farris not be allowed to return to Missouri. Nevertheless, Lincoln disregarded Dick's warning and ordered that Farris be allowed to return to his home there. Despite this, at least according to Farris's testimony, Dick refused to allow him to return home and he was forced to move to Chicago. Farris then appealed again to his friend Justice Davis, who personally went to the White House and obtained an order allowing Farris to return home unconditionally four months after his ordeal had begun.[20]

Another minister who soon found himself before a provost marshal was E. M. Bounds, a minister at Brunswick. Until just before the war, Bounds had worked as a lawyer in northeast Missouri and began his labors in the ministry as a circuit rider for the Methodist Episcopal Church South. Although he had taken the oath of allegiance to the Missouri and United States constitutions, Bounds refused to take the "convention oath," for it required its adherents to support the government of the United States against its enemies. As a southern sympathizer, Bounds admitted that he could not honestly swear to it. For this reason, he was arrested and sent to St. Louis, where in return for his release he agreed to exile and by Curtis's order "was sent South with [the] first lot." Apparently, Bounds did not seek the revocation of his banishment and spent the war traveling and preaching to southerners as he had done in Missouri. After the war he eventually became an editor for the *St. Louis Christian Advocate,* the premier publication of his denomination in the West.[21]

Another instance of the military's interference with the churches and their ministers occurred in Mexico, Missouri. In January 1863, the local provost marshal ordered James Morton, the minister of the Presbyterian church, to leave the state. As a British subject, he sought the aid of the British consul to appeal this decision, which was made without providing Morton a hearing and without even notifying Provost Marshal General Dick. J. Edward Wilkins, who, as a representative of the British government, had interceded on behalf of other citizens of his country, requested that Morton receive a hearing and be allowed to return to Missouri to collect proof of his neutrality in the conflict. From the evidence presented against Morton, however, it appears that his behavior was not always friendly toward Union forces, although his anger may have been provoked by the bad behavior of troops who, toward the end of 1861, had taken possession of the Presbyterian church in Mexico where he preached. Morton testified that in early 1862 soldiers under the command of John B. Henderson came to the church and disrupted a prayer meeting and stole coal belonging to the church. Morton sent a deacon to request the soldiers to stop until the service was over. About half of the church was filled with soldiers attending the services. Afterward Morton explained to the soldiers, who were angry that he had "reproved" them for swearing and taking the coal, that it had been purchased with difficulty by the poor parishioners but that they would give it up willingly if the soldiers brought an order from an officer. Some of these soldiers recognized that they had behaved badly and returned later to hear him preach. Nevertheless, some overzealous Union supporters claimed that this incident demonstrated Morton's disloyalty. From then on he was "the subject of insult and persecution."[22]

On January 11, 1862, Captain Herron took possession of the church. Morton went to Herron and Colonel Henderson to request that the soldiers occupy other quarters, as there were other places where they could stay. Henderson and Herron rejected Morton's request and, according to him, were generally unfair and ungentlemanly in their behavior. More serious than this was the behavior of the soldiers, who insulted him and threatened his life. "On the eve of their departure a Company of Dutch Soldiers, I believe they belong to the 1st Missouri Home or Reserve Guards, entered the Church and occupied it until about the middle of April, when they were removed to some other point." The two companies did considerable damage to the church, in which the soldiers chopped wood and rode their horses.[23]

After a few months' respite from military occupation, on November 19, 1862, Company A of the 10th Missouri State Militia took possession of the church and, like their military predecessors, damaged the church substantially. "On the doors inside the Church they cut or carved the most obscene language which had to be filled up lest the eyes of any lady might see it." After this, Morton refused to pay a $10 fine for the militia services as to do so, he believed, would associate him with "southern sympathizers." He also argued that he was exempt as a British subject and strictly neutral in the conflict. On November 29, 1862, Major Woodson, commander of the post at Mexico, ordered Morton jailed for two days and nights after he compared the militia unfavorably to Merrill's Horse. This regiment, Morton declared, would not shelter themselves in a church. These comments were made in earshot of the militia. Responding to this insult, Lieutenant Hopkins called Morton "a damned rebel," to which he protested that the officer had no right to call him names. A soldier pulled his pistol and threatened to shoot Morton if he did not remain quiet, while another ordered him to leave "in the most abusive language." Claiming that he had honestly mistaken this soldier for "a Yellow negro," he replied "that no negro should order me to leave." At this, as might be expected, the soldiers became more abusive, and one of them attempted to hit Morton but was prevented. While jailed, Morton caught a cold and infection of the lungs. This confrontation with the military led to his banishment.

While he could not claim to have behaved always prudently, Morton denied that he had ever done anything in word or deed which could be considered disloyal. He promised to produce witnesses, including soldiers of the enrolled militia, who would support his claim to have acted in a strictly neutral manner. Provost Marshal Gardner contradicted these assertions and claimed that Morton had told acquaintances that he favored the South, although the provost marshal did not provide names of his witnesses. Gardner also argued that Morton's return to Mexico would have a bad affect upon the community, providing Secessionists with a victory, demoralizing Unionists, and undermining his authority. General Curtis, who had been made aware of Morton's case by the British Consul Wilkins, revoked Morton's banishment on March 18, ruling that he could remain in Missouri anywhere except in Audrain County. Later, after Curtis and Dick were no longer in authority in Missouri, Morton appealed the order preventing him from returning to Mexico, but his request was denied.[24]

The case of Samuel B. McPheeters, minister of the Pine Street Presbyterian Church of St. Louis, was the most important of those cases concerned with the proper policy of the military toward ministers and churches. It was the adjudication of this case which eventually caused Lincoln to intervene decisively to prevent the military from interfering with the churches. Writing a week after inquiring concerning the case of Farris, Provost Marshal General Dick was concerned that Curtis's new policy (which would be made public in just a few days) ordering the summary arrest, imprisonment, or banishment of ministers with southern sympathies might be rescinded or at least undercut through Lincoln's intervention. In a special order, Dick provided the rationale and justification for the arrest and banishment of McPheeters and his wife and the policy promulgated in General Orders No. 35. In this special order, a copy of which he sent to Lincoln, Dick argued that McPheeters had encouraged members of his congregation and others to rebel by refusing publicly to support the United States government or to denounce the Confederacy. In other words, according to Dick's strange logic, McPheeters encouraged rebellion by remaining absolutely neutral concerning the war. He maintained his silence despite his wife and other relatives supporting the South. In addition to banishing McPheeters and his wife to the South, Dick "ordered that the Church edifice, books and papers, at the corner of Eleventh and Pine Streets be placed under the control of those loyal members of Pine Street Church." Moreover, in a letter to Lincoln, Dick pressed his case that this policy of banishing influential supporters of the rebellion to the South was necessary, for these persons convinced many young men to join guerrilla bands, which had destroyed many lives and much property in Missouri.[25]

As was often the case in matters regarding Missouri, Lincoln soon received contradictory reports and advice. Once again, Lincoln's friend Justice Davis was asked to intervene with the president, this time to stop the banishment of McPheeters. Another correspondent, Archibald Gamble, brother of Governor Gamble, wrote to Attorney General Bates noting that McPheeters did not preach politics from the pulpit and arguing that it was wrong for him to be banished "without a hearing" of any sort. McPheeters also wrote to Bates, explaining the circumstances which led to the controversy between himself and some members of his congregation. According to him, a small minority of the members demanded that he publicly state his views on "civil & political questions," which he refused to do. In a newspaper editorial, McPheeters observed that as a minister of the gospel his spiritual duty was to stand aloof from controversies preventing their entrance "into the house of God." Moreover, he stood upon the principle of "the complete and absolute separation" of church and state.[26]

Lincoln reluctantly entered the McPheeters controversy at a time when in the short span of a couple of months he had already found it necessary to referee the question between Gamble and Halleck concerning the governor's authority to dismiss officers from the Missouri State Militia and to intervene in the matter of Robert P. Farris. At the same time Lincoln was also involved in reviewing the extent to which martial law should remain in force in Missouri, in assessing whether it was prudent to hand over control of northern Missouri to the state authorities, and, as seen below, in considering Curtis's policy of imposing assessments against disloyal persons. On December 27, Lincoln met with McPheeters at the White House. He explained his side of the controversy and sought the repeal of his banishment upon the principle that the military should not have authority over the churches and their ministers. Unsure about the proper decision, Lincoln that same day telegraphed Curtis to suspend his order banishing McPheeters. Curtis promptly repealed the banishment order but left in place that part of it handing over control of the church to McPheeters's antagonists. To Lincoln, Curtis responded that McPheeters was "evidently a bad rebel, doing injury here, and his removal is, so far as I can learn, universally approved by Union men." However, as seems obvious from Dick's special order banishing him, no evidence existed proving McPheeters's disloyalty. Lincoln, unlike Curtis, knew that not all Unionists favored the expulsion of "Rebel priests" generally, and that some were opposed to McPheeters's expulsion in particular. For this reason, Lincoln considered it prudent to determine whether or not it would be just to banish McPheeters and to consider the implications of Curtis's General Orders No. 35. Of Curtis's assertion that "Rebel priests are dangerous and diabolical in society," Lincoln undoubtedly considered this statement too universal in scope and typical of the rhetoric of Radicals who too often dealt in absolutes, ignoring important nuances of opinion and lumping together all supporters of slavery and those advocating a moderate war policy as disloyal.[27]

In his reply to Curtis's letter of December 29, Lincoln demonstrated an independence of mind and sophisticated understanding of the differing motivations, biases, and emotions of the disputants, all of which were weighed in consideration of what would be just to McPheeters, best for Missouri, and proper in respect to the support he owed his commander of the department. Lincoln, perhaps hoping to persuade Curtis that his policy was ill-conceived and unjust, explained that he had looked into the matter carefully during a meeting with Attorney General Bates and McPheeters. After examining a copy of the oath the minister had signed, Lincoln found nothing in the charges presented against him to conclude that McPheeters had violated it. Moreover, after talking with the minister, Lincoln concluded that he was "a man of unquestioned good moral character," although he also believed him to "sympathize with the rebels." Nevertheless, Lincoln thought it bad policy to exile a man because "he has a rebel wife & rebel relations, that he sympathizes with rebels, and that he exercises rebel influence." In the end, however, Lincoln decided that if Curtis believed that McPheeters should still be banished then he would not interfere, as such a decision could only be made by the commander "on the spot." Perhaps, having already intervened in several cases in Missouri, Lincoln feared that he might have undercut Curtis's authority a great deal and wanted to discourage others from seeking his intervention in the internecine struggles among Unionists in Missouri. Whatever the reason, Lincoln's decision not to intervene would mean that the controversy, much to his chagrin, would remain unsettled. In making this concession, the president also reminded Curtis "that the U. S. government must not, as by this order, undertake to run the churches."[28]

For whatever reason, Curtis allowed McPheeters to remain in St. Louis but did not permit him to resume his duties as a minister. Whether it was done intentionally or not, Curtis's failure to repeal that part of the special order prohibiting McPheeters from preaching was contrary to Lincoln's decision. Some months later, when McPheeters's friends petitioned to have him restored to his pulpit, the president was incredulous that Curtis had ignored his command not "to run the churches," provoking him to note on the petition "that, in no event, was any one to interfere by my authority, as to who should, or should not preach in any church. . . . The assumption that I am keeping Dr. M. from preaching in his church is monstrous. If any one is doing this, by pretence [sic] of my authority, I will thank any one who can, to make out and present me, a specific case against him." In a letter to one of the petitioners, Lincoln defensively asserted that he had never sought to meddle in the affairs of the churches and had ordered Curtis and his subordinates not to do so also. He was astonished to learn that his order might have been disobeyed. In the end, on December 31, 1863, more than a year after the controversy concerning McPheeters first had been presented to him, the president communicated through Attorney General Bates his desire that McPheeters should "quietly resume the exercise of all the rights, duties, and functions of [his] office, as if no interruption had occurred." From that point forward, Lincoln proved to be more aggressive in stopping any improper interference of the military in ecclesiastical affairs.[29]

After the McPheeters controversy, General Curtis and Provost Marshal General Dick were more cautious in their treatment of ministers and during the remainder of their tenures tried to avoid similar disputes, although they still investigated ministers suspected of being disloyal. One of these ministers was S. J. P. Anderson, who apparently was less scrupulous in maintaining neutrality than was McPheeters, having expressed support for the South privately. In May 1863, Dick interrogated him and became convinced that he was disloyal. However, Anderson appealed to Attorney General Bates, his fellow sectarian, and Dick felt constrained to submit Anderson's case to a military commission. After hearing evidence, the commission found Anderson guilty and sentenced him to be sent South. By the time of the trial, General John M. Schofield was in command and he "disapproved" of the proceedings on the grounds that the commission did not have "the minimum [members] prescribed" by orders. And indeed, as became evident soon after his assumption of command, General Schofield did not single out ministers for special scrutiny and punishment nor were they provided any special protections. For this reason, Lincoln would not again find it necessary to resolve any ecclesiastical conflicts until the McPheeters matter once again erupted at the end of the year. So long as a minister swore an oath of allegiance and maintained silence concerning the war and politics, he could expect to pursue his ministry without interference. However, any minister refusing to conform himself to these requirements soon faced arrest and possible imprisonment or banishment.[30]

Apparently, the expulsion of a number of ministers created a strong demand for replacements, especially for those regions where strong secessionist sentiment existed and much guerrilla warfare continued. One of the towns where few ministers wished to serve was Boonville. Located near the Missouri River in the central part of the state, the pulpit of the Episcopal church there had remained empty for a year. In the summer of 1863, however, a young minister, F. R. Holeman, accepted a call to serve there. How well Holeman understood the circumstances into which he entered is unclear, but it was not long before the local provost marshal had arrested and placed him on parole. Like McPheeters, Holeman insisted on maintaining strict neutrality but carried the application of this principle a step further, insisting that taking the oath of allegiance would mean that he was taking "part in the deplorable discord of our country." Apparently, no evidence existed that Holeman had said or done anything disloyal or had ever challenged the authority of the military over him. Moreover, realizing that the state would not recognize marriages performed by ministers refusing to take the oath, he had declined conducting them. Holeman, in a letter to the district commander, General E. B. Brown, argued that no oath should be required of loyal citizens. He also believed that the oath requirement was an unwarranted intrusion of the state upon the church. The bishop of the Episcopal church in Missouri, Cicero S. Hawks, regarded Holeman's position as an odd one and felt he was taking the principle of neutrality too far. He thought it strange that Holeman declared his loyalty but was unwilling to obey the powers over him, preferring instead to be banished rather than to take the oath. Perhaps Holeman simply disliked his new position and sought some excuse to leave. This impasse eventually resulted in Holeman, who had requested time to prepare for his departure, being ordered to Canada, where he preferred to live during the remainder of the war until he could return and coexist in peace with his fellow countrymen.[31]

It must be remembered that "Rebel priests" were not the only targets of General Orders No. 35. While it singled out those considered by General Curtis as the most influential members of society, the order did not exclude less prominent persons who encouraged rebellion. As noted above, the policy of banishing persons who were secretly helping or persuading others to participate in the rebellion was not a new one. At the beginning of his command, General Halleck had employed this power in a public manner—such as in the case of Samuel Engler—to deter others from challenging military authority. He also expelled southern sympathizers from Missouri because of their influence and capacity to cause trouble during wartime. However, when General Schofield inquired about his authority to expel disloyal persons of wealth and influence in St. Louis for secretly establishing "a military organization extending all over the State and embracing very large numbers," Halleck replied that as commander of the department he had the power to banish "all persons who endanger the public peace and safety. But this power should be sparingly exercised," he added, "as it is not good policy to increase the ranks of the enemy by sending South all their friends and sympathizers." However, at least some of the district commanders did not exercise such restraint. General

Benjamin Loan, commander of the central district headquartered at Jefferson City, arrested many disloyal persons, presumably attempting to apply Curtis's directions for determining loyalty, allowing the "milder" Secessionists to leave the state within ten days. Loan believed that the more dangerous persons must be held in prison during the war. Of all the district commanders, General Merrill probably arrested and exiled more persons than any other. By late 1862, Merrill stated that he had arrested fifteen hundred persons whom he had released on taking the oath and posting a bond. Of these, he claimed not to know that any of them had "faithfully kept their promises to behave in all respects as loyal citizens." For this reason, he had exiled many others, especially "the designing, unscrupulous, shrewd, and unprincipled leaders," who used their influence to cause their neighbors to aid the rebellion while they remained safely at home. Both Loan and Merrill had complained about interference from outside and convinced Provost Marshal General Dick of the wisdom of their policy. While Lincoln expressed reservations concerning the policy, even temporarily ordering its suspension, for the most part he was reluctant to hinder the efforts of his commanders. However, in the case of McPheeters, he had advised caution in the exercise of such a discretionary power. With a Union victory far from certain after more than a year and a half of war, Lincoln was willing to accept the restriction of civil liberties where military necessity seemed to require it, reserving for himself as commander in chief the right to mitigate the actions of his commanders whenever he deemed it preferable or necessary.[32]

After Lincoln's warning to proceed cautiously in employing his authority to banish persons from Missouri, Curtis modified General Orders No. 35, commanding that no one be banished from the state without a trial by military commission, thereby removing the major objection to his policy. Nevertheless, the number of persons Curtis and Dick expelled from Missouri was significant and undoubtedly exceeded those exiled by their predecessors. Most of them were removed for providing support to the enemy in some manner or actually participating in guerrilla activities. Recognizing that most of their actions could not be scrutinized by the president, who had much more than Missouri to monitor, for the most part Curtis and Dick were able to pursue their policies unhindered, so long as their actions did not affect the friends of persons with access to Lincoln. In most such cases, the president brought the matter to Curtis's attention, asking only that he look into it. Overwhelmed and overworked, the president sought to disentangle himself from "Missouri matters" to the extent that he could. Moreover, it is clear that Curtis and Dick, as was customary in observing the proper chain of command, brought most policy questions for resolution to the War Department, where severe measures received a much more favorable hearing than they sometimes did from Lincoln. Thus Provost Marshal General Dick gained permission from the War Department to arrest and exchange "citizen prisoners," many of whom were held in overcrowded and unhealthy military prisons.

The War Department also approved the arrest and banishment of influential women against whom Dick had acquired proof through the capture of a Rebel mailbag that they were encouraging rebellion and providing information to the enemy. Some of these women were the wives of the most prominent Rebels from Missouri and included the wife of Trusten Polk, a former United States senator then serving as a judge in the Confederacy, and others whose husbands were generals or congressmen in the South. Undoubtedly recognizing that the banishment of such high-profile women without prior permission to do so could soon generate a wave of protests from their friends and petitions to Lincoln, Dick undercut such efforts by gaining the imprimatur of no less than Judge Advocate Joseph Holt, who stated unequivocally that "the policy which [Dick] indicates for the treatment of incorrigible Rebels is unquestionably the true one and a policy less lenient than this cannot be safely pursued anywhere but especially in the State of Missouri." Upon this recommendation, Secretary of War Stanton approved the policy, thus reducing greatly the likelihood that Lincoln would intervene in the matter. By the end of Curtis's tenure as commander in Missouri, the president apparently agreed with the policy and communicated his unwillingness to intervene in most cases, although, as in the case of Samuel B. Churchill, Lincoln mitigated his banishment and allowed him to live in Louisville, Kentucky, after Lincoln's good friends James and Joshua Speed requested this modification. These interventions by the president, as discussed in the next chapter, ensured that he could not disentangle himself from affairs in Missouri, for both Radical and Conservative Unionists had gained some success in presenting their disputes to him. Thus, short of refusing to consider any more petitions from Missouri, which he was unwilling to do, Lincoln should not have been surprised that he continued to receive appeals seeking his settlement of policy disputes.[33]

7

RADICAL POLICIES AND THE REMOVAL
OF GENERAL SAMUEL R. CURTIS

AS NOTED IN CHAPTERS 2 AND 3, different military commanders in Missouri had ordered the confiscation of property through assessments to provide funds for loyal war refugees and to cover the expense of restoring property damaged by guerrillas or by General Sterling Price's army. Generally, these funds were collected from disloyal persons, although, as in the case of John Pope in northern Missouri very early in the war, an entire community, including its *loyal* members, was made responsible for all depredations and property damage occurring in a town and the surrounding area. This policy was exceptional and in a brief time Pope repealed it after complaints from Governor Hamilton R. Gamble and Congressman Frank P. Blair Jr., who both objected to treating Unionists and Secessionists alike, considering it unwise and detrimental to the war effort. General Henry W. Halleck's assessment and confiscation policy sought only to punish the disloyal and to benefit war refugees from southern Missouri. Under nineteenth-century international law, Halleck's order was legal as an emergency war measure. Moreover, it was considered acceptable under the laws of war for regiments while in the field to seize civilian property, which could be useful to the war effort or to deny its use to the enemy. This is still true today. Generally, compensation for the value of the loss of property thus seized was made only to loyal persons. Much property in Missouri and elsewhere was lost or destroyed in this manner.[1]

General John M. Schofield, who in 1862 succeeded Halleck to command in Missouri, also issued an order assessing upon Rebels and their supporters a "sum of $5,000 for every soldier or Union citizen killed; from $1,000 to $5,000 for every one wounded; and the full value of all property destroyed or stolen by guerrillas." These seizures were made in accord with military law. Recognizing that money and supplies were streaming into the South from areas well outside of the war zones and thus not subject to military law, Congress in

August 1861 passed a law to seize any property intended for the enemy. In July 1862, Congress enacted another law allowing for the seizure of property in the North or in captured territory belonging to all officers of the Confederate government, civil and military, and the possessions of disloyal persons. Once such property was identified, district attorneys began proceedings for seizure in the territorial and federal court systems. For this reason, when Secretary of War Stanton directed him to enforce the Confiscation Act in Missouri, General Schofield, as he recounted in his memoirs many years later, expressed the opinion that the command was unlawful, for only the courts could enforce the statute. Nevertheless, not wishing to behave in an insubordinate manner, he issued an order directing the provost marshal general to seize the property of disloyal persons according to the statute and to provide to the district attorney the evidence against them for trial. In this order Schofield was careful to make clear that only the courts were to determine the final status of the property. Other departmental commanders and provost marshals were not as scrupulous about adhering to the letter of the law as was Schofield. Interestingly, just as there had been "hundreds of treason indictments but no punishments, so there were many confiscation cases, but only a small amount of property confiscated." Moreover, later the Supreme Court of the United States ruled that the seizure of real property under the second Confiscation Act could not extend beyond the life of the owner, its possession reverting to his or her heirs.[2]

Under the rules of martial law of that time, however, it must be remembered that the military still retained its authority summarily to seize or destroy any property so long as it served a legitimate military purpose. Thus persons living in the war zones were still subject to martial law and commanders could, and often did, act apart from the civil laws upon the grounds of military necessity. Of course, commanders had to employ such authority skillfully and with caution, not forgetting that the power was only temporary and must be relinquished as soon as the necessity had passed. The responsibility for determining this was the burden of the departmental commander, who had continually to monitor the circumstances and be willing to diminish his and his subordinates' authority as soon as civil control was reestablished. Many years after the war, the Supreme Court of the United States would uphold Schofield's actions from this period regarding the military's seizure of rents in a case originating from St. Louis in *Mitchell v. Clark* (1884).[3]

After the failure of the guerrilla uprising in the summer of 1862 in which many irregulars were killed, captured, or driven into hiding, the district militia and federal division commanders ordered assessments against persons who had supported the uprising. These assessments upon those responsible for the uprising were intended to compensate loyal persons for the damage sustained in the guerrilla raids and to supply and pay the enrolled militia, for which the state had no funds. These district commanders established boards to determine the losses in property and the expense of supplying and paying the enrolled militia. The boards identified disloyal persons in the community to pay according to their means and their support of the guerrilla outbreak. Some of the military commanders provided scant direction to these committees' work. Others, such as General Lewis Merrill, who by the fall of 1862 had acquired extensive experience fighting guerrillas and their supporters, gave detailed instructions to the committees ordering them to document the evidence, testimony, and their deliberations in determining who should pay and how much. On October 10, 1862, Provost Marshal General Thomas T. Gantt, who had been appointed by General Schofield, sent out a circular to the district and division commanders ordering the suspension of these assessments, asserting that they were in violation of the Confiscation Act of July 1862. It is unclear whether this order led to Gantt's dismissal and the appointment of Franklin A. Dick to the position. Whatever the reason, it is clear that his understanding of the jurisdiction and effect of the congressional statute was not shared by General Samuel R. Curtis and President Abraham Lincoln. Later, when he ordered the suspension of assessments, the rescission of the authority was based upon the determination that the military necessity for it no longer existed.[4]

While in many of the militia districts assessments continued to the end of 1862, in others commanders suspended county-board assessments and military seizures after they learned that some militia units had abused this authority. Having received reports that some enrolled militia units, who had been given authority to forage in the field, were pillaging the communities in which they were operating, General John McNeil, commander of the eighth military district of Missouri, ordered these units to disband and that an accounting be made of all property seized by the militia and that the assessments be discontinued. Other complaints surfaced regarding some of the seizures and some excessively large assessments, such as Colonel Richard C. Vaughan's assessment of $85,000 on the people of Chariton County. Moreover, in one instance, at least, some confusion existed concerning to whom the proceeds should go from the sale of "contraband property," after the commander of United States forces claimed that a local enrolled militia unit had sold property belonging to his command.[5]

Further confusion existed concerning who had authority, Governor Gamble as commander in chief of the enrolled militia or General Curtis as departmental commander, to suspend these assessments. Because General Schofield as departmental commander in August 1862 had ordered the establishment of a board in St. Louis County to make assessments there, Gamble believed that Curtis had the power to suspend them. However, Curtis was reluctant to take the responsibility, for he believed that Schofield had exercised this authority as commander of the enrolled militia, the command of which Gamble had retained, denying it to Curtis when he had succeeded Schofield. For his part, apparently unknown to Gamble and Curtis, Schofield stated that his authority to order the assessments had derived from his command of the District of Missouri as a United States officer. To resolve the matter, Gamble wrote to Lincoln requesting the suspension of the assessment on the grounds that the emergency under which Schofield had ordered it no longer existed. Gamble also considered this action prudent, given the "very many outrageous blunders both as to the sentiments of persons assessed and their ability to pay money for the purposes expressed in the order. Very loud complaints are made by very many citizens not only against the principle upon which the assessment is made but against the action of the board in carrying out the order." In addition to recognizing that the board had often assessed the wrong persons, even supporters of the policy believed that the board had erred in conducting its hearings in secret and not providing to persons accused of being disloyal or supporting the rebellion the chance to hear and rebut the testimony against them.[6]

In response to Gamble's request, Lincoln, who had become increasingly concerned about the propriety and legality of property seizures, suspended the assessment in St. Louis County and requested that Curtis provide him with "a statement of facts pertinent to the question, together with your opinion upon it." Curtis replied that he had suspended the assessment and agreed with Gamble that the "military necessity" justifying its implementation probably no longer existed. Absent military necessity, he concluded, the continuance of the assessments would violate the Confiscation Act of July 1862. However, Curtis argued that the assessment in St. Louis County should not be revoked, for the threat of its being reinstated would serve as a warning to anyone who might be tempted to help insurgents or the Confederacy. Apparently, General Halleck and Secretary of War Edwin M. Stanton had independently concluded also that the assessments in Missouri were then unnecessary and should be suspended. Governor Gamble, believing that all assessments should be suspended immediately, not just the one in St. Louis County, ordered all assessments by the enrolled militia stopped and asked Lincoln to order the revocation of those by United States officers as well. This action, coupled with the overwhelming opposition to the assessments, including all of Missouri's members of Congress except one, prompted Lincoln to write to Curtis requesting that he consult with Gamble on this and other matters. Moreover, having heard that some of the assessments had been fraudulently made to enrich the assessors, the president expressed grave reservations about them and noted that whether the report was factual, "nothing but the sternest necessity can justify the making and maintaining of a system so liable to such abuses."[7]

Apparently, because the president had not peremptorily ordered Curtis to stop them all, some of the assessments outside of St. Louis County continued. Congressman Thomas L. Price requested that General Benjamin F. Loan's assessments in central Missouri be suspended at least temporarily, noting that they could always be renewed if necessary. This request and General Merrill's January 15, 1863, order to assessment boards to collect $300,000 in the northeast district convinced Lincoln to suspend such collections for the time being. This decision, it is clear, did not please Curtis, some of his commanders (most notably Merrill and Loan), and some Radicals. In particular, General Loan reacted badly to the suspension order, publishing a general order commanding his commissioned officers to execute "promptly" all Confederate recruiters and persons providing aid and comfort to the enemy. Moreover, he ordered the destruction of the homes of those providing aid to the enemy and the seizure of their personal property to help Unionists who had suffered loss at the hands of guerrillas. While this order did not technically violate the suspension of assessments, it violated the spirit of the policy, which was intended to allow circumstances in Missouri, so long as no new uprisings occurred, to return to normal.[8]

Another issue creating some controversy was the military's regulation of trade in Missouri. Soon after taking command, General Curtis ordered that "no public trade or commercial business shall be carried on within the department except by persons strictly loyal." In this he was complying with War Department orders that sought to interdict the delivery of supplies and wealth into the South. He also ordered that no trade be conducted with those places where the rebellion continued. While he generally favored severe policies, Curtis permitted traders to purchase goods from disloyal persons, believing that not enough supplies were available for civilian and military needs if only acquired from loyal sellers. Moreover, he later decided to allow disloyal individuals who had recently taken the oath to receive licenses to trade goods, believing that such a policy would encourage them to remain loyal if for no other reason than to serve their own economic interests. General Loan, commander of the central district, objected to this as an unwise policy, noting that he had evidence that some of these traders were disloyal and should not profit from the war, especially when so many loyal men could not participate in such activities and were neglecting their own affairs to serve in the enrolled militia. These men could hardly be blamed for their outrage at seeing persons they considered disloyal prosper while they, supporters of the Union, suffered financial loss. Moreover, Loan claimed to have uncovered evidence that some of these dealers had traded with William C. Quantrill, the infamous guerrilla leader, thus providing their enemies with funds to continue their activities. These dealers also gathered information for the enemy as they traveled through the state unhindered.[9]

As with so many other policy matters, Lincoln also heard complaints from a group of merchants in Quincy, Illinois, about the policy restricting trade into Missouri from across the Mississippi River. Unwilling to act without first consulting with Treasury Secretary Salmon P. Chase, Lincoln commented that the merchants' request to gain unrestricted access to the Missouri market seemed reasonable and asked if any harm to the war effort would result from granting their request. A short time later, Chase sent to Lincoln a report by a special agent of the Treasury Department who explained that within the past few days authorities had intercepted powder, shot, and a six-pounder cannon being smuggled from Quincy or its vicinity into Missouri. All of these items had been concealed within or under other merchandise when it was discovered. The agent believed that without the restrictions upon trade a great deal of war contraband would fall into the hands of the enemy and recommended that the restrictions not be rescinded. Apparently, this information convinced Lincoln that a change in policy would be a mistake.[10]

In earlier chapters (see especially 2 and 4), First Amendment policies adopted under Curtis's predecessors are considered. Under the common law, permissible speech included the criticism of others, political leaders, and policies, but even during peacetime freedom of speech was not absolute, for judicial remedies against those slandering others and inciting violence, for instance, were maintained. During wartime, free speech rights were restricted further, as one might expect, leading to the decision of the military and political leadership, both Conservative and Radical, to suppress speech or arrest persons making disloyal statements. These actions appear to have been taken upon the premise that some freedoms must be curtailed, especially when their exercise could divulge important information to the enemy and lead to the death of others or even the defeat of federal forces in battle. Moreover, the authorities in Missouri particularly sought to suppress any speech meant to incite others to violence against Unionists or to join the Confederate military or guerrilla forces. Distinguishing between acceptable dissent or criticism and statements actually disruptive of the peace was not an easy task. As noted above in chapter 6, Curtis, recognizing the difficulty of discerning who was truly disloyal, provided guidelines to follow in the determination of an individual's status. Nevertheless, even if a person was considered to be disloyal, if they did or said nothing harmful to the war effort the authorities really had no reason to arrest or imprison them, although they lost certain civil liberties such as the rights to hold office and to vote. More difficult even than determining the loyalty of persons was the task of discovering those who were inciting violence and rebellion. This was complicated by the false testimony of persons harboring personal grudges against those who were really loyal or neutral. Provost marshals were often confronted with conflicting testimony about which the truth could not be ascertained, or if ascertainable, only after the expenditure of a good deal of time and effort. As with the exercise of so many of their extraordinary powers, provost marshals were expected to use good judgment and common sense in the application of departmental orders and in keeping the peace.[11]

Unfortunately, military commanders and provost marshals sometimes demonstrated their willingness to abuse their power to indulge personal animosities or to punish fellow Unionists with whom they disagreed on policy matters, especially on the issue of slavery. Such appears to have been the motivation of General Loan, commander of the central district, in the arrest of Sample Orr. It is clear that Orr was a loyal and conservative Unionist who as a member of the state convention had used his influence from the beginning of the rebellion to prevent Missouri from seceding. Ever since his gubernatorial campaign in 1860, when he had run as the Union candidate against Claiborne F. Jackson, Orr held the reputation of being a forceful and witty public speaker whose opponents respected and often feared his sharp and formidable rhetoric. General Loan could not have been unaware of this record and reputation. Orr had been arrested after having spoken publicly in Jefferson City criticizing Loan's assessments and the president's emancipation policies and suspension of the privilege of the writ of habeas corpus. Apparently, Governor Gamble considered Orr's criticisms well within the bounds of acceptable dissent, for he ordered Orr's release, who, although remaining free, was charged with expressing "disloyal sentiments and opinions with the purpose and object of encouraging opposition and disloyalty to the Government of the United States and counseling resistance to the authority of the same." In June 1863, a military commission tried Orr over three days, hearing testimony from enrolled militia officers, grand jury members, and newspaper editors, all of whom believed him to be thoroughly loyal, only disagreeing with some of the methods used to put down the rebellion. The military commission found him not guilty, apparently agreeing with Orr's lawyer, Alexander W. Doniphan, that the arrest and charges were nothing more than General Loan's attempt to silence a critic of his radical tactics.[12]

Curtis, from the very beginning of his command, sought to provide clear guidance on departmental policy to his subordinates. While less uncertainty and danger then existed in Missouri than before, nevertheless it was his judgment that without various military controls a return of widespread guerrilla violence was possible. Perhaps this, in part, explains his decision not to intervene in Orr's case. Moreover, probably under the sway of General Merrill and Provost Marshal General Dick, when dealing with disloyal persons Curtis distinguished between influential persons (like Orr) and those deemed less dangerous. In particular, as already noted, Curtis marked ministers for special scrutiny as they held important positions of responsibility in the community and wielded considerable capacity to influence others for ill as well as good. In this, Curtis went too far and actually forgot or ignored his own rules for determining the loyalty of suspected persons. In particular, the case of Samuel B. McPheeters was an example of this, for he had taken the oath of allegiance and no evidence was ever found that he had violated it. According to Curtis's own circular on loyalty, as McPheeters pointed out to him, such a circumstance was to be considered *"prima facie"* proof of loyalty. Despite his failure to enforce his own rules consistently, Curtis, as a military commander where much bitter guerrilla conflict had already occurred, was correct to attempt to anticipate potential dangers and prevent them. In this respect, his responsibilities were very different from those of law-enforcement officials whose authority only began when evidence of the commission of a crime was discovered. Thus, Curtis also ordered the arrest of persons attempting to discourage the enlistment of soldiers or to incite violence.[13]

Curtis's speech policies were moderated somewhat, especially after Lincoln's intervention in the cases of McPheeters and others made clear that only on the basis of military necessity could speech be suppressed or punished. In other words, the president insisted that the military should not suppress or punish speech except when it could cause harm to others or to the war effort in Missouri. Ironically, during this period the number of arrests for disloyal speech apparently increased substantially, largely because provost marshals and military forces were able to exploit the relative peace Missouri then enjoyed after the guerrilla uprising of the previous summer. The military's focus soon became the identification of persons attempting again to stir up trouble. Inevitably, mistakes were made and many persons were arrested who represented little or no threat. Some of those arrested were the victims of personal enemies who had falsely accused them, thus using the military authorities to exact a measure of personal revenge. As in Orr's case, some of these animosities resulted from political controversies, especially among Unionists who disagreed with Lincoln's emancipation policy. Another group arrested included persons who had made their disloyal remarks while intoxicated or out of anger but had never intended to challenge the authority of the military. After their arrest, they endured the unpleasant task of explaining their behavior to the military authorities. From the available evidence, it appears that most of these persons obtained their release after taking the oath of allegiance and posting a bond.[14]

In considering these policies it is useful and interesting to compare them to those of a later conflict. During the First World War, President Woodrow Wilson allowed the suppression of practically all dissent, leading to many unnecessary arrests and considerable abuses of power under his administration. That he did not exercise the same restraint as Lincoln had in prohibiting arrests except in cases where military necessity required them was especially unjustified given that no warfare existed within the territory of the United States, and indeed, the nearest battles were fought in Europe thousands of miles away. Among the critics of the suppression of speech during this time was Harvard law professor Zechariah Chafee, who argued that only speech which directly incited others to aid the enemy or commit violence should be suppressed or punished. The debate over these arrests became the basis of a long reconsideration of the extent to which government should limit speech, leading to the protection of speech rights in all but the most clear instances where great and irreparable damage might result from its exercise.[15]

Closely related to speech policy was the extent to which the First Amendment protected the press from interference or suppression. Under Curtis's predecessors, the military had prevented the distribution of out-of-state newspapers considered disloyal, a policy he continued. To enforce this, provost marshals monitored the newsstands and bookstores. In November 1862, George J. Jones, the owner of a bookstore in St. Louis, was arrested for selling copies of the *Montreal Commercial Advertiser* in which was published an essay by an anonymous writer from St. Louis. The paper had been prohibited from the military district because it was "hostile to the US [sic] Government and that the circulation may be productive of injury." Jones, who was a British subject and had been arrested the previous spring (see chapter 4), refused to tell the provost marshal who had written the essay or even who purchased the Canadian newspaper from him. For this reason, Jones was imprisoned at the Gratiot Street Prison for a few days and interrogated again about the matter. Claiming that cooperation with the authorities would be a violation of his neutrality, a status he was duty bound to maintain as a British subject, Jones continued to refuse to provide any names to the provost marshals. For this reason, he was required to report daily at ten in the morning at the provost marshal's office for a month and a half and then afterward on Mondays, Wednesdays, and Fridays. In March 1863, the United States Police closed Jones's bookstore and arrested him again for "giving aid & comfort to the enemy by engaging in the sale and distribution of papers, pamphlets &c [sic] encouraging the rebellion and in opposition to the Government in its efforts to suppress it." Jones remained imprisoned until late May when General Schofield, a short time after assuming command of the Department of the Missouri, ordered Jones's release and that he be allowed to resume his business. Thus his circumstances would remain, until an undercover agent was able to gain his confidence and confirm many of the accusations against Jones and more.[16]

In considering his policy toward the press it should be remembered that by the time Curtis had taken command no secessionist newspapers were being published in Missouri and many of their editors had been arrested or banished from the state. As with his policy regarding speech, Lincoln's opinion toward the proper extent of freedom of the press during wartime slowly evolved until he concluded that the power to suppress newspapers should be exercised only sparingly. Perhaps after more than a year of war, the president recognized that wartime restrictions upon the press should not extend beyond the publication of information of military value to the enemy. Moreover, he may have feared a public backlash for suppressing dissent. Whatever the reasons, and guided again by the test of military necessity, Lincoln became increasingly reluctant to leave the decision concerning the extent of First Amendment rights to the discretion of his military commanders. Having dealt with a number of controversies and corresponded with the president concerning similar issues, Curtis was aware of the president's desire to allow for greater freedom where military necessity did not require restrictions and to avoid further controversies if possible. As noted above, Lincoln had impressed upon Curtis the necessity of gaining cooperation from Radical and Conservative Unionists alike, without whose support new troubles would arise.

Nevertheless, it is clear that Curtis treated Radical and Conservative newspapers differently. An instance of his willingness to tolerate abundant misbehavior from a Radical newspaper editor is evident in Curtis's handling of a dispute between the editor of the *St. Joseph Herald*, Smith O. Scofield, and Conservative and proslavery General Odon Guitar. Apparently Scofield had attacked Guitar as a "petty tyrant, seeking a brigadiership." Curtis believed that such a statement was "subversive of all military power" and directed the local provost marshal to warn the editor not to indulge in editorial commentary of this sort again. Curtis also asserted that even proslavery Unionists were important to the success of the war effort in Missouri—no small concession from a Radical—and that it would be unwise to "throw away any of our Union strength." Curtis also wrote to General Guitar, no doubt fearing that he might arrest the editor or suppress his newspaper. He requested that Guitar act with good judgment and moderation. In summing up, Curtis stated the proper policy well: "There must be no needless ground for charges of military oppression, but military power must not be despised and degraded."[17]

At about the same time that Curtis intervened in the controversy between General Guitar and Scofield, Curtis declined Governor Gamble's demand to suppress the radical German language newspaper the *Neue Zeit* after it had published articles criticizing the governor as disloyal and calling for Radicals to rebel against him. The governor believed "that in the present condition of affairs a paper which under pretence of loyalty seeks to overthrow the Government ought to be instantly suppressed. Their disloyalty is as dangerous as secession or any other kind of treason." Gamble also appealed to Provost Marshal General Dick to suppress the *Kansas City Journal of Commerce* edited by D. K. Abeel. In a March 5, 1863, editorial Abeel had accused the governor of "courting popularity with the secession sympathizers" rather than suppressing the rebellion and enforcing the civil laws. Moreover, Abeel asserted that "Governor Gamble, as he evinces by every act, adheres strongly to the 'States Rights' doctrine; and the question now is, whether Gamble is trying to accomplish covertly what Claiborne F. Jackson endeavored to do openly." Dick, who undoubtedly consulted Curtis concerning the matter, refused Gamble's request to arrest the Radical editor. These refusals to take action against Radical newspapers angered Gamble and his supporters and became part of the complaint made later against Curtis, leading eventually to his removal as commander in Missouri.[18]

Another cause of Conservative complaint was Curtis's and his subordinates' often severe treatment of Conservative Unionist editors who had criticized military authorities and opposed emancipation. An example of this was the case of James Monaghan, who had received permission to establish a newspaper "in favor of a vigorous prosecution of the War in suppressing the present rebellion and for the Union first last and always." Established in northeastern Missouri, the *Weekly Louisiana Union* was first published on May 14, 1863. That same day Provost Marshal D. P. Dyer suspended publication and arrested Monaghan, who accused Dyer of having abused his authority to help the Radicals in the last election. To justify this arrest, Dyer claimed that these criticisms had undermined "the confidence of the people in those who are administering the Government." After his arrest, Monaghan was sent to St. Louis and held in the Gratiot Street Prison. Just days before this, General Ambrose E. Burnside had arrested Clement L. Vallandigham. In a letter to Provost Marshal General Dick, Dyer noted Lincoln's support of Burnside's action, indicating that these events had emboldened him to arrest Monaghan. A major difference between the cases of Vallandigham and Monaghan, however, was that the former opposed the war while the latter supported it. Indeed, apart from emancipation, Monaghan did not oppose the policies employed to win the war, but instead criticized the local military authorities for their conduct during a recent election. In fact, testimony of some indicated that Dyer had arrested Monaghan at least as much from personal and partisan animus as from any real or imagined military necessity that existed. Among the several persons who vouched for Monaghan's loyalty was General Ulysses S. Grant's brother-in-law, Alexander Sharp, who had served for a time as a military aid to his famous relative and was considered to be thoroughly loyal. In early June, after reviewing the evidence and depositions presented against Monaghan, the provost marshal general's office ordered him released. Nevertheless, he was not allowed to resume the publication of his newspaper for several months. In November Monaghan wrote to Lincoln complaining that he had been unfairly treated and that he was loyal. The president directed his secretary John Hay to write to General Schofield, who was then in command in Missouri, to look into Monaghan's case. This led to the decision by the end of the year to allow Monaghan again to publish his newspaper. Unfortunately, this would not mark the end of his troubles with the military authorities.[19]

Another Conservative Unionist editor to be arrested for his opposition to Lincoln's emancipation policy was C. P. Anderson. A little more than a year before (see chapter 4), the military authorities had held him for a brief period before releasing him upon the intercession of Congressman Thomas Price. In the April 25, 1863, issue of the *California News,* Anderson had written a very critical editorial of the president and his policies toward African Americans. Anderson had stated that the North and South then comprised distinct nations. He also represented Confederate President Jefferson Davis as being universally supported by Southerners, while Lincoln did not have similar support among Northerners. The main difference of opinion, Anderson claimed, was in the attitudes of both sections toward African Americans. "Mr. Lincoln's Government holds that Negroes are naturally entitled to impartial freedom and every where within its jurisdiction it carries this into practice. It has abolished all distinction of the whites and negroes in the Federal districts, in the territories and everywhere within the jurisdiction of that government." Anderson thought it preferable to "perish . . . by the sword" than be subjugated and made to accept such principles. He described the United States as a "mongrell [sic] government or a government that includes negroes." He also asserted that Davis was administering his government in accord with the past and that Lincoln was the innovator and destroyer of the principles upon which the country had been founded. As he expressed it, "Davis represents the true principles of 1788–1860." Moreover, Anderson complained that Lincoln adhered only "to the outward symbols of the 'Union'" in much the way Augustus had established the Principate while pretending to restore the Republic of ancient Rome. In early June, a military commission tried Anderson for "aiding and abetting" the rebellion. While finding him guilty of having written and published the April 25 editorial, the military officers did not believe that he had supported the enemy in it, for they found him not guilty of the charge. Nevertheless, the military commission required Anderson to post a bond of $1,000 and prohibited him from leaving his county, although this prohibition was rescinded later.[20]

As noted in chapters 5 and 6, by the fall of 1862, the newly created Enrolled Missouri Militia had soundly defeated a guerrilla uprising which had threatened to plunge the state into chaos. After this victory, the prospect for peace and a return to civil government seemed highly probable if not inevitable. Governor Gamble believed no further necessity existed for the garrisoning of large numbers of federal troops in Missouri, for little danger remained that a Confederate army large enough to overwhelm Missouri's militia forces would invade the state, especially given the successes of the Union military in the West. Thus, when Lincoln asked the governor whether he thought it necessary to retain federal forces in Missouri he had replied without hesitation that so long as Missouri's militia forces, both the Missouri State Militia and the Enrolled Missouri Militia, were provided adequate supplies and arms no necessity remained for the retention of federal troops north of the Missouri River.[21]

General Curtis disagreed with the governor's analysis, arguing that only severe measures would maintain the peace. Thus he had implemented a very harsh regime of confiscations, assessments, arrests, and banishments. These policies convinced Gamble that Curtis intended to impose Radical rule upon Missouri, which, the governor believed, would lead to renewed guerrilla warfare and more turmoil among the slave population. And indeed, it is clear from his policies that Curtis particularly sought to undermine the state's support for slavery, an institution that he, along with his fellow Radicals, blamed for the beginning and continuance of the war. The institution of these policies was aided significantly in Curtis's appointment of Radicals as local provost marshals throughout the state and most importantly Franklin A. Dick as provost marshal general to direct them. Under Dick these provost marshals could be expected to use their military police powers vigorously to enforce the congressional acts which freed the slaves of disloyal persons. In General Orders No. 35, issued on Christmas Eve 1862, Curtis ordered his provost marshals and those of his forces in the United States service to protect slaves who came into their lines and were owned by disloyal persons as directed by the War Department. These congressional measures, it is clear, were intended to operate in enemy territory, a very different circumstance from that of Missouri, a loyal state where no military necessity existed for such a policy. Presumably, Congress intended to diminish the labor available to the enemy and punish those who remained in rebellion to the government of the United States. Therefore, as already noted in chapter 6, in January 1863 Lincoln ordered the suspension of General Orders No. 35 and the end of the provost-marshal system. Only after Curtis protested that these measures were necessary to maintain the peace did Lincoln reconsider their suspension, ultimately reversing his decision. Later that month, Lincoln also suggested that Curtis adopt the same policy General Gordon Granger had implemented in Kentucky, another border state, prohibiting all noncombatants (especially runaway slaves) from his military lines. Curtis breezily rejected this advice, arguing that only the disloyal and those of lukewarm loyalty complained of his policy. Again, Lincoln, who was reluctant to overrule his commanders in the field, did not insist upon the policy change. This decision proved to be unfortunate, for the interference of federal troops with slavery, more than any other policy, undermined what little support that remained among Conservatives and Moderates for General Curtis's leadership and led to an effort by well-placed men, both in Congress and Lincoln's cabinet, to seek the Radical commander's removal.[22]

Curtis's belief that only disloyal persons and lukewarm patriots were opposed to allowing slaves within his military lines was far wide of the reality, for many Unionists, including those who had opposed secession from the beginning of the conflict, disliked federal troops interfering with slavery. Moreover, Governor Gamble and many other civil authorities were determined to enforce state law preserving the institution of slavery for loyal citizens, believing that Curtis's radical policies were causing a good deal of suffering among the slaves, who, having been encouraged to escape from their masters, were often left to fend for themselves. Another important consideration was the congregation of large groups of runaways who threatened to become more than a nuisance when out of desperation they resorted to theft and other crime to sustain themselves. It was also feared that these fugitive slaves would encourage even more of their fellow bondsmen to run away, thus increasing the humanitarian disaster then developing. Another concern was that Curtis's policies would provoke more proslavery Unionists and southern sympathizers to aid or join guerrilla bands, or at the very least refuse to support efforts to reassert Union control. Many Unionists living near the border of Kansas complained bitterly that Radical troops had collected together groups of fugitive slaves and brought them into Kansas, some of whom had been organized into military groups and under the leadership of antislavery commanders had returned to Missouri, where they looted and stole slaves.

Because of these abuses and policies, Gamble refused to place the enrolled militia under Curtis's command and ordered them to aid the civil authorities in retrieving fugitive slaves. The governor felt justified in this because of Curtis's refusal to revise military policies that were in conflict with state law once their necessity no longer existed. Thus, in support of the governor's policy, United States Senator John B. Henderson wrote to Lincoln stating that by his own observation he had found "much angry excitement in the country in consequence of negroes, the slaves of loyal men and even emancipationists, being held as servants and waiting men in federal camps, and it is believed that Genl [sic] Curtis might stop this work by a simple order, keeping out, all persons white & black from the lines."[23]

Most slaves entering Union military lines arrived without possessions or food and presented federal commanders with the difficult task of caring for and feeding them. Unlike some of their predecessors, when fugitives accused their owners of disloyalty, many of the Radical provost marshals were willing to accept these slaves' claims at face value, expending little effort to corroborate them. Providing them with freedom papers, the military included some explanation for granting the slave's freedom. Usually the reasons given concerned the owners' disloyalty or activities in aiding the rebellion. Sometimes the state authorities, both civil and military, recaptured these newly freed slaves, believing that they had been emancipated wrongly. The files of some of these emancipated slaves contained depositions detailing the disloyalty of their masters. In a few instances, slave owners presented witnesses and depositions demonstrating that they were loyal citizens and that their slaves had misrepresented them to the provost marshal. Thus John Garr sought the revocation of freedom papers given to one of his slaves. Apparently he was able to prove his loyalty to the satisfaction of Provost Marshal Robert S. Moore in Chillicothe, for he recommended revoking the slave woman's freedom papers, noting that Garr's "negress is at home working for him at present."[24]

In determining the status of slaves, many of the provost marshals under Curtis were especially sceptical of southern sympathizers' testimony supporting a slave owner in his effort to recover a slave. For instance, R. C. Hancock, provost marshal in Chariton County, refused to turn over Abe to his master Colin Coy despite the depositions of a number of his neighbors supporting his request. They all asserted that Abe should not be believed when he claimed to have been directed by Coy to bring food to bushwhackers and to care for their horses. Hancock explained to Provost Marshal General Dick that he had "given the boy free papers and hired him out to a good union man and am exercising guardianship over him." Fearing that he had acted imprudently, Hancock requested direction concerning what to do under such a circumstance, although he expressed his reluctance "to revoke papers unless compelled to do so by higher authority." Moreover, Hancock was suspicious of Coy's witnesses, for all were southern sympathizers. He may also have suspected that the witnesses had coordinated their statements, for they were very similar in detail. Significantly, in a sworn statement Coy admitted that Abe had provided aid to guerrilla forces but claimed that he had acted without Coy's direction.[25]

Distrust existed not only between the military authorities and Secessionists, as was to be expected, but also between Radical and Conservative Unionists, especially in the determination of the status of slaves. At times this animosity between them, demonstrating slavery's great power to divide, even rivaled the hostility that each felt toward the enemy. One is left with this impression from the dispute concerning some of Charles Jones's slaves, who had run away and been recaptured upon a state's warrant in April 1863. Colonel J. T. Vitt, the local commander of enrolled militia troops garrisoned at the town of Union, doubted the loyalty of Jones, who was a prominent lawyer and state legislator. Despite the testimony of many of Jones's neighbors that he was a loyal man, Vitt and Provost Marshal Henry C. Eitzen doubted this loyalty was genuine, believing that Jones would switch back to the other side if he thought it had a fair chance of success. Apparently there was some reason to doubt his loyalty, for according to William Van Ness Bay, a judge of the Supreme Court of Missouri and a longtime friend, Jones sympathized with the South, although from the beginning he had thought that secession was a great exercise in folly. For this reason, and perhaps to protect his wealth, Jones opposed secession. Judge Bay also noted that, although Jones was proslavery and owned approximately sixty slaves worth tens of thousands of dollars, he was very different from most slave owners, for despite the danger of losing his entire investment Jones refused to sell any of his slaves and treated them with the greatest kindness.[26]

Eitzen, who was unimpressed with or ignorant of Jones's benevolence to his slaves, wrote to Provost Marshal General Dick concerning Jones's case, noting his suspicion that he was only a fair-weather supporter of the Union, and this only "to save [his] negro property." Eitzen suggested that Dick talk to Bernard G. Farrar, former provost marshal general, for his opinion of Jones. Eitzen also pointed out that Captain Crandall, who had refused to release Jones's slaves to him, had recently sent home slaves belonging to a loyal man, demonstrating that he would do his duty and follow orders regarding slavery. After Crandall had refused to release his slaves, Jones next acquired an arrest warrant for them in which they were accused of having committed theft. Believing that he could not refuse this warrant, Crandall handed the slaves over to the local sheriff who placed them in jail awaiting trial. According to Captain Amos P. Foster, Jones had obtained the warrant as a ruse to gain the removal of his slaves from the control of the military and that "a mock trial" of the slaves had been held and they were then in the custody of Jones, who had moved with them to St. Louis. Thus, Jones had outmaneuvered and outwitted his Radical protagonists. Later, Jones wrote to Provost Marshal General James O. Broadhead explaining the difficulties he had experienced and requesting an introduction to General John M. Schofield, to whom he wanted to make clear that he was an unconditional Unionist whether "with negroes, or without negroes." A year later, apparently having cleared himself with the military authorities, Jones was again living in the town of Union with his slaves. According to letters written at this time, he had already allowed ten slaves to enlist into the United States service and wished to see ten more be of some service to the government. He expressed the desire to no longer be a slave owner and thought it best that his slaves be free.[27]

While the vast majority of militia officers were proslavery and under the authority of Governor Gamble, occasionally militia officers refused to return fugitive slaves to their owners. In these cases, Gamble and his subordinates had the officer arrested and replaced. Another controversial issue regarded the proper treatment of contraband slaves, who, having fled from their disloyal masters into Union lines, were without any means of supporting themselves or their families. Some of them were employed as servants to Union officers, while others were given a variety of tasks including cutting wood for the railroads or steamboats, general labor for farmers and others, building fortifications, work as teamsters, unloading freight from steamboats, and even grave-digging duty, among other things. Believing that such examples of slaves being employed by the military would encourage more of them to throw off their fetters, some white Missourians drove them away. These actions sometimes brought civilians into conflict with the local military authorities.[28]

Despite these incidents, slaves continued to escape and seek the protection and support of Union soldiers, especially further South where their numbers sometimes overwhelmed resources and the commanders' capacity to protect and employ them. This situation led to the decision to put philanthropists in charge of fugitive slaves, establishing for them camps providing shelter, food, and jobs. One of these camps was located near Helena, Arkansas, and was called "Camp Ethiopia," holding from two to three thousand slaves consisting of men, women, and children, all of whom were desperate to cling to the Union army for fear that they would be captured and returned to slavery. Unfortunately, the conditions in these camps were very poor, with many of the former slaves living in makeshift shelters they built themselves or in condemned army tents. Often the unhappy inhabitants of these camps were not paid for their labors and were pressed into labor gangs in which they were sometimes mistreated in a manner not unlike their experiences as slaves.

Two military chaplains, Jacob G. Forman and Samuel Sawyers, were placed on detached service to work with the Western Sanitary Commission to provide what aid they could to the destitute and sick in Camp Ethiopia.[29]

Because of these very difficult circumstances, one of the duties of Sawyers as superintendent of contrabands was to find suitable placements for these newly freed slaves. On February 18, 1863, Charles Frank, a St. Louis saloon keeper and a sutler to the army, applied to Sawyer in Helena for "two young contrabands to be raised in his own family." Sawyer and Frank went to Camp Ethiopia and found two free black children, a brother and sister, Tom and Anna, promising to clothe and educate them and to hand over the girl to her mother America Smith whenever she called for her at his residence in St. Louis. Frank also promised that he would educate the children and they would remain free. Despite this agreement, when at the end of March 1863 Smith traveled to St. Louis and called upon Frank for her daughter Anna, who was then only nine years of age, she learned that Frank no longer had the girl or boy. Fearing that Frank had sold them, Smith turned to the provost marshal's office for help in regaining them. When questioned about what had happened to the children, Frank claimed that he had given them away to two merchants who lived south of Cairo, Kentucky, but could not remember their names. From May 11 to May 23, Frank was held in the Myrtle Street Military Prison and again imprisoned on September 18 for eleven days. After his second imprisonment, a report to Provost Marshal General Broadhead, who had by then replaced Dick, indicated that it was suspected that Frank had feigned forgetting to whom he had "given" the children and that really he had sold them. Thus, Frank refused to divulge this information for fear he would be punished for the violation of his agreement with Captain Sawyer and for selling free children into slavery. The military again arrested him in January of 1864, holding him for twelve more days. As before, Frank was placed on parole and was prohibited from leaving St. Louis, a restriction which he claimed prevented him from making a living. One official, writing in May, noted that the children's mother had continually sought to recover them and in particular was "constantly exhibiting the most touching solicitation for her daughter." After evidence was finally gathered of his sale of the children, Frank was arrested in September 1864 and was tried before a military commission sometime after November 25, 1864. Nevertheless, nothing in the file indicates that the children were ever recovered or even specifies the outcome of Frank's trial.[30]

From the outset in the fall of 1862, a number of prominent critics opposed the appointment of General Curtis as commander in Missouri. Lincoln's choice of him for the top command in Missouri seemed logical, for he was next in rank to General Schofield and had much military experience in Missouri. The president, however, failed to consult with Governor Gamble and other important political leaders to gain their advice and cooperation in this decision. Thus, without this advice Lincoln could not know about the serious reservations many loyal Missourians held concerning Curtis's appointment. If the president had learned about these critics' concerns he might have chosen another officer better suited for the command. The critics disliked Curtis's radical politics and his strong antislavery views and considered him unequal to meeting the challenges of his new command. The most important of these critics were Governor Gamble, Missouri's congressional delegation, and Attorney General Edward Bates. In particular, the opposition of Gamble alone should have disqualified him for the post, for Curtis's primary task was to cooperate with the governor to coordinate the efforts of the militia and federal troops to maintain the peace.[31]

Whether fairly or not, after a series of policy blunders during the first few months of Curtis's command, Gamble felt confirmed in his initial assessment that Curtis lacked the judgment and skills necessary for success as the department commander in Missouri. For this reason, the governor and others influential with the administration, especially United States Senator John B. Henderson and both members of the cabinet from Missouri, Bates and Montgomery Blair, began to lobby the president for Curtis's removal. Henderson, an important War Democrat ally, threatened to resign if Lincoln retained Curtis. Apparently, the demand of Henderson, who had risked his seat to support the administration in some of its more unpopular measures, convinced the president that he must find a new commander in Missouri. Finally in March 1863, Lincoln chose Major General Edwin V. Sumner, who had served in territorial Kansas and for a short period in St. Louis as commander of the Department of the West just before the outbreak of war. Born in 1797, Sumner was then the oldest major general in the federal army, and although antislavery in sentiment, had proven himself a soldier devoted to duty, not inclined to interpose his own views when orders dictated a different course of action. Unfortunately, Sumner died before he could assume his new post in Missouri. Thus Curtis remained for two months more before another satisfactory replacement could be found. This delay came despite Curtis making clear after Sumner's death his desire for another command. In the end, after looking far and wide for a new commander, Lincoln chose as Curtis's successor his predecessor General Schofield. Having already endured a dose of Missouri troubles, the new commander was reluctant to return, finally accepting his assignment more as an unpleasant and unavoidable task than as an opportunity and challenge.[32]

8

EMANCIPATION AND CIVIL LIBERTIES

THE STRENGTHS AND WEAKNESSES of President Abraham Lincoln's decision making are evident in his appointments and removals of commanders in
Missouri. The examples of William S. Harney, John C. Frémont, and Samuel R.
Curtis, who in the end were all removed because of the lackluster performance
of their duties, demonstrate the president's willingness to retain officers even
after they had demonstrated their inability to adapt to the special complexities
of Missouri's circumstances and politics. Lincoln's reluctance to remove commanders, even after the exertion of abundant pressure upon him, was partly
due to his understanding that most men are flawed. For this reason, the president was willing to tolerate some measure of incompetence and insubordination—a prominent case in point being General George B. McClellan.

While he willingly conceded the truth of many complaints made against
military leaders, Lincoln often doubted the likelihood of finding another officer capable of performing better than the commander then in place. More
times than not, Lincoln may have been correct, but the downside to retaining
a truly incompetent commander could be the unnecessary loss of life. Another consideration that may have influenced Lincoln not to remove commanders unless absolutely necessary was the inevitable period of confusion
resulting from the change. Moreover, frequent changes of commanders could
undermine confidence in the administration. Nevertheless, this consideration unfortunately led occasionally to the retention of commanders ill-suited
for their duties. Such were the cases of Frémont and Curtis. In particular,
Lincoln blundered when he failed to consult Missouri's political leadership
before appointing Curtis. This mistake was compounded when Lincoln ignored the warnings and complaints of Governor Hamilton R. Gamble, whose
confidence and cooperation were absolutely necessary to the success of any
commander's efforts in Missouri. The choice of General John M. Schofield,

however, was excellent, for the former commander was acceptable to the governor, who met the news of Schofield's appointment with relief. The Radicals, however, were angered by Curtis's relief and from the beginning of Schofield's tenure sought to undermine his authority.

Soon after the appointment, Lincoln wrote to Schofield to guide him in the conduct of his responsibilities. By the summer of 1863, the president had grown impatient with the factionalism among Unionists in Missouri. Both the Radicals and Conservatives distrusted one another and no end to their disputes seemed imminent. The Radicals questioned the loyalty of anyone, including those who had opposed secession from the very beginning, who held proslavery sentiments or believed that emancipation should be instituted only gradually. For their part, Conservatives considered the Radicals unreasonable and demagogic in their demands for immediate emancipation. This factionalism had made cooperation among Unionists nearly impossible and Lincoln had relieved Curtis from command because he had become a leader of the Radicals. Thus, the president advised Schofield to maintain his independence of thought and action from both factions "and do right for the public interest." He warned that this would not be easy but "so much greater will be the honor if you perform it well. If both factions, or neither, shall abuse you, you will probably be about right. Beware of being assailed by one, and praised by the other."[1]

In his reply, Schofield thanked Lincoln for his support and promised to maintain a proper neutrality befitting his role as commander of the department. He also expressed the hope that he might mediate rather than participate in the factional disputes then raging in Missouri. Moreover, the new commander expressed the earnest desire "that the Missouri State Convention at its approaching session will adopt such measures for the speedy emancipation of slaves as will secure the acquiescence of the large majority of Union men. If this hope be realized, one of my most embarrassing difficulties will be removed, or at least greatly diminished."[2]

By the time of Schofield's reappointment to command in Missouri, much had changed since the border state congressmen, including most of Missouri's delegation, had rejected Lincoln's plan for compensated, gradual emancipation the previous summer (see chapter 4). The majority of the Missouri State Convention had considered the call for emancipating the slaves to be premature, believing that no necessity then existed compelling them to take such a radical step. This attitude changed as the war continued and public opinion turned against the institution of slavery. A major obstacle to emancipation, however, remained in the question of the status of the newly freed slaves. Most whites, even those in favor of emancipation, were adamantly opposed to social and political equality for the former slaves.[3]

Despite these reservations, by the end of 1862 Governor Gamble believed that slavery was doomed and that passage of a bill emancipating Missouri's slaves would hasten peace. Moreover, in the fall of 1862 a majority of candidates in favor of emancipation was elected to the state legislature. Separate action on emancipation was necessary, for Lincoln's proclamation of January 1, 1863, only affected those states still in a condition of rebellion. Therefore, in a message to the state legislature Gamble urged its members to pass legislation emancipating Missouri's slaves. In preparation for this, the governor had employed federal judge Charles Gibson and Charles L. Bernays, editor of a German language newspaper, to rally support among Germans living in St. Louis for an emancipation plan which Gamble was about to propose. According to his plan, only those slave children born after the plan's passage would be freed. To insure that they would not abandon their responsibility to them, the owners of these slaves' mothers would be required to raise them until they reached maturity and could take care of themselves. This plan, although not freeing all of the slaves then living before the bill's passage, had the advantage of reducing significantly the cost of compensating slave owners and circumventing the need to gain their consent, both requirements of the state constitution. Gamble believed that gradual, compensated emancipation had the additional advantage of encouraging free immigration into Missouri, thus securing the state for the Union.[4]

Despite a majority of the legislators favoring emancipation, a bill abolishing the institution was not passed. A major reason for this failure was that a significant minority of abolitionists were unwilling to compromise to gain passage of legislation for anything less than immediate, or close to immediate, emancipation. Ironically, these hardliners were joined by proslavery legislators in defeating the bill. The action of these Radical Republicans in preventing a compromise measure from passing alienated many moderates of their party who were willing to accept a gradual emancipation bill. Eventually this led to a permanent break between the right and left wings of the Republican Party in Missouri. After it became clear that no emancipation bill could be passed, some of the Radicals (or Charcoals, as they were sometimes called) sought to pass legislation for the election of a new state convention, which could then meet and ensure the passage of an immediate emancipation bill, or at least one much more to their liking. Given the results of the previous election, the Radicals expected the members of this new convention would be more Radical than that of the old. In the end, however, the legislation failed and it appeared that the matter could not be addressed until the next session of the legislature.[5]

This failure led Governor Gamble, who was convinced that slavery would not survive the war, to call the state convention into a final session to consider "some scheme of Emancipation" to be adopted. Undoubtedly, he trusted the Conservative members of the state convention to devise a more reasonable plan to end slavery than the legislature and was probably relieved when it had failed to create a new convention. Moreover, by the spring of 1863, if for no other reason than to settle once and for all an issue dividing the Unionist effort, the governor recognized that slavery must be abolished.[6]

Before the convention reconvened in June 1863, the Radicals in St. Louis increased their attacks upon the governor, whom they distrusted, believing him still to be secretly proslavery. These attacks, published in the German language newspapers in St. Louis, accused Gamble of only calling the convention together to preempt the establishment of a new convention, which would pass an immediate emancipation ordinance. In an effort to place pressure on Lincoln to adopt their agenda, the Radicals of St. Louis held a meeting at which they passed resolutions calling upon Lincoln to remove both of his Missouri cabinet members, Montgomery Blair and Edward Bates, and for the sacking of General in Chief Henry W. Halleck, whom they regarded as too conservative. The meeting also asserted that only an immediate emancipation plan would be acceptable to them. Lincoln, who was by then impatient to disentangle himself from Missouri matters, firmly rejected the Radicals' demands and made it clear that he preferred the policy of gradual to immediate emancipation. Thus matters stood on the eve of the Missouri State Convention's final session, which convened in Jefferson City on June 15, 1863.[7]

In a message to the convention, Governor Gamble explained that the state constitution, which required the consent of slave owners and compensation before slaves could be emancipated, had made it impossible for the legislature to pass an emancipation ordinance; therefore, only through amendment or the action of an extraconstitutional body, such as the convention, could the is-sue of slavery be resolved conclusively. Noting that the members represented a wide range of opinion on the slavery issue, he urged them to work together to find a reasonable compromise. Gamble also recommended that they take care not to deprive citizens of their rights "farther than is necessary to make the public benefit certain and sure."[8]

The convention responded by establishing a committee on emancipation and appointing the governor as chair. With the majority of delegates Conser-vative, it was no surprise when the committee presented a plan for gradual emancipation. In the proposal, the committee repealed those sections of the state constitution requiring the consent and compensation of owners. Slavery would end on July 4, 1876, a century after the traditional date of the signing of the Declaration of Independence. The plan also prohibited the importation of new slaves on penalty of their owners forfeiting them as property. A member of the committee had sought an earlier date for emancipation and a ban on all slave sales. Another, taking a very different view, argued that blacks benefited from slavery and that the plan would harm many white families.[9]

At first, some expressed concern that Lincoln would find this plan for gradual emancipation unacceptable. Lincoln learned of this when General Schofield sent a telegram requesting his direction in the matter. The president replied that he would respect the convention's plan if military necessity did not dictate otherwise. He also stated his preference for gradual emancipation as a policy most beneficial to "both black and white." The probability of the military intervening in this matter, he believed, was small, especially if the transitional period from slavery to freedom was brief.[10]

Having gained some assurances from the president that their decisions would be respected, the delegates debated the committee's emancipation plan. Amendments were offered to address a number of concerns and objections to the plan. Charles D. Drake, one of the new members of the convention, proposed that the slaves be emancipated on January 1, 1864, and that a period of apprenticeship follow to help in making the transition from slavery to free-dom smooth. This plan was rejected. As the debate unfolded, Drake accused the governor of having called the convention together to pass an ordinance "so feeble and inert as to prolong Slavery in this State, with a continuance of the wretchedness it has brought upon us, until some distant day." Later Drake proposed that slavery end on January 1, 1866, and challenged Gamble to vote for it. Whatever his reason, perhaps to demonstrate that he was not conspiring to save slavery, the governor voted for the amendment. As was the tendency of the Radicals, Drake then moved the bar, calling for the immediate emancipation of Missouri's slaves. United States Senator John B. Henderson, who was also a member of the convention, drew attention to Drake's shifting positions and accused him and the Radicals of being more interested in preserving slavery as a political issue than in abolishing it. This accusation seemed to be confirmed when later Radical and proslavery delegates joined in support of an amendment which would have required a vote of the people on any emancipation measure passed by the convention.[11]

As debate continued for some time without any progress, Gamble, a shrewd parliamentarian, proposed that the issue be tabled and that a new convention be established to decide the matter later. To the Conservative members, the prospect of a new convention dominated by Radicals deciding upon emancipation was all the motivation necessary to bring the majority together upon a compromise measure. The ordinance repealed the state constitution's prohibitions upon emancipation, abolished slavery on July 4, 1870, and established an intermediate status for freedmen as "servants," allowing for a smooth transition for both slave and master and preventing an interruption in the supply of labor that many feared. Those slaves who were over forty years of age on July 4, 1870, would remain servants for life, while those younger than twelve would not gain full freedmen status until the age of twenty-three. All the rest would gain their freedom on July 4, 1876. Anticipating the possibility that the South might win its independence, the ordinance also prohibited the sale of slaves or their removal from Missouri after July 4, 1870.[12]

The passage of this emancipation measure, much to Lincoln's chagrin, did not end the controversy among Unionists in Missouri. The Radicals soon criticized the convention for not ending slavery immediately. Moreover, while the issue of free-state soldiers interfering with slavery became much less of a problem after General Scholfield sent the vast majority of federal troops to reinforce General Grant at Vicksburg and elsewhere, other difficulties concerning African Americans continued to create friction between Radicals and Conservatives. An issue soon to grow in importance was the decision of the United States government to employ African Americans as soldiers. As with all slaveholding societies, Missourians feared violence from their former slaves. Before Lincoln permitted the recruitment of African Americans into segregated regiments, Radical commanders in Kansas had illegally formed fugitive slaves into military units. To Missourians living along the border of Kansas, these efforts represented a great threat of violence, leading to a group of prominent and loyal members of Clay and Jackson counties to travel to St. Louis "to confer with the government of the State" to determine what could be done. In a petition sent to the president in September 1862, they stated their fear that "an armed band of negroes" would soon invade Missouri. Apparently, to prevent this danger Secretary of War Edwin M. Stanton wrote to United States Senator James Lane, who was then recruiting troops in Kansas, to remind him that he was authorized to recruit "loyal white men" only.[13]

In January 1863, at the same time that he published the Emancipation Proclamation, Lincoln announced "that colored men of suitable condition would be received into the war service." At first, the administration was cautious about the implementation of this policy in the loyal border states. During the summer of 1863, General Lorenzo Thomas, adjutant general of the United States, authorized Colonel William A. Pile of the 33rd Missouri Volunteers to raise "colored troops" in Missouri upon the condition that he gain the permission of Governor Gamble. Missouri's executive was unopposed to Pile's efforts so long as he did not interfere "with the slaves of loyal owners and avoid[ed] any violation of the laws of the State." General Schofield, recognizing that the cooperation of Governor Gamble was necessary for success, cautiously supported these efforts and was careful to inform him of what was being done. Thus, when General Thomas Ewing, commander of the Department of the Border, sought to recruit African Americans along the Kansas-Missouri border, Schofield notified the governor to gain his assent and to ensure that Missouri would get credit for the regiments raised.[14]

By the end of the summer, it became evident to Schofield, however, that Governor Gamble's conditions prevented the recruitment of the vast majority of African Americans at a time when the military's demand for troops was tough to meet. For this reason, Schofield suggested that Lincoln order the recruitment of "all able-bodied negroes in Missouri" wanting to enlist, providing vouchers to their owners for reimbursement. This policy was advantageous, Schofield believed, for then recruiters would not have the complicating task of determining the loyalty of slave owners, a question best left to a board appointed by the president or the governor. In this way loyal owners would be compensated and the military's resources could concentrate on winning the war. No response to his suggestion came immediately and Schofield, who had requested guidance on the slavery issue before, concluded that Secretary of War Stanton wished to avoid the issue altogether.[15]

In this, Schofield was mistaken, for in early October 1863, the War Department established a secret policy regarding the enlistment of slaves in the loyal border states allowing for more aggressive recruiting among free blacks and slaves, although it still required the consent of masters before enlisting their property. After thirty days, however, if recruiters had failed to fill their quotas, the general order removed restrictions upon the recruitment of slaves. Loyal masters would still be able to apply for compensation for their losses but could no longer prevent their slaves from enlisting. This conditional provision was instituted when the ranks of "colored regiments," as they were then called, remained unfilled. Thus in November, when the results of the recruiting efforts among African Americans proved less than satisfactory, General Halleck notified Schofield of the administration's decision to remove some of the restrictions preventing the successful recruitment of slaves. Upon receiving the new regulations, Halleck requested that Missouri's department commander offer suggestions "to suit them to the peculiar condition of your department." Schofield again recommended that recruiters no longer be required to gain the consent of masters. Because loyal owners would be compensated for the loss of their slaves, he also suggested "that no compensation be paid for the services of any slave who has at any time since the beginning of the rebellion belonged to a person who has been in or given aid to the rebellion. This is necessary to prevent persons who can prove their loyalty from buying the slaves of Rebels and selling them to the Government." Moreover, to prevent trouble, Schofield sought to control who would be allowed to recruit among African Americans. He proposed to give this duty to provost marshals, who were under his command and whom he could strictly control.[16]

Secretary of War Stanton approved Schofield's suggestions and General Orders No. 135 was issued on November 14. All African American recruits were to be freed in return for their service and were placed under the command of Colonel Pile at Benton Barracks in St. Louis. His task was to organize and train the new soldiers and prepare them for military service. Interestingly, neither the supporters nor the opponents of slavery in Missouri opposed this new policy. Because it so completely conformed to the position of the Radicals, they had nothing upon which to hang any criticism. The Conservatives, on the other hand, who had just expended considerable effort to defend Schofield against a recent attempt to oust him (see chapter 9), were unprepared to attack him, although they would not have hesitated to heap scorn upon his predecessor, General Samuel R. Curtis, if he had attempted the same. However, while this new policy provided a means by which slaves eligible for military service could gain their freedom, African Americans still faced threats to their liberty. A lawless element, possibly with the aid of a provost marshal near St. Louis, attempted to turn the new circumstances to their advantage by kidnapping some of the new recruits and bringing them to Louisville, Kentucky, where they were sold into slavery.[17]

Not long before he was relieved of command, General Curtis had refused a request from the War Department to send federal troops to General Grant at Vicksburg. Curtis feared that he would be left with too few troops if General Sterling Price or another Confederate commander invaded Missouri. Schofield, however, considered the risk of invasion small and promptly sent most of the remaining federal regiments in Missouri to General Grant. Schofield also understood that opening up the Mississippi River to the gulf would make Missouri and the rest of the West more secure. And indeed, Schofield's gamble paid off when, after capturing Vicksburg, Grant returned enough troops to enable Schofield to capture Little Rock and establish a line of defense along the Arkansas River. This move made Missouri more secure against an attack from the South, although the guerrilla threat continued to grow. With their defeat on the battlefield, many Missourians from the vanquished Confederate armies returned home. While probably only a small percentage of this group then became guerrillas, the group was still large enough to cause many problems. In his autobiography written after the war, however, Schofield admitted that he could not have transferred federal troops from Missouri to Vicksburg if he had not been given command over the enrolled militia forces, an advantage denied to General Curtis "because of the unfortunate antagonism between him and the State Government."[18]

While it was fortunate, indeed, that Schofield had the confidence of Governor Gamble, many problems associated with the militia forces remained. First, Missouri's militia, like that of most state forces, lacked the proper training and discipline to operate efficiently in the field. Schofield believed that although the enrolled militia had performed well against the guerrilla insurgency of 1862, the size of the militia forces required to win was twice that necessary if federal regiments had been employed instead. Second, too many of the militia, whether officers or men, abused their power to gain vengeance against personal and political enemies. For this reason, in General Orders No. 63, issued on July 7, 1863, Schofield reminded these forces of their purpose and responsibilities as soldiers. Despite martial law being in force throughout much of the state, the military's primary task was to put down the rebellion and restore civilian authority as soon as possible. Moreover, as circumstances permitted, the military was to support the civil authorities in their responsibility to administer and enforce local and state law. This included permitting these officials "to execute civil process in all camps and posts," unless in so doing the action would somehow hinder the military in its duties or would violate congressional law or a presidential proclamation. However, only the local commanding officer could make such a determination, which then must be reported promptly to the department commander.[19]

Unfortunately, this cooperation between the civil and military authorities was threatened later when Schofield ordered the militia no longer to participate in efforts to capture fugitive slaves. In March 1863, Congress had already prohibited the United States military participation in slave catching. As noted in chapter 7, Gamble had refused to place the enrolled militia under Curtis's command, in part at least, because the governor suspected the general would order the militia to discontinue aiding owners and state officers, as was required by state law, in the capture of fugitive slaves. In late July, Schofield, much to the surprise of Gamble, extended the congressional prohibition upon slave catching to the enrolled militia in General Orders No. 75. When this order was issued, Gamble's first inclination was to rescind Schofield's command over the enrolled and provisional militia. However, as he was then in Philadelphia and about to meet with the president in Washington D.C., the governor may have hoped to resolve this and other matters at the White House. In his absence, Lieutenant Governor Willard P. Hall decided that it would be imprudent to relieve Schofield from the command of state forces, concluding that in retaliation he might order the military no longer to supply the provisional militia, which would force the state to disband them almost immediately. As Hall expressed his dilemma, "it will be said that because the militia were not permitted to arrest runaway negroes, I have exposed white men to be ruined by bushwhackers." Upon his return to Missouri, Gamble, recognizing his weak position and the necessity of working with Schofield, decided to place all of Missouri's militia forces under Schofield's command "until further orders."[20]

As the summer progressed, despite his reservations concerning their efficiency, Schofield believed the enrolled and provisional militia forces had accomplished much since their organization and did not want them discharged until they could be replaced by regular forces raised in Missouri. By the time the draft and new enlistments were implemented, Schofield hoped to reduce significantly the number of provisional regiments in active service. Due to serious revenue shortfalls Missouri would soon have no money to pay the militia, prompting the governor to propose that recruiters for the United States military be permitted to recruit among the provisional militia. This plan would help relieve the state's revenue shortfall by converting a number of militia into United States troops whose pay would then be the responsibility of the federal government. If regular troops were not raised soon, however, the militia would be forced to serve without pay, a circumstance which could lead to much dissension and possibly mutiny in the ranks.[21]

On March 3, 1863, Congress had passed a measure which prepared the way for conscription, authorizing the president to suspend the privilege of the writ of habeas corpus for the duration of the war. The measure was introduced in December 1862, but it encountered strong opposition delaying its passage to the end of the congressional session. Importantly, the bill protected members of the military from prosecution and civil suits for any actions taken under the president's or a subordinate's order. This provision was later upheld by the Supreme Court of the United States in *Mitchell v. Clark* (1884). The first draft under the new law began in July 1863. In preparation for it, and to insure it was properly administered, the solicitor of the War Department, William Whiting, issued a series of circulars explaining the duties of the provost marshals in respect to it. The act provided for the arrest of anyone seeking to persuade others to resist the draft, or in any other way to impede it. Whiting explained who was eligible for the draft and that those refusing to report when called were to be arrested as deserters and sent to the nearest military authority. Moreover, he explained that provost marshals were not to obey writs of habeas corpus issued from the state courts and provided instructions for how to refuse their orders respectfully. Lincoln also prohibited all persons liable to the draft from leaving the country.[22]

During the summer of 1863, federal provost marshals and enrollment boards established by Congress to implement the draft were assigned to districts to begin the labor of enrolling white men between the ages of twenty and forty-five, excepting only immigrants who had not filed for citizenship. Of those selected to report, many were exempted because of physical or mental disabilities or because they were the only source of support for dependents such as siblings and widowed mothers. Those not exempted could still legally avoid service by paying a $300 commutation fee or providing a substitute, someone willing to enlist in his place. Many more of the draftees simply refused to report as ordered and were officially designated as deserters subject to court-martial. In practice, only a small percentage of the men drafted (7 percent) were actually inducted into the military service. Instead, the threat of conscription and the inducement of a bounty stimulated enlistments and filled the ranks of the military. Without this carrot and stick approach, the federal army would have been reduced significantly in a brief period of time.[23]

From the start, some conscripts applied to their local state and federal courts to gain writs of habeas corpus. This was possible because Lincoln allowed the process to continue until September 15 when he finally suspended the privilege of the writ. Over the previous two and a half months, those opposed to the draft had sought to combat it through both legal and illegal means. Men in New York City, opposed to the war for a variety of reasons, had rioted against the draft, killing over one hundred people and destroying considerable property. Others had appealed to the state and federal courts seeking a writ of habeas corpus. While many of the courts did not issue writs, some state and federal judges made rulings apparently intended to obstruct the draft. One of these rulings claimed that a man could not be designated a deserter until after he had reported to the military authorities and subsequently fled. This ruling by a state judge, however, was in contradiction to a precedent of the Supreme Court of the United States, *Houston v. Moore* (1820), in which Justice Bushrod Washington had established the principle that military service, and thus jurisdiction of military law, began at the time designated for men to report for duty.[24]

To sort all of this out through the courts would take much time, for presumably various challenges to the law and federal authority must maneuver their way through the state and federal courts to the United States Supreme

Court, where a final decision could be rendered. By September, Lincoln had received a report from Secretary of War Stanton indicating that challenges to the draft were beginning to have some effect in undermining public support for it and rallying those opposed to the war around the issue. For this reason, the president composed a direct appeal to the public in which he explained why a draft had become necessary. After two years of war, voluntary enlistments had largely dried up. This left conscription as the only means of filling the ranks of the military. Without the draft, the president believed, the war was lost. Opponents to the draft, he noted, argued that it was unconstitutional, for the Framers had never enumerated it among congressional powers. Lincoln, however, thought that such reasoning was flawed, for the Constitution had expressly delegated to Congress the authority "to raise and support armies" without designating any particular mode for exercising this power. If its absence from the text of the Constitution prevented Congress from conscripting men into the military, then one must conclude that voluntary enlistments were unconstitutional as well, for they are not found in the document either. Such a conclusion was unavoidable.[25]

On September 14, a special cabinet meeting was held to consider the practicability of suspending the privilege of the writ of habeas corpus. According to Secretary of the Navy Gideon Welles, the president complained that municipal and state judges were "defeating the draft" by releasing conscripts "under *habeas corpus.*" Considering such proceedings "factious and mischievous," in an uncharacteristically passionate manner Lincoln expressed his determination to send these judges "after Vallandigham" if necessary. Lincoln sought advice from his cabinet upon what course of action he should follow. Although they disagreed concerning its source, some believing it an inherent commander-in-chief power and others that only Congress could grant it, the consensus of the cabinet was that Lincoln should proclaim the privilege of the writ suspended upon the basis of the March 3 "act relating to *habeas corpus.*" Welles believed that only a United States judge should have the power "to decide in these naval and military cases affecting the law and service of the United States," for with it judges could "interrupt great military movements by an abused exercise of this writ,—could stop armies on the march." In a document drafted by Secretary of State William Seward and revised upon recommendations of the cabinet, Lincoln announced the suspension of the privilege of the writ of habeas corpus on September 15. The proclamation was primarily concerned with stopping resistance to the draft and the military according to the law of war. However, throughout the country the writ could still be issued to challenge the arrest of persons in matters unconnected with the military.[26]

While the rules were clear concerning the draft for United States troops, as was often the case these issues were more complicated in Missouri, especially as they related to the militia. As already noted in chapter 5, during his first tenure in command of the department, General Schofield had established the enrolled militia, a draft to meet the emergency of a guerrilla uprising in the summer of 1862. After these guerrilla forces had been defeated, most of the enrolled militia were then disbanded, although they remained subject to recall in the event of another emergency. In early 1863, Governor Gamble created the provisional militia, regiments handpicked from the enrolled militia, to meet the need for troops in Missouri. However, during its first legislative session since May 1861, the General Assembly in Jefferson City passed an act allowing any member of the militia to pay a $30 commutation fee to escape service. This amount was very low and it was feared that, given the low pay and the hardships experienced by the militia, the vast majority of men would opt to pay the fee rather than to serve. Another obstacle to maintaining the enrolled militia was the increasing opposition of the Radical Republicans, who viewed them as a predominately disloyal and proslavery force.[27]

Before the president put a stop to it, another obstacle to raising troops in Missouri was the inevitable resort to the local courts seeking a writ of habeas corpus, which, as noted above, had become a favorite tactic of those opposed to the war, or at least those unwilling to serve. Thus, in July 1863 John C. Cook appealed to Probate Judge J. M. Gilstrap for a writ to be issued to Provost Marshal Thomas Crampton to explain the reason for Cook's arrest. Crampton did not reply and Gilstrap ordered the sheriff to request of General Odon Guitar that he command Crampton "to make his proper return to said writ to the end that the laws of the land may be executed." Guitar, himself a lawyer, declined to intervene until it was demonstrated that the civil authority was unable to enforce its order. Eventually, the habeas hearing was held in which Crampton responded that as a military officer in the service of the United States he had arrested Cook as a deserter. Cook denied this. The judge ruled that Cook had never been in the United States service, and although he had served in the Eleventh Missouri State Militia Cavalry he was entitled to a discharge and the judge ordered him released. However, apparently this order was ignored, for Cook remained in the military until September 1 when he was discharged. Interestingly, less than a year later Cook served in the Forty-second Enrolled Missouri Militia, when guerrilla activity had again increased significantly.[28]

As in other parts of the country, delays in the implementation of the draft in Missouri were causing unanticipated problems. As the enrollment was being made, many who supported the South went "to the brush to avoid the draft" and fought as guerrillas. On August 15, in a letter to Assistant Adjutant General E. D. Townsend, General Schofield argued that no further delay should occur, for once the draft was finished then Union forces would need "to fight only that portion of [southern sympathizers] who happened to be drafted." For this reason, Schofield requested that a final decision concerning the institution of the draft be made immediately. Unfortunately, the department commander's concerns apparently went unheeded and no acceleration of the process occurred.[29]

Just days later, Schofield's task was further complicated in the aftermath of William C. Quantrill's sack of Lawrence, Kansas. During the summer, opposition to departmental policies had grown and Radicals immediately blamed Schofield and the enrolled militia for the disaster. Editors of radical newspapers demanded that regular forces replace the enrolled militia, whom the Radicals believed were either incompetent or disloyal and thus unwilling to prosecute the war vigorously against guerrilla forces. This opposition apparently encouraged some members of the enrolled militia to resist their call-up by applying to local judges for writs of habeas corpus. However, at least one state circuit-court judge, George W. Miller, rejected such an appeal, declaring the enrolled militia and its draft to be legal, although he also made it clear that a man could easily escape service by simply paying the $30 commutation fee as provided by the law.

Perhaps Miller's decision disappointed some, for Federal District Judge Robert W. Wells was asked: "Is the Enrolled Missouri Militia amenable to the United States authorities?" Wells ruled that they were. All of these questions, however, became irrelevant soon thereafter, when the president suspended the privilege of the writ on September 15, the day after Wells had given his opinion. At least that was the perspective of even a newspaper as radical as the *St. Louis Missouri Democrat,* which noted on September 17 that applications for writs of habeas corpus had been made to Judge Clover of the St. Louis criminal court by two enrolled militiamen, John Falck and H. J. Bockrath, who had been ordered to serve in provisional regiments. Despite Lincoln's suspension, Judge Clover issued writs to Colonel Henry H. Catherwood of the Eleventh Provisional Regiment. At this point apparently no more action was taken in the criminal court, which is what one would expect if the military refused to surrender the men. Moreover, during the next few months, whatever resistance remained to the enrollments and the selection of conscripts was unavailing, for 15,000 new men were mustered into the Department of the Missouri, bringing the total in arms to 50,374. This success was all the more remarkable given that the enrollments in some of the regions, especially along the Kansas-Missouri border, could not be completed because of the continued guerrilla warfare there.[30]

Even before the Civil War, hostility had existed between the people of Kansas and of Missouri. Before 1854, the Missouri Compromise had prohibited slavery from the territory of Kansas. After Congress passed the Kansas-Nebraska bill, however, the restriction upon slavery was repealed and residents were given the authority to organize a territorial government and decide whether to permit slavery there. This action turned Kansas into a battleground, leading to violence between proslavery and antislavery forces. Abraham Lincoln, then a successful lawyer and former congressman, was so incensed by the Missouri Compromise's repeal that he reentered politics with a renewed vigor and zeal to stop the further extension of slavery, eventually becoming a leader of the fledgling Republican Party in Illinois. In late 1859, Lincoln traveled to Kansas to see the circumstances there firsthand and to speak at several towns along the Missouri border. As a moderate, however, he opposed the tactics of John Brown, strongly criticizing his effort to foment a slave insurrection in the South. After spending almost a week in Kansas, the future president returned to Springfield, Illinois.[31]

Despite both states' decisions to reject secession in 1861, much bitterness and distrust remained between Kansans and Missourians from the long struggle of the past decade. Moreover, as already noted in chapters 3 and 4, the major obstacle to effective cooperation remained the issue of slavery. In order to strike a blow against this hated institution, in Kansas James H. Lane and Charles R. Jennison raised regiments of men eager to wreak vengeance upon slaveholders and to free as many slaves as possible, whether they were the property of Secessionists or not. Many Missourians suffered a variety of indignities and lived under difficult circumstances as long as these forces remained in the region. Early in the war, numerous reports from various parts of Missouri, especially along its border with Kansas, demonstrated that some Kansas regiments were looting and destroying property and stealing slaves. General Henry W. Halleck, soon after taking command of the department in November 1861, ordered federal troops not to interfere with slavery but found that he had little power to stop many of the depredations being committed.

The problem along the Kansas-Missouri border was an especially difficult matter to solve, for even after ordering Kansas regiments out of Missouri's border counties, the attacks upon civilians and the theft of slaves continued. Because Lane had encouraged these activities, when Lincoln decided to make Kansas a separate military department from Missouri, Governor Gamble, Lieutenant Governor Hall, General Halleck, and many residents in the Missouri border counties wrote to express their strong disapproval of placing Lane in command there. Apparently, Lincoln had intended to appoint Lane but, after receiving such opposition, instead prudently selected David Hunter for the command, although it is also clear that the president did not lose his confidence in Lane—an unfortunate misjudgment—for he appointed him as a brigadier general. Lincoln noted that "it is insisted by some that Lane must be kept out of Missouri, which is doubtful with me. . . . With his knowledge of the country and the men, I expect him to be a valuable officer."[32]

While the seizure or destruction of civilian property was often necessary during a time of war, many reports circulated of pillaging by German home guard and Kansas volunteer regiments led by Lane and Jennison. Believing that such behavior, which had become common under Frémont's command, could seriously undermine support for the Union in Missouri, Halleck began to deal with those responsible. First, he ordered all soldiers committing depredations to be "arrested and placed in irons." Officers failing to do all in their power to prevent such outrages were to be prosecuted as accomplices in the crimes. Halleck especially blamed Lane and Jennison for allowing their forces to act with great inhumanity and without discrimination between loyal and secessionist Missourians. These depredations, Halleck believed, had "done more for the enemy in this State than could have been accomplished by 20,000 of his own army." Later, despite his efforts to stop such crimes, Halleck admitted that Kansas regiments continued to "cross the [Missouri] line, [to] rob, steal, plunder, and burn whatever they can lay their hands upon. They disgrace the name and uniform of American soldiers and are driving good Union men into the ranks of the secession army." To end these raids, Halleck ordered General John Pope to force all Kansas regiments from Missouri and to arrest those who resisted him.[33]

During the early part of 1862, despite Hunter's appointment, the problems along the border continued and Halleck ordered two regiments to patrol Jackson County in northwestern Missouri, where much of the violence was then occurring. Because of guerrilla activity throughout much of Missouri, Halleck was unable to station more troops there. While the troubles along the border were attributable in large part to the lawlessness of Kansas troops, Halleck knew that enemy guerrillas and federal troops from other free states were responsible too. Recognizing that many of the officers of these out-of-state forces encouraged, or at least condoned, slave stealing and the commission of other crimes against the laws of war, Halleck removed them in the hope that their replacements would obey orders and prevent their subordinates' misconduct. Nevertheless, Halleck believed, without at least fifty thousand more troops he could not stop the depredations. His analysis turned out to be far too accurate and Lincoln, who had hoped that the violence along the border would end soon, learned from Governor Gamble that "a military force from Kansas" had entered Missouri, seized a group of citizens, and brought them across the border. These citizens had earlier arrested a Kansan for allegedly committing a crime in their community. Gamble noted the importance of preventing any further interference with the civil courts and ensuring that the fall election be held without incident. As he explained to Lincoln, the provisional government must prove that it can protect its citizens and their property or its failure to do so would soon mean its downfall.[34]

The situation along the border, however, seemed to be worsening. After receiving more reports of the misbehavior of troops and civilians from Kansas, Gamble again wrote to Lincoln in September 1862, explaining that runaway slaves were being organized into military units and that soon these forces were expected to invade Missouri and attempt to emancipate the slaves there. While regretting the necessity, Gamble made it clear "that if such invasion is made I will resist it with all the force I can command" and promised "to give to the people of Kansas a taste of the evils of war in their own territory." It was at this critical time that Lincoln replaced Schofield with General Samuel R. Curtis as commander in Missouri, an appointment which displeased Gamble very much. Curtis also made little progress in defusing the circumstances along the border, which remained tense despite continued efforts to pacify the region.[35]

Unfortunately, some of the measures used to counter the guerrilla threat, especially the enrolling of militia, had unintended consequences leading to more trouble. Under General Orders No. 24, southern sympathizers were exempted from military service. Along the Kansas-Missouri border, loyal men were in the minority and thus shouldered a majority of the burden of patrolling and fighting the guerrillas and their supporters. These men were thus unable to attend to their professions while disloyal men, because they were exempted from military service, could pursue their business interests and even profited from military contracts. Some of these men, having received passes from the provost marshal to trade, used the privilege to provide livestock and other supplies to Quantrill, perhaps the most ruthless and cruel guerrilla leader the war produced. This circumstance caused much resentment among loyal men.[36]

In early May 1863, Governor Gamble again wrote to Lincoln, asserting that the circumstances had not improved, in part because of the actions of Kansas regiments, which General James G. Blunt had ordered into Missouri a short time before and which had committed a number of atrocities. The Kansans, claiming to have killed guerrillas, had actually "shot down" both southern sympathizers and Unionists, all of whom, according to sources Gamble claimed to be credible, "were men shot down on their own farms or in their own houses, peaceably pursuing their own occupations." From late spring into August 1863, it became evident that much destruction of property and life continued and that both bushwhackers and Kansas regiments or "Red Legs," as they were sometimes called, were responsible. Hoping to stop this type of violence, General Thomas Ewing Jr., who had been placed in charge of the border region to provide a buffer between Kansas and Missouri, issued General Orders No. 10 in which he commanded persons known to have aided guerrillas arrested, although he also exempted from detainment those who were "compelled by threats or fears to aid the rebels." However, this judicious enforcement of martial law was implemented for only a few days when news was learned of Quantrill's raid against Lawrence, Kansas.[37]

When assigning motivation for the destruction of Lawrence and the slaughter of its unarmed male residents, one must be careful not to attach too much certainty to any of the possible reasons. In his colorful account of the massacre Jay Monaghan posited as Quantrill's primary motive for the raid his desire to reestablish his authority as guerrilla chief along the border. At first guerrilla chiefs, including such notables as George Todd, William "Bloody Bill" Anderson, Frank James, and Cole Younger, were reluctant to recognize Quantrill's leadership and were unenthusiastic about his suggestion that they make a raid against Lawrence. However, these guerrillas apparently embraced the opportunity after the deaths of one of Anderson's sisters, a female cousin of Younger, and three other young women. They had died in the collapse of a building in Kansas City where Union authorities had imprisoned them. Although this tragedy was the result of an accident, such a distinction mattered little to the guerrillas, who blamed all Unionists for the women's deaths. Therefore, a raid on Lawrence to avenge the death of these women, despite the obvious danger entailed in committing such an atrocity, appealed to the guerrillas who agreed to Quantrill's plan. Moreover, to the guerrillas Lawrence was the residence of the worst element of their enemy, the abolitionists, and of James H. Lane, the inveterate enemy of guerrillas and slavery. Arriving at dawn on August 21, the guerrillas found the town asleep and defenseless. Killing nearly two hundred men and boys, the guerrillas quickly returned to western Missouri, where the rough terrain of woods and brush would conceal them from retaliation. A short time after the massacre, General Schofield wrote to Lincoln and conjectured that the guerrillas may have been retaliating for Ewing's decision to remove the families of the guerrillas from the border region. Ewing's order had been issued on August 18, just three days before the raid. Whatever the reason, the Lawrence massacre led Ewing and Schofield to take severe and controversial action of their own.[38]

One of the first demands for vengeance came from Kansas Governor Thomas Carney, who wrote to Schofield soon after the massacre, demanding that those in western Missouri be punished, for "no body of men large as that commanded by Quantrill could have been gathered together without the people residing [there] . . . knowing everything about it." From two to three thousand Kansans were then in arms preparing to carry out raids into Missouri. Among these was one of the survivors of the attack, United States Senator Lane, who, along with Congressman Abel C. Wilder, sent a telegram to Lincoln demanding the removal of Schofield, whose "imbecility & incapacity" they blamed for the atrocity. In response, Lincoln urged Schofield to do all in his ability "to give them future security and to punish their invaders." In reply to the president's letter, Schofield noted that the difficult circumstances along the border had existed throughout the war and that none of his predecessors had prevented violence there as well. He reminded the president that because he had sent troops to Grant during the Vicksburg campaign, the number available for service in Missouri had been much reduced. After the citadel's capture, many paroled troops from Missouri's Confederate regiments had returned home and some of them had undoubtedly joined the guerrillas. Moreover, these irregular forces received aid in supplies and intelligence from the locals who were overwhelmingly in favor of the South, enabling the marauders to operate with impunity along the northern border region of Kansas and Missouri. Schofield also warned the president that Senator Lane, the mayor of Leavenworth, and others were preparing to lead an armed mob into Missouri and that it would be his duty as department commander to stop them.[39]

Efforts to punish Quantrill's guerrillas were reasonably successful, forces in Kansas and Missouri killing about one-third of those responsible for the massacre. In the wake of the Lawrence disaster, without first consulting with Schofield, on August 25 Ewing published General Orders No. 11. While, as noted above, he had already ordered the families of some of the most notorious guerrillas to leave northwestern Missouri, it was clear that Ewing issued this much more comprehensive evacuation measure to demonstrate to Lane and other Kansans that he was serious about stopping guerrillas from coming into Kansas. Thus he ordered the evacuation of all persons living in the counties of Jackson, Cass, and Bates, as well as parts of Vernon, excepting only those living in certain towns or townships he designated. Anyone could gain an exemption with proper documentation demonstrating their loyalty, but even these persons must stay at the nearest military post in their region. All other residents, however, must leave within fifteen days. Another provision ordered all hay and grain then in the fields to be harvested and brought "within reach of military stations," which would be collected after September 9. The commanders of these posts were to record the names of loyal owners and the amounts provided for the purpose of compensating them later. Presumably disloyal persons would not be paid. Ewing also ordered all hay and grain destroyed which was not in a place where the military could use it. While it is unclear exactly when Lincoln learned about General Orders No. 11, he most probably knew just days after the order was published, if not sooner, and could have intervened, although the outcry from Kansas and Radicals would have been great. Moreover, no doubt exists that Lincoln knew about the order by October 1, for in a letter to Schofield the president approved the policy "of removing the inhabitants of certain counties en masse; and of removing certain individuals from time to time, who are supposed to be mischievous."[40]

On August 31, General Schofield traveled to Kansas and conferred with Governor Carney, Senator Lane, General Ewing, and others about the crisis. In these consultations, Schofield sought to work out a security arrangement to keep Kansans out of Missouri, but in the end settled for issuing his own proclamation "forbidding armed men not in the regular military service from crossing the line [into Missouri]." For a time, because Senator Lane was then touring the state inciting Kansans to arm themselves and organize into a large force with which to enter Missouri, there existed the possibility that a clash might occur between Lane's force and Missourians. Ostensibly, Lane claimed that the expedition was not to avenge Lawrence, but rather to "recover their stolen property." It was clear to everyone, however, that vengeance was the primary purpose of the proposed expedition. To prevent Kansas's militia from joining Lane, Schofield ordered that the militia of both states were to be employed "only for the defense of their respective states," unless otherwise ordered by their district commanders. Moreover, Ewing greatly reduced the possibility of trouble when he had the ferry on the Missouri River near Leavenworth seized, making it impossible for Kansans to cross into Missouri there. By September 9, the day Lane had chosen to rendezvous with his force at Paola and to then move into Missouri, most Kansans had lost their enthusiasm for the adventure and only "a few hundred people" arrived and, after listening to speeches by Lane and others, soon dispersed, most of them returning to their homes.[41]

While in northwestern Missouri, Schofield inspected the region to strengthen the defenses and to prevent a repeat of the Lawrence disaster. He also characterized Ewing's evacuation order as "wise and necessary." Without such a measure Schofield believed that the loyal and innocent could never live there. The situation was "the old border hatred intensified by the rebellion and by the murders, robberies, and arson which have characterized the irregular warfare carried on during the early periods of the rebellion, not only by the rebels, but by our own troops and people." The vast majority living along the

border in Missouri "were open rebels" who willingly provided intelligence
and resources to the guerrillas. Thus Union troops could not move against
the guerrillas there without being detected, and guerrillas had the further advantage that the terrain was "remarkably well adapted by nature for guerrilla
warfare." Under these circumstances the only "remedy" was the mass removal
of the inhabitants from along the border.[42]

To carry out this policy, Ewing ordered commanders of military posts to
ensure that only loyal persons be allowed to remain in the affected counties.
Seeking to protect property, he provided specific rules for the confiscation
of abandoned livestock and other supplies useful to the military, prohibiting the taking of nonmilitary items such as household articles. Unfortunately,
despite this order, much looting of abandoned homes occurred. Moreover,
by requiring everyone to leave within fifteen days without providing transport and aid to the vast majority of refugees, Ewing and Schofield must be
held at least partly responsible for the human suffering and deaths resulting
from the order. This was certainly the position of some contemporary critics, most notably George Caleb Bingham, who produced a painting of the
evacuation, in which he made Ewing the central villain of his work. However,
one must not forget that Quantrill and his raiders were ultimately responsible
for much of what happened in the aftermath of the Lawrence raid, including
the removal of the relatives and supporters of the guerrillas. It is also clear
that without the removal policy the retribution against them would have been
even more severe than it was. This was recognized by the families themselves,
most of whom out of fear complied willingly with the order, making its enforcement easy.[43]

The consequences of Ewing's order were quite dramatic. A witness to
this was Major Bazel F. Lazear of the Twelfth Missouri State Militia Cavalry,
who participated in the pursuit of Quantrill and fought skirmishes with the
guerrillas. Lazear and his command killed a number of them and recovered
stolen property discarded by the guerrillas to escape their pursuers. Afterward, he and his troops continued to scour parts of the evacuation zone and
found themselves moved to compassion because of the plight of the evacuees,
some of whom were on foot or in old wagons with only the possessions they
could carry with them. To enforce the order, Ewing commanded Kansas regiments into the counties to push the inhabitants out. While some accounts
of this episode were embellished by those wishing to portray the federal

government as despotic and unjust, others are credible, especially those of loyal men such as Martin Rice, a Unionist who testified that a squad of the Ninth Kansas had ruthlessly murdered six of his neighbors with whom he had been traveling. Each of the counties were largely abandoned and many homes were destroyed by fire, so much so that these counties came to be known as "the burnt district."[44]

In contrast to the criticism of the evacuation order by southern sympathizers and some Conservatives, the Radical press, in particular, attacked not only Generals Schofield and Ewing, but also Governor Gamble, much of the provisional government, and the enrolled militia for the disaster. The Radicals charged that the military authorities and the provisional government were disloyal and, if not exactly supporters of the Lawrence atrocity, at the very least they had acquiesced in it and other guerrilla raids committed since General Curtis's removal in late May. The purpose of these attacks, which appeared primarily in German newspapers and the *St. Louis Missouri Democrat,* was to gain the removal of Schofield and Gamble and the disbanding of the enrolled militia. In their place the Radicals demanded federal troops and the appointment of a Radical military governor. These and other demands, including an end to Schofield's suppression of freedom of the press, challenged Lincoln's skills as a leader and statesman.[45]

9

LINCOLN'S SHOWDOWN
WITH THE RADICALS

DURING THE SUMMER OF 1863, the Missouri Radicals, despite the state convention's passage of a gradual emancipation bill by late June, continued to organize their opposition to the leadership of General John M. Schofield and Governor Hamilton R. Gamble. They also pressed President Abraham Lincoln to impose radical policies upon Missouri despite his protests that he had "been tormented beyond endurance for months by both sides" with their disputes and demands. The Radicals' activism was partly retaliatory against Gamble, whom they blamed along with other Conservatives for the removal from command of General Samuel R. Curtis. As noted in chapter 8, in late May Lincoln had warned Schofield to stand aloof from all factions and "let your military measures be strong enough to repel the invader and keep the peace, and not so strong as to unnecessarily harrass [sic] and persecute the people." This advice was sound as a goal but, as it turned out, was unachievable in practice.[1]

When he wrote this letter, Lincoln had hoped that Schofield could somehow avoid becoming involved in the strife which then existed between the Conservatives and Radicals, not an easy task. In the letter, the president described the Radicals and Conservatives as Unionist factions led by Curtis and Gamble involved in an unfortunate struggle, which he felt it was necessary to break up somehow. Thus, as he explained his decision to Schofield, because "I could not remove Gov. Gamble, I had to remove Gen. Curtis." This characterization of his action was accurate as far as it went, but Lincoln omitted stating that he would not have sacked Curtis had the Conservatives not badgered him into it. Of course, it would have been unwise for the president to admit this, as well as his earlier mistake in appointing Curtis in the first place. Perhaps belatedly, Lincoln recognized the necessity of having a commander there who could work with the provisional government. During his previous stint as commander in Missouri, Schofield had already proven his ability to

cooperate with Gamble and his subordinates, was familiar with the department, and had shown no inclination to become embroiled in politics. Therefore, if he had not been Curtis's replacement, Schofield's prospects for success
would have been promising. Ironically, with its publication, the letter itself
soon became the object of much bitter dispute and further controversy, leading eventually to Schofield's decision to suppress elements of the Radical press
in Missouri.[2]

After writing his letter on May 27, Lincoln had a copy sent to Curtis as
well. Undoubtedly, the president wished to demonstrate to his former commander, who had by then returned to Iowa, that he had not lost confidence in
him. It was common at the time, and something that Lincoln himself did frequently, for writers to mark their correspondence as confidential when they
wished for it to be kept secret. Indeed, Lincoln had indicated on a letter written the day before that it should remain private, but failed to insist that Curtis
not share his letter with anyone else. As Curtis explained to one of his staff,
Richard McAllister, such an omission meant that the letter "could not have
been sent solely for my own eye." He also requested that if McAllister went to
Washington D.C. that he "inform the President of my innocence in the publication of his letters and assure him it was against my injunctions & wishes.
That I sought only to show copies to friends but they thought it necessary to
vindicate the President and myself against falsehood & convict the real actors
in their duplicity." More than likely, either Curtis or one of his friends, such
as United States Senator from Kansas James H. Lane, had sent the letter to the
St. Louis Missouri Democrat for publication.[3]

When the letter was published, Schofield had been away from St. Louis,
but he soon sought answers from the editors of the *St. Louis Missouri Democrat*. After learning that William McKee was responsible for the letter's publication, Schofield requested that he come to his headquarters and explain
the matter to him. McKee ignored both this and a written request to discuss
the matter, which led to Schofield ordering his arrest. At the provost marshal
general's office, McKee would only say that no one on Schofield's staff had
leaked the letter to him. After this interview, the editor was allowed to leave
by "simply giving his verbal parole," but he was also given just ten days to tell
the military the culprit's name. This "nominal" arrest, as Schofield described
it to Lincoln, was not politically motivated, despite what the Radicals claimed.
Interestingly, some years before in a deposition before a justice of the peace,

McKee had refused to divulge the source of some information which had appeared in a newspaper he edited. For this he had been arrested. In the October 1853 term, the case had come before Governor Gamble when he was chief justice of the Supreme Court of Missouri. In his decision Gamble had ruled in response to the writ of habeas corpus that McKee could be held in prison for contempt of court until he testified. It is probable that Schofield knew about this incident through Gamble, with whom he would have naturally consulted as the president's letter concerned him as well. If so, it may explain Schofield's decision to press McKee to divulge his source.[4]

While he did not believe that Schofield's arrest of McKee was politically motivated, Lincoln still feared that his action had forever lost to him "the middle position," that is, a position disassociated from both Unionist factions. As soon as he had learned about McKee's arrest, the president sought to defuse the controversy by appealing to his friend and Radical congressman Henry T. Blow, noting that "the publication of a letter without the leave of the writer or the receiver I think cannot be justified, but in this case I do not think it of sufficient consequence to justify an arrest; and again, the arrest being through a parole merely nominal, does not deserve the importance sought to be attached to it. Cannot this small matter be dropped on both sides without further difficulty?" Lincoln also readily seized upon Schofield's suggestion "to stop proceedings in the matter." Thus the matter was dropped, although the Radicals continued to criticize Schofield's action.[5]

However, as Schofield would write many years after the war, the chance of fostering cooperation between the factions, or even to get them to leave one another alone, was by this period impossible. As he explained in a letter to General in Chief Henry W. Halleck, although Governor Gamble was willing to compromise, noting his willingness to meet the Radicals halfway on the emancipation issue, for their part, the Radicals would be dissatisfied "short of the overthrow of the existing State government." Moreover, Schofield thought that the president did not understand "the nature of this quarrel in Missouri," for Lincoln thought that both the Conservatives and Radicals were equally opposed to his policies. Such a circumstance was a major concern to Lincoln with a presidential election looming in 1864. Schofield argued that the Conservatives, in actuality, "were sincere in their friendship and support of Mr. Lincoln, and desired his renomination, while the Radicals were intriguing for Mr. Chase or some other more Radical man."[6]

As noted in chapter 8, the Radical press blamed Schofield for the Lawrence, Kansas, massacre of August 21. This criticism led to calls for his removal and the appointment of a Radical military general to take more comprehensive control of Missouri. These newspapers also demanded resistance to calls for service in the enrolled militia and accused Gamble of despotism and protecting slavery. Moreover, at least one Radical editor blamed Lincoln for the continued turmoil and troubles in Missouri and did not consider him a friend. Gathering together at Jefferson City, the Radicals aired many of their grievances against the civil and military government and organized their opposition. These events eventually led to Schofield's decision to issue on September 17 General Orders No. 96 in which he declared that the president's suspension of the privilege of the writ of habeas corpus for persons drafted into the military would pertain to militia forces in Missouri. More important, he announced that from thenceforward he would "rigidly" enforce martial law throughout the department against "all persons who shall in any manner encourage mutiny, insubordination, or disorderly conduct, or endeavor to create disaffection among troops." Schofield also warned that he would not tolerate anyone communicating "words calculated to excite insurrection or lawless acts among the people, or [those] who shall publish falsehoods or misrepresentations of facts calculated to embarrass or weaken the military authorities." Persons guilty of violating this general order, Schofield warned, would be liable to arrest and trial before a military commission and if convicted would be fined and imprisoned. Newspapers in violation of these new rules would be suppressed. Believing that at least some of the criticism of his policies had originated with the officers and men under his command, Schofield ordered his troops to obey the army regulation forbidding either praise or criticism of their superiors and the publication of unauthorized correspondence and other literature.[7]

Schofield explained to General Halleck that the Radicals in Missouri, especially in St. Louis, had for some time sought to gain control of the state government and affect national policy. Most seriously, Radical opposition to Schofield was responsible for the mutiny of the 11th Provisional Regiment and the attempt by the Radical officers and men of the 23rd Missouri Volunteers to gain the removal of their commanding officer Quinn Morton. This was hardly surprising, Schofield believed, given the scandalous and misleading articles then being published in the newspapers, bringing him to the conclusion that only "a strong remedy" could arrest their demoralizing affect upon the troops. Even in deference to the president's "well-known wishes . . . relative to freedom of speech and the press," Schofield considered it impossible longer to delay taking this corrective action. He then asked Halleck to place this order before the president, noting that his approval would make clear to the Radicals that their efforts could not succeed. On September 26, Halleck replied, enclosing the president's written approval of Schofield's order. Halleck counseled Schofield to be very careful in the use of this new authority, for otherwise the Radicals might "incite public sympathy" by claiming that they were being persecuted. A few days later, Lincoln himself wrote to Schofield and reminded him that his main duty was to keep the peace. He also ordered Schofield not to arrest anyone, to stop any public assembly, or to suppress any newspapers except when it was absolutely necessary to prevent "injury to the military." Later that month, Schofield reported to Lincoln of the success of his policy and that he had found it necessary only to arrest one person.[8]

At the time of his approval of General Orders No. 96, Lincoln was preparing to meet with a Radical delegation from Missouri whose demands included Schofield's removal. It is clear that the president had supported the policy only reluctantly, in part because of his principle of not interfering with commanders in the field and in part to protect Schofield, who was then vulnerable to attack. This position was pragmatic, for clearly Lincoln could not run any of the several military departments himself, all of which had their own unique and complex set of circumstances and problems, none more so than Missouri. Not wishing to become embroiled in the many and varied difficulties of the military departments, the president avoided involvement in decision making as much as possible, even when he thought a commander's policies were imprudent. In this instance, he supported Schofield's measure but privately warned him not to enforce it except under extreme circumstances. Another instance of this was in Lincoln's very public support of General Ambrose E. Burnside's arrest of Clement Vallandigham, an antiwar Democrat politician, for denouncing the war and asserting that it was "a war for freedom of the blacks and the enslavement of the whites." While Burnside's policy and action in Vallandigham's arrest and imprisonment were contrary to administration policy and potentially embarrassing, Lincoln probably calculated that more harm than good would result from his undermining Burnside's authority.[9]

In the three weeks prior to the Radical delegation's arrival in Washington D.C., Lincoln received a number of letters from both Conservatives and Radicals, who provided contradictory information to him concerning conditions in Missouri. Conservatives and others warned Lincoln that the Radicals were primarily interested in obtaining political power, that they had very limited support among Missourians, and that a majority of the delegates supported someone other than Lincoln for the Republican presidential nomination next year. Supporters of the Radicals declared themselves earnest backers of Lincoln and the war effort, attacked Governor Gamble as disloyal, and provided a variety of reasons for sacking General Schofield and replacing him with a Radical. Both General Schofield and Governor Gamble defended themselves in letters. As noted above, Schofield argued that the president was mistaken in believing that both the Radicals and the Conservatives were equally responsible for the factionalism in Missouri. Gamble, who to this time had been reluctant to defend himself against his critics, after prodding from friends and relatives, wrote to the president defending his administration and appealing to him for support against the Radicals.[10]

Lincoln, whose time was being occupied increasingly with Missouri matters, found himself in the unenviable position of trying to understand and cope with the Byzantine politics of Missouri. As he had advised Schofield, Lincoln sought to remain apart from their factional dispute and to deal fairly with both groups, each of which he needed to maintain control of Missouri and the gains of the military in the West. At their recent convention held in Jefferson City, the Radicals had chosen a delegation of seventy to travel to Washington D.C. to meet with the president and present to him their demands. This delegation was headed by Charles D. Drake, one of the harshest critics of both Lincoln and Gamble. One of the members of the president's cabinet, Secretary of the Navy Gideon Welles, viewed the arrival of these Radicals as most unwelcome, characterizing them as "extreme party men" whose "hate and narrow partisanship" made difficult the compromise and cooperation needed among Unionists to fight the war effectually. While considering the Radicals' policies more in agreement with his own than the Conservatives, the president was also aware that the Radicals were some of his most vocal critics. Despite needing their support for reelection, however, Lincoln was determined to pursue the course he thought best in Missouri.[11]

On September 30, 1863, Lincoln met with the delegation for two hours at the White House. Drake read from a prepared statement, presenting the Radicals' version of events in Missouri. Beginning with the premise that the war could only be won by the complete and immediate abolition of slavery, he asserted that anyone opposed to this policy must be disloyal. However, he did not attempt to reconcile this statement with the actions of Governor Gamble and the majority of the state convention, who were proslavery and from the beginning of the war had supported the Union and Lincoln and had prevented Missouri's secession. Moreover, many of these Conservatives were the first to enlist into military service when it was unclear which way the state would go, while many Radicals like Drake had not become soldiers and were on the sidelines during this critical period.[12]

Drake also accused Governor Gamble of seeking to prevent the passage of immediate emancipation when he called the state convention together just months before. The adoption of a plan for gradual emancipation was intended to blunt the momentum for slavery's eradication and thus was "adverse to true loyalty, and to the vital interests of our State. . . . The policy of our State Executive represses and chills the loyal heart of Missouri, as a pro-Slavery policy represses and chills loyal hearts everywhere." Moreover, Drake asserted that Gamble's war policies treated disloyal persons too gently and demonstrated the governor's secret purpose of undermining the Union effort.[13]

As Lincoln had been warned, the main goal of Drake's presentation was the removal of General Schofield, replacing him with General Benjamin Butler. This was necessary, Drake argued, for Schofield was supporting the Conservatives, suppressing freedom of speech and the press, was illegally extending Lincoln's suspension of the privilege of the writ of habeas corpus to include men drafted into the militia, and had removed federal troops from Missouri. Finally, Drake asserted that because of these policies, during the brief period of Schofield's command circumstances in Missouri had deteriorated significantly.[14]

Drake's presentation, it soon became clear, did not have the effect he and his fellow delegates had hoped. The president's private secretary John Hay, who listened to the entire speech, was unimpressed by the Radicals' arguments, which he thought unconvincing and empty of substance. Hay believed that Lincoln's response demonstrated the superiority of his intellect and character over that of his critics. At the end of their meeting, Lincoln promised to send his decision regarding their demands in writing.[15]

While he considered his response, Lincoln continued to receive letters from both Radicals and Conservatives in which they sought to sway his decision. To refute the accusations that he was responsible for the deteriorating circumstances in Missouri, Schofield both wrote to Lincoln directly and provided a memorandum to Congressman James S. Rollins, which he used in composing a letter urging the president to reject the Radicals' demands. Gamble also wrote to Lincoln and enlisted friends to write defenses of himself. In particular, Gamble resented the charge that he was somehow disloyal and accused the Radicals of attempting to overthrow the provisional government. Noting that under the Constitution of the United States, the executive had the duty to protect the states from rebellion, Attorney General Edward Bates pressed Lincoln to intervene militarily to stop the Radicals. Another Missourian and a relative by marriage to both Gamble and Bates, Federal Judge Charles Gibson leaked to the *New York Times* Gamble's demand for support from Lincoln, hoping that public pressure might force him to act. However, Lincoln declined to move precipitously, believing that circumstances did not warrant such drastic measures, observing that while a small number of Radicals had advocated a violent insurrection against Gamble and Schofield, the resolutions passed at the Radicals' convention were political rather than revolutionary. Nevertheless, Lincoln declared that once the danger presented itself he would not hesitate to move against it.[16]

In his written reply to the Radical delegation published in mid-October, Lincoln provided his own analysis of Missouri's wartime troubles. The Radicals, he observed, had demanded that he remove General Schofield, replace the state militia with federal regiments, and enforce the election laws. In his presentation Drake had justified Schofield's removal by documenting the great amount of suffering among Unionists which had occurred since he had taken command in Missouri. The Radicals argued that Schofield and Gamble were responsible for these circumstances and that a change was necessary. Lincoln, however, rejected this analysis, noting that "the whole can be explained on a more charitable and, as I think, a more rational hypothesis. We are in civil war."[17]

Lincoln also rejected the idea that only the Radicals were truly loyal, and especially the idea that the Conservatives were disloyal. To illustrate his point, the president described the various Unionist factions in Missouri. Of these there were those who are for the Union with, but not without, slavery; those for it without, but not with; those for it with or without, but prefer it with; and those for it with or without, but prefer it without. Among these, again, is a subdivision of those who are for gradual, but not for immediate, and those who are for immediate, but not for gradual, extinction of slavery. It is easy to conceive that all these shades of opinion, and even more, may be sincerely entertained by honest and truthful men, yet all being for the Union, by reason of these differences each will prefer a different way of sustaining the Union. At once sincerity is questioned and motives are assailed. Actual war coming, blood grows hot and blood is spilled; thought is forced from old channels into confusion; deception breeds and thrives, confidence dies, and universal suspicion reigns.[18]

Noting that Missouri's political and military affairs had been in turmoil since the beginning of the war, Lincoln did not hold Schofield and Gamble responsible for them as did Drake and the Radicals. Thus, the president refused to remove Schofield. As for sending more federal troops to Missouri, Lincoln wanted to know from where they could be spared. Moreover, he observed that those regiments Schofield had sent to General Ulysses S. Grant had played a very important role in the capture of Vicksburg, especially in thwarting Confederate General Joseph E. Johnston's attempt to reinforce the citadel. Concerning the enforcement of Missouri's election law, however, Lincoln promised to ensure that only those eligible to vote could do so.[19]

Apparently, soon after their meeting with the president, the Radicals concluded that they had failed to convince him of their diagnosis and remedy for the troubles in Missouri and had returned home rather downcast. Lincoln's later written response confirmed their conclusion and effectively ended their efforts to undermine Schofield's authority. Interestingly, Drake quickly changed tactics, visiting Schofield on October 24 and requesting that he modify an order enforcing Missouri's election law. Having gained the president's support, Schofield probably secretly enjoyed refusing Drake's request.[20]

Before the election on November 3, Lincoln, in addition to the complaints of the Radicals, had received letters from other Missourians requesting that he protect the political process and enforce Missouri election law. One of the regions where trouble was expected was in Buchanan County in northwestern

Missouri. Just north of the counties evacuated by General Thomas Ewing Jr.'s General Orders No. 11, Radicals accused Gamble of arming former Confederate soldiers and other disloyal persons to interfere with the right of legal voters to cast their ballots. While he doubted the veracity of these accusations, Lincoln still requested that Schofield look into the matter and ensure that Missouri's election laws were enforced, that only those eligible voted, and that soldiers in no way interfered with the balloting.[21]

Just prior to the election, Schofield issued two general orders in which he warned soldiers and civilians alike not to interfere with the right of anyone to assemble and express their political opinions or to attempt to intimidate voters or stop the voting in any way. Violators would be tried by court-martial or military commission. Schofield also warned election judges that they were responsible for ensuring that only persons eligible could vote and provided them with the ordinance of the state convention passed on June 10, 1862, to guide them. "Any action on their part excluding qualified voters from the polls, or admitting those who are not qualified as stated, will be punished as a military offense." Schofield also ordered that all troops were to be absent from the polls and in camp on the day of the election unless they were needed to provide security. He also sternly warned commanders that they would be held responsible for any misbehavior of their troops. Soldiers were to vote in camp at their company polls in accordance with state law. Because of the concern for security at some of the polling sites, such as those in Buchanan County, Schofield ordered commanders to take the precaution of stationing troops on election day where they could protect the election judges and voters.[22]

The election, which was primarily to choose new judges for the Supreme Court of Missouri, was conducted with only a few reported problems. Most of these complaints concerned claims, which (even if all were true) were minor incidents involving only a few individuals being prevented from voting. In one instance, a private soldier of the 7th Cavalry Missouri State Militia against orders had entered Sedalia on the day of the election and sought to prevent loyal men from voting for the "Copperhead ticket." Private Harmon Teppencamp, according to the record of his trial before a military commission, went so far as to tear up Alfred Forbes's ticket. For his actions, Teppencamp was sentenced to six months' hard labor with a ball and chain attached to his left leg. However, because this type of thing was exceptional, Schofield was able to report to Lincoln six days after the election that it had "passed off in perfect quiet and good order. . . . The prospects of future peace in this State are highly encouraging."[23]

Soon after the election of November 3, 1863, the state legislature convened in special session to elect two United States senators. Once again the Radicals and Conservatives struggled for preeminence, but neither held a majority and each must either compromise with the other or with the Democrats. In conversation with Illinois Congressman Elihu B. Washburne, Schofield expressed the opinion that the Conservatives and Radicals so disliked one another that little chance existed that they would ever conclude a deal. This assumption led Schofield to write to Conservative candidate James O. Broadhead asking him to withdraw his name from consideration. Not long after, another Conservative, John B. Henderson, and a Radical, B. Gratz Brown, were chosen, ending the controversy. Nevertheless, after returning to Washington D.C., Washburne reported to Lincoln that Schofield had opposed cooperation between the Radicals and Conservatives and had used his influence to oppose the election of Brown. This report, according to his secretary John Hay, "displeased" the president very much. Moreover, Brown reported to Lincoln that Schofield opposed the convening of a new convention for the purpose of drafting a new state constitution. These reports led to Lincoln's decision to summon Schofield to the White House.[24]

In his account of the White House meeting, Schofield claimed that after Lincoln heard his version of his conversation with Washburne, the president immediately believed him, stating that "I believe you, Schofield; those fellows have been lying to me again." Nevertheless, it became clear to Lincoln that a controversy was about to erupt concerning Schofield's interference with the legislature, in which both sides would accuse the other of misrepresentations. Such a circumstance, the president was convinced, "will create an additional amount of trouble, not to be overcome by even a correct decision of the question. [Therefore] the question itself must be avoided." Thus, Lincoln agreed to remove Schofield, but not before promoting him to major general. With the promotion, the president could then appoint him to another command. However, the president considered it impossible to gain the United States Senate's consent without the support of Brown. To break this impasse, Lincoln agreed to appoint Rosecrans to the Department of the Missouri and Curtis to the Department of the Kansas, two appointments

Brown and the Radicals wanted very much, in return for Brown supporting Schofield's promotion. A short time later, after agreeing to these terms,
Brown secretly schemed to organize opposition against Schofield among fellow senators by providing to Massachusetts Senator Charles Sumner a radical protest to the appointment. This led Lincoln to comment, after learning
of it, that he was "very much disappointed at Brown. . . . [and considered it]
rather a mean dodge to get Sumner to do it in his stead." Thus matters stood
until the command of the Department and Army of the Ohio became available and General Ulysses S. Grant requested that it be filled by either James B.
McPherson or Schofield. When General Halleck asked him whether such a
position might be to his liking, Schofield replied: "That is exactly what I
want; nothing in the world could be better." He then went to the president
and expressed his desire for the position, even at the cost of losing his promotion. Lincoln enthusiastically agreed to this plan, noting that thus the
Missouri problem was solved. Soon thereafter, the order was published announcing William S. Rosecrans as the new commander of the Department
of the Missouri.[25]

In a letter to Secretary of War Edwin M. Stanton, Lincoln admitted that
the appointments of Rosecrans and Curtis were not "in a purely military
point of view . . . indispensable, or perhaps, advantageous." Lincoln had offered this concession to Stanton who considered Rosecrans insubordinate
for refusing to obey orders promptly to attack the army under Confederate
General Braxton Bragg at Chattanooga during the Vicksburg campaign. This
attack would have brought relief to General Ulysses S. Grant's forces at an
opportune time when forces under Confederate General Joseph E. Johnston
were then attempting to break the siege of Vicksburg. After his victory, Grant
was appointed commander of the Military Division of the Mississippi. Given
the choice to relieve Rosecrans, Grant readily accepted the appointment of
General George H. Thomas in his stead. Thus, by the end of 1863 Rosecrans
was without a command, a circumstance which presented Lincoln with a
problem because of Rosecrans's influential connections in Congress. At the
same time that a suitable replacement for Schofield was needed, Ohio Congressman James A. Garfield was lobbying Lincoln to find another command
for Rosecrans. And so, over the opposition of both Halleck and Stanton,
Lincoln appointed Rosecrans to command of the Department of the Missouri
and in so doing solved a pair of problems, which only a short time before had

seemed insoluble. At this turn of events, Lincoln expressed to Schofield his satisfaction, saying, "Why Schofield, that cuts the knot, don't it? Tell Halleck to come over here."[26]

On January 29, 1864, Rosecrans arrived in St. Louis and remained only a short time before traveling to Nashville, Tennessee, to testify before courts of inquiry into the actions of some of his subordinates at the Battle of Chickamauga. Returning to Missouri, Rosecrans investigated the circumstances of his new command and considered the posts and fortifications, the resources, and the troops available for its defense. Believing that more troops were necessary for Missouri's security, Rosecrans immediately requested that two infantry and four cavalry regiments be sent to him, which he preferred over Missouri troops. Upon the arrival of these federal forces, he intended to disband the twenty-five hundred enrolled and provisional Missouri militiamen then operating in the field, although he hoped that many of these could be persuaded to enlist in the United States service. The elimination of militia forces, Rosecrans believed, would be best, for outsiders would do "justice to all parties . . . nor [be] interested in local politics." However, he soon learned that his request for out-of-state troops was denied, for the military situation in Missouri was considered stable. To understand Rosecrans's request, it is necessary to consider the various reports he received concerning the circumstance of Missouri's militia forces.[27]

Rosecrans's early views concerning the need to replace militia forces with United States troops was probably strongly influenced by various reports of the misbehavior of militia. While by the time Rosecrans accepted command in Missouri, most of the out-of-state forces were gone, having been ordered to other regions, there still existed the problem of troops from Kansas crossing the border and committing depredations. These out-of-state forces, just like Missouri's militia, were tainted by their participation in local affairs and their harboring of past wrongs. While on patrol, Kansas cavalry forces sometimes treated civilians roughly, especially if they believed them to be disloyal. If the patrol was led by a Radical, any slaveholders or persons supporting the peculiar institution were often treated as Rebels or southern sympathizers, even though many of them were opposed to secession. In addition to plundering whatever valuable property was available, when the opportunity presented itself these patrols also stole slaves or encouraged them to escape to Kansas. Other patrols, although less dogmatic in their opposition to slavery, were often motivated by a desire to avenge the Lawrence massacre, for which they believed themselves justified in their looting and threatening of Missourians. Sometimes, as Assistant Adjutant General O. D. Greene expressed it, both Kansas and Missouri patrols were "guilty of tyrannical excesses toward citizens."[28]

Missouri's militia forces, however, seemed to be motivated in their commission of "excesses" more by local politics or other internal considerations. Their depredations could be as serious as those committed by Kansas troops, especially when a militia force, primarily composed of Radicals or Conservatives, was garrisoned in a community of the opposite political faction. As noted above in this chapter, this factionalism was intense and led to much bickering and animosity between Conservative and Radical Unionists. After the Radicals had failed to persuade Lincoln to remove Governor Gamble and General Schofield, the legislature, then under the Radicals' control, passed a resolution in early December 1863 to form a committee "to investigate the management and conduct of the Missouri State Militia, the Missouri Enrolled Militia, and the Provisional Regiments, and all other State organizations of Militia." While justifying this investigation on the grounds that the militia had been organized and led in direct violation of Missouri's constitution and laws and contrary to War Department orders, the transcripts of the numerous interviews demonstrate that the Radicals on the committee, comprising seven of its nine members, were primarily interested in condemning the actions of Conservative military and political leaders and promoting the radical agenda.[29]

It seems unlikely that General Rosecrans ignored this report, although, given its length of over four hundred pages, he probably tasked a member of his staff to read and summarize its contents for him. The report goes far toward explaining his disenchantment with Missouri's militia forces. Interestingly, however, in contradiction to the committee's professed objective of investigating violations of state law, some of the interviews demonstrated that the Radical majority objected to the enforcement of laws they disliked. For instance, one section of the report focused upon the use of the Enrolled Missouri Militia to catch fugitive slaves, which remained one of the state militia's responsibilities until General Schofield was given command over them and intervened, ending their slave-catching activities in the summer of 1863. In particular, it is clear that the Radicals resented Governor Gamble's refusal to place the Enrolled Missouri Militia under the authority of Radical General Curtis earlier that year. While documenting the enforcement of Missouri's slave law, such as in refusing to recognize free papers illegally issued to African Americans, the majority also revealed their strong commitment to abolition, even when their devotion tended to promote lawlessness and in some cases anarchy. Moreover, the majority on the committee expended a good deal of energy finding examples of officers and soldiers opposed to the recruitment of African Americans as troops, although in the end they found few instances of actual violations of the law.[30]

Another aspect of the majority's Radical agenda revealed in the report was the criticism of Conservative Governor Gamble's use of his authority as commander in chief of state forces to remove Radical officers, to refuse to replace Conservative officers, and the appointment of former southern sympathizers. The committee accused the governor of removing Radicals for no other reason than their political beliefs. Nevertheless, no evidence was presented showing that the governor had abused his power or acted beyond the limits of his authority. The Radicals also criticized General Schofield for enforcing the fifth article of war, a provision which they also disliked, in which soldiers were prohibited from criticizing the president, vice president, the Congress, and the governors and legislatures of states. For this, the committee in its majority report complained that Schofield sought "to muzzle the voices [of militiamen] in the exercise of their rights as citizens, in discussing the political necessities of their own State, which they suppose themselves to be entitled to govern according to their own intelligence and old-fashioned notions about civil freedom in a republic!" This complaint, in particular, is odd given the long-standing practice of limiting the rights of soldiers, especially during wartime. These restraints upon the soldiery are necessary for the civilian and military leadership to maintain proper discipline and control over the troops. The partisan nature of the majority's report is also revealed in its inclusion of the reports of both Charles D. Drake and James Taussig, both of whom had led Radical delegations to Washington D.C., to urge that Lincoln adopt radical measures in Missouri.[31]

In their minority report, the two Conservative members of the committee, Joseph Davis and R. B. Palmer, provided a succinct summary of events in Missouri from the time of Governor Claiborne F. Jackson's inaugural to contextualize much which had happened in Missouri. In their summary, the minority detailed the difficulties of Governor Gamble's position, listing some of the personal sacrifices he had made to prevent secession and how he had been severely criticized by the majority. Davis and Palmer also noted that the Radical Republicans had opposed Governor Gamble despite his attempts to compromise on the issue of slavery and to support the president. In the matter of appointing and removing officers from the militia and federal forces, Davis and Palmer remarked that the governor from the beginning of the war had appointed at a bare minimum 2,280 officers. The minority also observed that these appointments were made from "every county in the State, and unavoidably in most cases [relied] upon the information of others." Moreover, in reviewing the interviews of removed Radical officers it was noted that one of these officers candidly admitted that his participation in a political meeting would cost him his commission and that he would deserve it, while it was clear that others were sacked because of "bad conduct." No evidence existed that the governor had sought to remove Radical officers for any reason other than for incompetence or the disobedience of orders. One of the most serious charges against the governor concerned the use of former Confederate soldiers, who had returned to Missouri, sworn oaths of allegiance to the state and national governments, and had enlisted in the militia service. According to the Radicals, this policy was dangerous to the security of the state. However, from the testimony published in the report it was clear that the so-called Paw-Paw regiments had done much good service and certainly had not engaged in more wrongdoing than other militia units. In summing up their conclusions, the minority stated that one must remember that from the beginning of his choice by the state convention Governor Gamble had confronted a very difficult situation in which "anarchy bore sway and a deep gloom had seized upon the hearts and hopes of the loyal portion of our people." From this circumstance he had established "a regularly organized government" and had returned order to most of the state where the courts again operated and the people were free to pursue their interests. This, Palmer and Davis believed, was not an accident, but instead was evidence of wise governance and vigorous opposition to the rebellion. Indeed, they believed that "it is a standing commendation of the energy and forecast with which our military affairs have been conducted. It is a silent rebuke to the murmurings of malcontents amongst us."[32]

While it is unclear exactly when the report to the Missouri House of Representatives was published, it probably was available to Rosecrans sometime in late February or early March. If so, this publication went far in explaining his negative view concerning the militia and his wish to replace them with federal forces. It was clear from the report that many of the problems in Missouri resulted from the awkward command structure, where the state was "governed by too many different and conflicting authorities." Under Rosecrans the state was divided into five districts controlled by subordinates and further subdivided into several subdistricts. While the district commander was in overall control, his authority was undercut because the provost marshal and assistant provost marshals remained directly answerable to the provost marshal general and often received orders "independently of, and in many instances without the knowledge of" the district commander. This unwieldy structure was further complicated in the governor's retention of some control over the enrolled and provisional militia, which he could either order into the field or recall. Thus, it is understandable that Rosecrans sought to transform militia forces into United States troops who would all be under his absolute authority.[33]

Perhaps hoping to escape these problems by taking the field in active operations, to Secretary of War Stanton Rosecrans proposed "sweep[ing] the country west of the Mississippi to the Gulf." Another alternative was to drive Confederate forces south of the Arkansas River or occupy southern Missouri to prevent guerrilla depredations against farmers who otherwise would be unable to plant their crops that spring. None of these proposals gained support, for the new General in Chief Grant considered Missouri and the region west of the Mississippi River of secondary importance and he was willing to accept the possibility of fields remaining unplanted and some guerrilla activity in southern Missouri for the indefinite future. He believed that focusing instead upon the destruction of the Confederate armies in the East was far more important than attending to what were primarily mopping-up operations in the West. Once the remaining major Confederate armies were destroyed, men and resources could be shifted westward to complete the pacification of Missouri. However, this strategy required stripping to bare bones all forces from other commands, including those from Missouri.[34]

Given these priorities, Rosecrans soon turned to the less heroic work of providing greater security to Missouri with the men and resources he had. One of his first concerns was the reorganization of the provost-marshal system and the appointment of a new provost marshal general and assistant provost marshals, men from other states who would bring to their duties sound judgment and none of the local prejudices and animosities often harbored by Missourians. While both Stanton and Halleck agreed with the policy of appointing persons without ties to Missouri, in the end the need for competent officers elsewhere placed Rosecrans's request very low on their, and more importantly Grant's, list of priorities. With Missouri divided into five military districts, Missouri's new commander ordered that each be divided into subdistricts over which an assistant provost marshal was placed. This arrangement meant that a provost marshal general, five district provost marshals, and numerous assistant provost marshals were given the primary duty of administering martial law and maintaining peace in the state. These men were stationed in towns and cities where they could ensure military law was enforced with the support of local militia and federal forces.[35]

The choice of provost marshal general was particularly important, and from the beginning Rosecrans had in mind John P. Sanderson for the position. Sanderson was a Pennsylvania politician who had parleyed his friendship with Lincoln's first secretary of war, Simon Cameron, into a colonelcy. Both Stanton and Assistant Secretary of War Charles A. Dana were opposed to Sanderson's appointment. Despite their opposition, after Rosecrans interceded directly with the president, Lincoln ordered Sanderson's appointment on February 22, 1864. On March 4, Rosecrans announced Sanderson as the new provost marshal general and Lieutenant Colonel A. Jacobson of the 27th Missouri Volunteers as his assistant. Located in "a large three story double brick building," the headquarters of the provost marshal general housed a large staff of over forty persons already knowledgeable and experienced in their jobs. While confident of his ability to handle the new position, Sanderson was surprised to learn "of the extent of the operations of the business devolving upon me. . . . The Provost Marshal of this Department is now, in the present condition, in truth, a power, and has devolving upon him an enormous amount of duty, responsibility, & patronage." He also soon discovered that the duties were difficult, requiring long hours and "all the mind, energy, skill, tact, & talent I can command."[36]

With his team in place, Rosecrans still confronted formidable problems as commander of the Department of the Missouri. The state militia, which he had hoped either to convert into United States troops or to replace, was under both his command and the command of Governor Willard P. Hall, who had become the state's chief executive after Governor Hamilton R. Gamble's death in late January 1864. How well such an arrangement worked depended much upon their relationship. Thus, when Halleck and Schofield were in command, few problems emerged because of the trust they developed with Governor Gamble. At first, Rosecrans and Governor Hall apparently worked well together, although by the summer their relationship had deteriorated significantly. One of the major difficulties was the overlap of command, or as Lincoln's personal secretary John G. Nicolay described the situation in June 1864 while on a fact-finding mission in northwestern Missouri, the state was "governed by too many different and conflicting authorities." So long as the governor, department commander, the district commanders, and provost marshal general and his subordinates cooperated, command problems could be avoided. Fortunately, in the first months of Rosecrans's command, many of these problems were still in the future.[37]

Nevertheless, other problems did present themselves. One of those emerging soon after Rosecrans had taken command was the interference of the courts in military affairs. One of the issues first confronted during Schofield's command was resistance to the draft. As noted in chapter 8, some draftees sought to avoid military induction by filing applications in civil court for writs of habeas corpus. While he had the authority to suspend the privilege of the writ, initially Lincoln had allowed the applications to proceed in the courts until he judged that without his intervention the draft might be seriously delayed at a time when the United States military was in serious need of men. During this time, Schofield had established rules for Missouri, issuing General Orders No. 63 on July 7, 1863, in which he declared that Missouri's troops were to encourage the restoration of civil authority and to support civil officers in the administration of their duties, except when in so doing military security and authority might be undermined. Moreover, he warned soldiers that they would not be shielded from prosecution in the civil courts for any crimes they might commit. Rosecrans established a similar policy ordering the reading of General Orders No. 63 to every company of troops. Nevertheless, while reiterating Schofield's policy, Rosecrans also made clear that he would not allow proceedings which had been instituted to punish officers and soldiers in the exercise of their military duties, especially prosecutions instituted by "men distinguished for their sympathies with the rebellion, or, at best, for their want of sympathy with the Union cause."[38]

On March 5, 1864, five days after Rosecrans had declared his intention to shield his troops from malicious civil prosecutions, newspaper editor James Monaghan appealed to departmental headquarters for permission to proceed with a lawsuit he had brought against the commander and the provost marshal at Louisiana in northeastern Missouri. Monaghan was suing William C. Allison and David P. Dyer of the First Provisional Enrolled Missouri Militia "for false imprisonment and stopping the publication of his newspaper," the *Weekly Louisiana Union* in May 1863. According to the testimony of several persons, Monaghan was a firm supporter of the Union, although he was also adamantly opposed to emancipation. In his newspaper, he had criticized the provost marshal for his actions during the previous election. Monaghan had been arrested and his paper closed for this and other fault finding which, according to the military authorities, was designed "to break down the confidence of the people in those who are administering the Government and in the acts of the authorities to put down the rebellion." Most of the testimony, however, including that of Alexander Sharp, a brother-in-law of General Grant, supported Monaghan's claim that he was a loyal War Democrat, although opposed to many of the policies of the Lincoln administration.[39]

From May 14 until June 2, 1863, Monaghan remained in custody, a part of which was spent at the Gratiot Street Military Prison. After an investigation, the provost marshal general's office concluded that "Monaghan is an unconditional Union man in favor of crushing the Rebellion in any manner, is antirepublican but a War Democrat. Is pro-slavery in principle but truly loyal." More importantly, the report noted that Dyer, who was primarily responsible for his arrest, was a political enemy of Monaghan and that without some evidence of wrongdoing or disloyalty he should be given his "unconditional release." A day after Monaghan's release, Dyer recommended that Monaghan be banished from the state. If, indeed, Dyer had arrested the editor to silence a political enemy, then certainly Monaghan had a strong case to sue in civil court for damages.[40]

Before making a decision about Monaghan's case, Rosecrans sought the advice of General Odon Guitar, a district commander and lawyer who had practiced in Missouri for many years. Guitar replied that Monaghan had always been a loyal man and that the county, court, and jury was loyal and could be trusted to adjudicate the matter justly. He recommended that the military not interfere in the suits. This was not the end of Monaghan's travails, however, for just two months later a mob of soldiers and civilians broke into his printing office and destroyed valuable property, including his printing press worth $1,000. According to Monaghan, a soldier fired a pistol at him but missed, and another pulled the trigger of his weapon but it failed to fire. As a Union man, Monaghan demanded protection and the prosecution of the soldiers involved in the incident. Provost Marshal General Sanderson noted in the file that he had requested a report on the incident from the provost marshal there.[41]

While it seems clear that Monaghan's case against Allison and Dyer should have gone forward, two cases in the Boone County Circuit Court against Pearce Buffington, one criminal and the other civil, were different. The cases concerned Henry and Henderson Bryant, two slaves of James I. Hickman, who had fled to Jefferson City where the provost marshal gave them certificates of freedom to which they were entitled for their work in the quartermaster's department. Afterward, both worked for Buffington "at his mill near Claysville" until they enlisted in the United States service in March 1864. The grand jury of the Boone County Circuit Court "indicted Buffington for unlawfully dealing with slaves." Hickman brought suit against him for $1,276 in damages. General Clinton B. Fisk, the commander of the District of North Missouri, stopped these proceedings and wrote to Rosecrans for instructions. According to Fisk, Hickman was a Secessionist and according to a bill passed in Congress the two Bryants were free. Moreover, this case was just one of many similar cases in his district—and presumably others throughout Missouri—in which persons "had employed contrabands." Such prosecutions in state courts, it was clear, would undermine congressional law and military authority and unfairly expose both civilians and soldiers to litigation despite their operating under the new rules. Thus, James F. Dwight, acting judge-advocate, in reporting about the Buffington case noted that under the law these slaves were free and "if General Fisk is authorized to check such proceedings now, it may save much trouble and annoyance in the future."[42]

As can be ascertained from Monaghan's situation and many other incidents (about which more below), while warfare was primarily limited to clashes between Union troops and small bands of guerrillas in early 1864, keeping the peace, especially between Radicals and Conservatives, remained a challenge for Rosecrans and his forces. Despite having reorganized the provost-marshal system and placed it under the authority of Sanderson, problems remained in regions where some of the assistant provost marshals and military leaders proved to be incompetent or corrupt and where a large part of the population was sympathetic to the Confederacy. Moreover, after over two and a half years of war, past outrages were not easily forgotten, leading some to attack those who had wronged them. These animosities sometimes led to a cycle of violence such as that along the Kansas-Missouri border, where the commission of atrocities often escalated until it became very dangerous to live there. Thus, General Samuel R. Curtis, who had been appointed to command of the Department of the Kansas at the same time Rosecrans received his command, believed it was best for past wrongs to be forgotten and to "let old sores alone and attend to recent matters."[43]

However, while sounding reasonable, letting bygones be bygones proved to be difficult, especially in the midst of a bitter conflict where much distrust existed. While there were regions where the population was largely loyal and little opportunity existed for trouble such as "in Atchison, Holt, Nodaway, Andrew, Gentry, northern De Kalb, Harrison, Mercer, Daviess, [and] Grundy" counties, the majority of the state required at least some troops to protect against guerrilla attacks and to prevent violence among the people. Additionally, because of guerrilla violence and the disloyalty of a large minority, often the civil courts could not function, requiring the continued imposition of martial law and the trial of civilians before military commissions. In some instances, the population was trustworthy enough to entrust the trial of criminals before their juries and judges, although they still needed the military's help in enforcing the law and capturing outlaws.[44]

In late February 1864, Rosecrans ordered the sale of arms and ammunition restricted to loyal persons. General John C. Frémont had instituted such a measure in 1861, which had remained in force under General Henry W. Halleck until July 1862, when General John M. Schofield called out the enrolled militia to counter a major guerrilla uprising. However, despite these measures everyone recognized that many weapons remained in the hands of disloyal persons and guerrillas. While the military had some arms available in armories and forts, for the most part these militiamen provided their own weapons and were commanded to seize arms and ammunition from disloyal persons. Schofield also ordered disloyal men and southern sympathizers "to report at the nearest military post or other enrolling station . . . [and] surrender their arms." After this, various policies in the different districts were instituted including the attempt to remove all weapons from both loyal and disloyal persons in some regions. In the aftermath of the Lawrence, Kansas, massacre, Schofield intervened and ordered that "all loyal and peaceable citizens in Missouri will be permitted to bear arms." This policy seemed best, for it was clear that despite efforts to prevent weapons from falling into the hands of the disloyal, then as today such prohibitions were ineffective.[45]

Nevertheless, some sought to persuade Rosecrans that because many disloyal persons possessed arms, great danger of a general uprising existed. Fearing that Rosecrans might decide to prohibit all weapons from civilians, some political and military leaders argued that restrictions upon weapons and ammunition were futile. One aspect of the problem was that the prohibition on sales could not extend to bordering states where by 1864 all types of weapons were available, some of which were superior to those issued to federal and militia troops. In the opinion of General Guitar, who admitted to originally supporting the ban on gun ownership of disloyal persons, experience had proven that not "a solitary rebel soldier, guerrilla, thief, or marauder in Missouri [was ever found] in want of arms and ammunition." Moreover, his report and the letters of others, including the brother of the governor, Congressman William A. Hall, argued that any attempted ban would result in "law-abiding men" being unilaterally disarmed and left at the mercy of criminals and guerrillas. Therefore, while it was true that by allowing the ownership of weapons some persons could use them to disrupt the peace and support the rebellion, it was believed that many more serving as militiamen or in defending their homes would bear arms for good purposes. This seemed especially prudent given the vulnerability of unarmed persons to guerrilla attacks. After receiving conflicting advice, and recognizing that each region had differing circumstances, Rosecrans wisely left such policy decisions to district commanders, who were better informed about the character of the inhabitants and the dangers to which they were exposed. Later that summer, after a general uprising of guerrilla forces threatened the peace and prepared the way for another invasion of a Confederate army under General Sterling Price, some blamed Rosecrans and his district commanders for not having adopted measures to confiscate the weapons of disloyal persons. Given the great difficulty, if not the impossibility, of restricting the possession of arms, these criticisms were unfair and ignored the resourcefulness and ingenuity of those seeking to undermine Union control in Missouri. In his efforts to pacify the state, as seen in the next chapter, Rosecrans employed a number of measures intended to deter or punish those inclined to help the rebellion. Such policies, along with those suppressing dissent, were a continuation of methods employed by previous commanders and would have similar results as before.[46]

10

GENERAL WILLIAM S. ROSECRANS
AND PRICE'S RAID

AS HE FAMILIARIZED HIMSELF with his new command and put in place key persons of his team, General William S. Rosecrans also learned of the policies instituted by his predecessors and confronted various issues like the practicability of the civil courts taking over at least some of the cases which had formerly been adjudicated before military tribunals during the war. While small bands of guerrillas still operated intermittently in various regions, the trouble they caused was minor when considered in the context of what had transpired there before. Despite this, Rosecrans was prudent in not moving quickly to dismantle the provost-marshal system or to send home precipitously militia forces scattered throughout the state at military posts. A lessening of guerrilla activity during the winter months was normal as the guerrillas and their supporters awaited spring when the lush foliage returned, enabling bushwhackers more easily to elude Union patrols. Moreover, some of the more notorious and dangerous of the guerilla bands, including that led by William C. Quantrill, had wintered in Texas but would soon return to Missouri. Interestingly, the Confederates were anxious to see Quantrill and his band go north, for they had looted and killed Texans in the same manner they had treated Missourians and Kansans. As seen below, the renewal of guerrilla activity was coordinated by Confederate General Sterling Price to provide a diversion and to occupy at least a portion of the Union forces in preparation for a raid just prior to the fall election.[1]

Despite this period of relative calm, different problems arose which Rosecrans found necessary to address. One regarded a petition asking the military to help "the destitute families of Rebels in Benton County." To this request, Rosecrans directed that those persons suffering within Missouri should be sent "to their natural protectors beyond our lines if practicable," although he also conceded that under some circumstances common humanity might

require furnishing aid to the friends of enemies. As department commander
he also reviewed banishment orders. In one instance, Rosecrans modified the
banishment order of an elderly woman who had sought to help a prisoner,
Otho Hinton, escape from custody. The decision was made to send her to
Indiana where two of her brothers lived, despite her willingness, as she expressed it, to have the guard murdered to free the prisoner. In another case,
Rosecrans was less lenient toward a Mrs. Ward of St. Louis. She had been banished from Missouri to the region east of Illinois and north of the Ohio River.
Despite this, she had traveled to Washington D.C., which was not within the
area designated for her exile, and had gained an interview with the president.
Lincoln telegraphed Rosecrans stating that she wished to be allowed to return
to her home and was willing to take the oath of allegiance and post a bond for
her good behavior. The president requested that Rosecrans look into the matter. The next day he replied that strong opposition existed against her return
and that her case was "a very bad one." For this reason he declined to allow her
to return.[2]

Other matters of importance were the regulation of travel and trade in
and out of the department. In August 1861, Provost Marshal Justus McKinstry
instituted a system in which only persons acquiring passes from his office
could travel in and out of St. Louis County (see chapter 2). Soon after taking command, General Henry W. Halleck discontinued this passport system,
declaring it unnecessary, only requiring passes for persons crossing military
lines (see chapter 3). In December 1862, General Samuel R. Curtis, recognizing that disloyal persons were conveying various supplies, weapons and ammunition, and military intelligence to the enemy, sought to restrict trade and
travel to loyal persons. Lincoln approved these restrictions after Secretary of
the Treasury Salmon P. Chase had investigated complaints against the policy
and found evidence of smuggling by disloyal persons (see chapters 6 and 7).
As noted in chapter 9, General Rosecrans turned his attention primarily to
restricting the sale of arms and ammunition, which, according to reports, was
getting into the hands of disloyal persons. He also supported the decision of
some provost marshals to prevent the sale of liquor. Moreover, in southern
Missouri Rosecrans sought to stop trade with rebels in Arkansas.[3]

Another policy continued during Rosecrans's command was the practice
of arresting persons speaking out against Lincoln, his administration, and its
policies. Most of the time, a detective or soldier arrested civilians who were

overheard expressing themselves in a public place. Often they spoke out when they were drunk or in an argument with a neighbor or acquaintance, who then reported the statement to authorities. Most of these persons were without any influence and their arrests in retrospect seem unnecessary today. Most were released soon after their arrest, upon taking the oath of allegiance and posting a bond. Moreover, some arrests resulted more from the strong animosity between Conservative and Radical Unionists than from any real disloyalty expressed. These arrests invariably were instigated by Radicals against Conservatives. A prominent example of this was the detainment of a congressman and brother of the governor, William A. Hall, who had served as a delegate to the state convention in March and April 1861. As part of the committee on foreign relations, Hall had supported the majority report rejecting secession and during the convention's July 1861 session had served on the committee that had recommended the ouster of the state government under Governor Claiborne F. Jackson.[4]

According to eyewitness accounts, a soldier of the First Iowa was seated on a train behind Hall, who was in conversation with another man. The soldier claimed to have overheard Hall criticize the president's policies as more destructive to the government than those of Jefferson Davis, the president of the Confederacy. Isaac Gannett, provost marshal at Mexico, reported to Provost Marshal General John P. Sanderson that although Hall had been a firm supporter of the Union at the beginning of the war,

> for some time past he has been sliding away from the morings [sic] of a true patriot and he at present is of that party that are so strongly opposed to the administration that they think Jeff Davis but little inferior if not superior to President Lincoln. Hall is an influential man in these parts and therefore the language he used at the Depot in this place (which I firmly believe he did use and which he does not deny) is the more disloyal because of its influance [sic].

However, testimony of others who also overheard the conversation disagreed with the soldier's account. Gannett, who was a lieutenant of the Seventh Kansas Cavalry and a supporter of Radical policies such as emancipation and the use of African-American regiments, wrongly asserted (whether purposely or mistakenly) that Hall had never denied the charge against him, and

Gannett probably regarded Congressman Hall to be disloyal for his support of slavery and his political opposition to the Radicals. Whatever the motivation for his arrest, Hall was not held for long, likely in part because the accusation against him was contradicted by Hall himself and others, and partly because Governor Hall had written to Rosecrans requesting him to intervene in his brother's case.[5]

Another civil liberties issue with which General Rosecrans was confronted after taking command in Missouri concerned the press. James L. Fawcett, former editor of the *St. Louis Herald,* requested that the order suppressing his newspaper be rescinded. Fawcett had served as one of the secretaries of the 1860 Democratic state convention, which had nominated Claiborne F. Jackson as its gubernatorial candidate. In 1861, before General John C. Frémont had ordered Fawcett to stop publication, the paper had gained the reputation as "a half-starved secession bantam." Because of its financial problems, some suspected that Fawcett had purposely provoked Frémont to shut down the paper's printing operation and thus "avoid forfeiture of bond money on a city printing contract it had failed to fulfill." In reply to Fawcett's request, Rosecrans directed that the publication of the *Herald* be allowed to resume "so long as it shall appear to be truly loyal in its tone and sentiment, of which the major-general commanding (or higher military authority) will judge." He also warned that he would suppress any paper that published articles "tending to weaken the military power of the nation by exciting resistance to the constituted authorities." These stipulations, in practice, despite Rosecrans's obligatory promise not to interfere in political questions, if strictly enforced would have effectually prohibited criticism of his command and the Lincoln administration. A short time later, Rosecrans published General Orders No. 38 in which he rescinded all orders "prohibiting the sale or distribution of any newspaper or periodical" within the department. Moreover, he commanded that any order suppressing a publication must first be approved by him. While one interpretation of this order might be that he had a change of heart about censorship, another more probable motivation was his desire to take this important policy decision from his district commanders. As seen below, General Orders No. 38 did not end the curtailment of the First Amendment in Missouri.[6]

In late March 1864, Provost Marshal General Sanderson ordered the suppression of the sale of pro-Confederate books and biographies of famous southern generals. Perhaps more important, little was done to punish mob violence against newspaper editors, such as James Monaghan (see chapter 9) and others. A short time after the attack upon Monaghan, another editor in the same town of Louisiana in northeastern Missouri was attacked by a mob—probably the same one responsible for the earlier attack—destroying the press. According to the account of Samuel T. Glover, a St. Louis lawyer and friend of Lincoln, the paper had endorsed the president for reelection. Glover believed that the Radicals from Missouri were conspiring to gain Treasury Secretary Chase's nomination at the upcoming convention and were instigating violence against Conservatives. These same events were reported by James O. Broadhead, another friend of Lincoln from St. Louis and former provost marshal general, although he feared that the president would do nothing to help or protect his supporters. According to Attorney General Edward Bates, to whom Broadhead had sent his letter, after reading about the atrocities committed in Missouri the president "seemed deeply moved, but said not a word." Moreover, Bates claimed to have been fighting daily for the rule of law with the military authorities who had arbitrarily wielded power and trampled upon the law. "The President can *see,* as well as any man, what is good for his country. O! that he could *act* as well as *see*! But men do tell us that '*Hell* itself is paved with good int[ent]ions!! He wishes well to his Country, but lacks the faculty to control—the *will* to punish the abuses of his power, which, rampant & unrebuked, are rapidly bring[ing] him & his good cause, to sorrow & shame." Still unclear, if these accounts and Lincoln's reaction to them are true, are the reasons for his failure to intervene in Missouri's affairs yet again. At least in part, Lincoln was probably trying to avoid becoming again ensnared in the highly partisan politics of Missouri. Another consideration may have been his wish not to offer any reason for the Radicals to take further offense at his policies in the months leading up to the presidential election. That Lincoln was very concerned about his prospects in Missouri is evident, for at different times in 1864 he sent his personal secretaries to the state to learn about the circumstances and attitudes there. Moreover, in doling out patronage and public offices, such as administration advertisements to newspapers and positions like postmaster, Lincoln warned that only those publications and persons supporting his reelection and other candidates of the Union Party could benefit from governmental largess.[7]

At approximately the same time that he was handling matters relating to freedom of speech and the press, General Rosecrans found himself managing another First Amendment issue, the guarantee to the free exercise of one's faith. As noted in chapter 6, President Lincoln had intervened when General Samuel R. Curtis sought to remove disloyal ministers from their churches. At first, Lincoln had expressed his opinion that the government should not be running the churches, and while he did not explicitly order Curtis to reinstate Samuel B. McPheeters as minister of the Presbyterian church in St. Louis, the clear corollary to his advice was that the pastor should be allowed to resume his ministry. Thus, believing that the matter had been resolved, Lincoln was genuinely surprised to learn in late 1863 that some in McPheeters's congregation were petitioning to allow him to resume his ministry. If, after ordering McPheeters's return to the pulpit, Lincoln had expected this to be the end of religious controversies in Missouri, the president was disappointed, for soon another order, this time from the War Department, gave extraordinary authority to Bishop Ames, a Methodist-Episcopal Church North minister, to replace ministers of the Methodist-Episcopal Church South with those he considered loyal in the departments of the Missouri, the Tennessee, and the Gulf. According to the order, departmental commanders were "expected to give him all the aid, countenance, and support practicable in the execution of his important mission." This measure, it was hoped, would "restore tranquility to the community and peace to the nation."[8]

Learning of this order, on February 11, 1864, Lincoln wrote to Secretary of War Edwin M. Stanton explaining his action in the McPheeters case and quoting his own strong statements eschewing any intention or desire to interfere with or run the churches. Unfortunately, this latest order from the War Department instituted a different policy and caused Lincoln much "embarrassment," as he described it. Not wishing to revoke Stanton's order peremptorily, the president asked the secretary, "What is to be done about it?" The next day, while the War Department considered how to respond, Bishop Ames arrived in St. Louis and presented his commission to General Rosecrans. Being ignorant of what had transpired the year before and more recently, in an effort to bring his command into compliance with the War Department directive, he promptly issued a circular ordering his subordinates to report all Methodist-Episcopal Churches South within their commands where disloyal ministers still presided. This circular, perhaps, accelerated the speed with which the War Department responded, for on February 13 Rosecrans received a note from Lincoln, hand delivered by Congressman John Hogan, explaining that the Ames directive was not intended to be operative in Missouri. Despite this, on February 28 Rosecrans had still not revoked his circular and wrote to Stanton asking for clarification of the government's policy. Presumably, Stanton or a subordinate promptly notified him of the order's revocation. Nevertheless, before the president had corrected the secretary of war's mistake, the Stanton-Ames order was strongly condemned as an abuse of military power. As one critic asked: "Where is the end to be? and what principle of American constitutional law will remain if freedom of religion and of conscience is at the mercy of any commander of a military post ?"[9]

Just days after resolving the question of Bishop Ames's authority over the Methodist-Episcopal Church South in Missouri, Rosecrans requested his provost marshal general to devise a policy by which to ensure the loyalty of the members of "religious convocations . . . whose function is to teach religion and morality to the people." This, he believed, could be accomplished by requiring that members of such assemblages "give satisfactory evidence of their loyalty to the Government of the United States" in some manner. Apparently, reports had reached Rosecrans of a conspiracy to use an upcoming denominational meeting "ostensibly for ecclesiastical purposes, but really and truly to aid the rebellion by bringing the rebel leaders" from the South into Missouri. In order to thwart this plot, on March 7 Provost Marshal General Sanderson issued Special Orders No. 61 requiring the members of all religious convocations to certify to the local provost marshal that everyone participating had sworn to a loyalty oath. Military authorities determining that a conference was not in compliance with this provision were to disband it immediately. Moreover, assistant provost marshals were ordered to attend the meetings of these conferences and inform members of the new regulation.[10]

Opposition to Special Orders No. 61 arose after its publication and soon came to the attention of Lincoln. The most cogent objection to it was that all serving ministers in Missouri had already sworn allegiance to Missouri and the United States as citizens, but this oath was required of them as "church officers" and therefore was unacceptable. Unintentionally, it seems, Rosecrans had violated the spirit, although not the letter, of Lincoln's main objection to the Stanton-Ames order and was inadvertently and unnecessarily interfering in the affairs of the Church. Moreover, if allowed to stand, Special Orders No. 61 could end in many loyal preachers refusing to swear the required oath as a matter of conscience. Thus, it was argued, thoroughly loyal men would soon be prohibited from serving Christ, a prohibition only He had authority to enforce. From Lincoln's April 4, 1864, letter to Rosecrans, it is clear that although the president was not altogether convinced by this argument, he wished to avoid such a showdown and believed that other objections to the order were more compelling. One of these stemmed from a basic understanding of human psychology, the reluctance of loyal men, who had never before been accused of disloyalty, to swear an oath as a requirement for the enjoyment of their civil liberties. Moreover, Lincoln noted that Rosecrans's order also had the unintended consequence of exposing the government and military to the charge "that while men may without an oath assemble in a noisy political meeting, they must take the oath to assemble in a religious meeting." In this way, without ordering Rosecrans directly, Lincoln communicated his desire to have Special Orders No. 61 modified. In compliance with the president's wish, assistant provost marshals no longer attended religious meetings and only those ministers who had not previously sworn a loyalty oath were required to swear to the new oath.[11]

During the winter and spring of 1864, the varied and difficult issues concerning slavery and the treatment of African Americans in Missouri continued to be a source of friction between Radical and Conservative Unionists and between the military and civil authorities. Moreover, with large numbers of runaways, many of whom were sick and destitute—especially among women, children, and the elderly—a humanitarian crisis presented to the authorities problems not easily solved. From the beginning of the war, fugitive slaves had come into Union military lines and had been employed as workers building trenches and fortifications. In July 1862 Congress passed a law freeing all slaves employed in this manner by the military. In Missouri, reluctant to undermine Unionist support among slaveholders and other proslavery loyalists, Lincoln refused to allow interference with the institution of slavery there. Over time, however, as the war progressed and Missouri became secure for the Union many persons, including the president, became convinced that the abolition of slavery would hasten the war's end. In response to this change in circumstances, Congress passed laws providing for the emancipation of those slaves who had been employed in the Confederate war effort or were owned by persons who had aided and abetted the rebellion. While the Emancipation Proclamation of January 1, 1863, only freed those slaves in regions still in rebellion, which did not include Missouri, by June of that year the state convention had passed a bill providing for their gradual emancipation. In November, after some hesitation by the War Department and Lincoln, the United States military issued an order authorizing the recruitment of all suitable African Americans regardless of their owners' status.[12]

After many slaves had fled from Missouri to other states, the number of African Americans available to meet the needs of labor and the United States military was reduced significantly. For this reason, General Schofield in November 1863 ordered that slaves not be permitted to leave Missouri. Nevertheless, soon after taking command in late January 1864, General Rosecrans allowed women and children and African American men unfit for military service to leave the state if their owner was loyal. Apparently, this measure was operative until March 1 when the department commander repealed it, justifying the change in policy by noting the labor shortage, the smuggling trade of stolen slaves and kidnapped free blacks, and the need for African American soldiers.[13]

Under General Rosecrans's command the efforts to recruit African Americans were intensified. This occurred because of the increasing need for troops and the slow progress in raising African-American regiments. This explains Congress's interest in learning why the War Department was not enrolling slaves for the draft in loyal states like Missouri in late 1863. Secretary of War Stanton explained that enrollment for the draft under the congressional act of March 3, 1863, pertained only to "citizens of the United States" and therefore under the current law slaves could not be enrolled, citing the Dred Scott decision, which had ruled that slaves were not citizens. As this decision was then still in force, and Congress had not included slaves as part of those liable to enrollment, the War Department could not enroll them. Of course, slaves were able to enlist voluntarily and many were enthusiastic about the opportunity, for in return for their service they received freedom for themselves and their families. To maximize the number of blacks recruited in Missouri, Schofield, as already noted in chapter 8, gained permission to allow recruiters to enlist slaves of both loyal and disloyal masters. Before this, loyal masters could refuse to allow their slaves to serve in the military. Still, even after losing the power to prevent their slaves from enlisting, loyal masters had the advantage over their disloyal counterparts in that they were eligible for a $300 bounty paid as compensation for the loss of their property.[14]

Despite the inducements to slaves and their masters to join the United States military, some recruiters encountered opposition to their efforts. Guerrilla activity also increased as those most adamantly opposed to emancipation and the employment of black soldiers "went to the brush" or provided aid to others who did. Those who threatened recruiters and provided support to bushwhackers were sometimes arrested, as in the case of John Watson, who lived near Glasgow and had threatened to "feed and hire Bushwackers to kill all such men [recruiters]." Watson was arrested and imprisoned at the state penitentiary in Jefferson City and later transferred to the Myrtle Street Prison, where he remained at least until April 11, 1865. Because of these threats, some provost marshals, who were given the major responsibility of overseeing the recruitment efforts, requested more troops to protect the recruiters and families of slaves, some of whom were being sold or mistreated by their former owners.[15]

While opposition to voluntary enlistments was not permitted, the tactics of some recruiters in forcing slaves and free blacks into military service violated the law. Thus complaints about these impressments were investigated. While some of the reports proved to be untrue, others were substantiated and arrests were made. Such was the circumstance of Washington, a slave owned by Curtis F. Wells. In a sworn affidavit, Wells testified that Captain Lucas at Paynesville had arrested his slave and was "kept in camp by force Contrary to Law and Orders." According to Joseph Mclean, a member of the local county committee, Wells, a loyal man whose son had served in the army from the war's beginning, had no objection to his slave Washington, who was unwilling, serving as well. Moreover, Mclean claimed that several other slaves had been impressed into military service. Other instances of lawlessness associated with the recruitment of black soldiers occurred, as in the instance of a slave owner, Washington Watts. Although willing to allow his slaves to enlist, the local garrison prevented him from taking home two of his slaves, who had been rejected as unfit for the service, helping them to run away. Such behavior tended to undermine support for the enlistment of slaves and led to complaints, some of which had reached Lincoln. In a letter to Rosecrans, the president noted that "it is complained that the enlistment of negroes is not conducted in as orderly a manner, and with as little collateral provocation, as it might be." Nevertheless, Lincoln reassured Rosecrans that he considered his handling of this and other matters to have been "better than I had dared to hope." Fortunately by August 1864, these "provocation[s]" soon largely came to an end, when almost every African American fit for service had been recruited, comprising from four and a half to five black regiments, and it was estimated that at best enough men might be found to fill one more regiment. This recruitment had reduced the number of black laborers in Missouri to such an extent that labor costs had risen dramatically.[16]

After a period of relative calm during the first months of Rosecrans's command in Missouri, guerrilla activity began to increase during the spring, although many of these depredations were committed by small bands. As had been the case throughout the war, because of the difficulty of identifying who the guerrillas were, these bands were difficult to eradicate. This problem was especially challenging where a majority of the population was composed of southern sympathizers who supported the guerrillas. These supporters often allowed them to camp upon their property, fed the guerrillas and their horses, and provided information concerning the location and movements of Union troops during their stay. Moreover, after displaying oaths of allegiance some captured guerrillas were able to convince Unionists of their loyalty and gain their release. The oath similarly shielded guerrillas in Kentucky.[17]

To stop their activities, the troops under Rosecrans employed a number of the usual methods. As noted in the introduction and earlier chapters, guerrillas captured in the act of committing depredations were often summarily executed, a policy Lincoln officially approved in the spring of 1863 and almost certainly knew about much earlier. In June and July 1864, a period of intensified guerrilla activity, an estimate of seventy and eighty guerrillas, respectively, were killed and "few, if any, prisoners of war of this class [were] taken." Moreover, those suspected of being guerrillas or their supporters were arrested and tried before military commissions. In these trials the court and most of the military officers acting as jurors provided due process to the defendants and rendered verdicts based upon the evidence. Thus, many of the defendants were acquitted on at least some of the charges or specifications brought against them. For those convicted, the sentences were typically proportionate to the seriousness of the crimes committed; although the death penalty was rare, incarcerations ranged from six months to life imprisonment. Sometimes imprisonment included the added penalty of hard labor or with "ball and chain." Moreover, the department commander, the judge advocate's office in the War Department, and the president exercised a routine review of cases and sometimes reduced the punishment or pardoned a prisoner. In other instances, because of some irregularity in the proceedings, the case was ordered to be retried.[18]

On June 28, 1864, recognizing that guerrilla depredations were increasing, General Rosecrans issued General Orders No. 107, in which communities were directed to establish committees of safety and county committees to organize against the guerrilla threat. He also commanded these communities to form two companies of select men from the local enrolled militia of men known for their "courage, energy, and willingness to serve." These measures were probably intended to provide greater security not only against the guerrilla threat, but also against the increasing likelihood of an invasion by a Confederate army. According to his report composed after leaving the department, "early in the spring" Rosecrans began to suspect that General Price was using guerrilla forces to gather intelligence and make other preparations for an invasion into Missouri. Another very real danger was the operation of Confederate saboteurs, who sought to disrupt traffic upon the Mississippi and Missouri rivers, which was important for the movement of supplies, soldiers, and communications. Thus, Rosecrans issued a series of general orders to protect shipping. Moreover, he took the extraordinary measure of forbidding laborers involved in the production of war goods from organizing themselves into unions and striking. Lincoln received protests against this policy but did not intervene, perhaps believing that military necessity justified Rosecrans's order.[19]

During this period, Rosecrans and Provost Marshal General Sanderson became increasingly concerned about a conspiracy which they believed sought to aid Price's expected raid. The Order of American Knights (OAK) was a secret organization claiming to have many members in the border and loyal states. Those disaffected with the war rallied under its banner, although often for varied reasons and with different purposes. To facilitate and coordinate their purpose, John H. Taylor, the supreme commander of the OAK in Missouri, ordered its members to seize weapons, ammunition, and strategic points throughout the state and to recruit and gather men to join the invading force. Taylor also appointed General Price as the overall commander of forces there. For his part, Price welcomed the help of the OAK, for his expedition was undermanned, especially in the accomplishment of its primary goal of seizing St. Louis, from where (it was hoped) the remainder of the state might be controlled with the help of southern sympathizers and guerrillas. With the war going badly, Price feared that a peace treaty might be negotiated in which Missouri would be bargained over to the Union. To prevent this, he believed it was important for the Confederacy to have control of some part of Missouri, even if it was only for a short time. If St. Louis could not be captured, the Confederate general hoped to gain possession of Jefferson City and to install Confederate Governor Thomas C. Reynolds at the governor's mansion. The Confederate governor might be there only briefly, but even this would be a propaganda victory, Price and Reynolds believed. While in Missouri, both hoped to hold an election, which they thought would be useful to legitimize Missouri's Confederate government and delegitimize the Unionist provisional government. If none of these purposes for the invading force could be achieved, at the very least Price intended to recruit into his army many southern sympathizers and members of the OAK, destroy property valuable to the enemy, and draw off Union forces which would otherwise have been sent east to reinforce the Union armies then confronting the Confederate armies in Georgia, Tennessee, Virginia, and elsewhere. Another expected ancillary benefit was the chance to hurt Lincoln and other Republican candidates in the fall election.[20]

In the months leading to Price's raid, Sanderson gathered evidence concerning the OAK and its purpose to overthrow the United States government, or at the very least to form "a northwest confederacy." This task apparently consumed the provost marshal general, who by June 22 had compiled a thousand-page report about the conspiracy. Before this, Rosecrans had requested the president to permit a trusted officer to travel to Washington D.C. to explain the conspiracy, which, as Rosecrans described it, was "of high national importance." Lincoln, who seemed to be dubious of the importance of the information, wanted it sent by express. By this time, Missouri's department commander, perhaps seeing conspirators hiding behind many, if not every door, again requested permission to send an aide. After receiving a letter from Illinois's Governor Richard Yates, Lincoln instead decided to send his personal secretary John Hay to hear what Rosecrans had to communicate. Arriving in St. Louis on June 13, Hays met with Rosecrans and Sanderson for several hours and concluded that their information was important. The next day, Rosecrans wrote to the president again explaining the plans of the OAK, which, in addition to overthrowing the government, included sabotage, espionage, acquiring military supplies for the South, and spreading false rumors. Moreover, Rosecrans again pressed the president to allow one of his aides to visit the White House and explain more fully the danger the conspiracy posed to the government. Lincoln was adamantly opposed to this, for Rosecrans was attempting to circumvent a War Department order prohibiting officers from coming to Washington D.C. without permission.[21]

Believing that the president would give a favorable response to his request, Rosecrans sent Sanderson east, where he stopped in Harrisburg, Pennsylvania, awaiting permission to proceed on to Washington D.C. While at Harrisburg, Sanderson conferred with various persons, including Pennsylvania's Governor Andrew G. Curtain. Another officer, Captain J. B. Devoe, who was apparently not prohibited from traveling to the nation's capitol, was dispatched to confer with various members of the House and Senate and to secure for Sanderson a meeting with the president. Eventually, Devoe was able to speak to Hay, who had returned to the White House, and lay before him the evidence of the OAK's conspiracy. At the time, Lincoln happened to be at the War Department and so Devoe returned the next morning and met the president with Congressman James A. Garfield. Apparently, Sanderson was not permitted to meet with the president, who by this time had concluded that Rosecrans and his provost marshal general had expended much time and trouble to uncover a conspiracy, which, while involving numerous persons in several states, was not as dangerous as the officials supposed. In summing up his conclusion concerning the OAK in the North, Lincoln stated that it was "not especially worth regarding, holding it a mere political organization with about as much of malice and as much of puerility as the Knights of the Golden Circle." In this judgment, Lincoln may have been too dismissive concerning the threat the OAK presented, for in July Sanderson's detectives infiltrated the organization further, especially in St. Louis, and arrested and gained confessions from several of the secret organization's leadership. These arrests may have crippled the organization somewhat, although many of its members were still able to help Price during his raid into Missouri.[22]

Another important incident, influencing Lincoln's judgment of Sanderson's and Rosecrans's interpretation of the circumstances in Missouri, concerned the employment of Jacob W. Terman, alias Harry Truman—no relation to President Truman—from northwest Missouri as a scout. During this time, Lincoln's secretary John G. Nicolay was in St. Joseph gathering information about security almost a year after the evacuation of much of the region by General Thomas Ewing Jr's General Orders No. 11. In a letter Nicolay explained the various difficulties still existing in Missouri and provided his own analysis of the Truman matter. Nicolay believed that Sanderson and Rosecrans had been deceived by Truman into believing that he would "be able to ferret out a great conspiracy which had for its object the capture of Hannibal, Quincy, and other points by guerrillas." They accepted his plan to collect a group of men and disguise them as guerrillas to act as spies and capture the conspirators. Unfortunately, Truman turned out "to have been a very bad character, illiterate, intemperate, immoral, and subsequently criminal." Even after receiving reports of his misdeeds, Sanderson and Rosecrans allowed Truman and his band to continue their operations, leading to the summary killing of seven men, who had not been captured with weapons or in the field. This action caused a panic among men in the region, and thirteen Union men were "murdered in retaliation." Finally, this led to Truman's arrest. This report eroded Lincoln's trust in the judgment of both Rosecrans and Sanderson, for the president apparently ordered no extraordinary measures be taken to counter the threat of the OAK. Truman, for his violation of orders and the laws of war, was tried before a military commission in November and sentenced to death. This sentence was disapproved by Rosecrans, who ordered him to be held until further orders. In March 1865, Truman was released but soon returned to his past bad behavior, resulting in his arrest again in June.[23]

While they were wrong about the extent of the OAK's influence and power, Rosecrans and Sanderson had gathered substantial evidence of Price's impending invasion. The activities of the OAK and others supporting the southern cause were then well along in their preparations. Just before he invaded Missouri, Price had sent John Chestnut and other agents "into Missouri to gather intelligence, raise recruits, and circulate propaganda." This activity increased just prior to the invasion and as Rosecrans later explained guerrilla activity in northern Missouri grew markedly and "the most cold-blooded and diabolical murders" of Union men were committed then.[24]

To meet the emergency Rosecrans raised five complete and five incomplete regiments of twelve-month men to protect against the guerrilla uprising and prepare for Price's impending invasion. To punish those supporting the guerrillas, assessments were made against southern sympathizers. On September 19, General Price with his Army of Missouri, comprising approximately twelve thousand men, entered southeastern Missouri. This force, a mix of cavalry, infantry, and artillery, moved toward St. Louis and against Price's orders looted many unfortunate Missourians along the way. After some hesitation, Price concluded that the fortifications and forces arrayed at St. Louis were too formidable for his force, and he turned his attention instead to Fort Davidson located at Pilot Knob, where one thousand militia and civilians under the command of General Thomas Ewing Jr. confronted him. Despite being outnumbered greatly, Ewing refused to surrender and was able through skill, luck, and because of Price's inept tactics to kill and wound approximately fifteen hundred Confederates before retreating and destroying the munitions and artillery left behind in the fort. This defeat caused Price to be much more cautious when he approached the fortifications at Jefferson City, deciding on October 8 to continue west without attacking. Over the next two weeks, numerous skirmishes and battles were fought with Union cavalry and infantry forces in pursuit of Price's army on its raid from Jefferson City to Kansas. On October 23, an important battle was fought near Kansas City at Westport, where the Confederates encountered mostly Missouri and Kansas militia forces. A lively fight ensued until the Confederate battle line collapsed after the arrival of General Alfred Pleasonton's cavalry. Retreating south along the state line road, on October 25 a decisive battle was fought at Mine Creek, Kansas, during which Price's army was smashed and thrown into confusion. Losing several generals, including division commanders John S. Marmaduke and William L. Cabell, and approximately twelve hundred casualties in killed, wounded, and missing, the Battle of Mine Creek was very close to a complete disaster for Price, who then was faced with the possibility of complete annihilation. Only the exhausted condition of Price's pursuers, both men and horses, saved the Army of Missouri.[25]

As noted in chapter 3, Price had violated the laws of war in commissioning guerrillas to operate behind Union lines in Missouri. Therefore it was hardly surprising that he employed guerrillas to create chaos in Missouri before and during his invasion. For those individuals falling into the hands of these outlaws, the consequences were devastating, often ending in their property being looted, their homes burned to the ground, and their lives lost. Perhaps Price's most inexcusable action was his willingness to provide the guerrilla leader William "Bloody Bill" Anderson, a psychopathic murderer, with a captain's commission and to send him into the region north of the Missouri River where he continued his bloody career until killed in late October. Price also sought to employ Quantrill, despite his experience with him and his command in Texas, where earlier in the year they had practiced their special skills upon Confederate citizens (see above). When he failed to find Quantrill, Price commissioned George Todd, who led a remnant of the former guerrilla chief's band and was as violent and ruthless as the rest. Later, when before a Confederate court-martial to defend the conduct of his expedition, Price denied his use of guerrilla forces, wishing thereby to conceal his connection to the atrocities committed by them before and during the raid.[26]

During this crisis, Rosecrans and his district commanders instituted various emergency measures to prevent more damage to the infrastructure, to protect loyal civilians and military supplies, to retaliate severely against those violating the laws of war, and to punish disloyal persons supporting Price's raid. While the Confederate army besieged Fort Davidson at Pilot Knob, abolitionist Brigadier General Clinton B. Fisk, district commander of North Missouri, ordered some of the most prominent supporters of the South to constitute "a citizen telegraph guard" responsible for the maintenance of the telegraph line from Boonville to Allen. This duty, especially during this period of widespread guerrilla activity, was very dangerous and thus it seemed appropriate to Fisk for those supporting the rebellion to endure its attendant hardships and dangers. One of the most notorious of these men was Reverend William G. Caples, who had served as a chaplain in Price's army in 1861 until he was captured and paroled. Despite this, Caples continued to express his devotion to the southern cause, thus making himself obnoxious to the military authorities at Glasgow where he lived. Ironically, just a few days after Fisk had published his order, on October 8 during a rebel attack upon the town Caples was struck by a cannon ball and died four days later.[27]

Another measure instituted in late September was General John McNeil's order declaring the town of Rolla "a military camp." Coming under martial law, no one could pass through the pickets of the militia there without permission from the military authorities. All men were ordered to report within twenty-four hours for defensive duty. Those failing to obey would then be liable to punishment as deserters. Other measures established throughout Missouri included the summary execution of guerrillas and those prisoners of war captured wearing federal uniforms, who were considered spies and probable members of Anderson's guerrilla band responsible for the murder of over twenty unarmed federal soldiers then on furlough at Centralia. Moreover, in some places those "found guilty of harboring and feeding guerrillas will be warned out of the State and their houses burned, their fences and crops destroyed." Apparently, after Price had been driven from Missouri and much of the trouble had ended, General Rosecrans, fearing that some of the emergency policies had been too harsh, ordered his district commanders to suspend all banishment orders until evidence could be gathered to determine who deserved exile.[28]

During the guerrilla uprising intended to prepare for Price's raid, some Union commanders threatened retaliation against captured guerrillas and their friends, especially when Unionists had been taken hostage. Sometimes, these measures simply punished the supporters of the guerrillas for a recent raid. This was the case in Marshall, where Colonel Bazel F. Lazear arrived soon after the courthouse and another building there had been destroyed by fire. In Frankford, this same band had killed and wounded ten African Americans and a German man, burning down twelve homes in the process. When a man refused to provide information about the guerrillas, Lazear had him shot. He also "arrested ten Rebels," whom he promised to kill whenever another Union supporter was murdered. This action and his arrest of several women caused many in the county to flee to parts unknown, for, as Lazear expressed it, they were "the worst scared people" he had ever seen.[29]

Perhaps the most disturbing incident of retaliation, however, occurred during Price's raid when six federal soldiers were shot several days after being captured at Pilot Knob. According to the testimony of Union prisoners of war, on October 3 Major James Wilson and five members of his command were handed over to the guerrilla Tim Reves, who was then commanding a regiment in Marmaduke's division. As Wilson and his soldiers were Union soldiers enlisted according to the laws of war, their surrender to the Confederate military entitled them to humane treatment. After their bodies were found, Rosecrans ordered that one Confederate major and six enlisted men be chosen from their prisoners to be shot in retaliation. On October 29, a firing squad shot six Confederate enlisted men. Rosecrans had also ordered that a suitable Confederate major should be found for execution. However, soon after Enoch O. Wolf was selected, Lincoln intervened on his behalf and he was eventually exchanged. Several Unionists had written to Lincoln protesting the shooting of the Confederate prisoners of war and arguing that such retaliatory measures stained the Union cause. To these criticisms, Rosecrans replied that if the United States military was unwilling to retaliate for the murder of its soldiers the Confederates would have no incentive to stop such outrages. In particular, the Confederate leadership sought to blur the lines between the treatment of regular soldiers, deserving to be handled as prisoners of war, and the treatment of those who, because they fought outside the accepted laws of war, were to be treated summarily. While the retaliatory execution of Confederate prisoners of war was severe in the extreme, many Union military leaders considered it a necessary deterrent and legal under the laws of war then in force. As already noted, Price had long ignored this distinction in his employment of brutal guerrilla bands, understanding that they occupied large numbers of United States troops in Missouri who otherwise could be sent elsewhere.[30]

One of General Price's goals for his raid into Missouri was to create enough havoc to disrupt the fall election, or at least to shake confidence in Lincoln and cause many to vote for the Democrats' candidate, George B. McClellan. In this, as in his other purposes, Price was largely unsuccessful. Lincoln had long been concerned about his chances of winning Missouri in the 1864 presidential election and may have decided to replace General John M. Schofield with Rosecrans, in part, because he knew that it would please the Radical Republicans, who by then were the dominant political group in Missouri. While he largely avoided becoming involved in the internecine squabbles that often erupted between Unionists, the president did use the powers and patronage of his office to improve his chances in the fall. Thus, learning that the *St. Joseph Tribune*, which received advertising revenue from the War Department and the Commission of Indian Affairs, was publishing editorials criticizing his administration, the president threatened to direct such business to another publication. Moreover, believing that the soldiers' vote would favor him significantly, he wrote to Rosecrans expressing his concern that the military have the opportunity to participate. The general soon reassured him that he would interpose no obstacles in their way.[31]

Having received various and contradictory reports about the political campaign, in October Lincoln again sent his personal secretary John G. Nicolay to Missouri to provide him with information and analysis concerning the relative strengths and positions of the different political factions and their attitudes toward his reelection. Nicolay, who had been there in June, met with political operatives and others to determine what the prospects were for the president and other candidates of the Union Party. Arriving during Price's raid, Nicolay found the Conservative and Radical Unionists at odds with one another and that "things are in a pretty bad tangle, but I think they are gravitating towards an understanding—temporary at least if not permanent—which will unite the vote of all the Union men on the electoral and State ticket." After meeting with numerous operatives in St. Louis and Springfield and spending more than a week in Missouri, Nicolay concluded that most of the quarrels between Unionists were the result of "little else than personal animosity and the usual eagerness to appropriate the spoils, that is left to prevent a full and harmonious combination of all the Union voters of Missouri. Even these obstacles are fast giving way before the change and pressure of circumstances, and the mere lapse of time." Moreover, instead of turning the electorate against Lincoln, Price's raid probably helped the president and the Union Party's candidates gain more votes than they lost, at least this was the opinion of some observers on the scene.[32]

During the campaign, two incidents in September, and perhaps more, of soldiers breaking up political rallies led to investigations and orders reiterating the policy that soldiers were not to interfere with lawful public assemblages. One of these occurred in Kansas City, where the frequent candidate for public office, James H. Birch, was running for the United States Congress. According to one report, soldiers of the Second Colorado drew their pistols and drove Birch from the speaker's rostrum before he could finish his speech. Colonel Ford, upon learning of the incident, offered to accompany Birch and prevent any further interference, but the candidate declined to return.[33]

Another, more serious incident occurred in St. Louis during a Democratic rally for their nominee McClellan. According to an account by one of the event's organizers, Charles C. Whittelsey, a group of "mutinous and lawless soldiers" sought to stop the meeting, which was being held in front of the Lindell Hotel. The soldiers assembled near the hotel and began "shouting for Abe Lincoln, damning McClellan, and doing everything to provoke a breach of the peace, that they might have some excuse for a riot." The soldiers then began throwing stones and soon stormed the speakers' stand, destroying political paraphernalia and seizing an American flag. The main participants of this riot were members of the 6th Missouri Cavalry, Merrill's Horse, and the Tenth Kansas regiments. These soldiers with others had come into

St. Louis to attend a rally for Colonel Thomas C. Fletcher, the Radical guber-natorial candidate, and had only learned about the Democratic meeting after coming into town. After this incident, Colonel J. H. Baker, then in command of the post where the incident occurred, issued a general order in which he promised that soldiers interfering with political meetings would be arrested and severely punished. Officers found wanting in their efforts to prevent soldiers from breaking up such assemblages would be summarily dismissed from the service. Moreover, he ordered the provost guard to attend political meetings with a strong enough force to prevent any further problems. While another Democratic meeting was dispersed by soldiers before Baker's order was published, apparently no other similar incidents occurred in St. Louis after this.[34]

As the election neared, some Missourians worried that the laws prohibiting certain classes of people from voting would not be enforced. Both Lincoln and Rosecrans received written and verbal appeals requesting that measures be taken to ensure the integrity of the election. After the president inquired about his plans, Rosecrans explained that he was then drafting a general order for the election, which he would issue soon. In it, the department commander ordered that only those qualified according to state law would be allowed to vote. Anyone who had taken up arms against the United States was prohibited from voting. Election judges were ordered to prevent anyone from voting who was ineligible according to state law. Rosecrans also excluded from serving as an election judge anyone who had borne arms against the United States or assisted the enemy. Moreover, he warned against interference with legal voters and ordered soldiers not to misbehave at the polls. All company commanders were to make arrangements for their soldiers to vote in the field or in camp and commanders of posts were responsible for providing military guards at the polls where needed. This order was issued before Price's army had been driven from Missouri. Fortunately, the election went forward as planned without hindrance and most troops, having returned home or to their posts, were able to participate without the need for special arrangements. Rosecrans, recognizing the importance of the military's participation, even ordered a commander in the field not to call out troops until after the election unless some compelling military necessity required it. Some suspicion existed that General James Craig had ordered his Radical troops into the field to prevent them from voting.[35]

While most of the usual politicking had probably ceased during Price's raid, the election was held as scheduled and apparently Rosecrans's measures prevented violence and other problems at the polls. For instance, in Buchanan County where disturbances at polling places were not uncommon even during peacetime, General Fisk noted that "the election passed off through-out the district with remarkable quietness. I have learned of but little trouble. There was a slight friction at the polls in Saint Joseph, but that is annual on this border, where so many of the sovereigns have been in the habit of voting 'early, late, and often,' and on both sides of the Missouri River." In consider-ing the results statewide, it is notable that fifty-two thousand fewer voters went to the polls than in 1860. This reduction occurred largely, although not exclusively, because of the exodus of many persons from Missouri during the war and the loyalty oath requirement, which made ineligible many persons who had voted in the former presidential election. Violence and organized efforts to prevent eligible voters from exercising the franchise undoubtedly occurred, but apparently these were not widespread. In the end, Lincoln must have been satisfied with the manner in which the election was held and es-pecially with the results, for he won with a forty thousand vote majority, the same as the Radical gubernatorial candidate Thomas C. Fletcher. Gaining re-election, the president planned for an end to military rule and the war. With a Radical governor and a new military commander in Missouri, Lincoln hoped for a smooth transition to peace and the reestablishment of civilian control, a goal for which he had long labored and could then perceive was within his grasp.[36]

11

LINCOLN AND THE RETURN
TO CIVILIAN RULE IN MISSOURI

AFTER THE DEFEAT OF Confederate General Sterling Price's invading army and the conduct of a successful wartime election in Missouri, General William S. Rosecrans may have expected a restoration of his prestige as a military man and department commander. This was not to be. His removal from command of the Department of the Missouri marked the end of his active military career, although he remained nominally on duty until December 1865. General Ulysses S. Grant's decision to replace him was based as much on Rosecrans's past performance at the battles of Corinth and Chickamauga as on his deficiencies in Missouri. Grant had considered Rosecrans incompetent in his defense of the federal entrenchments at Corinth, Mississippi, and slow in his pursuit of Confederate General Earl Van Dorn when speed and energy would have destroyed the enemy's army. Furthermore, after pursuit was no longer feasible and Grant had recalled him, Rosecrans ignored his order to return to Corinth and thus exposed his army to annihilation. During his siege of Vicksburg, Grant had ordered Rosecrans, then with an independent command in Tennessee, to move against Confederate General Braxton Bragg to prevent him from detaching any of his troops to operate against federal forces at Vicksburg. Despite General Henry W. Halleck's repeated orders to advance, Rosecrans did not move until it was too late, leading to the disaster at Chickamauga. Such insubordination had led to Grant's removal of Rosecrans at Chattanooga and would lead to his replacement as commander in Missouri.[1]

Given this past experience, it is unsurprising that Grant was predisposed to believe that Rosecrans should have countered Price's threat before he had reached Pilot Knob, thus driving him back into Arkansas before he could do further damage in Missouri. This analysis was probably unfair to Rosecrans, who found it necessary to keep his forces scattered throughout Missouri to counter guerrilla activity until Price's invasion. Moreover, it is clear that Grant thought Rosecrans had more troops available to him than he in fact did. Still, with better preparation, he had at least four months' notice of the invasion, and greater speed in movement to concentrate his troops, Rosecrans should have stopped Price before he had traveled very far into Missouri. This conclusion was confirmed in part by a report of Rosecrans's refusal to move swiftly in pursuit of Price's army after the Battle of Westport. This report had been sent to Halleck by General Samuel R. Curtis and forwarded to Grant. According to a conversation recorded in it, Rosecrans justified his slow and ineffectual pursuit of Price as preferable to relentlessly dogging the enemy until he was brought to bay. Despite examples to the contrary, Rosecrans argued that wearing out troops in pursuit of the enemy would only render them incapable of striking a decisive blow. In the end, although based upon some misconceptions and personal prejudice, Grant was correct in believing that more foresight and energy should have resulted in the annihilation of Price's army. And so in December 1864, Grant removed Rosecrans and refused to send him to another command, noting that he "will do less harm doing nothing than on duty. I know no department or army commander deserving such punishment as the infliction of Rosecrans on them."[2]

As it turned out, Grant probably felt free to dismiss Rosecrans because of the availability of General Grenville M. Dodge for the command of the Department of the Missouri. In 1861 Dodge had served in Missouri first as colonel of the 4th Iowa at Rolla, eventually becoming commander of the post there. During the battle for Atlanta in 1864, Dodge was commander of a part of the 16th Corps under General William T. Sherman when he received a head wound on August 19. For two days Dodge was unconscious and not expected to survive, but to the surprise of many he slowly began to recover. However, by the end of the year both Grant and Sherman regarded Dodge still too unwell to endure the strains and rigors of the field and apparently considered the command in Missouri an excellent place where the talents of the efficient, young general of thirty-three years could be employed. While he had hoped to command in the field again, Dodge accepted the independent command with some knowledge of the difficulties that awaited him in the troublesome Department of the Missouri. While no large, armed enemy force threatened the state at the beginning of his tenure, many small guerrilla bands still plundered and murdered citizens, thereby keeping pressure

on the military and political leaders to find means by which to end these depredations once and for all. However, this task was further complicated when
General Halleck ordered Dodge to send to General George H. Thomas whatever federal troops he could spare. Thus fourteen infantry and four cavalry
regiments were removed from his command.[3]

When Dodge took command in December 1864, several military commission trials were then convened to punish persons accused of various misdeeds
during Price's raid. Two men, Simon Hausman and Henry Mason, for example, were convicted of "enticing soldiers in the service of the United States to
desert" and received $5 fines and sentences of two years' imprisonment. Oth-
ers were accused of various forms of misconduct including consorting with
guerrillas and providing them with intelligence and material aid, various associations with Confederate soldiers, espionage, conspiring to help prisoners
of war escape, and a number of depredations including looting and murder.
Many of these persons were convicted and sentenced to imprisonment during the war, although a good number were allowed to go to the Confederacy,
if they preferred, so long as they did not return during the war. Others had
no choice and were banished, some in spite of having been acquitted of the
charges brought against them. One of these cases involved Ruth Briscoe, who
despite admitting to the arresting soldier that she had indeed been with Bill
Anderson's guerrillas and had purchased goods with Confederate money at
a merchant's store, was acquitted when it was discovered that the witnesses
against her were no longer available in Cooper County where she lived. Nevertheless, the military authorities believed her guilty and probably suspected
that the witnesses for the prosecution had been harmed or intimidated, and
thus she was ordered to leave the state.[4]

On December 21, General Dodge wrote to Halleck requesting that he
inquire with Secretary of War Edwin M. Stanton and President Abraham
Lincoln concerning a policy of banishment he intended to implement. Dodge
believed that by banishing the families of guerrillas and notable southern
sympathizers he could deny to them the support network which had enabled
guerrillas to operate successfully every spring and summer. To accomplish
this Dodge intended to draw up a list of persons known to have aided and
abetted guerrillas or Price's efforts during his raid. His policy was announced
on January 8, 1865, as General Orders No. 7. In it he ordered all persons to
oppose and report upon guerrillas in their communities. Those failing in

this responsibility would have their property seized and they and their families would be banished to the South. Moreover, Dodge encouraged southern sympathizers to leave the state voluntarily by giving them time to put their affairs in order and permitting them to take some of their property with them. Interestingly, this policy in some measure resembled Lincoln's treatment of Clement L. Vallandigham, the infamous Copperhead Democratic congressman from Ohio, who was banished to the South. Noting that these Missourians and Vallandigham greatly favored the South, both Lincoln and Dodge accommodated them in so far as to send them to live with their friends under the Confederate government, which they apparently preferred.[5]

This measure was vigorously enforced throughout the state. Perhaps the most enthusiastic supporter of this policy was General Clinton B. Fisk, district commander of North Missouri. Two days after Dodge had issued his general order, Fisk ordered Dr. Hosea R. C. Cowden and his family to leave Rocheport, a small town along the Missouri River in the central part of the state, and settle east of Indiana within three weeks. Written testimony confirmed that Cowden had supported Governor Claiborne F. Jackson in 1861 and had recruited men for the Confederate cause after the Battle of Boonville, paying two men $25 a month to serve. Later Cowden had conspired with William "Bloody Bill" Anderson to transport his slaves to the South in August 1864, when the guerrilla leader and his band had occupied Rocheport and terrorized its inhabitants. Upon receiving the order to leave Missouri, Cowden circulated a petition requesting the revocation of his banishment. However, Fisk declared to a subordinate, Brigadier General J. B. Douglas, that he was inclined to banish all persons signing such a petition, as well. Moreover, probably upon Fisk's request, Douglas provided a list of persons whom he wished banished. Apparently, Dodge's order led to the banishment of a large number of southern sympathizers, sometimes with unexpected results. Several years after the war when he was working for the Union Pacific Railroad, Dodge happened to be near Boise, Idaho. Leaving the train to inspect "an irrigation project," he was surprised upon his return to find "his car well stocked with Boise Valley fruit." After inquiry, he learned that a group of men he had banished from Missouri had left the fruit in genuine appreciation for their forced emigration. "They had explained everything to the station agent and said that there was a time when they would have hanged Dodge if they could have captured him in Missouri, but they were now thankful that his severe methods had driven them into the wonderful Boise Valley." If this story is true, the number of Missourians forced to leave during the last few months of the war was large and this may have removed many of the remaining supporters of the guerrillas, as Dodge intended, from the state.[6]

As he had done throughout the war, Lincoln intervened in cases when he suspected that the punishments were too harsh or to ensure that a person had been treated fairly. An instance of this concerned Anna B. Martin, who had been banished from Missouri. However, according to the records, she had requested in writing her banishment to avoid further imprisonment, but without permission she had returned to Missouri and thus was again incarcerated. Another banishment case involved Nancy Thompson, whose record evidently provided little if any reason for her expulsion. Lincoln, who was then concerned to diminish the violence in Missouri and to reconcile all parties there, ordered General Dodge to suspend her banishment and inquired of him to "ascertain and report to me whether there is any thing, & what, against her, except that her husband is a rebel." While her file shows that the order expelling her was suspended, no other record apparently exists beyond this, indicating that Thompson most probably was allowed to remain. Another woman, Elizabeth Arnold, after she was ordered to leave Missouri, convinced the authorities of her loyalty, and the banishment order against her was revoked. However, others, despite Lincoln's intervention, were not as fortunate, or it turned out that the information the president had acted upon was inaccurate. In other instances, friends in high places like former governor Austin A. King requested that Lincoln only modify a banishment order to allow John Ecton and Wesley Martin to live in the loyal states instead of in the South, where evidently many supporters of the South were unwilling to immigrate. Apparently, their devotion to the Confederate cause did not extend to voluntarily reaping the rewards of the seeds of rebellion they had helped to sow.[7]

As Dodge pursued his banishment policy, on January 15 Lincoln suggested that the prosecution of such vigorous and severe measures was counterproductive to achieving the goal of ultimate reconciliation among various factions in Missouri. Believing that victory was near, the president wanted to start the transition from war to peace as soon as possible. One way to achieve this, he proposed, was for communities to hold meetings at which factions would find ways to work together to end the strife that had prevailed for too long between neighbors. Such a reconciliation could lead to the withdrawal of troops and a return to normalcy. Dodge, who was unpersuaded by Lincoln's proposal, wrote to Governor Thomas C. Fletcher to gain his perspective upon it. Fletcher replied that the president evidently did not understand the circumstances then facing Missouri, where trouble with guerrillas continued and only the organization of reliable veteran soldiers and loyal men into new military units could stop the violence. The governor also believed that attempts to compromise with or appease the enemy and southern sympathizers would only embolden them. After consulting with Fletcher, Dodge explained to the president that many guerrillas remained in the state, especially north of the Missouri River, and he had very few soldiers to confront them. His banishment policy, therefore, was the only means by which loyal Missourians could remain. While some of Lincoln's correspondents agreed with him, most notably Congressman William A. Hall, probably a majority of Missouri's political leadership sided with Dodge in his dread of the coming spring and a renewed outbreak of guerrilla violence.[8]

At the end of his command in Missouri, General Rosecrans had sought to begin the transition to civilian rule by providing a heavy military guard to protect judges and their records with the eventual purpose of substituting civil tribunals for military commissions. Soon after it had convened in late December 1864, Missouri's General Assembly sent a memorial to Lincoln warning that the removal of military authority from the state was dangerous. This message reflected the anxiety caused by the withdrawal of nineteen federal regiments from Missouri. Thus, the General Assembly wished Lincoln to exercise "great Caution in rescinding or modifying in any way orders that have injurious & coercive influences only upon our enemies and the enemies of our common country. At the present time in many parts of our State the Civil law is to a large extent powerless." Despite this message, as noted above, Lincoln sought to encourage both General Dodge and Governor Fletcher to organize community meetings at which efforts would be made to conciliate different factions to one another in the common goal of ending the violence and returning Missouri to its status before the war.[9]

A month after first proposing it, Lincoln again wrote to Governor Fletcher urging that he implement his plan of holding "neighborhood meetings." Initially, the governor again reacted negatively to this proposal, writing to Dodge that he would try Lincoln's policy but expected it to fail and he wanted to be prepared militarily when it did. "With your knowledge and mine of the real condition of the state, it is heart-sickening to be put off by such a policy." In a letter written shortly after his to Dodge, Fletcher provided Lincoln with his analysis for why such a policy would fail. The problem, as he saw it, was that only loyal men could be trusted to adhere to their promises and that guerrilla bands would use the lessening of military control as an opportunity to continue plundering and murdering their fellow citizens. Only "the unconditional submission of the authority of the law" could bring peace. Nevertheless, Fletcher promised to confer with Dodge and others concerning Lincoln's plan and seek to determine how best to implement it. The governor also intended to go where the violence was worst and attempt to persuade Missourians to reconcile with one another.[10]

Thus matters stood when General Grant's plan "to merge the Departments of Missouri, Kansas, and the Northwest into a military division" finally came to fruition. This meant that General Dodge, although remaining as commander of the Department of the Missouri, would then be subordinate to General John Pope, to whom Grant had offered this command in late November 1864. Upon his arrival in Missouri, Pope determined it important for Dodge, who subsequently was given the responsibility of commanding the Department of Kansas as well, personally to travel to the plains and mobilize and lead an expedition to stop the plains tribes' depredations then being committed in retaliation for the massacre at Sand Creek, which had occurred the previous November. One of the major goals of the expedition was the reopening of the overland mail route. These duties removed Dodge from active participation in Missouri's affairs until the first of April, when he returned to St. Louis.[11]

This circumstance changed the dynamics in Missouri significantly, for General Pope's attitude toward martial law and the provost-marshal system was very different from Dodge's, and much more in agreement with the president's. In a letter to the commander of the new military division, Lincoln requested that Pope investigate a report he had received concerning the unilateral decision of provost marshals to forfeit bonds posted by Missourians to ensure their loyalty. These provost marshals acted as judges and juries in seizing and selling property to satisfy these bonds, prompting the president's intervention. Pope responded that he considered "the provost-marshal system . . . oppressive and absurd. I am examining into and will correct the whole matter," he promised.[12]

At the same time, Lincoln received other reports of an assessment against disloyal persons in St. Louis County to benefit refugees. This matter had come to the attention of Missouri's congressional delegation in Washington D.C., of which only three members thought such a policy appropriate, the rest protesting it as an unnecessary disturbance of the peace. In particular, the assessment against Charles McLaren was considered excessive, especially because he had kept his promise since 1861 to in no way aid the rebellion, despite his being "a gentleman of strong southern feeling." Thus, according to Congressman Henry T. Blow, to punish someone of integrity like McLaren in the same manner as oath breakers and active supporters of the southern war effort seemed to be both ethically wrong and poor policy. In justifying his decision to institute this assessment, General Dodge explained that when he had taken command he had learned that a large number of refugees were then being housed and supported by the government. Concerned about the expense, he wrote to General Halleck to learn what he should do. Halleck replied in late 1864 that the federal government would not pay such an expense and that if the local authorities refused to shoulder the burden, then Dodge should make an assessment against disloyal persons. In December 1861, Halleck had himself made disloyal persons in St. Louis County support Union refugees in this manner. After consulting with representatives of the Western Sanitary Commission in St. Louis, Dodge gained the agreement of this charitable organization to take responsibility for the welfare of the refugees if "the old Lawson Hospital" was repaired and made comfortable for them. This was accomplished at the cost of $10,000. The assessment was made "to reimburse the quartermaster's department for amount expended and debt incurred, and if stopped will bring the whole matter back on Government." In regard to the assessment against McLaren, Dodge noted that he too had thought the assessment too large and had already reduced it by $1,500, noting that the vast majority of the assessments had been "levied upon the property of rebels who had fled the State, gone South or to Europe."[13]

In early March 1865, having been in command only a month, General Pope explained to Governor Fletcher his determination to end martial law and to begin the process of fully turning control of the state over to the civil authorities. Pope admitted that before taking command in Missouri he had expected to return the state immediately to the full exercise of its civil authority and "dispense entirely with the cumbersome, inefficient, and altogether anomalous machinery of the provost-marshals, provost guards, and military supervision." This expectation was premised on his knowledge of Missouri's successful fall elections and the establishment of a loyal government. For these reasons, he had originally thought it impossible that there remained any need for martial law and provost marshals. Since then, however, he had realized that returning civilian control to Missouri would not be as easy as he had originally supposed, forcing him to move more slowly than he had hoped. Nevertheless, Pope feared that the character of the people might be permanently harmed if this military system continued much longer. He thought it imperative then that the people be forced to look to themselves and their civil institutions for protection. Moreover, citing recent examples of provost marshals abusing their power and authority, Pope argued that such abuses were common and threatened to undermine republican government in Missouri.[14]

Thus, Pope proposed to Governor Fletcher that in those regions where it was possible, the civil authorities should once again take control. Recognizing that this transition might still be difficult or even impossible in some places, he favored a gradual reimposition of civil law to avoid a general upheaval. Moreover, Pope noted that regular troops could have little success against guerrillas without help from the people. With the people's full support, however, little chance existed for failure. Once Missouri was again fully controlled by its civil authorities, other states would have a fit example by which to model their own progress toward ending martial law and recovering their full rights as citizens, especially those in the South.[15]

Governor Fletcher responded to Pope's proposal much more favorably than he had to Lincoln's. On March 7, the governor published a proclamation incorporating many of Pope's ideas in which he requested all law-abiding citizens to work together, regardless of their past disagreements, to restore peace. He also ordered judges and justices of the peace to hold court wherever possible and to request military protection if necessary. After Fletcher's proclamation was published, Pope wrote to Lincoln explaining his plans more fully and providing some advice. Noting Missourians' dependency upon the military, he urged that the federal government no longer support the Missouri State Militia after May 1, when the allocated funds for its support expired. Where the civil courts were operative, Pope wanted to suspend martial law privately by ordering troops and provost marshals to be withdrawn. Then whenever emergency powers were needed, instead of using federal troops, the governor would employ state militia to stabilize the situation until civil control could be reasserted. The expense of this would then be borne by the state, and Pope believed that this in itself would greatly dampen the people's enthusiasm for such measures. This policy was then possible, he asserted, because the state government and a large majority of the people were loyal, making federal intervention no longer necessary. Pope noted that this could work only so long as the president and his administration refused to be enticed into intervening and instead referred all appeals and petitions to the state government. In implementing this policy, however, he believed that "an abrupt and sudden abrogation of martial law would create much alarm and discontent among a certain class of people in the State and would meet with violent [dis]approbation. I propose, therefore, to get rid of it gradually, and without any public order suffer it to die out for want of exercise, so that the people will be unconscious of it until they cease to regard martial law necessary or desirable."[16]

President Lincoln, who had long ago wearied of involvement in Missouri's affairs, agreed to Pope's plan. Just as important was Governor Fletcher's willingness to attempt the experiment of weaning Missouri from its dependence upon the military. On March 17, Pope issued Special Orders No. 15 in which he ordered his provost marshals, once the civil officers and courts had resumed their duties, to confine themselves exclusively to military affairs. The military was not to interfere with any cases coming under civil jurisdiction. Any prisoners held as guerrillas, against whom evidence sustained charges of murder and other crimes "cognizable by civil courts," were to be surrendered to the local authorities. Where it was necessary, however, persons could still be detained "in military custody" and tried before military commissions. Moreover, Pope ordered that after their civilian trials, regardless of the outcome, the civil authorities were to return the defendants to the custody of the local provost marshals. Thus, it is clear that Pope's vaunted faith in civil authority and distrust for martial law and the provost-marshal system was not as profound and thorough as he had represented when he first took command in Missouri and as he would state later in his memoirs many years after the war. Confronted by circumstances and reality, he was forced to adjust his policy and retain the military in Missouri. The transition from military to civilian control would not be as easy as he had first thought, which he admitted in his special order.

The attempt to restore civil administration in Missouri after the State has been so long under the jurisdiction of martial law will doubtless give rise to many perplexing questions between the military and civil authorities, but all such questions should be considered and decided in a spirit of candor and forbearance. It is expected and requested that the civil authorities will not hesitate to appeal from decisions of military commanders in any case which seems proper to the commanding general of this military division, who will not fail to give any such appeal careful and dispassionate examination.[17]

Necessary to the implementation of Pope's plan was the strengthening of the state militia through the establishment of yet another organization, this time referred to as the Missouri Volunteer Militia. This force was considered necessary because of the problems associated with the Enrolled Missouri Militia and the Provisional Militia, both of which often were ineffectively led by line officers elected by their men. While some militia units had proven themselves effective and well-disciplined, others were considered responsible for many outrages and for abusing their powers to punish southern sympathizers and Unionists with whom they disagreed politically, but who were otherwise peaceful and law-abiding citizens. Thus, it was considered important to dismiss all but the best of the enrolled and provisional militia and replace them with companies of men who would be led by proven military men taken from veterans, some of whom were then returning from the East. Although these arrangements reduced the number of militia available for duty, Pope intended to improve their quality and discipline substantially. Moreover, efforts were made to arm them with "Spencer rifles and Colt revolvers," weapons better suited for confronting guerrillas than the outdated and often unreliable weapons issued to militia units previously. Eventually, thirty-one companies were raised and stationed in the remaining troublesome regions of Missouri, mostly along the Missouri and Mississippi rivers where small guerrilla bands still operated.[18]

Undoubtedly wearied by the long war and encouraged by the prospect of a return to normalcy, men like General Fisk, commander of the North Missouri district, actively worked to protect the operation of the civil courts, some of which had not held proceedings for some time. He also personally inspected all the prisons in his district and corrected corruption and abuses committed by his provost marshals. At St. Joseph, Fisk uncovered a plot between the assistant provost marshal and some attorneys there to use their authority for gain. After interrogating thirty witnesses and taking some one hundred pages of testimony, Fisk discovered that for some time the assistant provost marshal had caused wealthy persons living some distance from the post to be arrested. False affidavits accusing these persons of disloyalty were made and the prisoners were not permitted visitors, either family or lawyers, for several days. Thus a prisoner, seemingly forgotten and destined to indefinite incarceration, would be desperate to extricate himself from this situation. It was at this point, when the despair of the prisoner was profound and deep, that an attorney who was part of the scheme would visit the prison, ostensibly on other business, and would be called upon by the prisoner for help. The attorney would then feign great concern over what he had heard about the charges against their mark and the almost certain sentence of long imprisonment or worse which awaited him. The prisoner, the attorney would then assert, could not escape his fate without the aid of his influence upon the military authorities, but for which he would need to pay $1,500. In this manner, the attorneys and assistant provost marshal had defrauded several persons. Fisk provided this evidence to the local circuit court judge, who presented it to a grand jury, who indicted two of the lawyers involved.[19]

Other encouraging signs of progress were evident, although President Lincoln, who was assassinated on April 14 of that year, never learned about most of them. On March 31, all restrictions upon the ownership of arms and ammunition were removed, although merchants were still required to maintain an accurate account of what was sold and to whom. Just two days before Lincoln's death, Pope proposed to Governor Fletcher the quiet return of power to the civil authorities in northern Missouri, excepting only the region bordering along the Missouri River. He intended to remove all the provost marshals from there and to concentrate the remaining troops in the river counties. No announcements were made of this so that the transfer could occur without notice or dissent. Pope also noted that those who were opposed to this policy could no longer argue that it was premature, because the war was not over. After the surrender of Lee to Grant, such arguments lost much of their force. Because the courts were then in session there, Fletcher agreed to the removal of all provost marshals and troops north of the Hannibal and St. Joseph Railroad, although he suggested caution in the regions along both the

Mississippi and Missouri rivers where guerrilla activity was expected to erupt soon. On April 19 Pope was confident enough in the success of these efforts that he wrote to General Grant relating his expectation that "in a few months" he could "leave Missouri entirely to the State authorities and remove all the military forces from the State." Of course, this success would be contingent upon whether or not significant guerrilla activity occurred again in the upcoming spring and summer. To counter this danger, he considered the proposals of others like Congressman James S. Rollins, who suggested that it would be wise to establish armed boat patrols and post military guards at the ferry crossings on the Missouri River. These measures had been effective during the early part of the war in preventing guerrillas from crossing the river.[20]

Investigations of military interference with the civil authorities also continued. On March 25 Pope ordered Dodge to prohibit the military from hindering John Ryland, district attorney in Jackson County, in the performance of his duties. Moreover, Pope ordered the investigation of the provost marshal at Lexington for arresting persons with weapons after the restrictions upon possessing arms had been lifted. Another concern of the division commander was the effort to make an assessment against Secessionists on behalf of Dr. D. J. Martin, a prominent Unionist whose property had been destroyed by the enemy. Such a return to martial law would be a step backward, Pope believed, and therefore the matter was referred to Governor Fletcher to be handled under Missouri's civil laws. Pope noted that many other Unionists besides Martin had valid claims to profit from assessments against Secessionists, but it would be a mistake to return to martial law in this way.[21]

By May 1865, the military's correspondence turned to the subject of the proper terms upon which to accept the surrender of Confederate soldiers and officers. Some of these Missourians wanted assurances that they could return to their homes without fear of imprisonment or harassment. This came in the form of a general order in which all returning Confederate soldiers would receive pardon upon reporting to the local provost marshal in their community and taking the oath prescribed in Lincoln's amnesty proclamation of December 8, 1863. The oath taker promised to "support, defend, and protect the Constitution of the United States" and to uphold all congressional acts and Supreme Court decisions regarding slavery. In one instance, there arose the question of upon what terms a "rebel Congressman" might surrender. Provost Marshal General J. H. Baker replied that no terms could be offered as he was a civil officer of the Confederate government and thus was exempted from the benefits of Lincoln's proclamation. Baker ordered his correspondent to arrest the Confederate congressman, if possible. In his report of July 18, General Dodge noted that after Confederate General Robert E. Lee's surrender to General Grant, he had demanded the surrender of all Confederate forces within his command and that around ten thousand officers and men in Missouri and Arkansas had surrendered "under the Grant-Lee agreement." In the case of irregular forces, Dodge allowed them to surrender with the promise that the United States military would take no action against them. This promise, however, left "the civil authorities unrestrained to deal with them for the crimes they had committed in violation of the laws of the State and of the United States and contrary to usages of war."[22]

Unfortunately, the end of the war did not mean the cessation of violence, for some guerrilla activity, although greatly reduced from its wartime levels, continued and remained a problem. In 1866, after General Pope had refused to provide federal troops "to assist certain sheriffs in executing writs against bushwhackers who threatened the peace," Governor Fletcher called out the militia to support the civil authorities. Unfortunately, the militia was controlled by the Radicals and some of these units treated Conservatives and southern sympathizers rather roughly. Moreover, during this period arose vigilante groups calling themselves "Regulators," who acted in secret as paramilitary groups doling out severe punishment upon those they deemed to be troublemakers. Later, as a result of complaints from Missouri's Conservatives, President Andrew Johnson replaced Pope with General Winfield Scott Hancock, who was able to persuade "Fletcher to reorganize the militia on a less partisan basis and promised that some federal troops would be available for support duty where needed. Eventually, three companies of Regulars performed spot patrols that fall."[23]

Of course, the most profound consequence of the war was the end of slavery in the United States. On January 11, 1865, Arnold Krekel, the president of the state constitutional convention then in session, wrote to Lincoln announcing the convention's decision to abolish slavery immediately. This decision, however, did not alleviate the terrible circumstances in which African Americans found themselves during the last months of the war and after. Guerrilla bands continued to murder blacks, driving most into the towns where they could not subsist themselves, thus becoming a burden upon their communities. To meet the needs and end the suffering of the dispossessed former slaves, superintendents of freedmen provided supplies and rations. In July 1865, according to the records of the Freedmen's Bureau, a federal agency established during the war to help freedmen adjust to life after slavery, three thousand freedmen and their families received rations and other support. The numbers of freedmen receiving this dole, however, declined rapidly after this, indicating that by the winter of 1865–1866 most blacks had found employment, many of them returning to the countryside and their former masters to support themselves. Others preferred to find work in towns and cities doing a variety of menial jobs. Although free, African Americans were restricted under special discriminatory laws instituted throughout the former slaveholding South and little provision was made for the education of black children. In some cases, African American schools were burnt down, but such tactics sometimes backfired when military officials ordered the seizure of local white churches to supply a school meeting place. The most important debility of all, however, was that African Americans were denied the right to vote under the new state constitution. This would not change until 1870 when the Fifteenth Amendment to the Constitution of the United States guaranteed to male blacks the right to vote. Freedom brought with it many new and often puzzling problems for the freedmen, many of which would not gain redress for another century.[24]

Given its circumstances at the beginning of the war, it is difficult to imagine a scenario in which Missouri came through the conflict without a great amount of trouble and at least some significant curtailment of civil liberties. In retrospect, with the vast majority of the population identifying with the South and favoring slavery, it is remarkable that a majority rejected secession. It should be remembered, however, that many of Missouri's leaders, including the governor and lieutenant governor, a majority of state legislators, and many community leaders actively supported secession and sought to make the state part of the Confederacy. Under the leadership of former Governor Sterling Price, who then was serving as commander of the state militia, war erupted between the militia and federal forces led by General Nathaniel Lyon. Moreover, many Missourians, although unwilling to join Price's army, operated secretly as guerrillas or provided support to them. Within a short period many Missourians had taken sides and were fighting one another on the battlefield or in their backyards. A bitter conflict ensued in which few

Missourians escaped without suffering some loss in property or from the violence. Under these circumstances, Lincoln and Missouri's Unionist leadership could not permit the state to descend into chaos and were justified in the establishment of a provisional government and a military commander with expanded authority to ensure the public safety.

This circumstance was not inevitable, for without Price's encouragement of guerrilla activity and his repeated invasions of the state despite little prospect for success, Missouri could have settled down after 1861 to relative peace. This was not to be and led to the establishment of martial law, a provost-marshal system, and military tribunals to try civilians for wartime offenses. Nothing like it before or since has ever been created in United States history. In considering these events and measures one must remember that no one had any idea what the future held and certainly could not know the result of the war. Such an observation, while seemingly pedestrian and obvious, is sometimes forgotten by those considering these events and judging the decision making of Lincoln and others. Today's knowledge of a northern victory is ever present, at least in one's subconscious, and if not guarded against can cause one to dismiss the real dangers, anxieties, and uncertainties experienced by the Civil War generation. Indeed, many European military experts of the time thought it highly unlikely that the South could be conquered. Thus, it is important to understand the events from the perspective of those who endured them without our knowledge of a northern victory as preordained and inevitable.

One of the great difficulties for Lincoln, military leaders, and the provisional government in establishing policy was to gain accurate knowledge of circumstances in Missouri. From the very beginning, often two and more versions of an event were presented in which it was sometimes impossible to ascertain what was accurate, or even most true. Understanding much of what happened was complicated by the testimony of persons who testified to events from a perspective often tainted by prejudice and personal and political biases. For this reason, Lincoln relied upon his commanders and certain trusted persons to come to some understanding of Missouri's situation for the purpose of establishing policy. More times than not, the president, responsible for the overall conduct of the war everywhere, did not have sufficient time to look into allegations of wrongdoing on the part of military and political leaders and their subordinates. To gain the perspective of an outsider, Lincoln frequently sent trusted military and political advisers and even his personal secretaries to Missouri. Increasingly, however, as the war progressed Lincoln sought to disentangle himself from Missouri's affairs, an understandable desire, but sometimes it was at the expense of fairness to persons who had real grievances and legitimate concerns which he needed to address. Moreover, perhaps all too cognizant of his own fallibility, Lincoln was reluctant to dictate measures and policy to military and political leaders more familiar with the circumstances than himself. Hardly someone conspiring to establish himself as a dictator, the president wished to diminish his involvement in Missouri's affairs rather than accrue more power and authority to himself. The record demonstrates that he desired to return the country as quickly as possible to its prewar status and provide its citizens with all the attendant political and civil liberties enjoyed under the Constitution of the United States.

While Lincoln and his military and political counterparts made many mistakes of commission and omission, when one considers the difficulty of their task one must marvel at the overall effectiveness of their efforts to prevent Missouri's secession, to restore order, reestablish government, and to hold elections in the midst of much turmoil, many military setbacks, and the often bitter internecine struggles which erupted among Unionists. Often these achievements came at the cost of civil liberties, but it is clear from the outset that without martial law and the firm hand of military rule, Missouri's situation would have been far worse than it was. Having said this, it must also be noted that Lincoln failed occasionally to stop unfortunate abuses of power and unnecessary restrictions upon civil liberties. Perhaps the most egregious of these was his acceptance of the summary execution of guerrillas caught in the field in arms. This policy is at least partly responsible for the bitterness and intensity with which the irregular conflict was conducted throughout the war. While guerrillas should not have been granted prisoner of war status, they might have been accorded some status comparable to that of spies and others acting outside the acceptable modes of warfare. In this manner, these irregular combatants might still receive severe punishment, although only after having been tried before a military commission.[25] Moreover, the military's curtailment of religious liberty and freedom of speech and the press were largely unnecessary and the full exercise of these rights should have been restored much earlier during the war. Of course, once again, it is much easier for one looking back with full knowledge of the war's outcome to make such judgments and one cannot say with certainty how such moderations in measures and policies would have altered events. However, the experiment should have been tried and could have been ended upon evidence that a firmer hand was still needed. There was little to lose and much to gain in such a test.

Another aspect of Lincoln's role was that of a moderator of disputes, often intervening on behalf of persons, some deserving and others not, who were suffering under some measure instituted by a provost marshal or military commander. Many examples in the pages of this book demonstrate that Lincoln sought to mitigate the severity of war and military rule when he thought commanders or military tribunals were too harsh in their punishments or when he believed that persons deserved an opportunity to redeem themselves. His instincts were not of a despot but of a reluctant warrior who wished to gain victory and return the country to peace and stability as soon as possible. This is best demonstrated in Lincoln's desire to minimize the number of military arrests and to restore civil authority to Missouri during the commands of Halleck, Curtis, and Dodge before the war was won.[26] These episodes demonstrate best the unfairness of the anti-Lincoln theses which, for various reasons, seek to portray the president as power hungry and intent upon transferring power from the states to the national government and from the legislative to the executive branch. When one considers the moderation of his proposed reconstruction plan, which sought the swift restoration of the seceded states into the Union with full constitutional rights, the persuasiveness of the anti-Lincoln arguments is diminished substantially if not completely. Given the great difficulties through which he directed the ship of state into safe harbor, Lincoln richly deserves his reputation as one of our greatest presidents.

Notes

Epigraph. Abraham Lincoln, *The Collected Works of Abraham Lincoln,* ed. Roy P. Basler, vol. 4 (New Brunswick, NJ: Rutgers University Press, 1959), 426.

1. Abraham Lincoln to Henry T. Blow, Charles D. Drake, and others, 15 May 1863, Lincoln, *Collected Works,* vol. 6, 218.

2. Harry V. Jaffa, *Crisis of the House Divided: An Interpretation of the Issues in the Lincoln-Douglas Debates,* with a new preface (Chicago: University of Chicago Press, 1982), 204–32, 280–81, 286–87, and 303–04. Lincoln, *Collected Works,* vol. 1, 108–15. For a nice overview of the anti-Lincoln historiography see Don E. Fehrenbacher, *Lincoln in Text and Context: Collected Essays* (Palo Alto: Stanford University Press, 1987), 197–213. Herman Belz, *Abraham Lincoln, Constitutionalism, and Equal Rights in the Civil War Era* (New York: Fordham University Press, 1998), 17–43. Harold M. Hyman, *A More Perfect Union: The Impact of the Civil War and Reconstruction on the Constitution* (Boston: Houghton, Mifflin, 1975), 62–64 and 75–77. Daniel Farber, *Lincoln's Constitution* (Chicago: University of Chicago Press, 2003), 144–46. Mark E. Neely Jr., *The Fate of Liberty: Abraham Lincoln and Civil Liberties* (New York: Oxford University Press, 1991), 231–32. Thomas J. DiLorenzo, *The Real Lincoln: A New Look at Abraham Lincoln, His Agenda, and an Unnecessary War* (New York: Crown Publishing, 2002), 130–70.

3. Lincoln to Joshua F. Speed, 24 August 1855; and Lincoln to Lyman Trumbull, 10 December 1860, Lincoln, *Collected Works,* vol. 2, 320–23, and vol. 4, 149–50. Don E. Fehrenbacher, *Prelude to Greatness: Lincoln in the 1850's* (Palo Alto: Stanford University Press, 1962), 21–25.

4. Lincoln to David Hunter, 23 December 1861, Abraham Lincoln Papers, Library of Congress, Washington D.C. See also chapter 3.

5. Richard Shelly Hartigan, *Lieber's Code and the Law of War* (Chicago: Precedent Publishing, 1983), 1–7 and 21–23. Frank Freidel, *Francis Lieber: Nineteenth-Century Liberal* (Baton Rouge: Louisiana State University Press, 1947), 340. Lewis R. Harley, *Francis Lieber: His Life and Political Philosophy* (New York: Columbia University Press, 1899), 153–54. William T. Sherman learned of Lincoln's pragmatic approach to the military immediately after the First Battle of Bull Run. *Memoirs of General W. T. Sherman* (New York: Library of America, 1990), 208.

6. Lincoln to Erastus Corning & others, 12 June 1863, Abraham Lincoln Papers, Library of Congress, Washington D.C.

7. Neely, *Fate of Liberty,* 45–46. The estimated number of cases in the Adjutant General Records is according to Thomas P. Lowry, who, along with his wife Beverly, has researched these records extensively and created a database for many of the cases. *Moyer v. Peabody* (1909), 212 *U.S.* 78–86. Louis S. Gerteis, "'An Outrage on Humanity': Martial Law and Military Prisons in St. Louis During the Civil War," *Missouri Historical Review* 96, no. 4 (July 2002): 303–04.

8. The law codes I have in mind particularly are the Code of Hammurabi (early eighteenth century B.C.) of ancient Mesopotamia and Dracon's Code, the first written legal code of Athens (late sixth century B.C.). The Latin sentence is the motto of Missouri.

9. Hugo Grotius, *The Rights of War and Peace Including the Law of Nature and of Nations,* with an introduction by David J. Hill (Boston: Adamant Media Corporation, 2003), 9–10, 21–26. Emmerich de Vattel, *The Law of Nations: or Principles of the Laws of Nature applied to the Conduct and Affairs of Nations and Sovereigns,* trans. Joseph Chitty and with additional notes and references by Edward D. Ingraham (Philadelphia: T. and J. W. Johnson and Company, Law Booksellers, 1883). Theodore Dwight Woolsey, *Introduction to the Study of International Law Designed as an Aid in Teaching and in Historical Studies,* revised and enlarged by Theodore Salisbury Woolsey (New York: Charles Scribner's Sons, 1871; sixth edition, 1892), 412–13. Burrus M. Carnahan, "Lincoln, Lieber and the Laws of War: The Origins and the Limits of the Principle of Military Necessity," *The American Journal of International Law* 92, no. 2 (April 1998): 214.

10. General Order No. 100, articles 1–30. Captain James G. Garner, "General Order 100 Revisited," *Military Law Review* 27 (January 1965): 9. Carnahan, "Military Necessity," 213–31.

11. Lieber Code, article 82, *The War of the Rebellion: A Compilation of the Official Records of the Union and Confederate Armies,* 128 vols. (Washington D.C.: Government Printing Office, 1880–1902), series 3, vol. 3, 157.

12. Lieber Code, articles 155–57, *Official Records,* series 3, vol. 3, 163. Garner, "Order 100," 33. Lincoln to Erastus Corning & others, 12 June 1863, Lincoln Papers. Freidel, *Lieber,* 317–41. Carnahan, "Military Necessity," 223–25. The example of General Don Carlos Buell in Tennessee in 1862 demonstrated the effectiveness of Confederate guerrilla tactics when a Union commander refused to employ vigorous measures against them. James M. McPherson, *Tried by War: Abraham Lincoln as Commander in Chief* (New York: Penguin Press, 2008), 103–05 and 115–17.

13. Hamilton R. Gamble to Abraham Lincoln, 2 May 1863, Hamilton R. Gamble Papers, Missouri Historical Society, St. Louis, Missouri.

14. Lincoln's Message to Congress in Special Session, 4 July 1861, quoted in Michael P. Johnson, ed., *Abraham Lincoln, Slavery, and the Civil War: Selected Writings and Speeches,* Bedford Series in History and Culture (Boston: Bedford/St. Martin's Press, 2001): 128–29.

15. Ibid., 130–31. James G. Randall, *Constitutional Problems under Lincoln,* rev. ed. (Urbana: University of Illinois Press, 1964), 120–24.

16. Roger B. Taney, *Reports of Cases at Law and Equity and in the Admiralty Determined in the Circuit Court of the United States for the District of Maryland* (Philadelphia: Kay and Brothers, 1871), 246–70. McPherson, *Tried by War,* 27–30. It is next to impossible, even after according the chief justice every benefit of the doubt, to conclude that his only motive in issuing his decision in Merryman was to explicate the Constitution of the United States and to preserve essential rights to individuals. His strong sympathy with the South was no secret and his subsequent behavior, the preparation of various "opinions-without-cases declaring unconstitutional the nation's

conscription, emancipation, and legal-tender policies," demonstrated his intention through judicial action to hamstring the Lincoln administration and the military. See Hyman, *A More Perfect Union*, 81–98 and 256–60.

17. Washington D.C. *Daily National Intelligencer*, 21 August 1861. Horace Binney, *The Privilege of the Writ of Habeas Corpus under the Constitution*, part one (Philadelphia: C. Sherman and Sons, Printers, 1862), 12. Freidel, *Lieber*, 309–12.

18. Binney, *Privilege of the Writ*, 21–24, 26, 29, 31, 36, and 40. Sydney G. Fisher, "The Suspension of Habeas Corpus During the War of the Rebellion," *Political Science Quarterly* 3, no. 3 (September 1888): 457 and 484–85. Despite the practical considerations, it should be noted that after the war several states in adopting new constitutions "included provisions absolutely prohibiting suspension of the writ" and the general consensus remained that such action was a legislative rather than an executive power. Two exceptions were South Carolina and Florida, which, in 1858 and 1868 respectively, granted the authority to the governor. See Dallin H. Oaks, "Habeas Corpus in the States: 1776–1865," *The University of Chicago Law Review* 32, no. 2 (winter 1965): 250–51 and 266–67. For an interesting and informative assessment of the scholarly debate concerning suspension of the writ today, see Farber, *Lincoln's Constitution*, 157–62.

19. In his treatment of this controversy, James A. Dueholm argues that the *grant* of power to suspend the privilege of the writ is found only in article 2 of the Constitution and therefore it must be an exclusively executive power. Here both Taney and Binney disagree with Dueholm that the grant of power is in the suspending clause itself, which provides the authority and limits its suspension to two specific instances, "rebellion or invasion." See Dueholm, "Lincoln's Suspension of the Writ of Habeas Corpus: An Historical and Constitutional Analysis," *Journal of the Abraham Lincoln Association* 29, no. 2 (Summer 2008): 47–66.

20. Neely, *Fate of Liberty*, 20. Edward Bates to Hamilton R. Gamble, 24 July 1862, Bates family papers, Missouri Historical Society, St. Louis, Missouri. For the cases of well-connected persons I have in mind those of Ebenezer Magoffin, the brother of the governor of Kentucky, Beriah Magoffin, and Nathaniel Watkins, half-brother of Henry Clay, but there are many other examples.

21. Dennis K. Boman, "All Politics Are Local: Emancipation in Missouri," in *Lincoln Emancipated: The President and the Politics of Race*, ed. Brian R. Dirck (DeKalb: Northern Illinois University Press, 2007), 130–54.

22. Carnahan, "Military Necessity," 217–19 and 228–29. Randall, *Constitutional Problems*, 351–65. Randall, who lived through both world wars of the twentieth century and was deeply troubled by German claims of military necessity to justify acts of genocide and other violations of international law, rejected the concept as a fraud, claiming that "one does not plead military necessity for an act of unquestionable validity or of normal legality." Nevertheless, Randall contradicted himself in favorably noting elsewhere that Lincoln had himself appealed to military necessity in justifying his decision to emancipate the slaves, see xviii–xix.

23. William Whiting, *War Powers under the Constitution of the United States: Military Arrests, Reconstruction, and Military Government. Also now First Published, War Claims of Aliens, with Notes on the Acts of the Executive and Legislative Departments During Our Civil War and a Collection of Cases Decided in the National Courts*, forty-third ed. (Boston: Lee and Shepard Publishers; New York: Lee, Shepard and Dillingham, 1871), 162–67. Farber, *Lincoln's Constitution*, 146–52.

24. See chapters 6, 7, and 8 of this book for Lincoln's involvement in the commands of Generals Curtis and Schofield.

25. Randall, *Constitutional Problems,* 176–79. James M. McPherson, *Battle Cry of Freedom: The Civil War Era,* vol. 6 of *The Oxford History of the United States,* ed. C. Vann Woodward (New York: Oxford University Press, 1988), 596–97 and 599. David Herbert Donald, *Lincoln* (New York: Simon and Schuster, 1995), 419–21.

26. Lincoln to Stanton, 11 February 1864, Lincoln, *Collected Works,* vol. 7, 178. Circular of the Department of the Missouri, 12 February 1864; and Rosecrans to Edwin M. Stanton, 28 February 1864, series 1, vol. 34, part 2, 311 and 452–53. Lincoln endorsement concerning letter of Reverend John Hogan, 13 February 1864, Lincoln Papers.

CHAPTER ONE

1. "Lincoln's First Inaugural Address," in *Documents of American History,* ed. Henry Steele Commager (New York: Appleton-Century-Crofts, 1949), 385–88. Lincoln to Lyman Trumbull, 10 December 1860, in Abraham Lincoln, *The Collected Works of Abraham Lincoln,* ed. Roy P. Basler (New Brunswick, NJ: Rutgers University Press, 1959), vol. 4, 150. It should be noted here that the original draft of Lincoln's inaugural took a more stern stance; in it, he promised to use "all the power at my disposal" to reclaim the property of the United States seized by the South and to enforce the laws and Constitution. However, Lincoln moderated his message upon the advice of Secretary of State William Seward and others. See David M. Potter, *The Impending Crisis, 1848–1861,* completed and edited by Don E. Fehrenbacher, the New American Nation Series, ed. Henry Steele Commager and Richard B. Morris (New York: Harper and Row, 1976), 565–66.

2. William E. Parrish, *Turbulent Partnership: Missouri and the Union, 1861–1865* (Columbia: University of Missouri Press, 1963), 5–6.

3. Galusha Anderson, *The Story of a Border City During the Civil War* (Boston: Little, Brown, 1908), 82–83.

4. Walter H. Ryle, *Missouri: Union or Secession* (Nashville, TN: George Peabody College for Teachers, 1931), 176, 178, 181–83, 193, and 235–36. Christopher Phillips, *Missouri's Confederate: Claiborne Fox Jackson and the Creation of Southern Identity in the Border West* (Columbia: University of Missouri Press, 2000), 236. Arthur Roy Kirkpatrick, "Missouri on the Eve of the Civil War," *Missouri Historical Review* 55 (January 1961): 100, 102–03. Aaron Astor, Belated Confederates: Black Politics, Guerrilla Violence, and the Collapse of Conservative Unionism in Kentucky and Missouri, 1860–1872 (Ph.D. dissertation, Northwestern University, 2006), 127–28.

5. *Journal of the Missouri State Convention, Held at Jefferson City, July 1861* (St. Louis: George Knapp and Co., 1861), 19 and 34–37. John F. Philips, "Hamilton Rowan Gamble and the Provisional Government of Missouri," *Missouri Historical Review* 5 (October 1910): 1–6. Parrish, *Turbulent Partnership,* 10–13. Anderson, *Border City,* 40, 48–50, and 54–62. For the secessionist viewpoint on the convention see Thomas L. Snead, *The Fight for Missouri: From the Election of Lincoln to the Death of Lyon* (New York: Charles Scribner's Sons, 1886), 78–96.

6. Phillips, *Missouri's Confederate,* 241, 243–45, and 248–49. C. F. Jackson to J. W. Tucker, 28 April 1861, James O. Broadhead Papers, Missouri Historical Society, St. Louis, Missouri.

Anderson, *Border City*, 10–20 and 71–72. *The War of the Rebellion: A Compilation of the Official Records of the Union and Confederate Armies*, 128 vols. (Washington D.C.: Government Printing Office, 1880–1902), series 1, vol. 2, 798.

7. Thomas L. Snead, "The First Year of the War in Missouri," in *Battles and Leaders of the Civil War*, ed. Robert Underwood Johnson and Clarence Clough Bue, 4 vols. (New York: Century Company, 1887–1888), vol. 1, 264. Broadhead, "St. Louis During the Civil War," 9–16, 32–35, 39–41, 43–46, Broadhead Papers. Peter Cozzens and Robert I. Girardi, eds., *The Military Memoirs of General John Pope* (Chapel Hill: University of North Carolina Press, 1998), 6. Christopher Phillips, *Damned Yankee: The Life of General Nathaniel Lyon* (Columbia: University of Missouri Press, 1990), 140–42, 150–52, 154, 159–64. John M. Schofield, *Forty-six Years in the Army*, with a foreword by William M. Ferraro (New York: Century Co., 1897; reprint, Norman: University of Oklahoma Press, 1998), 33–34. Anderson, *Border City*, 73–75 and 84–85. Arthur Roy Kirkpatrick, "Missouri in the Early Months of the Civil War," *Missouri Historical Review* 55 (April 1961): 251 and 253. Parrish, *Turbulent Partnership*, 17–19 and 25. For a more detailed account of Frank P. Blair Jr.'s activities during this crisis, see William E. Parrish, *Frank Blair: Lincoln's Conservative* (Columbia: University of Missouri Press, 1998), 89–111. For an interesting estimate on the importance of breaking up Camp Jackson, see Grant's comments in John Russell Young, *Around the World with General Grant: A Narrative of the Visit of General U. S. Grant, Ex-president of the United States, to Various Countries in Europe, Asia, and Africa in 1877, 1878, 1879 to which are added Certain Conversations with General Grant on Questions Connected with American Politics and History*, vol. 2 (New York: Subscription Book Department, the American News Company, 1879), 465–68.

8. Snead, "First Year," 264–65. Anderson, *Border City*, 92–93, 97, and 102–03. Phillips, *Lyon*, 177–94. Silvana Siddali, ed., *Missouri's War: The Civil War in Documents*, The Civil War in the Great Interior (Athens: Ohio University Press, 2009), 66–68.

9. Parrish, *Turbulent Partnership*, 25–28. Charles Gibson to Thomas T. Gantt, 13 May 1861, Charles Gibson Papers, Missouri Historical Society, St. Louis, Missouri. Mark E. Neely Jr., *The Fate of Liberty: Abraham Lincoln and Civil Liberties* (New York: Oxford University Press, 1991), 5. Phillips, *Lyon*, 199–200. Lincoln to Frank P. Blair Jr., 18 May 1861, Lincoln, *Collected Works*, vol. 4, 372–73. Lincoln also received letters from friends in St. Louis whom he trusted. See Lyman Trumbull to Lincoln, 15 May 1861, and Samuel T. Glover to Lincoln, 24 May 1861, Abraham Lincoln Papers, Library of Congress, Washington D.C.

10. Charles Gibson to Thomas T. Gantt, 13 May 1861, Gibson Papers.

11. "To the People of the State of Missouri," 14 May 1861; William S. Harney to Simon Cameron, 15 May 1861; Harney to Col. E. D. Townsend, 17 May 1861, *Official Records*, series 1, vol. 3, 371–74.

12. Snead, *Fight for Missouri*, 171–72. Anderson, *Border City*, 115–17.

13. Harney to Judge Treat, 15 May 1861; and report of Colonel Richard H. Wightman, 17 July 1861, *Official Records*, series 1, vol. 3, 25; and series 2, vol. 1, 115–16. Record book of the St. Louis Criminal Court, vol. 11, 17 and 24 July 1861. Judge Treat's decision in *In re McDonald*, 16 Federal Case No. 8751 (1861), 17–33, dealt almost exclusively with the jurisdictional issue of the case in which he ruled in MacDonald's favor. Nothing in the opinion provided any information about MacDonald's fate.

14. Joint proclamation of Harney and Sterling Price, 21 May 1861; Frank P. Blair Jr. to Cameron, 24 May 1861; and Lorenzo Thomas to Harney, 27 May 1861, *Official Records*, series 1, vol. 3, 374–76. James O. Broadhead to Montgomery Blair, 22 May 1861, Broadhead Papers. Snead, "First Year," 266.

15. Parrish, *Turbulent Partnership,* 29–30. Kirkpatrick, "Early Months," 236–39. Dennis K. Boman, *Abiel Leonard: Yankee Slaveholder, Eminent Jurist, and Passionate Unionist, Studies in American History,* vol. 38 (Lewiston: Edwin Mellen Press, 2002), 222–23. Abiel Leonard to James O. Broadhead, 3 June 1861, Broadhead Papers. James O. Broadhead to Abiel Leonard, 5 June 1861, courtesy of William Everett, private collection of descendant of Abiel Leonard. Frank P. Blair Jr. to Simon Cameron, 24 May 1861; Unknown to O. D. Filley, 22 May 1861; Unknown to Frank P. Blair Jr., undated; S. Williams to Sterling Price, 23 May 1861; William S. Harney to Price, 24 and 27 May 1861; Price to Harney, 24, 27, 28, and 29 May 1861; Harney to Lorenzo Thomas, 31 May and 5 June 1861; and General Orders, No. 5, 31 May 1861, *Official Records,* series 1, vol. 3, 375–76, 378–81, and 383. Lincoln to Frank P. Blair Jr., 18 May 1861, Lincoln, *Collected Works,* vol. 4, 372–73.

16. Thomas C. Reynolds to Jefferson Davis, 3 June 1861, *Official Records,* series 1, vol. 53, 692–94.

17. Geoffrey Perret wrongly credited John C. Frémont with Jackson's ouster. See Perret, *Lincoln's War: The Untold Story of America's Greatest President as Commander in Chief* (New York: Random House, 2004), 82. Thomas C. Reynolds to Jefferson Davis, 3 June 1861; Nathaniel Lyon to Lorenzo Thomas, 3 and 13 June 1861; General Orders, No. 30, 6 June 1861; Simon Cameron to Lyon, 11 June 1861; B. Gratz Brown to T. W. Sweeny, undated, *Official Records,* series 1, vol. 3, 382–84 and series 1, vol. 53, 692–94. Note of Lincoln on back of letter from Governor Richard Yates, 14 June 1861, Lincoln, *Collected Works,* vol. 4, 407. Snead, "First Year," 267.

18. General Orders, No. 30, 6 June 1861; George B. McClellan to Chester Harding Jr., 18 June 1861; and General Orders, No. 40, 3 July 1861, *Official Records,* series 1, vol. 3, 384–85 and 390.

19. Snead, "First Year," 264. Lincoln's Address to Congress, 4 July 1861, *Official Records,* series 3, vol. 1, 311–15.

20. Constitution of the United States, article 1, section 9. Memorandum of Titian J. Coffey, April 1861; Lincoln to Winfield Scott, 25 April 1861; and Edward Bates to Lincoln, 5 July 1861, Lincoln Papers. William S. Harney to Judge Treat, 15 May 1861; Harney to E. D. Townsend, 18 May 1861; and Thomas C. Reynolds to Jefferson Davis, 3 June 1861, *Official Records,* series 2, vol. 1, 114–16, and series 1, vol. 53, 692–94. Daniel Farber, *Lincoln's Constitution* (Chicago: University of Chicago Press, 2003), 17–19 and 157–63. See also my discussion of suspension of the writ in the introduction of this book.

21. "Memorandum: Military Arrests," Lincoln, *Collected Works,* vol. 4, 372. Report of Nathaniel Lyon on the Battle of Boonville, 22 June 1861; M. Jeff Thompson to Jefferson Davis, 2 July 1861; and L. Polk to L. P. Walker, 23 July 61, *Official Records,* series 1, vol. 3, 11, 601–02, and 612–14.

22. Lyon to Cameron, 29 June 1861; Special Orders, No. 1, 29 June 1861; Lyon to Chester Harding Jr., 2 July 1861; M. Jeff Thompson to Joseph Tucker, 16 July 1861; and John M. Schofield to Harding, 26 July 1861, *Official Records,* series 1, vol. 3, 386–88, 407, and 608–09.

23. Anderson, *Border City,* 166. James Peckham, *Gen. Nathaniel Lyon and Missouri in 1861: A Monograph of the Great Rebellion* (New York: American News Company, 1866), 286–89. Charles Elliott, *Southwestern Methodism: A History of the M. E. Church in the South-west from 1844 to 1864, comprising the Martyrdom of Bewley and Others; Persecutions of the M. E. Church and its Reorganization,* edited and revised by Leroy M. Vernon (Cincinnati: Poe and

Hitchcock, 1868), 287, 291–94. In his biography of Jackson, *Missouri's Confederate: Claiborne Fox Jackson and the Creation of Southern Identity in the Border West* (Columbia: University of Missouri Press, 2000), 249, Christopher Phillips claims that the letter found in the Broadhead papers was a forgery, basing his opinion upon the handwriting. However, several contemporaries who knew Jackson quite well, including Thomas L. Price, a congressman and fellow Democrat, testified that the handwriting was Jackson's. Moreover, Deputy Marshall of the United States Ephraim H. Tunnicliff testified that he executed the search warrant on the office of the *State Journal* and that Tucker directed him to Jackson's letter, which he found in the desk at which Tucker was sitting. Claiborne F. Jackson to Joseph W. Tucker, 28 April 1861; and "Mem of notes taken on Examination of J. W. Tucker of the State Journal on prosecution for treason," Broadhead Papers. Perhaps the letter in the Broadhead papers is a copy of Jackson's original, which was presented in court as evidence.

24. *Journal of the Missouri State Convention, Held at Jefferson City, July 1861* (St. Louis: George Knapp and Co., 1861), 9–12; *Proceedings of the Missouri State Convention, Held at Jefferson City, July 1861* (St. Louis: George Knapp and Co., 1861), 14. Parrish, *Turbulent Partnership*, 36–41.

25. *Journal, July 1861*, 9–12. Parrish, *Turbulent Partnership*, 36–41.

26. *Proceedings, July 1861*, 24, 83, and 95.

27. *Proceedings, July 1861*, 51–56, 73, and 131–33. Parrish, *Turbulent Partnership*, 41–45.

28. Parrish, *Turbulent Partnership*, 47. Anderson, *Border City*, 42. Walter H. Ryle, *Missouri: Union or Secession* (Nashville, TN: George Peabody College for Teachers, 1931), 181–83.

29. Simon Cameron to Hamilton R. Gamble, 3 August 1861; and Lincoln to Bates, 22 August 1861, Lincoln, *Collected Works*, vol. 4, 470–71 and 495. Bates to Lincoln, 14 August 1861, Lincoln Papers.

CHAPTER TWO

1. John M. Schofield, *Forty-six Years in the Army*, with a foreword by William M. Ferraro (New York: Century Co., 1897; reprint, Norman: University of Oklahoma Press, 1998), 37–49. Lincoln memorandum, 23 July 1861, Abraham Lincoln, *The Collected Works of Abraham Lincoln*, ed. Roy P. Basler (New Brunswick, NJ: Rutgers University Press, 1959), vol. 4, 457. John M. Palmer to Lyman Trumbull, 24 July 1861; John C. Frémont to Lincoln, 30 July and 5 and 17 August 1861, Abraham Lincoln Papers, Library of Congress, Washington D.C.

2. John C. Frémont to Col. Townsend, 18 July 1861; Pope to the People of North Missouri, 19 July 1861; and General Orders, No. 4, 19 July 1861, *The War of the Rebellion: A Compilation of the Official Records of the Union and Confederate Armies*, 128 vols. (Washington D.C.: Government Printing Office, 1880–1902) series 2, vol. 1, 187–88.

3. Unknown to George Nash, 21 July 1861; Notice, 21 July 1861; John Pope to Samuel J. Kirkwood, 23 July 1861; General Orders, No. 1, 24 July 1861; Hurlbut to Frémont, 27 July 1861; General Orders, No. 3, 31 July 1861; Pope to Col. J. D. Stevenson, 2 August 1861, *Official Records*, series 2, vol. 1, 189–97. Peter Cozzens and Robert I. Girardi, eds., *The Military Memoirs of General John Pope* (Chapel Hill: University of North Carolina Press, 1998), 24.

4. James M. McPherson, *Battle Cry of Freedom: The Civil War Era*, vol. 6 of *The Oxford History of the United States*, ed. C. Vann Woodward (New York: Oxford University Press, 1988), 329–31. Ulysses S. Grant, *Personal Memoirs of U. S. Grant, Selected Letters, 1839–1865* (New York: Literary Classics of the United States, 1990), 160–67. Bruce Catton, *Grant Moves South* (New York: Little, Brown, 1960; repr., Edison, NJ: Castle Books, 2000), 3–22. Stephen A. Hurlbut to J. M. Palmer, 14 July 1861; Hurlbut to Col. Smith, 14 July 1861, and General Orders, No. 2, 16 July 1861, *Official Records*, series 2, vol. 1, 186.

5. Ulysses S. Grant to Speed Butler, 22 August 1861, *Official Records*, series 1, vol. 3, 452. Schofield, *Forty-Six Years*, 48–49. Frémont to Lincoln, 30 July 1861, Lincoln Papers.

6. William M. Leftwich, *Martyrdom in Missouri: A History of Religious Proscription, the Seizure of Churches, and the Persecution of Ministers of the Gospel, in the State of Missouri During the Late Civil War and under the "Test Oath" of the New Constitution* (St. Louis: Southwestern Book and Publishing Company, 1870), vol. 1, 332–33. William M. McPherson to Hamilton R. Gamble, 29 July 1861, Hamilton R. Gamble Papers, Missouri Historical Society, St. Louis, Missouri.

7. Union Provost-Marshals' File of Papers Relating to Individual Citizens, 1861–1866, Record Group 109, National Archives and Records Administration, Washington D.C., microfilm reel no. 1469, J. B. Fuqua file.

8. John M. Palmer to Lyman Trumbull, 24 July 1861; John Howe to Montgomery Blair, 4 [11?] August 1861; Frémont to Lincoln, 5 and 17 August 1861; Frémont to John G. Nicolay, 6 August 1861; and Frank P. Blair Jr. to Montgomery Blair, 15 August 1861, Lincoln Papers. John S. Phelps and Frank P. Blair Jr. to Lincoln, 6 August 1861; and Thomas A. Scott to John S. Phelps, 8 August 1861, *Official Records*, series 1, vol. 3, 430; and series 3, vol. 1, 392. Lincoln to Simon Cameron, 7 August 1861, Lincoln, *Collected Works*, vol. 4, 475–76. John S. Phelps to Hamilton R. Gamble, 8 August 1861, Gamble Papers.

9. John T. K. Hayward to Frémont, 10 August 1861; Hurlbut to Col. R. F. Smith, 12 August 1861; Hurlbut to John Pope, 13 August 1861; Speed Butler to Hurlbut, 14 August 1861; C. A. Morgan to Hurlbut, 15 August 1861; John T. K. Hayward to J. W. Brooks, 13, 14, 17, and 19 August 1861; and J. W. Brooks to Simon Cameron, 27 August 1861, *Official Records*, series 1, vol. 3, 433–35 and 457–61; and series 2, vol. 1, 206–09.

10. It should be noted here that Hayward's main concern as supervisor of the Hannibal and St. Joseph Railroad was to prevent the continued destruction of its bridges, track, and other properties. Of course, the cessation of all guerrilla activities would help accomplish this goal. John T. K. Hayward to Frémont, 10 August 1861, *Official Records*, series 1, vol. 3, 433–35.

11. *St. Louis Missouri Republican*, 2 and 5 August 1861. Robert N. Smith to Gamble, 12 August 1861, Gamble Papers. Simon Cameron to Gamble, 3 August 1861; Special Order, 13 August 1861; Ulysses S. Grant to Speed Butler, 27 August 1861, *Official Records*, series 1, vol. 3, 463; series 1, vol. 53, 498; and series 2, vol. 1, 208. Edward Bates to Lincoln, 24 August 1861; and Gamble to Lincoln, 31 October 1861, Lincoln Papers.

12. L. W. Burris to Gamble, 8 August 1861; Charles Gibson to Gamble, 8 and 19 August 1861; George Brown to Gamble, 10 August 1861; J. T. K. Hayward to Gamble, 17 August 1861; E. B. Dobyns to Gamble, 18 August 1861; and Gamble to Lincoln, 26 August 1861, Gamble Papers. Special Orders No. 13, 30 August 1861, *Official Records*, series 2, vol. 1, 220–21. For a full discussion of the controversy between the Blair family and Frémont see William E. Parrish, *Frank Blair: Lincoln's*

Conservative (Columbia: University of Missouri Press, 1998), 112–39. The importance of slavery as a cause of secession is best demonstrated in Charles B. Dew, *Apostles of Disunion: Southern Secession Commissioners and the Causes of the Civil War* (Charlottesville: University of Virginia Press, 2001).

13. One of Fremont's first actions after this was to cause deeds of emancipation to be made out for the slaves of Thomas Snead, an aide to ousted Governor Jackson. As with much else, Frémont's actions were ill-conceived and precipitous, for the slaves turned out to belong to Snead's wife, thus making the freedom papers worthless. Proclamation of John C. Frémont, 30 August 1861; General Order No. 6, J. C. Kelton, 30 August 1861; Pope to Col. J. H. Eaton, 30 August 1861; and Proclamation of Frémont and deed of manumission, 12 September 1861, *Official Records*, series 1, vol. 3, 466–70 and series 2, vol. 1, 220 and 769–70. Cozzens and Girardi, *John Pope*, 24–27. Samuel T. Glover to Lincoln, 21 September 1861, Lincoln Papers. Galusha Anderson, *The Story of a Border City During the Civil War* (Boston: Little, Brown, 1908), 217–19.

14. Lincoln to John C. Frémont, 2 and 11 September 1861; and Frémont to Lincoln, 8 September 1861, *Official Records*, series 1, vol. 3, 477–78 and 485–86.

15. Daniel Farber, *Lincoln's Constitution* (Chicago: University of Chicago Press, 2003), 148–49.

16. Frémont to Colonel John McNeil, 28 July 1861; Proclamation, 30 August 1861, and Justus McKinstry to S. Burbank, 21 August 1861, *Official Records*, series 1, vol. 3, 410 and 466–67, and series 2, vol. 1, 128. *St. Louis Christian Advocate*, 23 May and 5 September 1861. Anderson, *Border City*, 213–14.

17. Stephen A. Hurlbut to John Pope, 13 August 1861; and Speed Butler to Hurlbut, 14 August 1861, *Official Records*, series 2, vol. 1, 207–09.

18. Paul Finkelman, "Civil Liberties and Civil War: The Great Emancipator as Civil Libertarian," *Michigan Law Review* 91 (May 1993): 1374–77.

19. James G. Randall, *Constitutional Problems under Lincoln*, rev. ed. (Urbana: University of Illinois Press, 1964), 481. Robert S. Harper, *Lincoln and the Press* (New York: McGraw-Hill, 1951), 142–44. William H. Rehnquist, *All the Laws but One: Civil Liberties in Wartime* (New York: Alfred A. Knopf, 1998), 46–48, 170, and 219. Charles Wiggins to Edward Bates, 24 April 1861, with a clip from the *St. Louis Evening News*, 23 April 1861, *Official Records*, series 1, vol. 1, 673–74.

20. *St. Louis Christian Advocate*, 24 January, 14 and 21 February, 21 March, 11 and 25 April, 16 and 30 May, 20 and 27 June, and 4, 11, 18, and 25 July 1861. After the war Charles Elliot provided an account of McAnally's wartime behavior in *Southwestern Methodism: A History of the M. E. Church in the South-west from 1844 to 1864, comprising the Martyrdom of Bewley and Others; Persecutions of the M. E. Church and its Reorganization*, edited and revised by Leroy M. Vernon (Cincinnati: Poe and Hitchcock, 1868), 239, 251, 257, 277, 280, 284–85, 294.

21. *St. Louis Christian Advocate*, 29 August 1861. Leftwich, *Martyrdom in Missouri*, vol. 2, 156–58. Robert S. Harper, *Lincoln and the Press* (New York: McGraw-Hill, 1951), 142. Later, McKinstry was arrested and convicted "of selling war contracts and dismissed . . . from the service." Louis S. Gerteis, "'A Friend of the Enemy': Federal Efforts to Suppress Disloyalty in St. Louis During the Civil War," *Missouri Historical Review* 96, no. 3 (April 2002): 169.

22. Leftwich, *Martyrdom in Missouri*, 3 and 108–24. *St. Louis Christian Advocate*, 4 and 11 July 1861; 29 August 1861; and 7 November 1861.

23. *St. Louis Christian Advocate,* 30 May and 7 November 1861. Leftwich, *Martyrdom in Missouri,* 108–24. Farber, *Lincoln's Constitution,* 171–75.

24. *St. Louis Christian Advocate,* 30 May and 7 November 1861. Leftwich, *Martyrdom in Missouri,* 108–24. Farber, *Lincoln's Constitution,* 171–75.

25. Mark E. Neely Jr., *The Fate of Liberty: Abraham Lincoln and Civil Liberties* (New York: Oxford University Press, 1991), 41. Francis Lieber, "Instructions for the Government of Armies of the United States in the Field," General Orders, No. 100 (Washington D.C.: Adjutant General's Office, Government Printing Office, 1898), article 13. Farber, *Lincoln's Constitution,* 146–52. Ulysses S. Grant to Speed Butler, 27 August 1861; and Grant to Chauncey McKeever, 29 September 1861, *Official Records,* series 1, vol. 3, 509; and series 2, vol. 1, 220. *St. Louis Republican,* 19 and 20 September 1861.

26. General Orders, No. 10, 12 September 1861, *Official Records,* series 2, vol. 1, 282. Some details about these prisoners is found in the *St. Louis Missouri Republican,* 10, 15, 19, and 20 September 1861.

27. Joseph Aubuchon, file II471, Judge-Advocate Papers, Record Group 153, National Archives, Washington D.C. General Orders, No. 12, 16 September 1861, series 2, vol. 1, 283. *St. Louis Missouri Republican,* 15 September 1861.

28. Special Orders, No. 2, 24 September 1861; and Special Orders, No. 10, 29 September 1861, *Official Records,* series 2, vol. 1, 283–84.

29. Dennis K. Boman, "Conduct and Revolt in the Twenty-fifth Ohio Battery: An Insider's Account," *Ohio History* 104 (Summer–Autumn 1995): 171–72. Lincoln to O. H. Browning, 22 September 1861, Lincoln, *Collected Works,* vol. 4, 531–32. Burrus M. Carnahan, "Lincoln, Lieber, and the Laws of War: The Origins and Limits of the Principle of Military Necessity," *The American Journal of International Law,* vol. 92, no. 2 (April 1998): 220–22.

30. Lincoln to O. H. Browning, 22 September 1861, Lincoln, *Collected Works,* vol. 4, 532.

31. Benjamin F. Butler to Winfield Scott, 24 and 27 May 1861; Simon Cameron to Butler, 30 May and 8 August 1861, *Official Records,* series 2, vol. 1, 752, 754–55, and 761–62.

32. Ulysses S. Grant to John C. Kelton, 30 August 1861; Justus McKinstry to Gordon Granger, 20 September 1861; and Grenville Dodge to Colonel Greusel, 4 November 1861, *Official Records,* series 2, vol. 1, 766, 771–72, and 775–76.

33. Cozzens and Girardi, *John Pope,* 28–29. See also the testimony in the case of *Orlando and Amanda Sawyer v. The Hannibal and St. Joseph Railroad Company,* which originated in the Buchanan County Circuit Court, was appealed to the Supreme Court of Missouri, and decided during the February 1866 term, Missouri State Archives, Jefferson City, Missouri.

34. Cozzens and Girardi, *John Pope,* 30–36. S. M. Breckinridge to Gamble, 3 August 1861; John M. Richardson to Gamble, 10 August 1861; and Charles Gibson to Gamble, 27 September 1861, Gamble Papers. Samuel T. Glover to Montgomery Blair, 2 September 1861; James O. Broadhead to Montgomery Blair, 3 September 1861; Winfield Scott to Lincoln, 5 September 1861; Lincoln to David Hunter, 9 September 1861; John B. Henderson to James O. Broadhead, 7 September 1861; John M. Shaffer to Winfield Scott, 14 September 1861; Francis P. Blair Jr. to Lincoln, 15 September, 1861; Samuel T. Glover to Lincoln, 20 and 21 September 1861; and John How to Montgomery Blair, 3 October 1861, Lincoln Papers. William E. Parrish, *Turbulent Partnership: Missouri and the Union, 1861–1865* (Columbia: University of Missouri Press, 1963), 52 and 66–68. Nathaniel

Lyon to Chester Harding Jr., 2 July 1861; M. Jeff. Thompson to Joseph Tucker, 16 July 1861; John M. Schofield to Chester Harding Jr., 26 July 1861; Ulysses S. Grant to William H. Worthington, 26 August 1861; Jefferson C. Davis to Frémont, 12 and 19 September 1861; Gamble to Frémont, 13 September 1861; Benjamin M. Prentiss to Frémont, 22 September 1861; W. E. Prince to James H. Lane, 23 September 1861; and Report of Lorenzo Thomas, October 1861, *Official Records,* series 1, vol. 3, 171–72, 174, 178, 183–84, 388, 407–08, 543–49, and 608–09; series 2, vol. 1, 217. Albert Castel, *General Sterling Price and the Civil War in the West* (Baton Rouge: Louisiana State University Press, 1968), 56–60. Robert E. Shalhope, *Sterling Price: Portrait of a Southerner* (Columbia: University of Missouri Press, 1971), 184–89. T. Harry Williams, "Frémont and the Politicians," *The Journal of the American Military History Foundation* 2 (Winter 1938): 182–83. James M. McPherson, *Tried by War: Abraham Lincoln as Commander in Chief* (New York: Penguin Press, 2008), 54–57.

35. *Journal of the Missouri State Convention Held at the City of St. Louis, October 1861* (St. Louis: George Knapp and Co., 1861), 17–20 and 110. Report of Quin Morton, 1 December 1862, and Benjamin M. Prentiss, 17 November 1862, *Official Records,* series 1, vol. 10, part 1, 277–80 and 291.

36. *Missouri State Convention, October 1861,* 4, 8, 9–32, 39–40, 50–51, 60–66, and 72–74.

37. Ibid., 4, 8, 60–66, and 72–74.

38. Gamble to Lincoln, 26 August 1861; Gamble to Charles Gibson, 20 September 1861; William M. McPherson to Gamble, 23 September 1861; Edward Bates to Gamble, 3 October 1861; and Gamble to Dr. John R. Moore, 30 November 1861, Gamble Papers. Gamble to Montgomery Blair, 5 October 1861; Gamble to William G. Elliot, 15 October 1861; Gamble to Lincoln, 31 October 1861; Gamble's memorandum on state militia plan, 31 October 1861; and Gamble to Henry W. Halleck, October 1862, Lincoln Papers.

39. Gamble's memorandum and letter to Lincoln, 31 October 1861, Lincoln Papers.

40. Memorandum and letter of Lincoln to Gamble, 4 November 1861; memorandum to Secretary of War, 4 November 1861, Gamble Papers. Gamble's proposal, 5 November 1861; Lincoln to Gamble, 6 November 1861; and General Orders, No. 96, 7 November 1861, *Official Records,* series 1, vol. 3, 565–66 and series 1, vol. 13, 9.

CHAPTER THREE

1. Charles Gibson to Hamilton R. Gamble, 10 November 1861, Gamble Papers, Missouri Historical Society, St. Louis, Missouri. John F. Marszalek, *Commander of All Lincoln's Armies: A Life of General Henry W. Halleck* (Cambridge: Belknap Press of Harvard University Press, 2004), 109–10.

2. General Orders, No. 97, 9 November 1861; George B. McClellan to Henry W. Halleck, 11 November 1861; General Orders, No. 1, 19 November 1861; Petition from a committee of Unionist residents in southwestern Missouri, 20 November 1861; General Orders, No. 8, 26 November 1861; Halleck to McClellan, 6 and 10 December 1861, *The War of the Rebellion: A Compilation of the Official Records of the Union and Confederate Armies,* 128 vols. (Washington D.C.: Government Printing Office, 1880–1902), series 1, vol. 3, 567–69, and vol. 8, 369–71, 380, 408, and 818.

3. Marszalek, *Halleck*, 110–11. Halleck to McClellan, 19 December 1861; Earl Van Dorn to Sterling Price, 7 February 1862; and Confidential Circular of G. T. Beauregard, 21 February 1862, *Official Records*, series 1, vol. 7, 899; and series 1, vol. 8, 448–49 and 748–49. Galusha Anderson, *The Story of a Border City During the Civil War* (Boston: Little, Brown, 1908), 168–69.

4. Anderson, *Border City*, 168–69 and 237–38. George E. Leighton Papers, 9 December 1861, Missouri Historical Society, St. Louis, Missouri. Robert A. Barnes Papers, General Orders, No. 1, undated, Missouri Historical Society, St. Louis, Missouri. General Orders, No. 19, 7 December 1861; General Orders, No. 16, 11 January 1862; General Orders, No. 41, 15 February 1862; General Orders, No. 55, 3 March 1862; General Orders, No. 3, 14 March 1862; Circular, 28 March 1862; Bernard G. Farrar to Major Hunt, 8 March 1862; Benjamin Loan to John M. Schofield, 18 and 25 March 1862; and Schofield to Loan, 21 March 1862, *Official Records*, series 1, vol. 8, 414, 495, 557, 586–87, 648, and 832; series 2, vol. 1, 173–74 and 271–73.

5. Gamble to Dr. John R. Moore, 30 November 1861, Gamble Papers. John Pope to Halleck, 2 December 1861; Charles Whittlesey to Halleck, 31 December 1861; and Halleck to Whittlesey, 2 January 1862, *Official Records*, series 1, vol. 8, 399 and 481, and series 2, vol. 1, 243–46.

6. General Orders, No. 96, 7 November 1861; and General Orders, No. 1, 25 November 1861, *Official Records*, series 1, vol. 3, 565, and series 1, vol. 8, 378.

7. *St. Louis Missouri Republican*, 26 November and 1 and 6 December 1861. Howard K. Beale, ed., *The Diary of Edward Bates, 1859–1866* (Washington D.C.: Government Printing Office, 1933), 219. Halleck to Gamble, 2 January 1862, Gamble Papers. Schofield to Loan, 10 December 1861; and Gamble to Halleck, 6 January 1862, *Official Records*, series 1, vol. 8, 422–23, and series 2, vol. 1, 252.

8. Lincoln to Governor Gustave P. Koerner, 15 January 1862; and Koerner to Lincoln, 26 January 1862, Abraham Lincoln Papers, Library of Congress, Washington D.C. Halleck to Frank P. Blair Jr., 6 January 1862; Halleck to McClellan, 14 January 1862; Lincoln to Halleck, 15 January 1862; Halleck to Curtis, 17 January 1862; Halleck to Lincoln, 21 January 1862; Halleck to McClellan, 2 February 1862; and McClellan to Halleck, 6 February 1862, *Official Records*, series 1, vol. 8, 490, 500–02, and 826–29; and series 1, vol. 7, 937.

9. Halleck to Schofield, 31 December 1861; Schofield to Kelton, 2 January 1862; Schofield to John B. Henderson, 2 January 1862; Schofield to Benjamin M. Prentiss, 3 January 1862; Halleck to McClellan, 14 January 1862; General Orders, No. 1, 22 March 1862; and General Orders, No. 5, 6 June 1863, *Official Records*, series 1, vol. 8, 479, 482, 500–03, 798–99, 823; and vol. 22, part 2, 860. Provost-marshal's record book, 6 January 1862, Arnold Krekel Papers, Missouri Historical Society, St. Louis, Missouri.

10. *St. Louis Missouri Republican*, 26 November 1861. Halleck to McClellan, 14 January 1861; General Orders, No. 28, 2 February 1862; and General Orders, No. 46, 22 February 1862, *Official Records*, series 1, vol. 8, 500–02, 542, and 563–64.

11. George E. Leighton to Halleck, 4 December 1861, *Official Records*, series 2, vol. 2, 139–41. Bernard G. Farrar to Leighton, 14 and 27 December 1861, Leighton Papers.

12. George E. Leighton to Halleck, 4 December 1861; and Leighton to William H. Seward, 6 December 1861, *Official Records*, series 2, vol. 2, 139–41 and 171.

13. Halleck to McClellan, 20 and 30 November 1861; Lincoln's endorsement, 21 November 1861; Lorenzo Thomas to Halleck, 25 November 1861; and Lincoln and William H. Seward, 2 December 1861, *Official Records*, series 2, vol. 1, 230–33.

14. General Orders, No. 13, 4 December 1861 and General Orders, No. 34, 26 December 1861, *Official Records*, series 1, vol. 8, 405–07 and 468.

15. General Orders, No. 39, 14 February 1862; and James Totten to the deputy sheriff and members of the grand jury in Moniteau County, Missouri, 10 April 1862, *Official Records*, series 1, vol. 8, 556 and 680–81. Henry W. Halleck, *Halleck's International Law or Rules Regulating the Intercourse of States in Peace and War*, revised by Sir G. Sherston Baker and Maurice N. Drucquer, vol. 2 (London: Kegan Paul, Trench, Trubner and Co., 1908), 466 and 470.

16. James B. Eads to Halleck, 23 November 1861; General Orders, No. 13, 4 December 1861; John Pope to Halleck, 11 December 1861; General Orders, No. 24, 12 December 1861; Orders No. 14, 18 December 1861; and Orders No. 16, 20 December 1861, *Official Records*, series 2, vol. 1, 150–51 and 230–31; and series 1, vol. 8, 405–06, 425–26, 446, and 452. Anderson, *Border City*, 242. Matthew M. Stith, "At the Heart of Total War: Guerrillas, Civilians, and the Union Response in Jasper County, Missouri, 1861–1865," *Military History of the West* 38 (2008): 1–27. Louis S. Gerteis, "'A Friend of the Enemy': Federal Efforts to Suppress Disloyalty in St. Louis During the Civil War," *Missouri Historical Review* 96, no. 3 (April 2002): 173–74.

17. Special Orders, No. 74, 24 January 1862, Barnes Papers. Halleck, *Halleck's International Law*, 2: 73–74, 86–87, and 91. Union Provost-Marshals' File of Papers Relating to Individual Citizens, 1861–1866, Record Group 109, National Archives and Records Administration, Washington D.C., microfilm reel no. 1238, citizen protest of William G. Clark et al. *John Decker v. Francis P. Blair Jr. et al.* and *James R. Shaler v. Nathaniel Lyon et al.*, cases 449 and 85 of the November 1861 term; and *Samuel Engler v. Henry W. Halleck et al.*, case 41 of the April 1862 term, St. Louis Court of Common Pleas.

18. Gamble to Halleck, 23 December 1861; Farrar to Commanding Officer at Cape Girardeau, 26 December 1861; Farrar to Halleck, 26 December 1861; Frank P. Blair Jr. to Halleck, 3 January 1862; Halleck to Blair, 6 January 1861; Farrar to Halleck, 1 March 1862; General Orders, No. 54, 3 March 1862; and General Orders, No. 109, 20 December 1862, *Official Records*, series 1, vol. 8, 490, 586, and 823–24; and series 2, vol. 1, 153, 155–56, and series 4, vol. 2, 248. *St. Louis Missouri Republican*, 16 December 1861 and 11 February 1862.

19. Anderson, *Border City*, 252–63. Order No. 2, Farrar to Leighton, 6 December 1861; and General Orders, No. 13, 4 December 1861, *Official Records*, series 1, vol. 8, 405–06 and 411.

20. Stephen A. Hurlbut to J. M. Palmer, 14 July 1861; General Orders, No. 2, 16 July 1861; General Orders, No. 6, 30 August 1861; Ulysses S. Grant to J. B. Plummer, 4 November 1861; General Orders, No. 8, 26 November 1861; and General Orders, No. 13, 4 December 1861, *Official Records*, series 1, vol. 3, 259 and 467–68; vol. 8, 380–81 and 405–07; and series 2, vol. 1, 185–86. William G. Clark, microfilm reel no. 1238, Union Provost-Marshals' File of Papers Relating to Individual Citizens, 1861–1866, Record Group 109, National Archives and Records Administration, Washington D.C., Missouri State Archives, Jefferson City, Missouri.

21. Provost-Marshal Records, microfilm reel no. 1218, Charlotte A. Armstrong. See also microfilm reel no. 1297, Thomas Davis; and no. 1348, Ashton P. Johnson or Johnston.

22. Provost-Marshal Records, microfilm reel no. 1237, Samuel B. Churchill. List of political prisoners, *Official Records*, series 2, vol. 2, 250.

23. Mary T. Valentine, *The Biography of Ephraim McDowell, M.D.: "The Father of Ovariotomy,"* second edition (Philadelphia: by the author, 1894), 158–80. Anderson, *Border City*, 187–89.

24. General Orders, No. 3, 31 July 1861; and General Orders, No. 32, 22 December 1861; *Official Records,* series 1, vol. 8, 463–64 and series 2, vol. 1, 195–96. *Liberty Weekly Tribune,* 3 January 1862.

25. General Orders, No. 13, 4 December 1861; Halleck to T. J. McKean, 22 December 1861; A. Krekel to Halleck, 23 December 1861; B. M. Prentiss to Halleck, 23 December 1861; Halleck to Prentiss, 23 December 1861; Halleck to Frank J. Herron, 23 December 1861; Halleck to John M. Schofield, 25 December 1861; Halleck to McClellan, 26 December 1861 and 9 January 1862; Schofield to Halleck, 1, 2, 8, and 10 January 1862; General Orders, No. 1, 1 January 1862; and General Orders, No. 39, 14 February 1862, *Official Records,* series 1, vol. 8, 405–07, 457–62, 475–79, and 556; and series 2, vol. 1, 252–53. Leander Stillwell, *The Story of a Common Soldier of Army Life in the Civil War, 1861–1865,* 2d ed. (Kansas City, Missouri: Franklin Hudson, 1920), 102 and 107–08.

26. Halleck to John Pope, 31 December 1861, *Official Records,* series 1, vol. 8, 822–23. Henry W. Halleck, "Military Tribunals and their Jurisdiction," *The American Journal of International Law,* vol. 5, no. 4 (October 1911): 958–67.

27. Sterling Price to Halleck, 12 January 1862; and Halleck to Price, 22 January 1862, *Official Records,* series 2, vol. 1, 255 and 258–59. See also the correspondence on this subject of John B. Clark and Confederate Secretary of War George W. Randolph in Silvana Siddali, ed., *Missouri's War: The Civil War in Documents,* The Civil War in the Great Interior (Athens: Ohio University Press, 2009), 147–48.

28. Sterling Price to Halleck, 12 January 1862; and Halleck to Price, 22 January 1862, *Official Records,* series 2, vol. 1, 255 and 258–59. *Ex parte Milligan,* 71 U.S. 2 (1866), 127. John M. Bickers, "Military Commissions Are Constitutionally Sound: A Response to Professors Katyal and Tribe," *Texas Tech Law Review* 34 (2003): 906.

29. Thomas Ewing to Halleck, 5 January 1862; Halleck to Gamble, 7 January 1862; Schofield to Halleck, 10 January 1862; Special Orders, No. 28, 10 January 1862; Special Orders, No. 10, 10 January 1862; Halleck to McClellan, 14 January 1862; Halleck to Lorenzo Thomas, 14 January 1862; C. S. Sheldon to Leonidas Horney, 27 January 1862; Britton A. Hill to Halleck, 31 January 1862; William F. Switzler to Halleck, 3 February 1862; A. S. Dinwiddie to Switzler, 9 February 1862; Circular, 14 February 1862; and General Orders, No. 44, 20 February 1862, *Official Records,* series 2, vol. 1, 251–65.

30. Halleck to John Pope, 31 December 1861; General Orders, No. 44, 20 February 1862; and General Orders, No. 20, 14 January 1862, *Official Records,* series 1, vol. 8, 561 and 822–23; and series 2, vol. 1, 405.

31. Joseph W. Bollinger, file KK 825, Judge-Advocate Papers, Record Group 153, National Archives, Washington D.C.

32. Jefferson F. Jones, file KK 834, Judge-Advocate Papers.

33. Ibid.

34. Apparently, General Schofield agreed with the commission that Jones was guilty of aiding and abetting the insurrection. Schofield to Jefferson F. Jones, 15 February 1862; and C. S. Sheldon to A. Krekel, 11 March 1862, *Official Records,* series 2, vol. 1, 264 and 269. Jefferson F. Jones, file KK 834, Judge-Advocate Papers.

35. John M. Schofield to Jefferson F. Jones, 15 February 1862; William F. Switzler to Halleck, 3 February 1862; A. S. Dinwiddie to Switzler, 9 February 1862; and General Orders, No. 44, 20 February 1862, *Official Records,* series 2, vol. 1, 262–65.

36. General Orders, No. 1, 13 March 1862; and General Orders, No. 2, 13 March 1862, *Official Records*, series 1, vol. 8, 611–12.

37. Michael Fellman, *Inside War: The Guerrilla Conflict in Missouri During the American Civil War* (New York: Oxford University Press, 1989), v and 23–29.

38. General Orders, No. 13, 4 December 1861, *Official Records*, series 2, vol. 1, 233–36. Robert T. McMahan Papers, Western Historical Manuscript Collection, State Historical Society of Missouri, Columbia, Missouri, journal entry of 26 April 1862. McMahan was a member of the Second Ohio Volunteer Cavalry.

39. Halleck to Benjamin Prentiss, 26 November 1861; John Pope to Kelton, 28 November 1861; Ulysses S. Grant to L. F. Ross, 4 December 1861; General Orders, No. 13, 4 December 1861; Halleck to Pope, 31 December 1861; General Orders, No. 1, 1 January 1862; Halleck to Schofield, 4 January 1862; Halleck to McClellan, 14 January 1862; George E. Waring Jr. to Halleck, 11 March 1862; Report of Waring, 12 March 1862; General Orders, No. 2, 13 March 1862; and Halleck to Edwin M. Stanton, 25 March 1862, *Official Records*, series 1, vol. 8, 187–89; 379–80, 500–02, 604, 611–12, 641–42; and 822–23; and series 2, vol. 1, 232–236, 251, and 477–78. Richard Shelly Hartigan, *Lieber's Code and the Law of War* (Chicago: Precedent Publishing, 1983), 41. Michael Fellman wrongly credits legal scholar Francis Lieber with establishing the policy to combat guerrillas and argued that Halleck only ratified what troops in the field were doing rather than setting policy himself. See Fellman, *Inside War*, 82 and 283, footnote 9.

40. General Orders, No. 2, 13 March 1862; and Report of Waring, 12 March 1862, *Official Records*, series 1, vol. 8, 187–89 and 611–12.

41. James Totten to J. H. Blood, 23 March 1862; Emory S. Foster to Totten, 25 and 28 March 1862; and General Orders, No. 17, 22 April 1862, *Official Records*, series 1, vol. 8, 349–50, 353–54, and 638–39; and series 2, vol. 1, 273 and 281–82.

42. Lincoln to Cuthbert Bullitt, 28 July 1862, Abraham Lincoln, *The Collected Works of Abraham Lincoln*, ed. Roy P. Basler (New Brunswick, NJ: Rutgers University Press, 1959), vol. 5, 344–46. Mark Grimsley, *The Hard Hand of War: Union Military Policy toward Southern civilians, 1861–1865* (New York: Cambridge University Press, 1995), 87. General Orders, No. 100, 24 April 1863, *Official Records*, series 3, vol. 3, 148–64. In Fellman's account, he is apparently unaware of Lincoln's deep involvement in supervising and modifying military policy from the beginning of the war, including the treatment of guerrillas, in Missouri. See Fellman, *Inside War*, 84–86.

43. General Orders, No. 252, 31 July 1863, *Official Records*, series 2, vol. 6, 163. Joseph T. Glatthaar, *Forged in Battle: The Civil War Alliance of Black Soldiers and White Officers* (New York: Free Press, 1990), 202–03. In his discussion of Lincoln's policy concerning the treatment of guerrillas, Fellman fails to distinguish between the treatment of guerrillas captured in the field in arms and those arrested on suspicion of being guerrillas. It is the latter group over whose cases Lincoln still exercised review of the proceedings, not the former. See Fellman, *Inside War*, 86. It should also be noted that after the Fort Pillow massacre, where defenseless black soldiers were murdered by Confederate troops under General Nathan Bedford Forrest, Lincoln and his cabinet recoiled from actually carrying out reprisal executions. Instead, they opted not to execute Confederate prisoners of war in retaliation, but to warn that any further incidents would result in such action. James M. McPherson, *Tried by War: Abraham Lincoln as Commander in Chief* (New York: Penguin Press, 2008), 215–16.

CHAPTER FOUR

1. General Orders, No. 19, 7 December 1861; Bernard G. Farrar to Major Hunt, 8 March 1862; and Circular, 28 March 1862, *The War of the Rebellion: A Compilation of the Official Records of the Union and Confederate Armies*, 128 vols. (Washington D.C.: Government Printing Office, 1880–1902), series 1, vol. 8, 414 and 648; and series 2, vol. 1, 173–74.

2. General Orders, No. 10, 8 January 1862, Robert A. Barnes Papers, Missouri Historical Society, St. Louis, Missouri. Lincoln to John M. Schofield, 20 July 1863, Abraham Lincoln Papers, Library of Congress, Washington D.C. Galusha Anderson, *The Story of a Border City During the Civil War* (Boston: Little, Brown, 1908), 142–43. James G. Randall, *Constitutional Problems under Lincoln*, rev. ed. (Urbana: University of Illinois Press, 1964), 477–510. Daniel Farber, *Lincoln's Constitution* (Chicago: University of Chicago Press, 2003), 170–75. John F. Marszalek, *Commander of All Lincoln's Armies: A Life of General Henry W. Halleck* (Cambridge: Belknap Press of Harvard University Press, 2004), 110 and 124–25.

3. General Orders, No. 48, 26 February 1862, *Official Records*, series 1, vol. 8, 568–69.

4. Record Book, U.S. Department of State, *Official Records*, series 2, vol. 2, 348. Depositions of Archibald K. Nisbet, 5 March 1862; J. C. Scott, 5 March 1862; Charles W. Hahn, 6 March 1862; Anthony F. Hahn, 6 March 1862; and J. Edward Wilkins to George E. Leighton, March 1862, microfilm reel no. 1351, Provost-Marshal Records.

5. Leighton to Wilkins, 7 and 10 March 1862, microfilm reel no. 1351, Provost-Marshal Records. The next commander in Missouri was Samuel R. Curtis, who took a tougher stance against persons suspected of disloyalty.

6. William M. Leftwich, *Martyrdom in Missouri: A History of Religious Proscription, the Seizure of Churches, and the Persecution of Ministers of the Gospel, in the State of Missouri During the Late Civil War and under the "Test Oath" of the New Constitution* (St. Louis: Southwestern Book and Publishing Company, 1870), vol. 2, 108–24.

7. Provost-Marshal Records, microfilm reel no. 1242, oath of A. F. Cox, editor of the *St. Louis Observer*, 14 February 1862. Benjamin G. Farrar to Thomas L. Price, 5 May 1862; *Official Records*, series 2, vol. 3, 520.

8. Trial of Edmund J. Ellis, 25 and 26 February 1862; and Edwin M. Stanton to Halleck, 5 April 1862, *Official Records*, series 2, vol. 1, 276 and 453–57. Later the military discovered that Ellis did not own the paper or its property, see Provost-Marshal Records, microfilm reel no. 1311, 8 July 1862.

9. See chapter 3 for the special circumstances and difficulties confronted by Missouri's civil and military government.

10. J. C. Kelton to J. B. Wyman, 7 August 1861; Executive Order No. 1, Relating to Political Prisoners, 14 February 1862; Circular, 14 February 1862; Halleck to J. W. Bell, 31 March 1862, *Official Records*, series 2, vol. 1, 125–26, 263–64; vol. 2, 221–23; and vol. 3, 413.

11. Report of George E. Leighton to William H. Seward, 3 March 1862, *Official Records*, series 2, vol. 2, 249–52. Microfilm reel nos. 1330 and 1471, Provost-Marshal Records.

12. Microfilm reel no. 1408, Provost-Marshal Records.

13. Microfilm reel no. 1465, Provost-Marshal Records.

14. Joseph B. Hussey, file KK 822, Judge-Advocate Papers, Record Group 153, National Archives, Washington D.C.

15. Microfilm reel no. 1400, Provost-Marshal Records. Jerry E. Wilson, "Willard Preble Hall (1820–1882)," in *Dictionary of Missouri Biography*, ed. Lawrence O. Christensen, William E. Foley, Gary R. Kremer, and Kenneth H. Winn (Columbia: University of Missouri Press, 1999), 366–67.

16. Microfilm reel no. 1471, Provost-Marshal Records. Leftwich, *Martyrdom in Missouri*, vol. 1, 177–78.

17. Leftwich, *Martyrdom in Missouri*, vol. 1, 128–42, 285–87, 308–31, and vol. 2, 365–67. John W. Davidson to James Peckham, 28 September 1862, *Official Records*, series 1, vol. 13, 681. The names of other ministers who fell victim to this type of arbitrary arrest were Jesse Bird, James Duval, and Caleb M. Colyear.

18. Leftwich, *Martyrdom in Missouri*, vol. 1, 376–91.

19. Once again, see chapter 2 for the details of these earlier events.

20. Leftwich, *Martyrdom in Missouri*, vol. 1, 287–90. Halleck to George B. McClellan, 20 December 1861; Farrar to commanding officer, 25 March 1862; and Special Field Orders No. 5, 27 September 1864, *Official Records*, series 1, vol. 8, 37, and vol. 41, part 3, 424–25; and series 2, vol. 1, 175–76. William Henry Lewis, *The History of Methodism in Missouri for a Decade of Years from 1860 to 1870* (Nashville, TN: Barbee and Smith, 1890), vol. 3, 289–91. Microfilm reel nos. 1277 and 1292, Provost-Marshal Records. *Liberty Weekly Tribune*, 17 August 1849. Enoch Mather Marvin, *The Life of Rev. William Goff Caples of the Missouri Conference of the Methodist Episcopal Church South* (St. Louis: Southwestern Book and Publishing Company, 1870), 260–84.

21. Joint proclamation of John C. Frémont and Sterling Price, 1 November 1861, *Official Records*, series 1, vol. 3, 563–64. Leftwich, *Martyrdom in Missouri*, vol. 1, 287–90.

22. Ibid., vol. 1, 297–308.

23. See chapter 2 for the details of the controversy surrounding slavery during Frémont's administration. The range of disagreement among Unionists, especially over slavery, would later lead to infighting and a less-than-effective strategy for winning the conflict in Missouri. This lack of concert greatly complicated Lincoln's task and exasperated him in dealing with Missouri matters. This noninterference policy toward slavery, which he had adopted years before, Lincoln had articulated best in a letter to Joshua Speed, saying that "I confess I hate to see the poor creatures [slaves] hunted down, and caught, and carried back to their stripes, and unrewarded toils; but I bite my lip and keep quiet." Lincoln to Joshua F. Speed, 24 August 1855, Abraham Lincoln, *The Collected Works of Abraham Lincoln*, ed. Roy P. Basler (New Brunswick, NJ: Rutgers University Press, 1959), vol. 2, 320.

24. Microfilm reel no. 1191, Samuel T. Sharp to Halleck, 14 February 1862; reel no. 1376, Gamble to Halleck, 8 January 1862; and Gamble to Farrar, 8 January 1862; and reel no. 1415, John M. Schofield order to Col. Williams, 27 February 1862; and James Dudley Wells to Halleck, undated, Provost-Marshal Records. John S. Phelps to Abraham Lincoln, 18 November 1861, Lincoln Papers.

25. Gamble to Halleck, 24 December 1861; and Halleck to Gamble, 26 December 1861, Hamilton Rowan Gamble Papers, Missouri Historical Society, St. Louis, Missouri.

26. Resolutions of the House of Representatives, 9 July and 9 December 1861; and General Orders, No. 3, 20 November 1861, *Official Records*, series 2, vol. 1, 759, 778, and 784. James G. Randall, *Constitutional Problems under Lincoln*, rev. ed. (Urbana: University of Illinois Press, 1964), 276 and 357. William E. Parrish, *Frank Blair: Lincoln's Conservative* (Columbia: University of Missouri Press, 1998), 137.

27. George E. Waring Jr. to Major General Asboth, 19 December 1861, *Official Records,* series 2, vol. 1, 789–90.

28. Henry W. Halleck to General Asboth, 26 December 1861; Halleck to Colonel Carlin, 9 January 1862; C. A. Morgan to Colonel, 30 January 1862; John Pope to Captain N. H. McLean, 10 February 1862; Order of Pope, 28 January 1862; and General Orders, No. 37, 14 February 1862, *Official Records,* series 1, vol. 8, 555–56; and series 2, vol. 1, 796, 799, 803–04, and 807. In his dissertation, Aaron Astor argued that Halleck's policy did little "to hold back the tide of fugitives." This, however, was not Halleck's purpose. Instead, he sought to implement faithfully Congress's slave policy as he understood it. Belated Confederates: Black Politics, Guerrilla Violence, and the Collapse of Conservative Unionism in Kentucky and Missouri, 1860–1872 (Ph.D. dissertation, Northwestern University, 2006), 146.

29. Microfilm reel no. 1315, list of black persons in jail; Farrar to Halleck, 17 December 1861, Provost-Marshal Records. Halleck to Farrar, 18 December 1861, *Official Records,* series 2, vol. 1, 788–89. Anderson, *Border City,* 241.

30. Farrar to Halleck, 4 February 1862; Farrar to Police Commissioners, 3 March 1862; Farrar to the Wiggins Ferry Company, 8 March 1862; Thomas C. Fletcher to John W. Harding, 18 March 1862; Farrar to Robert J. Rombauer, 2 April 1862; and Farrar to J. C. Kelton, 21 April 1862, *Official Records,* series 1, vol. 1, 805, 808–11, 814, and 816.

31. John B. Henderson, *Speech of Hon. J. B. Henderson of Missouri on the Abolition of Slavery delivered in the Senate of the United States, March 27, 1862* (Washington D.C.: L. Towers and Co., 1862), 1–15; Frank P. Blair Jr., *Speech of Hon. F. P. Blair Jr. of Missouri on the Policy of the President for the Restoration of the Union and Establishment of Peace delivered in the House of Representatives, April 11, 1862* (New York: Baker and Godwin, 1862), 3–8; E. H. Norton, *Speech of Hon. E. H. Norton of Missouri on Confiscation and Emancipation Delivered in the House of Representatives, April 24, 1862* (Washington D.C.: n.p., 1862), 2–8; John S. Phelps, *Confiscation of Property and Emancipation of Slaves: Speech of Hon. John S. Phelps of Missouri in the House of Representatives, May 22, 1862* (Washington D.C.: n.p., 1862), 1–8; and Frank P. Blair Jr., *Confiscation, Emancipation, and Colonization "Indemnity for the Past and Security for the Future": Speech of Hon. F. P. Blair Jr. of Missouri in the House of Representatives, May 23, 1862* (n.p., 1862), 1–7.

32. *St. Louis Missouri Republican,* 26 March 1862; 1 and 18 May 1862; 1, 5, 7, 10, and 22 June 1862; and 15 July 1862.

33. Translated excerpts from local German newspapers, the *Anzeiger des Westons* and the *Westliche Post,* in the *St. Louis Missouri Republican,* 1, 2, 13 May 1862 and 6 and 9 June 1862. *St. Louis Missouri* Republican, 3 June 1862. *Proceedings of the Missouri State Convention Held in Jefferson City, June 1862* (St. Louis: George Knapp and Co., 1862), 72–77.

34. *Proceedings, June 1862,* 82–84, 89–94, 103, 136–37, 227, and 239–41. William E. Parrish, *Turbulent Partnership: Missouri and the Union, 1861–1865* (Columbia: University of Missouri Press, 1963), 130–33.

35. Appeal to Border State Representatives to Favor Compensated Emancipation, 12 July 1862, Lincoln, *Collected Works,* vol. 5, 317–19. Border State Congressmen to Lincoln, 14 July 1862, Lincoln Papers.

36. John B. Henderson to Lincoln, 3 September 1862, Lincoln Papers.

CHAPTER FIVE

1. John M. Schofield, *Forty-six Years in the Army*, with a foreword by William M. Ferraro (New York: Century Co., 1897; reprint, Norman: University of Oklahoma Press, 1998), 54–56. Dennis K. Boman, *Lincoln's Resolute Unionist: Hamilton Gamble, Dred Scott Dissenter and Missouri's Civil War Governor* (Baton Rouge: Louisiana State University Press, 2006), 138–41. Report of John M. Schofield of operations in Missouri and northwestern Arkansas, April 10–November 20, 1862, *The War of the Rebellion: A Compilation of the Official Records of the Union and Confederate Armies*, 128 vols. (Washington D.C.: Government Printing Office, 1880–1902), series 1, vol. 13, 8.

2. General Orders, No. 13, 4 December 1861; and General Orders, No. 39, 14 February 1862, *Official Records*, series 1, vol. 8, 405–07 and 556. Galusha Anderson, *The Story of a Border City During the Civil War* (Boston: Little, Brown, 1908), 344.

3. Entries for 20, 26, 29, and 31 December 1861; 2, 3, 4, 6, 7, 9, 14, 18, 20, 21, 25, 30, and 31 January 1862; Arnold Krekel Record Book, 31 December 1861 to 30 July 1862, Arnold Krekel Papers, Missouri Historical Society, St. Louis, Missouri. In 1865, Krekel was president of the state convention which abolished slavery in Missouri several months before the passage of the thirteenth amendment to the Constitution of the United States.

4. General Orders, No. 13, 4 December 1861; General Orders, No. 19, 22 July 1862; and General Orders, No. 24, 4 August 1862, *Official Records*, series 1, vol. 8, 405–07 and vol. 13, 506 and 534–35. Entries of 2, 9, 10, 21, and 31 January; 1, 10, and 11 February; 10 and 20 March; and 23 July 1862, Krekel Record Book, Krekel Papers.

5. 4, 6, 8, 10, 13, 14, 16, 21, 27, and 28 January; and 4, 6, 10, and 11 February 1862, Krekel Record Book, Krekel Papers. Schofield to J. C. Kelton, 2 January 1862; *Official Records*, series 1, vol. 8, 503. Frederick H. Dyer, *A Compendium of the War of the Rebellion: Compiled and Arranged from Official Records of the Federal and Confederate Armies, Reports of the Adjutant Generals of the Several States, the Army Registers, and Other Reliable Documents and Sources*, part 3 (Des Moines, Iowa: Dyer Publishing Company, 1908), 305–06. T. M. Eddy, *The Patriotism of Illinois: A Record of the Civil and Military History of the State in the War for the Union*, vol. 2 (Chicago: Clark and Co., 1866), 480–81.

6. Proclamation of W. James Morgan to the citizens of Weston and Platte County, 9 December 1861; General Orders, No. 16, 11 January 1862; *Official Records*, series 1, vol. 8, 495; series 2, vol. 1, 238–39. Microfilm reel no. 1463, William D. Bacon, Union Provost-Marshals' File of Papers Relating to Individual Citizens, 1861–1866, Record Group 109, National Archives and Records Administration, Washington D.C.

7. General Orders, No. 30, 1 June 1862; and Report of John M. Schofield of operations in Missouri and northwestern Arkansas, April 10–November 20, 1862, *Official Records*, series 1, vol. 13, 8–9 and 409.

8. Schofield to Curtis, 4 June 1862; and Schofield to John C. Kelton, 17 June 1862, *Official Records*, series 2, vol. 3, 638; and vol. 4, 34–35.

9. Benjamin Loan to Schofield, 7 April 1862; Schofield to Loan, 12 April 1862; Schofield to J. C. McKibben, 10 June 1862; Halleck to Schofield, 16 June 62; Schofield to James Totten, 24 June 1862; and General Orders, No. 4, 27 June 1862, *Official Records*, series 1, vol. 13, 453; and series 2, vol. 3, 431–32, 447–48, and 672–73; and vol. 4, 26 and 59–60. For a good example of military commission trials brought during this period, see those held in Tipton in the spring of 1862. Out

of fifteen cases examined, nine defendants were found not guilty, and of the six convicted, only one was given what might be considered a significant punishment, imprisonment during the war. File II 999, Judge-Advocate Papers, Record Group 153, National Archives, Washington D.C.

10. William B. Hesseltine, ed., *Civil War Prisons* (Kent, Ohio: Kent State University Press, 1972), 5–8. James M. McPherson, *Battle Cry of Freedom: The Civil War Era*, vol. 4 of *The Oxford History of the United States*, ed. C. Vann Woodward (New York: Oxford University Press, 1988), 800–02. William T. Wells to Schofield, 27 August 1862, *Official Records*, series 2, vol. 4, 454–55. Louis S. Gerteis, "'An Outrage on Humanity': Martial Law and Military Prisons in St. Louis During the Civil War," *Missouri Historical Review* 96, no. 4 (July 2002): 304 and 311–12.

11. General Orders, No. 50, 28 February 1862, *Official Records*, series 2, vol. 1, 169–70.

12. George E. Leighton to Halleck, 4 December 1861; Schuyler Hamilton to J. M. Tuttle, 9 January 1862; Hamilton to J. J. B. Wright, 14 January and 8 February 1862; Hamilton to Mrs. M. McCree, 22 January 1862; Halleck to S. Burbank, 4 February 1862; General Orders, No. 33, 8 February 1862; and E. B. Brown to Schofield, 28 June 1862, *Official Records*, series 1, vol. 13, 454–56; series 2, vol. 1, 139–41, 164; and vol. 3, 185–86, 194, 209, 236–38, and 247. William C. Winter, *The Civil War in St. Louis* (St. Louis: Missouri Historical Society Press, 1994, reprint 1995), 79–80 and 152–54.

13. Hamilton R. Gamble to Edwin M. Stanton, 7 July 1862, *Official Records*, series 2, vol. 4, 143. Winter, *Civil War in St. Louis*, 82. William M. Leftwich, *Martyrdom in Missouri: A History of Religious Proscription, the Seizure of Churches, and the Persecution of Ministers of the Gospel, in the State of Missouri During the Late Civil War and under the "Test Oath" of the New Constitution* (St. Louis: Southwestern Book and Publishing Company, 1870), vol. 1, 288–89.

14. Halleck to S. Burbank, 4 February 1862; Thomas C. Fletcher to Bernard G. Farrar, 22 and 24 February 1862; and Halleck to the commanding officer at Alton, 28 February 1862, *Official Records*, series 2, vol. 1, 265–66, and vol. 3, 236–38.

15. Jacob G. Forman, *Western Sanitary Commission: A Sketch of its Origin, History, Labors for the Sick and Wounded of the Western Armies and Aid Given to Freedmen and Union Refugees with Accidents of Hospital Life* (St. Louis: R. P. Studley and Co., 1864), 13, 87, and 89. Charlotte C. Eliot, *William Greenleaf Eliot: Minister, Educator, Philanthropist*, intro. James K. Hosmer (Boston: Houghton, Mifflin, 1904), 226. J. C. Kelton to Schofield, 21 April 1862; George E. Leighton to C. W. Marsh, 22 May 1862; H. L. McConnel to Farrar, 23 June 1862; and William T. Wells to Schofield, 27 August 1862, *Official Records*, series 2, vol. 3, 467 and 574–75; and vol. 4, 57 and 454–55.

16. E. B. Brown to Schofield, 28 June 1862, *Official Records*, series 1, vol. 13, 454–56.

17. *St. Louis Missouri Republican*, 27 January 1862. James Totten to Schofield, 23 June 1862; and Schofield to Totten, 24 June 1862, *Official Records*, series 2, vol. 4, 55–56 and 59–60.

18. Forman, *Western Sanitary Commission*, 5–10 and 86–88. Eliot, *Eliot*, 216, 226–34.

19. Lincoln to John C. Frémont, 2 September 1861; John Pope to Halleck, 9 and 21 December 1861; F. Steele to Halleck, 9 December 1861; Steele to Pope, 9 December 1861; transcript of Ebenezer Magoffin's trial; Lorenzo Thomas to Halleck, 25 March 1862; J. F. Lee to Beriah Magoffin, 25 March 1862; J. F. Lee's report "in the matter of Ebenezer Magoffin," April 1862; Lincoln to Halleck, 9 April 1862; F. F. Flint to William Hoffman, 26 July 1862; and court of inquiry, 3 September 1862, *Official Records*, series 1, vol. 3, 469–70; vol. 8, 418 and 453; series 2, vol. 1, 236, 272, 276, 293–95, 298–300, 305, 358, 366, and 369–73; and vol. 4, 317–18 and 486–89. John J. Crittenden to Lincoln, 4 April 1862, Abraham Lincoln Papers, Library of Congress, Washington D.C. Ebenezer Magoffin,

file MM 2763, Judge-Advocate Papers, Record Group 153. Aaron Astor, Belated Confederates: Black Politics, Guerrilla Violence, and the Collapse of Conservative Unionism in Kentucky and Missouri, 1860–1872 (Ph.D. dissertation, Northwestern University, 2006), 127.

20. *Journal and Proceedings of the Missouri State Convention Held at Jefferson City and St. Louis March 1861* (St. Louis: George Knapp and Co., 1861), 34–37 and 267. Thomas C. Reynolds to Frémont, 15 August 1861; L. F. Ross to Watkins, 10 December 1861; L. F. Ross to Ulysses S. Grant, 12 December 1861; Ross to Halleck, 23 December 1861; and Halleck to Ross, 14 January 1862, *Official Records,* series 1, vol. 8, 432; and series 2, vol. 1, 126–27, 148–49, 154, and 159.

21. Ross to Watkins, 21 and 30 January 1862; Edward Bates to James O. Broadhead, 26 February 1862; Hamilton R. Gamble to Samuel R. Curtis, 22 October 1862, series 2, vol. 1, 160, 163, 168–69; and vol. 4, 642. Bates to Broadhead, 14 March 1862; and Greer W. Davis, 25 July 1862, the James O. Broadhead Papers, Missouri Historical Society, St. Louis, Missouri. Lincoln to Samuel R. Curtis, 16 December 1862, Abraham Lincoln, *The Collected Works of Abraham Lincoln,* ed. Roy P. Basler (New Brunswick, NJ: Rutgers University Press, 1959), vol. 6, 6. Watkins to Lincoln, 30 November 1862 and 22 February 1863; and statement of Albert Jackson, 25 December 1862, Lincoln Papers. Statements of Albert Jackson, 17 December 1862 and 3 January 1863, microfilm reel no. 1412, Provost-Marshal Records.

22. Hamilton R. Gamble to Edward Bates, 14 July 1862, Bates family papers, Missouri Historical Society, St. Louis, Missouri. Boman, *Hamilton Gamble,* 174–76. Tyler Dennett, ed., *Lincoln and the Civil War in the Diaries and Letters of John Hay,* with a foreword by Henry S. Commager (New York: Da Capo Press, 1988), 68–69. For letters asking for the commutation of death sentences see Sally C. Petty to Lincoln, 22 April 1862; and James S. Rollins to Lincoln, 2 May 1862, Lincoln Papers. For examples of Lincoln's interference in cases see trial record of Joseph P. Hussey; and Edwin M. Stanton to Schofield, 27 May 1862, *Official Records,* series 2, vol. 1, 178 and 494–503. See also "in the matter of Ebenezer Magoffin," *Official Records,* series 2, vol. 1, 369–73. Henry W. Halleck, *Halleck's International Law or Rules Regulating the Intercourse of States in Peace and War,* revised by Sir G. Sherston Baker and Maurice N. Drucquer (London: Kegan Paul, Trench, Trubner and Co., 1908), 30–41.

23. Bates to Gamble, 24 July 1862, Bates family papers.

24. General Orders, No. 18, 29 May 1862; H. Tompkins to Colonel Boyd, 27 June 1862; Schofield to J. M. Glover, 1 July 1862; Tompkins to Glover, 4 July 1862; Glover to Schofield, 6 July 1862; and affidavits of several officers and men concerning Tompkins's execution of Colonel Best; Special Orders No. 7, 7 July 1862; Schofield to John McNeil, 11 July 1862; and Report of Schofield of operations in Missouri and northwestern Arkansas, April 10–November 20, 1862; *Official Records,* series 1, vol. 13, 10–14, 402–03, and 467; and series 2, vol. 4, 92–93, 109, 137–42, and 145–46.

25. General Orders, No. 18, 29 May 1862; Schofield to John McNeil, 11 July 1862; Report of John M. Schofield of operations in Missouri and northwestern Arkansas, April 10–November 20, 1862; and Samuel R. Curtis to T. H. Holmes, 24 December 1862, *Official Records,* series 1, vol. 13, 10–14, 402–03, and 467; and vol. 22, part 1, 860–61.

26. Halleck to Gamble, 7 January 1862; Halleck to William M. McPherson, 3 April 1862; Schofield to J. C. Kelton, 27 July 1862; Gamble to Bates, 27 July 1862; O. H. Browning to Lincoln, 4 August 1862; McNeil to Colonel, 7 August 1862; excerpt from the *Palmyra Courier,* 15 August 1862; and Report of John McNeil, 17 September 1862, *Official Records,* series 1, vol. 8, 657–58; vol. 13, 211–16,

513–15, and 533–34; and series 2, vol. 1, 252; and vol. 4, 886–87. T. V. Munger to Amanda, 5 August 1862, Munger Family Civil War Letters Collection, Butler Center for Arkansas Studies, Central Arkansas Library System, Little Rock, Arkansas. *Richmond Daily Dispatch,* 10 September 1862.

27. Joseph B. Reavis to John M. Schofield, 30 August 1862; Special Orders No. 120, 12 September 1862; and Report of H. A. Gallup and statements of various officers, 18 September 1862; *Official Records,* series 2, vol. 4, 473, 512, and 532–40.

28. *St. Louis Missouri Republican,* 1 October 1862. *Richmond Daily Dispatch,* 8 October 1862. Lewis Merrill to Major Caldwell, 2 September 1862; Merrill to Major A. T. Denny, 23 September 1862; and Special Orders No. 35, 23 September 1862, *Official Records,* series 1, vol. 13, 611–12 and 660–61.

29. Schofield to Merrill, 9 September 1862 (2 letters); Merrill to Schofield, 9 September; T. C. Hindman to James Totten, 10 September 1862; and Totten to Hindman, 17 September 1862, *Official Records,* series 1, vol. 13, 621–23 and 647–48.

30. Thomas A. Harris to George W. Randolph, 23 June 1862; Randolph to Robert E. Lee, 29 June 1862; Lee to George B. McClellan, 6 and 11 July 1862; McClellan to Lee, 11 July 1862; McClellan to Stanton, 11 July 1862; Jefferson Davis to Lee, 1 August 1862; Lee to Henry W. Halleck, 2 August 1862 (two letters); Halleck to Lee, 7 and 9 August 1862, *Official Records,* series 2, vol. 4, 134–35, 170, 328–30, 350, 362, 784–85, 792–93, and 835.

31. William R. Strachan to Joseph C. Porter, 8 October 1862; meeting of officers of the First Missouri Brigade, 4 and 11 November 1862; Jefferson Davis to T. H. Holmes, 17 November 1862; *Memphis Daily Appeal,* 3 December 1862, *Official Records,* series 1, vol. 13, 719 and 908–10; and vol. 22, part 1, 816–19 and 861–67. For a minister's account of his ministrations to these ten prisoners in the hours leading up to their deaths, see Peter Donan, *Memoir of Jacob Creath Jr.* (Cincinnati: R. W. Carroll and Co., 1872), 179–81.

32. *Memphis Daily Appeal,* 3 December 1862; T. H. Holmes to Samuel R. Curtis, 7 December 1862; William R. Strachan to the editor of the *New York Times,* 10 December 1862; Curtis to Holmes, 24 and 27 December 1862; and E. Kirby Smith to Curtis, 3 June 1863, *Official Records,* series 1, vol. 22, part 1, 816–18, 860–67, and 879–80; and vol. 22, part 2, 307. Edward A. Pollard, *Southern History of the War: The Second Year of the War* (New York: Charles B. Richardson, 1864), 174–76. Richmond *Daily Dispatch,* 17 November and 10 and 13 December 1862.

33. William R. Strachan to the editor of the *New York Times,* 10 December 1862, *Official Records,* series 1, vol. 22, part 1, 861–67. D. W. Brewington to John McNeil, 16 July 1862; *Palmyra Courier,* 24 October 1862; Joseph R. Winchell to John B. Henderson, 12 December 1862; George E. Leighton to Henderson, 15 December 1862; E. K. Sayre to Henderson, 20 December 1862; R. E. Anderson to Henderson, 24 December 1862; petition to Lincoln, 1 January 1863; and Samuel T. Glover to Montgomery Blair, 13 June 1863, Lincoln Papers.

34. *St. Louis Missouri Republican,* 6, 10, and 18–21 June 1862. William E. Parrish, *Turbulent Partnership: Missouri and the Union, 1861–1865* (Columbia: University of Missouri Press, 1963), 90–98. John M. Schofield, *Forty-six Years in the Army,* with a foreword by William M. Ferraro (New York: Century Co., 1897; reprint, Norman: University of Oklahoma Press, 1998), 56–61. Frank P. Blair to Montgomery Blair, 8 August 1862, Lincoln Papers.

35. *Journal of the Missouri State Convention Held in Jefferson City June 1862* (St. Louis: George Knapp and Co., 1862), 11–12 and 19. *Proceedings of the Missouri State Convention Held in Jefferson City, June 1862* (St. Louis: George Knapp and Co., 1862), 200–01, 216–18, and 222.

36. Dennis K. Boman, *Lincoln's Resolute Unionist: Hamilton Gamble, Dred Scott Dissenter and Missouri's Civil War Governor* (Baton Rouge: Louisiana State University Press, 2006), 112–15 and 136–37.

37. *Journal, June 1862,* 10–16, 21–24, and 27–29. *Proceedings, June 1862,* 30–39, 43–71, 102–04, 111, 117–19, 130–31, 146, and 154–55. *Calder v. Bull,* 3 U.S. 386 (1798) and *Carpenter v. Pennsylvania,* 58 U.S. 456 (1855). It should be noted here that the Supreme Court of the United States in *Cummings v. Missouri,* 71 U.S. 277 (1867), declared a later loyalty oath unconstitutional on grounds not applicable to the loyalty oath passed by the state convention in June 1862. Even under the much more stringent test oath prescribed in Missouri's constitution of 1865, the Supreme Court of the United States in a split decision four to four did not declare the deprivation of the right to vote under it repugnant to the Constitution of the United States. No report of the Supreme Court of the United States on this case was published. However, for the report of Missouri's highest court see *Blair v. Ridgely,* 41 Missouri 63 (1866). See also Harold M. Hyman, *Era of the Oath: Northern Loyalty Tests During the Civil War and Reconstruction* (New York: Octagon Books, 1978), 117–18.

38. *Rolla Express,* 1 November 1862.

39. Microfilm reel no. 1465, James H. Birch file, Provost-Marshal Records. *St. Louis Missouri Republican,* 1 and 2 June and 17 November 1862. *Liberty Weekly Tribune,* 8 and 15 August, 3, 10, and 31 October 1862. James H. Birch to Hamilton R. Gamble, 7 September 1862, Hamilton R. Gamble Papers, Missouri Historical Society, St. Louis, Missouri. *Proceedings of the Missouri State Convention Held in Jefferson City, June 1863* (St. Louis: George Knapp and Co., 1863), 375–80.

40. Martin J. Hubble, *Personal Reminiscences and Fragments of the Early History of Springfield and Greene County, Missouri* (Springfield: Inland Printing, 1914), 81–88. Benjamin F. Loan to Samuel R. Curtis, 4 November 1862, *Official Records,* series 1, vol. 13, 806–07. Sample Orr, file LL 678, Judge-Advocate Papers, Record Group 153, National Archives, Washington D.C.

41. David W. Bartlett, *Cases of Contested Elections in Congress from 1834 to 1865 Inclusive* (Washington D.C.: Government Printing Office, 1865), 482–520. It is notable that in a report to General Henry W. Halleck just twenty days after the election, General Curtis referred to the incident in St. Joseph as the only instance of misconduct in an otherwise quiet election in which there was not "a particle of strife between soldiers and citizens." Curtis to Halleck, 24 November 1862, *Official Records,* series 1, vol. 22, part 1, 788–89.

42. Court-martial of Alexander S. Hughes, 15 November 1862 of the Sixty-fifth EMM; and General Orders, No. 2 of the Ninth Military District; Missouri Adjutant General Records, series: Enrolled Missouri Militia, Record Group 133, Missouri State Archives, Jefferson City, Missouri. Curtis to Halleck, 24 November 1862; and Curtis to Charles H. Howland, 22 February 1863, *Official Records,* series 1, vol. 22, part 1, 788–89; and vol. 22, part 2, 120–21. Frank P. Blair Jr. to Lincoln, 14 November 1862, Lincoln Papers.

CHAPTER SIX

1. Lincoln to Curtis, 17 December 1862, Abraham Lincoln, *The Collected Works of Abraham Lincoln,* ed. Roy P. Basler (New Brunswick, NJ: Rutgers University Press, 1959), vol. 6, 8.

2. *Liberty Weekly Tribune,* 9 January 1863.

3. Curtis to Lincoln, 17 and 20 December 1862; Dick to Lincoln, 19 December 1862; Dick to Montgomery Blair, 19 December 1862 and 26 January 1863; Charles D. Drake, 22 January 1863; J. T. K. Hayward to Lincoln, 27 January 1863; and Gilchrist Porter to John B. Henderson, 11 February 1863, Abraham Lincoln Papers, Library of Congress, Washington, D.C. Charles Gibson to Gamble, 4 January 1863; and Gibson to Lincoln, 23 February 1863, Hamilton R. Gamble Papers, Missouri Historical Society, St. Louis, Missouri. Edwin M. Stanton to Curtis, 14 January 1863; Benjamin F. Loan to Curtis, 27 January 1863; and Curtis to Odon Guitar, 1 March 1863, *The War of the Rebellion: A Compilation of the Official Records of the Union and Confederate Armies,* 128 vols. (Washington D.C.: Government Printing Office, 1880–1902), series 1, vol. 22, part 2, 41, 78–82, and 135–36.

4. Captain A. A. Stuart, *Iowa Colonels and Regiments: Being a History of Iowa Regiments in the War of the Rebellion and Containing a Description of the Battles in which They have Fought* (Des Moines: Mills and Company, 1865), 35–46. John M. Schofield, *Forty-six Years in the Army,* with a foreword by William M. Ferraro (New York: Century Co., 1897; reprint, Norman: University of Oklahoma Press, 1998), 56–57.

5. General Orders, No. 5, 1 October 1862, *Official Records,* series 1, vol. 13, 698–700. Circular from Curtis, 20 October 1862, Record Group 133, Adjutant General, series: General Orders Book, Missouri State Archive, Jefferson City, Missouri.

6. Dennis K. Boman, *Lincoln's Resolute Unionist: Hamilton Gamble, Dred Scott Dissenter and Missouri's Civil War Governor* (Baton Rouge: Louisiana State University Press, 2006), 118–19 and 138–40.

7. Hamilton R. Gamble to Henry W. Halleck, 22 September 1862; Halleck to Gamble, 27 September, 3 and 30 October 1862, *Official Records,* series 3, vol. 2, 579, 591–93, 646–47, 703–04. Gamble to Halleck, October 1862, Lincoln Papers.

8. Hamilton R. Gamble to Henry W. Halleck, 22 September 1862; Halleck to Gamble, 27 September, 3 and 30 October 1862, *Official Records,* series 3, vol. 2, 579, 591–93, 646–47, 703–04. Gamble to Halleck, October 1862, Lincoln Papers.

9. Gamble to Halleck, October 1862, Lincoln Papers. Halleck to Gamble, 30 October 1862; and Gamble to Halleck, 4 November 1862, *Official Records,* series 3, vol. 2, 703–04 and 735–36. In his November 4 letter, Gamble asserted he had not "designedly" made the document "ambiguous upon the question of the character of the force."

10. Gamble to Lincoln, 17 November 1862, Gamble Papers.

11. Gamble to Lincoln, 17 November 1862, Gamble Papers. Lincoln to Edward Bates, 29 November 1862; and Lincoln to Gamble, 30 December 1862, Lincoln, *Collected Works,* vol. 5, 515–16, and vol. 6, 23. Bates to Gamble, 2 December 1862, Edward Bates Papers, Missouri Historical Society, St. Louis, Missouri. Special Orders No. 417, 28 December 1862, and William Whiting to Stanton, 24 March 1864, *Official Records,* series 3, vol. 2, 955, and vol. 4, 196–97. Gamble to Lincoln, 13 July 1863, Lincoln Papers.

12. Lincoln to Gamble, 18 and 27 December 1862; Lincoln to Samuel R. Curtis, 19 December 1862 and 5 January 1863, Lincoln, *Collected Works,* vol. 6, 9–10, 21, and 36–37. Gamble to Lincoln, 18 and 27 December 1862; Curtis to Lincoln, 19 December 1862; Franklin A. Dick to Montgomery Blair, 19 December 1862; Dick to Lincoln, 19 December 1862; and Curtis to Lincoln, 20 December 1862, Lincoln Papers. Curtis to Colonel J. T. K. Hayward, 26 December 1862, *Official Records,* series 1, vol. 22, part 1, 875–76.

13. Curtis to Lincoln, 20 December 1862, Lincoln Papers. Curtis to Colonel J. T. K. Hayward, 26 December 1862, *Official Records*, series 1, vol. 22, part 1, 875–76.

14. William Sawyer to brother, 31 December 1862, Gamble Papers. Orwin C. Tinker to J. T. K. Hayward, 24 and 25 December 1862; Hayward to Tinker, 25 December 1862; Tinker to Thomas J. Bartholow, 29 December 1862; Hayward to J. D. Meredith, 29 December 1862; Lewis Merrill, 2 January 1863; Tinker to William D. Wood, 5 January 1863, Missouri Adjutant General Records, series: Enrolled Missouri Militia, Record Group 133, Missouri State Archives, Jefferson City, Missouri.

15. Curtis to Lincoln, 20 December 1862; Franklin A. Dick to Montgomery Blair, 26 January 1862; and Gamble to Lincoln, 4 February 1863, Lincoln Papers. Curtis to Hayward, 26 December 1862, *Official Records*, series 1, vol. 22, part 1, 875–76. Lewis Merrill to Gamble, 2 January 1863; Franklin A. Dick to William D. Wood, 8 January 1863; Tinker to Wood, 31 January and 4 February 1863; and Hamilton R. Gamble Jr. to Wood, 9 February 1863, Missouri Adjutant General Records, series: Enrolled Missouri Militia; William Sawyer to brother, 31 December 1862, Gamble Papers. Service record of Orwin C. Tinker, Record of Service Card, Civil War, 1861–1865, Missouri State Archives, Jefferson City, Missouri. Tinker was acquitted by special order on 1 May 1863.

16. Lewis Merrill to Franklin A. Dick, 15 December 1862, *Official Records*, series 1, vol. 22, part 1, 833–35.

17. General Orders, No. 23, 1 December 1862; and General Orders, No. 35, 24 December 1862, *Official Records*, series 1, vol. 22, part 1, 803–04 and 868–72. For the previous policy under the former provost marshal general, see Thomas T. Gantt to J. M. Bassett, 31 October 1862, *Official Records*, series 2, vol. 4, 670–71.

18. Lewis Merrill to Franklin A. Dick, 15 December 1862, *Official Records*, series 1, vol. 22, part 1, 833–35.

19. Dick to Montgomery Blair, 26 January 1863, Lincoln Papers. Union Provost-Marshals' File of Papers Relating to Individual Citizens, 1861–1866, Record Group 109, National Archives and Records Administration, Washington D.C., microfilm reel no. 1217, Bartlett Anderson file.

20. William M. Leftwich, *Martyrdom in Missouri: A History of Religious Proscription, the Seizure of Churches, and the Persecution of Ministers of the Gospel, in the State of Missouri During the Late Civil War and under the "Test Oath" of the New Constitution*, vol. 2 (St. Louis: Southwestern Book and Publishing Company, 1870), 83–93. Lewis G. Vander Velde, *The Presbyterian Churches and the Federal Union: 1861–1869* (Cambridge: Harvard University Press and London: Humphrey Milford, Oxford University Press, 1932), 133–34 and 325. Provost-Marshal Records, microfilm no. 1315, Robert P. Farris file, War Department Collection of Confederate Records, National Archives and Records Administration, Washington D.C. Dick to Lincoln, 12 December 1862, Lincoln Papers. Peter J. Barry, "'I'll Keep Them in Prison Awhile . . .': Abraham Lincoln and David Davis on Civil Liberties in Wartime," *Journal of the Abraham Lincoln Association* 28, no. 1 (Winter 2008): 20–29.

21. Provost-Marshal Records, microfilm no. 1233, E. M. Bounds file. Thomas M. Finney, *The Life and Labors of Enoch Mather Marvin, Late Bishop of the Methodist Episcopal Church, South* (St. Louis: James H. Chambers, 1880), 369. William Henry Lewis, *The History of Methodism in Missouri for a Decade of Years from 1860 to 1870*, vol. 3 (Nashville, TN: Barbee and Smith, 1890), 343.

22. Provost-Marshal Records, microfilm reel no. 1203, James Morton file.

23. Ibid.

24. Ibid.

25. Dick to Montgomery Blair, 19 December 1862; Dick to Lincoln, 19 December 1862; and Special Order No. 152, 19 December 1862, Lincoln Papers.

26. Newspaper clipping of Samuel B. McPheeters's letter, 19 December 1862; Hugh Campbell to David Davis, 20 December 1862; Archibald Gamble to Edward Bates, 22 December 1862; and Samuel B. McPheeters to Bates, 23 December 1862, Lincoln Papers.

27. Lincoln to Curtis, 27 December 1862, *Collected Works*, vol. 6, 20. Curtis to Lincoln, 27 December 1862, *Official Records*, series 1, vol. 22, part 1, 877–78. Dick to Lincoln, 19 December 1862 and 26 January 1863; Curtis to Lincoln, 28 and 29 December 1862; Apolline A. Blair to Montgomery Blair, 29 December 1862; and Lincoln to Curtis, 2 January 1863; Charles D. Drake to Lincoln, 22 January 1863, Lincoln Papers. Rev. John S. Grasty, *Memoir of Rev. Samuel B. McPheeters, D.D.*, with an introduction by Rev. Stuart Robinson (St. Louis: Southwestern Book and Publishing Company, and Louisville: Davidson Brothers and Company, 1871), 159–61. Edward McPherson, *The Political History of the United States of America During the Great Rebellion* (Washington D.C.: James J. Chapman, 1882), 534–37.

28. Lincoln to Curtis, 2 January 1863, Lincoln Papers. Terry Lee Beckenbaugh, The War of Politics: Samuel Ryan Curtis, Race and the Political/Military Establishment (Ph.D. diss., University of Arkansas, 2001), 90–91.

29. Curtis to McPheeters, 28 March 1863; McPheeters to Curtis, 31 March 1863; Curtis to Lincoln, 3 April 1863; John Whitehill and others to Lincoln, November 1863; Nathan Ranney to Edward Bates, 9 November 1863; O. D. Filley to Lincoln, 9 November 1863; John D. Coalter to Bates, 13 December 1863; and Lincoln to Filley, 22 December 1863, Lincoln Papers. McPherson, *Political History*, 534–37. For a detailed account of McPheeters's case from a pro-Confederate point of view, see Leftwich, *Martyrdom in Missouri*, vol. 2, 197–213.

30. Galusha Anderson, *The Story of a Border City During the Civil War* (Boston: Little, Brown, 1908), 133–35. Frederick A. Dick to Edward Bates, 15 May 1863; S. J. P. Anderson to Bates, 16 May 1863; Oliver D. Filley to Bates, 16 May 1863; and Bates to Lincoln, 20 May 1863, Lincoln Papers. McPherson, *Political History*, 537–38.

31. Microfilm reel no. 1475, F. R. Holeman file, Provost-Marshal Records.

32. John M. Schofield to J. C. Kelton, 30 August 1862; Henry W. Halleck to Schofield, 6 September 1862; Benjamin Loan to Curtis, 4 November 1862; Lewis Merrill to Frederick A. Dick, 15 December 1862; General Orders, No. 35, 24 December 1862; Edwin M. Stanton to Curtis, 14 January 1863; Halleck to Curtis, 15 January 1863; Curtis to Stanton, 15 January 1863; and Curtis to Lincoln, 15 January 1863, *Official Records*, series 1, vol. 13, 606, 616, and 806–07; and vol. 22, part 1, 41–43, 833–35, and 868–72.

33. Lincoln to Curtis, 5 January 1863; James Guthrie to Lincoln, 16 and 17 May 1863; Lincoln to Guthrie, 16 May 1863; James Speed to Lincoln, 17 May 1863; and James and Joshua Speed to Lincoln, 17 May 1863, Lincoln Papers. Lincoln to Edwin M. Stanton, 16 and 19 May 1863, *Collected Works*, vol. 6, 219 and 223. General Orders, No. 12, 7 February 1863; Dick to W. Hoffman, 5 March 1863; P. H. Watson to Dick, 24 April 1863; and Dick to T. I. McKenny, 12 May 1863, *Official Records*, series 1, vol. 22, part 2, 102–03; series 2, vol. 5, 319–21, 515, 599–600, 631, and 663–64. Microfilm reel no. 1293, Valentine P. Carney file; microfilm reel no. 1238, James W. Clark file; microfilm reel no. 1218, David H. Armstrong file; microfilm reel no. 1315, Catherine Ferrell file; microfilm reel no.

1185, John M. Childers file; microfilm reel no. 1239, Mary Cleveland file; microfilm reel no. 1305, John S. Downey file; microfilm reel no. 1477, Porter Jackman file; microfilm reel no. 1339, Richard Hardesty file; and microfilm reel no. 1289, William E. Caldwell file, Provost-Marshal Records. John Churchill to Captain Bryan, 18 May 1863, P. Taylor Bryan Papers, Missouri Historical Society, St. Louis, Missouri.

CHAPTER SEVEN

1. Henry W. Halleck, *Halleck's International Law or Rules Regulating the Intercourse of States in Peace and War,* revised by Sir G. Sherston Baker and Maurice N. Drucquer (London: Kegan Paul, Trench, Trubner and Co., 1908), 210–14. Hugo Grotius, *The Rights of War and Peace Including the Law of Nature and of Nations,* with an introduction by David J. Hill (Boston: Adamant Media Corporation, 2003), 332–44.

2. James G. Randall, *Constitutional Problems under Lincoln* (Urbana: University of Illinois Press, 1951; rev. ed., 1964), 275–315. John M. Schofield, *Forty-six Years in the Army,* with a foreword by William M. Ferraro (New York: Century Co., 1897; reprint, Norman: University of Oklahoma Press, 1998), 57–58. General Orders, No. 19, 11 September 1862, *The War of the Rebellion: A Compilation of the Official Records of the Union and Confederate Armies,* 128 vols. (Washington D.C.: Government Printing Office, 1880–1902), series 1, vol. 13, 624–25.

3. *Mitchell v. Clark,* 110 U.S. 633–51 (1884).

4. Special Orders, No. 3, 29 September 1862; Special Orders, No. 4, 30 September 1862; General Orders, No. 2, 1 October 1862; Special Orders, No. 22, 14 October 1862; Special Orders, No. 37, 17 November 1862; Special Orders, No. 58, 2 December 1862; and Special Orders, No. 60, 2 December 1862, *Official Records,* series 1, vol. 13, 691, 693, 700–02, 736–37, and 800; and vol. 22, part 1, 805–06. Circular of Provost-Marshal-General Thomas T. Gantt, 10 October 1862, Monroe County, Provost Marshal Papers, Western Historical Manuscripts Collection, State Historical Society of Missouri, Columbia, Missouri. Lafayette County Proceedings of the County Board, 2 October 1862, Western Historical Manuscript Collection, Columbia, Missouri. Liberty, Missouri, *Weekly Tribune,* 14 November 1862. Microfilm reel no. 1291, G. N. Caffee file, Union Provost-Marshals' File of Papers Relating to Individual Citizens, 1861–1866, Record Group 109, National Archives and Records Administration, Washington D.C. Schofield to James S. Thomas, 5 December 1862, Abraham Lincoln Papers, Library of Congress, Washington D.C.

5. Circular Order, John McNeil, 27 October 1862; Circular Order, 7 November 1862; Affidavit of W. Hammack, 15 August 1862–30 April 1863; Thomas J. Whitely to William Wood, 6, 13, and 18 December 1862; statement of Samuel Johnson, December 1862; and Lewis Merrill to Gamble, 2 January 1863, Missouri Adjutant General, series: General Orders Book, Record Group 133, Missouri State Archive, Jefferson City, Missouri.

6. William G. Eliot to Gamble, 1 December 1862; *Official Records,* series 1, vol. 22, part 1, 801–04. Gamble to Curtis, 1 December 1862; Gamble to Lincoln, 5 December 1862; Schofield to James S. Thomas, 5 December 1862; Richard C. Shackelford and T. J. Thompson to Abraham Lincoln, 5 December 1862; Samuel T. Glover to Montgomery Blair, 7 December 1862; and Curtis to Lincoln, 12 December 1862, Lincoln Papers.

7. Lincoln to Curtis, 10 December 1862; Curtis to Lincoln, 12 December 1862; John S. Thomas to Curtis, 16 December 1862; Lewis V. Bogy to Lincoln, 19 December 1862; St. Louis citizens to Lincoln, 19 and 30 December 1862; Gamble to Lincoln, 31 December 1862; California, Missouri, citizens to Lincoln, 1 January 1863; Missouri congressional delegation to Lincoln, 4 January 1863; Lincoln to Curtis, 5 January 1863; William A. Hall to Lincoln, 7 January 1863; James W. Sappington to John B. Henderson, 7 January 1863; Lincoln Papers. William G. Eliot to Halleck, 13 December 1862; *Official Records,* series 1, vol. 22, part 1, 830. Copy of Halleck to Curtis, 15 December 1862, William G. Eliot Papers, Missouri Historical Society, St. Louis, Missouri. Randall, *Constitutional Problems,* 279–80.

8. Thomas L. Price to Lincoln, 14 January 1863; Charles D. Drake to Lincoln, 22 January 1863; Franklin A. Dick to Montgomery Blair, 26 January 1863; and John T. Hayward to Lincoln, 27 January 1863, Lincoln Papers. Special Orders, No. 7, 15 January 1863; Edwin M. Stanton to Curtis, 20 January 1863; Lewis Merrill circular, 20 January 1863; and General Orders, No. 3, 20 January 1863, *Official Records,* series 1, vol. 22, part 2, 47–48 and 64–65.

9. General Orders, No. 5, 1 October 1862; Loan to Curtis, 16 November 1862; Executive Order, 21 November 1862; Clinton B. Fisk to Loan, 3 December 1862; Loan to Fisk, 17 December 1862; Loan to Curtis, 27 January 1863, *Official Records,* series 1, vol. 13, 698–700 and 798–99; vol. 22, part 1, 838–39; vol. 22, part 2, 78–82; series 3, vol. 3, 849. Microfilm reel no. 1219, Levy Ashbrook file; microfilm reel no. 1462, William H. Allen file; and microfilm reel no. 1312, Samuel Engler file, Provost-Marshal Records.

10. Lincoln to Salmon P. Chase, 5 December 1862; Chase to Lincoln, 7 December 1862; and William D. Gallagher to Chase, 11 December 1862, Lincoln Papers.

11. Circular from General Curtis, 20 October 1862, Missouri Adjutant General Records, series: General Orders Book.

12. H. M. Sumner to General Loan, 29 October 1862, H. M. Sumner Papers, Western Historical Manuscripts Collection, State Historical Society of Missouri, Columbia, Missouri. Loan to Curtis, 4 November 1862, *Official Records,* series 1, vol. 13, 806–07. File LL 678, Sample Orr trial, Judge-Advocate Papers, Record Group 153, National Archives, Washington D.C. Martin J. Hubble, *Personal Reminiscences and Fragments of the Early History of Springfield, Missouri, Greene County, Missouri* (Springfield: Inland Printing, 1914), 81–88.

13. General Orders, No. 35, 24 December 1862; Curtis to Lincoln, 15 January 1863, *Official Records,* series 1, vol. 22, part 1, 868–72; and vol. 22, part 2, 42–43. Samuel B. McPheeters to Curtis, 31 March 1863, Lincoln Papers.

14. Microfilm reel no. 1206, Henry Sexton file, 9 October 1862; reel no. 1349, Mrs. (Lottie?) Thomas C. Johnson file, 13 October 1862; reel no. 1244, Alexander Criddle file, 21 April 1863; reel no. 1408, William Turner file, 17 June 1863; reel no. 1285, Anderson Brown file, 17 June 1863; reel no. 1190, Harmon Haight file, 24 June 1863; reel no. 1408, John D. Turner file, 14 July 1863; and reel no. 1246, Pleasant W. Crump file, 13 October 1863, Provost-Marshal Records.

15. Zechariah Chafee Jr., *Freedom of Speech* (New York: Harcourt, Brace and Howe, 1920), 25 and 48–51. Richard Polenberg, *Fighting Faiths: The Abrams Case, the Supreme Court, and Free Speech* (Ithaca: Cornell University Press, 1999), 197–242 and 272–84.

16. Microfilm reel no. 1351, George J. Jones file, Provost-Marshal Records.

17. Lincoln to Curtis, 5 January 1863, Lincoln Papers. Curtis to Johnathan M. Bassett, 1 March 1863; Curtis to Odon Guitar, 1 March 1863; and Curtis to Smith O. Scofield, 1 March 1863, *Official*

Records, series 1, vol. 22, part 2, 134–37. Microfilm reel no. 1242, John S. Cowan file, Provost-marshal Records.

18. Gamble to Curtis, 9 February 1863; and Gamble to Lincoln, 2 May 1863, Hamilton Rowan Gamble Papers, Missouri Historical Society, St. Louis, Missouri. Samuel T. Glover to Edward Bates, 15 May 1863, Lincoln Papers. Charles D. Drake autobiography, 875–81, Western Historical Manuscript Collection, State Historical Society of Missouri, Columbia, Missouri.

19. Microfilm reel no. 1158, James Monaghan file, Provost-Marshal Records. David Herbert Donald, *Lincoln* (New York: Simon and Schuster, 1995), 419–21 and 441–44. Ulysses S. Grant, *Personal Memoirs of U. S. Grant, Selected Letters, 1839–1865* (New York: Literary Classics of the United States, 1990), 966 and 1055.

20. Microfilm reel no. 1217, C. P. Anderson file, Provost-Marshal Records.

21. Gamble to Lincoln, 18 and 27 December 1862, Lincoln Papers.

22. Curtis to Lincoln, 31 January 1863, Lincoln Papers. General Orders, No. 15, 4 November 1862; General Orders, No. 35, 24 December 1862; Edwin M. Stanton to Curtis, 14 January 1863; Henry W. Halleck, 15 January 1863; Curtis to Stanton, 15 January 1863; and Curtis to Lincoln, 15 January 1863, *Official Records*, series 1, vol. 22, part 1, 868–72; and vol. 52, part 1, 298–99; and vol. 22, part 2, 41–43.

23. Lebbeus Zevely to assistant adjutant-general of Missouri, 13 and 25 December 1862; and Hamilton R. Gamble Jr. to Henry Neill, 9 February 1863; Missouri Adjutant General Records, series: Enrolled Missouri Militia, Record Group 133, Missouri State Archives, Jefferson City, Missouri. Richard C. Vaughan to James O. Broadhead, 8 May 1863, James O. Broadhead Papers, Missouri Historical Society, St. Louis, Missouri. *St. Louis Missouri Republican*, 20 December 1862. Gilchrest Porter to Henderson, 11 February 1863; Henderson to Lincoln, 30 March 1863; and St. Louis citizens to Lincoln, 1 May 1863, Lincoln Papers.

24. Microfilm reel no. 1477, George Jackson file; microfilm reel no. 1409, Patience, Laura, and Ferdinand Tyler and Sally Green file; microfilm reel no. 1366, William B. Beasley file; microfilm reel no. 1468, Sophia Converse file; microfilm reel no. 1238, Hannah Clarke file; and microfilm reel no. 1189, John Garr file, Provost-Marshal Records.

25. Microfilm reel no. 1242, Colin Coy file, Provost-Marshal Records.

26. Microfilm reel no. 1350, Charles Jones file, Provost-Marshal Records. William Van Ness Bay, *Reminiscences of the Bench and Bar in Missouri* (St. Louis: F. H. Thomas and Company, 1878), 424–31.

27. Microfilm reels no. 1350 and 1351, Charles Jones file, Provost-Marshal Records.

28. William D. Wood to Hamilton R. Gamble, 10 November 1862, Gamble Papers. Microfilm reel no. 1205, Maurice D. Rees file; microfilm reel no. 1276, C. M. Waller file; microfilm reel no. 1311, Frank Ellington file; microfilm reel no. 1219, Major J. B. Rogers file; and microfilm reel no. 1218, Archer Alexander file, Provost-Marshal Records. Jacob Gilbert Forman, *The Western Sanitary Commission: A Sketch of its Origin, History, Labors for the Sick and Wounded of the Western Armies and Aid Given to Freedmen and Union Refugees with Incidents of Hospital Life* (St. Louis: R. P. Studley and Company, 1864), 110–11.

29. Forman, *Western Sanitary Commission*, 111–13.

30. Microfilm reel no. 1322, Charles Frank file, Provost-Marshal Records.

31. Gamble to Montgomery Blair, 24 September 1862, Lincoln Papers.

32. Charles Gibson to Lincoln, 23 February 1863; Henry T. Blow to Lincoln, 22 March 1863; Curtis to Lincoln, 23 March 1863; John B. Henderson to Gamble, 30 March 1863; St. Louis citizens to Lincoln, 1 May 1863; Joseph W. McClurg to Lincoln, 22 May 1863; and Lincoln to Schofield, 27 May 1863, Lincoln Papers. Lincoln to Stanton, 11 May 1863, Abraham Lincoln, *The Collected Works of Abraham Lincoln,* ed. Roy P. Basler (New Brunswick, NJ: Rutgers University Press, 1959), vol. 6, 210–11. Hamilton R. Gamble Jr. to Hamilton R. Gamble, 6 March 1863; Gamble to Lincoln, 2 May 1863; and John M. Schofield to Gamble, 26 May 1863, Gamble Papers. Howard K. Beale, ed., *The Diary of Edward Bates, 1859–1866* (Washington D.C.: Government Printing Office, 1933), 279 and 292. Galusha Anderson, *The Story of a Border City During the Civil War* (Boston: Little, Brown, 1908), 281–284. Terry Lee Beckenbaugh, The War of Politics: Samuel Ryan Curtis, Race and the Political/Military Establishment (Ph.D. diss., University of Arkansas, 2001), 97–104. Jay Monaghan, *Civil War on the Western Border, 1854–1865* (Lincoln: University of Nebraska Press, 1955), 38, 45, and 64–68.

CHAPTER EIGHT

1. Samuel T. Glover to Abraham Lincoln, 13 April 1863; Hamilton R. Gamble, 2 May 1863; Henry T. Blow to Lincoln, 5 May 1863; Glover to Edward Bates, 15 May 1863; Lincoln to Blow et al., 15 May 1863; Robert J. Rombauer et al. to Lincoln, 16 May 1863; Joseph W. McClurg to Lincoln, 22 May 1863; Lincoln to John M. Schofield, 27 May 1863; and Lincoln to Charles D. Drake et al., 5 October 1863, Abraham Lincoln Papers, Library of Congress, Washington D.C.

2. Schofield to Lincoln, 1 June 1863, *The War of the Rebellion: A Compilation of the Official Records of the Union and Confederate Armies,* 128 vols. (Washington D.C.: Government Printing Office, 1880–1902), series 1, vol. 22, part 2, 301.

3. *Proceedings of the Missouri State Convention Held in Jefferson City, June 1862* (St. Louis: George Knapp and Co., 1862), 72–77, 82–84, 89–94, 98–100, 103, and 136–37.

4. *St. Louis Missouri Republican,* 9, 12, and 18 November and 13 December 1862. Frank P. Blair to Abraham Lincoln, 14 November 1862; and Charles Gibson to Edward Bates, 9 December 1862, Lincoln Papers. William E. Parrish, *Turbulent Partnership: Missouri and the Union, 1861–1865* (Columbia: University of Missouri Press, 1963), 136–37.

5. *St. Louis Missouri Republican,* 16 December 1862, 17, 22, 23, and 31 January, 2, 6, and 19 February, and 9, 10, and 13 March 1863.

6. *Journal of the Missouri State Convention, Held in Jefferson City, June 1863* (St. Louis: George Knapp and Co., 1863), 3; *St. Louis Missouri Republican,* 6 February 1863.

7. The *St. Louis Missouri Republican* ran a series, entitled the "Spirit of the German Press," in which were provided translations of editorial columns critical of Gamble's administration primarily from the *St. Louis Neue Zeit* and the *Westliche Post.* For attacks on Gamble leading into the convention and Lincoln's reply to the Radical meeting's resolutions see the *St. Louis Missouri Republican,* 23 May, 3, 5, 6, 9, 11, and 12 June 1863 and Henry J. Raymond, *The Life and Public Services of Abraham Lincoln, Sixteenth President of the United States, Together with His State Papers,* etc. (New York: Derby and Miller, Publishers, 1865), 429–31.

8. *St. Louis Missouri Republican,* 17 June 1863; and *Missouri State Convention, June 1863* 3–6.

9. Journal, June 1863, 24; and *Proceedings of the Missouri State Convention Held in Jefferson City, June 1863* (St. Louis: George Knapp and Co., 1863), 135–36, 144–45, and 229.

10. James S. Rollins to Abraham Lincoln, 12 June 1863; John M. Schofield to Abraham Lincoln, 20 and 21 June 1863; and Abraham Lincoln to John M. Schofield, 22 June 1863, Lincoln Papers. Michael Burlingame and John R. Turner Ettlinger, eds., *Inside Lincoln's White House: The Complete Civil War Diary of John Hay* (Carbondale: Southern Illinois University Press, 1997), 88–89. John M. Schofield, *Forty-six Years in the Army*, with a foreword by William M. Ferraro (New York: Century Co., 1897; reprint, Norman: University of Oklahoma Press, 1998), 71–76.

11. *Journal, June 1863*, 12 and 27; and *Proceedings, June 1863*, 34–35, 285–86, 290, and 315–17.

12. *Proceedings, June 1863*, 344 and 367.

13. Schofield, *Forty-six Years*, 68–71. Edward M. Samuel et al. to Lincoln, 8 September 1862, and Edwin M. Stanton to James Lane, 23 September 1862, *Official Records*, series 1, vol. 13, 618–19 and series 3, vol. 2, 582.

14. James S. Rollins to Guitar, 1 February 1863, Odon Guitar Papers, Western Historical Manuscripts Collection, State Historical Society of Missouri, Columbia, Missouri. Joseph Medill to Lincoln, 15 May 1863; and John C. Frémont to Charles Sumner, 9 June 1863, Lincoln Papers. Schofield to Lorenzo Thomas, 10 June 1863; and Thomas to William A. Pile, 13 June 1863, *Official Records*, series 3, vol. 3, 328–29 and 356. Thomas Ewing Jr. to Col. C. W. Marsh, 4 July 1863, Missouri Adjutant General Records, series: Military Organization, Record Group 133, Missouri State Archives, Jefferson City, Missouri.

15. Lorenzo Thomas to Schofield, 21 September 1863; Schofield to Thomas, 26 September 1863; and Schofield to E. D. Townsend, 29 September 1863; *Official Records*, series 3, vol. 3, 847–48. Schofield, *Forty-six Years*, 99–100.

16. General Orders, No. 329, 3 October 1863; Schofield to Henry W. Halleck, 5 November 1863; Halleck to Schofield, 6 November 1863; Edwin M. Stanton to Schofield, 9 November 1863; and Schofield to Stanton, 12 November 1863, *Official Records*, series 1, vol. 22, part 2, 696; series 3, vol. 3, 860–61, 1003–04, 1009–10, and 1021–22.

17. Stanton to Schofield, 13 November 1863; General Orders, No. 135, 14 November 1863, *Official Records*, series 3, vol. 3, 1032 and 1034–36. David L. Phillips to Lincoln, 23 October 1863 and William G. Greenleaf to Lincoln, 16 December 1863, Lincoln Papers. H. H. Hine file, file LL 2648, Judge-Advocate Papers, Record Group 153, National Archives, Washington D.C.

18. Schofield, *Forty-six Years*, 69–71.

19. General Orders, No. 63, 7 July 1863, and Schofield to E. D. Townsend, 15 August 1863, *Official Records*, series 1, vol. 22, part 2, 357–58 and 451–52.

20. General Orders, No. 75, 29 July 1863; and General Orders, No. 24, 26 September 1863, *Official Records*, series 1, vol. 22, part 2, 408 and 577. John B. Gray to Hamilton R. Gamble, 1, 7, 10, and 15 August 1863; Edward Bates to Gamble, 3 August 1863; Willard P. Hall to Gamble, 10 and 19 August 1863; and Gamble to Hall, 15 August 1863, Hamilton R. Gamble Papers, the Missouri State Historical Society, St. Louis, Missouri.

21. Schofield to Lincoln, 20 October 1863, Lincoln Papers. Hall to Gamble, 19 August 1863, Gamble Papers.

22. William MacDonald, *Select Statutes and Other Documents Illustrative of the History of the United States, 1861–1898* (New York: Macmillan, 1903), 75–79. Circular No. 28, 16 June 1863;

Circular No. 29, 16 June 1863; Circular No. 36, 1 July 1863; Circular No. 47, 17 July 1863; Circular No. 51, 18 July 1863; Circular No. 52, 18 July 1863; and 8 August 1863, War Department order, *Official Records*, series 2, vol. 4, 358–59; and series 3, vol. 3, 368–70, 460–61, 523–24, and 535–36. *Mitchell v. Clark*, 110 U.S. 633–51.

23. James M. McPherson, *Battle Cry of Freedom: The Civil War Era*, vol. 4 of *The Oxford History of the United States*, ed. C. Vann Woodward (New York: Oxford University Press, 1988), 600–06. James G. Randall, *Constitutional Problems under Lincoln*, rev. ed. (Urbana: University of Illinois Press, 1964), 247–52.

24. McPherson, *Battle Cry of Freedom*, 609–11. Randall, *Constitutional Problems*, 257–59. *Houston v. Moore*, 18 U.S. 1 (1820).

25. Undated manuscript on the draft, Abraham Lincoln, *The Collected Works of Abraham Lincoln*, ed. Roy P. Basler (New Brunswick, NJ: Rutgers University Press, 1959), vol. 6, 444–49. George C. Gorham, *Life and Public Services of Edwin M. Stanton*, vol. 2 (Boston: Houghton, Mifflin, the Riverside Press Cambridge, 1899), 109–10.

26. Gideon Welles, *Diary of Gideon Welles: Secretary of the Navy Under Lincoln and Johnson*, with an introduction by John T. Morse Jr., vol. 1: 1861–March 30, 1864 (Boston: Houghton, Mifflin, the Riverside Press Cambridge, 1911), 432–34. MacDonald, *Select Statutes*, 75–79. Gorham, *Stanton*, 115–16. Proclamation suspending the privilege of the writ of habeas corpus, Lincoln, *Collected Works*, vol. 6, 451–52.

27. Edwin Draper to Samuel R. Curtis, 1 April 1863; and Schofield to Lincoln, 20 October 1863, *Official Records*, series 1, vol. 22, part 2, 270–72 and 666–68. Charles D. Drake, "Autobiography," 923, Western Historical Manuscripts Collection, State Historical Society of Missouri, Columbia, Missouri.

28. Writ of habeas corpus, 18 July 1863; J. M. Gilstrap, judge of probate court, order to sheriff, 21 July 1863; and Odon Guitar to Gilstrap, 21 July 1863, Odon Guitar papers. Finding and order of the Probate Judge of Macon County in the case of *John C. Cook v. Thomas Crampton*, 31 July 63; and service records of Cook, microfilm reels 835 and 864, Record Group 133, Missouri Adjutant General Records, series: Second Missouri State Militia Cavalry, Missouri State Archives, Jefferson City, Missouri. William E. Parrish, *A History of Missouri: 1860 to 1875*, vol. 3 (Columbia: University of Missouri Press, 1973), 110–11.

29. Schofield to E. D. Townsend, 15 August 1863, *Official Records*, series 1, vol. 22, part 2, 451–52.

30. *St. Louis Missouri Republican*, 10, 13, and 20 September 1863; *St. Louis Missouri Democrat*, 10–12 and 16–17 September 1863; General Orders, No. 315, 17 September 1863; General Orders, No. 96, 17 September 1863; and Ewing to Fry, 28 December 1863, *Official Records*, series 1, vol. 22, part 2, 546–47, 555–65, and 752–53; and series 3, vol. 3, 460, 817–18, and 1198. 17 September 1863, Record book of the St. Louis Criminal Court, vol. 12, St. Louis, Missouri.

31. David Potter, *The Impending Crisis: 1848–1861*, completed and edited by Don E. Fehrenbacher, the New American Nation Series, ed. Henry Steele Commager and Richard B. Morris (New York: Harper and Row, 1973), 156–63. Don E. Fehrenbacher, *Prelude to Greatness: Lincoln in the 1850s* (Palo Alto: Stanford University Press, 1962). Harry V. Jaffa, *Crisis of the House Divided: An Interpretation of the Issues in the Lincoln-Douglas Debates*, with a new preface (Chicago: University of Chicago Press, 1959; reprint, 1982). Lincoln, *Collected Works*, vol. 3, 495–505.

32. W. E. Prince to James H. Lane, 9 September 1861; James H. Lane to S. D. Sturgis, 3 October 1861; Gamble to O. G. Cates, 21 November 1861; Charles R. Jennison to the people of Jackson, Lafayette, Cass, Johnson, and Pettis counties, 27 November 1861; Isaac P. Jones to Halleck, 30 November 1861; Halleck to George B. McClellan, 19 December 1861; Halleck to Lincoln, 6 January 1862; Cates to Halleck, 27 January 1862; and Cates to Stanton, 26 February 1862, *Official Records,* series 1, vol. 3, 482–83, and 516; vol. 7, 532–33; vol. 8, 448–89; vol. 17, part 2, 91–94; and series 2, vol. 1, 231 and 779–81. Gamble to Lincoln, 18 October 1861; and Willard P. Hall to Lincoln, 18 October 1861, Lincoln Papers. *St. Louis Missouri Republican,* 26 November 1861. Lincoln to David Hunter, 23 December 1861, Lincoln Papers.

33. Proclamation of Charles R. Jennison, 27 November 1861; Halleck to George B. McClellan, 10 and 19 December 1861; General Orders, No. 2, 1 January 1862; Frederick Steele to J. C. Kelton, 14 January 1862; Halleck to Lorenzo Thomas, 18 January 1862; and Edwin M. Stanton to Thomas L. Price and James S. Rollins, 6 February 1862, *Official Records,* series 1, vol. 8, 448–49, 478, 507–08, 546–47, and 818–19; and series 2, vol. 1, 231–32.

34. Halleck to Edwin M. Stanton, 25 March 1862; and Gamble to Stanton, 4 June 1862; *Official Records,* series 1, vol. 8, 414, and 641–42. Gamble to Lincoln, 19 May 1862, Gamble Papers.

35. Halleck to Stanton, 12 July 1862; Edward M. Samuel to Lincoln, 8 September 1862; Samuel R. Curtis to Benjamin Loan, 29 September 1862; Willard P. Hall to H. Z. Curtis, 6 October 1862; and Loan to Samuel R. Curtis, 27 January 1863, *Official Records,* series 1, vol. 3, 618–19; vol. 13, 688–89, 712–14; vol. 17, part 2, 91; and vol. 22, part 2, 78–82. Gamble to Lincoln, 9 September 1862; and Gamble to Montgomery Blair, 24 September 1862, Lincoln Papers. Andrew Brownlow to Gamble, 1 August 1862, Gamble Papers.

36. General Orders, No. 24, 4 August 1862; and Loan to Samuel R. Curtis, 27 January 1863, *Official Records,* series 1, vol. 13, 534–35; and vol. 22, part 2, 78–82.

37. James G. Blunt to E. Lynde, 16 April 1863; and General Orders, No. 10, 18 August 1863, *Official Records,* series 1, vol. 22, part 2, 222–23 and 460–61. Gamble to Lincoln, 2 May 1863; Thomas Ewing to Lincoln, 27 June 1863, Lincoln Papers. A. Comingo to James O. Broadhead, 20 August 1863, James O. Broadhead Papers, Missouri Historical Society, St. Louis, Missouri.

38. Jay Monaghan, *Civil War on the Western Border: 1854–1865* (Lincoln: University of Nebraska Press, 1955), 279–81. Thomas Ewing Jr. to C. W. Marsh, 3 August 1863; William M. Wherry to Ewing, 14 August 1863; and General Orders, No. 10, 18 August 1863, *Official Records,* series 1, vol. 22, part 2, 428–29, 450–51, and 460–61.

39. Thomas Carney to Schofield, 24 August 1863; Sydney Clarke to James B. Fry, 25 August 1863; and Lincoln to Schofield, 27 August 1863, *Official Records,* series 1, vol. 22, part 2, 479, 489–90; and series 3, vol. 3, 719–20. James H. Lane and Abel C. Wilder to Lincoln, 26 August 1863, Lincoln, *Collected Works,* vol. 6, 415. Schofield to Lincoln, 28 August 1863, Lincoln Papers. Schofield, *Forty-six Years,* 80.

40. General Orders, No. 11, 25 August 1863; and Richard C. Vaughan to Edward Bates, 27 August 1863, *Official Records,* series 1, vol. 22, part 2, 473 and 484–88. Schofield to Lincoln, 28 August 1863; and Lincoln to Schofield, 1 October 1863, Lincoln Papers. Bazel F. Lazear to his wife, 10 and 27 September 1863, the Bazel F. Lazear Papers, Western Historical Manuscripts Collection, State Historical Society of Missouri, Columbia, Missouri.

41. Schofield, *Forty-six Years*, 80–83. Ewing to Schofield, 28 August 1863; Schofield to Carney, 29 August and 3 September 1863; and General Orders, No. 92, 4 September 1863, *Official Records*, series 1, vol. 22, part 2, 490 and 577–80.

42. Schofield to E. D. Townsend, 14 September 1863, *Official Records*, series 1, vol. 22, part 1, 572–76.

43. R. T. Van Horn to Ewing, 1 September 1863; General Orders, No. 92, 4 September 1862; General Orders, No. 16, 2 October 1863; General Orders, No. 20, 20 November 1863; and Ewing to Fry, 28 December 1863, *Official Records*, series 1, vol. 22, part 1, 575; vol. 22, part 2, 594–95, 713–14, and 752–53; and series 2, vol. 6, 245. Albert Castel, "Order No. 11 and the Civil War on the Border," *Missouri Historical Review* 57 (July 1963): 357–68. Jeremy Neely, *The Border Between Them: Violence and Reconciliation on the Kansas-Missouri Line* (Columbia: University of Missouri Press, 2007), 125–31.

44. Ann Davis Niepman, "General Orders, No. 11 and Border Warfare During the Civil War," *Missouri Historical Review* 66 (January 1972), 199–200, 204, and 208. Report of Bazel F. Lazear, 27 August 1863, *Official Records*, series 1, vol. 22, part 1, 587–88. Lazear to his wife, 10 and 27 September 1863, Lazear Papers.

45. Series of newspaper articles; *Official Records*, series 1, vol. 22, part 2, 549, 551–58, and 560–62. See *St. Louis Missouri Republican*, 28 August and 9, 10, and 13 September 1863; and *St. Louis Missouri Democrat*, 8, 10, and 16 September 1863.

CHAPTER NINE

1. Lincoln to Schofield, 27 May 1863, *The War of the Rebellion: A Compilation of the Official Records of the Union and Confederate Armies*, 128 vols. (Washington D.C.: Government Printing Office, 1880–1902), series 1, vol. 22, part 2, 293. Samuel T. Glover to Edward Bates, 13 April 1863; St. Louis Citizens to Lincoln, 1 May 1863; Henry T. Blow to Lincoln, 5 May 1863; Glover to Bates, 15 May 1863; Lincoln to Henry T. Blow and others, 15 May 1863; Lincoln to John M. Schofield, 27 May 1863, Abraham Lincoln Papers, Library of Congress, Washington D.C.

2. Lincoln to John M. Schofield, 27 May 1863, Lincoln Papers.

3. Lincoln to General Dix, 14 January 1863; Lincoln to Joshua F. Speed, 17 March 1863; Lincoln to Horatio Seymour, 17 March 1863; Lincoln to Isaac N. Arnold, 26 May 1863; and Lincoln to Schofield, 28 October 1863, Abraham Lincoln, *The Collected Works of Abraham Lincoln*, ed. Roy P. Basler (New Brunswick, NJ: Rutgers University Press, 1959), vol. 6, 56, 140, 145–46, 230–31, and 543–44. Curtis to Richard McAllister, 1 July 1863, and McAllister to Lincoln, 13 July 1863, Lincoln Papers.

4. Lincoln to Schofield, 13 July 1863; Schofield to Lincoln, 14 July 1863, *Official Records*, series 1, vol. 22, part 2, 366 and 373–74. *Ex parte McKee*, 18 Mo. Rep. 599–603.

5. Lincoln to Henry T. Blow, 13 July 1863; and Schofield to Lincoln, 14 July 1863; *Official Records*, series 1, vol. 22, part 2, 366 and 373–74. Lincoln to Schofield, 20 July 1863, Lincoln, *Collected Works*, vol. 6, 338. James L. McDonough, *Schofield: Union General in the Civil War and Reconstruction* (Tallahassee: Florida State University Press, 1972), 47–49.

6. John M. Schofield, *Forty-six Years in the Army*, with a foreword by William M. Ferraro (New York: Century Co., 1897; reprint, Norman: University of Oklahoma Press, 1998), 71–72 and

77. Henry W. Halleck to Schofield, 26 September 1863; and Schofield to Halleck, 30 September 1863, *Official Records,* series 1, vol. 22, part 2, 574–75 and 581–82.

7. Series of newspaper articles; and General Orders, No. 96, 17 September 1863; *Official Records,* series 1, vol. 22, part 2, 546–47, 549–58, and 560–62.

8. Special Orders, No. 255, 18 September 1863; Schofield to Halleck, 20 and 30 September 1863; Halleck to Schofield, 24 and 26 September and 5 October 1863; and Schofield to Lincoln, 25 October 1863, *Official Records,* series 1, vol. 22, part 2, 542–43, 546, 571, 574–75, and 581–82; and vol. 29, part 2, 261–62. Lincoln to Schofield, 1 October 1863, Lincoln Papers. Quinn Morton to Gamble, 28 September 1863, Hamilton R. Gamble Papers, Missouri Historical Society, St. Louis, Missouri.

9. James G. Randall, *Constitutional Problems under Lincoln,* rev. ed. (Urbana: University of Illinois Press, 1964), 176–79. James M. McPherson, *Battle Cry of Freedom: The Civil War Era,* vol. 4 of *The Oxford History of the United States,* ed. C. Vann Woodward (New York: Oxford University Press, 1988), 596–99.

10. James S. Rollins to Lincoln, 8 September 1863; Benjamin G. Brown, 9 September 1863; Joseph A. Hay to Lincoln, 11 September 1863; Rollins to Edward Bates, 13 September 1863; James F. Joy, 21 September 1863; James O. Broadhead to Bates, 22 September 1863; and C. E. Moss et al., 23 September 1863, Lincoln Papers. Bates to Broadhead, 26 September 1863, James O. Broadhead Papers, Missouri Historical Society, St. Louis, Missouri. Hamilton R. Gamble Jr. to Hamilton R. Gamble, 26 August and 6 September 1863; John B. Gray to Gamble, 9 September 1863; Samuel T. Glover to Gamble, 28 September 1863; Archibald Gamble to Gamble, 29 September 1863; and Hamilton R. Gamble to Lincoln, 30 September and 1 October 1863, Gamble Papers. Schofield to Halleck, 30 September 1863, *Official Records,* series 1, vol. 22, part 2, 581–82.

11. Michael Burlingame and John R. Turner Ettlinger, eds. *Inside Lincoln's White House: The Complete Civil War Diary of John Hay* (Carbondale: Southern Illinois University Press, 1997), 88–89. Joseph A. Hay to Abraham Lincoln, 11 September 1863, Lincoln Papers. Gideon Welles, *Diary of Gideon Welles,* vol. 1, 1861–March 30, 1864, with an introduction by John T. Morse Jr. (Boston: Houghton, Mifflin, the Riverside Press Cambridge, 1911), 448.

12. Charles D. Drake, "Autobiography," 918–22, Western Historical Manuscripts Collection, State Historical Society of Missouri, Columbia, Missouri. Charles Gibson and James S. Rollins to Abraham Lincoln, 11 October 1863, Lincoln Papers. For a particularly pointed reference to Drake's behavior during the early part of the war see Carl Schurz, *The Reminiscences of Carl Schurz,* vol. 3, with a sketch of his life and public services from 1869 to 1906 by Frederic Bancroft and William A. Dunning (New York: McClure Company, 1908), 299–300.

13. Drake, "Autobiography," 918–22.

14. Ibid., 923. Burlingame and Ettlinger, eds., *Diary of John Hay,* 88.

15. Ibid., 88–89.

16. Schofield, *Forty-six Years,* 89–99. Charles Gibson and James S. Rollins to Lincoln, 11 October 1863, Lincoln Papers. John M. Schofield to Henry W. Halleck, 30 September 1863; Lincoln to John M. Schofield, 1 and 4 October 1863; and John M. Schofield to Lincoln, 3 October 1863, *Official Records,* series 1, vol. 22, part 2, 581–82, 585–86, 595, and 601. Gamble to Lincoln, 30 September 1863, Lincoln Papers. Gamble to Lincoln, 30 September 1863; Charles Gibson to Gamble, 12 and 13 October 1863; and Lincoln to Gamble, 19 October 1863, Gamble Papers. Howard K.

Beale, ed., *The Diary of Edward Bates, 1859–1866* (Washington D.C.: Government Printing Office, 1933), 16 October 1863, 308.

17. Lincoln to Charles D. Drake, 5 October 1863, *Official Records*, series 1, vol. 22, part 2, 604–07.

18. Ibid.

19. Ibid., and General Orders, No. 101, 28 September 1863, *Official Records*, series 1, vol. 22, part 2, 577. No doubt, a reason for Lincoln's apparent exasperation with the Radicals was their demand that he appoint a military governor, something for which he had previously been criticized. See William C. Harris, *With Charity for All: Lincoln and the Restoration of the Union* (Lexington: University Press of Kentucky, 1997), 65–66.

20. James O. Broadhead to Edward Bates, 19 October 1863, Lincoln Papers. Schofield, *Forty-six Years*, 99–100.

21. Smith O. Scofield to Edwin M. Stanton, October 1863; Lincoln to Schofield, 1 and 28 October 1863; and Charles D. Drake to Lincoln, 3 and 10 October 1863, Lincoln Papers. Schofield to Lincoln, 25 October 1863, *Official Records*, series 1, vol. 22, part 2, 677.

22. General Orders, No. 101, 28 September 1863; General Orders, No. 120, 20 October 1863; Clinton B. Fisk to J. B. Rogers, 24 October 1863; Fisk to William T. Leeper, 25 October 1863; Schofield to Odon Guitar, 1 November 1863, *Official Records*, series 1, vol. 22, part 2, 577, 668–70, 676, 678, and 688.

23. T. Murphy to Judge Austin A. King, 3 November 1863, Broadhead Papers. Report of Robert McElroy, 9 November 1863, *Official Records*, series 1, vol. 22, part 1, 744. Schofield to Lincoln, 9 and 10 November 1863, Lincoln Papers. Harmon Teppencamp, file NN 1482, Judge-Advocate Papers, Record Group 153, National Archives, Washington D.C.

24. Lincoln to E. H. E. Jameson, 10 November 1863, *Collected Works*, vol. 7, 13. Schofield, *Forty-six Years*, 106–08. Lincoln to Schofield, 11 December 1863, *Official Records*, series 3, vol. 3, 1164. Burlingame and Ettlinger, eds., *Diary of John Hay*, 127.

25. Burlingame and Ettlinger, eds., *Diary of John Hay*, 127 and 129. Lincoln to Stanton, 18 and 21 December 1863, *Collected Works*, vol. 7, 78–79 and 84. Schofield, *Forty-six Years*, 107–10. General Orders, No. 19, 30 January 1864, *Official Records*, series 1, vol. 34, part 2, 188–89. William M. Lamers, *The Edge of Glory: A Biography of General William S. Rosecrans, U.S.A.* (New York: Harcourt, Brace, and World, 1961), 413.

26. Lincoln to Stanton, 18 December 1863, *Collected Works*, vol. 7, 78–79. Lamers, *Edge of Glory*, 413–16. Schofield, *Forty-six Years*, 110. Ulysses S. Grant, *Personal Memoirs of U. S. Grant* (New York: Library of America, 1990), 403–04.

27. Rosecrans to Halleck, 11 March 1864; and Rosecrans to Lincoln, 12 March 1864, *Official Records*, series 1, vol. 34, part 2, 566–68. Lamers, *Edge of Glory*, 418.

28. John B. Sanborn to O. D. Greene, 14 January 1864; Greene to Sanborn, 14 and 15 January 1864; Greene to Ewing, 14 January 1864; Ewing to Greene, 14 January 1864; E. B. Brown to Greene, 22 January 1864; James H. Young to Greene, 2 February 1864; Greene to Young, 3 February 1864; and Greene to Brown, 11 February 1864, *Official Records*, series 1, vol. 34, part 2, 80–82, 130, 226, 234, and 298–99.

29. *Report of the Committee of the House of Representatives of the Twenty-Second General Assembly of the State of Missouri appointed to Investigate the Conduct and Management of the Militia: Majority and Minority Reports* (Jefferson City: W. A. Curry, public printer, 1864), 7.

30. *Report on the Conduct and Management of the Militia*, 89–101.

31. Ibid., 102–58. See also, William Whiting, *War Powers under the Constitution of the United States: Military Arrests, Reconstruction, and Military Government. Also now First Published, War Claims of Aliens, with Notes on the Acts of the Executive and Legislative Departments During Our Civil War and a Collection of Cases Decided in the National Courts*, Forty-third ed. (Boston: Lee and Shepard Publishers; New York: Lee, Shepard and Dillingham, 1871), 162.

32. *Report on the Conduct and Management of the Militia*, 459–72.

33. John G. Nicolay to John Hay, 29 June 1864, Lincoln Papers.

34. Rosecrans to Stanton, 15 March 1864; and Rosecrans to Halleck, 16 March 1864, *Official Records*, series 1, vol. 34, part 2, 618–19 and 632. Lamers, *Edge of Glory*, 418. Grant, *Memoirs*, 781–87.

35. C. W. Marsh to Frank Eno, 23 February 1864; General Orders, No. 34, 4 March 1864; Rosecrans to Stanton, 5 and 15 March 1864; Stanton to Rosecrans, 5 March 1864; Halleck to Rosecrans, 14 March 1864; General Orders, No. 53, 9 April 1864; Frank S. Bond to Marsh, 21 April 1864; and Charles A. Dana to Rosecrans, 18 July 1864, *Official Records*, series 1, vol. 34, part 2, 404–06, 498, 505–06, 603, and 618–19; vol. 34, part 3, 107–08 and 248; and vol. 41, part 2, 235.

36. Rosecrans to Lincoln, 12 February 1864; Rosecrans to Henry Blow, 14 February 1864; General Orders, No. 36, 4 March 1864; Rosecrans to Halleck, 22 March 1864; and Rosecrans to James L. Thomas, 28 April 1864, *Official Records*, series 1, vol. 34, part 2, 304–05, 324, 498, 695; and vol. 34, part 3, 321–22. Rosecrans to Lincoln, 20 February 1864, Lincoln Papers. Lincoln to Rosecrans, 22 February 1864, *Collected Works*, vol. 7, 198. Frank L. Klement, *Dark Lanterns: Secret Political Societies, Conspiracies, and Treason Trials in the Civil War* (Baton Rouge: Louisiana State University Press, 1984) 75–76. 4, 5, 8, 12 March 1864, John P. Sanderson Journal, Ohio Historical Society, Columbus, Ohio.

37. John G. Nicolay to John Hay, 29 June 1864, Lincoln Papers.

38. General Orders, No. 63, 7 July 1863; and General Orders, No. 34, 29 February 1864, *Official Records*, series 1, vol. 22, part 2, 357–58; and vol. 34, part 2, 464–65.

39. Microfilm no. 1158, file of James Monaghan, Union Provost-Marshals' File of Papers Relating to Individual Citizens, 1861–1866, Record Group 109, National Archives and Records Administration, Washington D.C.

40. Ibid.

41. Ibid.

42. Clinton B. Fisk to Rosecrans, 31 May 1864; and memorandum of Acting Judge-Advocate James F. Dwight, 3 June 1864, *Official Records*, series 1, vol. 34, part 4, 191–94.

43. Samuel R. Curtis to Colonel Woodson, 27 January 1864; John B. Sanborn to N. H. Burns, 15 March 1864; Clinton B. Fisk to John Holdsworth, 9 June 1864; Fisk to Governor Willard P. Hall, 14 June 1864; and Fisk to S. Porter, 14 June 1864, *Official Records*, series 1, vol. 34, part 2, 168–69 and 620–21; and vol. 34, part 4, 287, 368–71.

44. E. G. Evans to C. C. Manwaring, 13 February 1864; General Orders, No. 34, 29 February 1864; Fisk to Holdsworth, 9 June 1864; *Official Records*, series 1, vol. 34, part 2, 436–37, 464–65; and vol. 34, part 4, 368–69. Randall, *Constitutional Problems*, 169–74.

45. General Orders, No. 19, 22 July 1862; General Orders, No. 24, 4 August 1862; General Orders, No. 86, 25 August 1863; General Orders, No. 32, 27 February 1864; General Orders, No. 36,

4 March 1864; John P. Clark to A. A. Rice, 10 March 1864; and Odon Guitar report, 28 March 1864, *Official Records,* series 1, vol. 13, 506 and 534–35; vol. 22, part 2, 474–75; vol. 34, part 2, 434, 498, 554–56. See chapters 2 and 5 for details about the restriction of arms under Frémont, Halleck, and Schofield.

46. R. B. Palmer to Rosecrans, 24 February 1864; William A. Hall to Rosecrans, 11 March 1864; Guitar report, 28 March 1864; General Orders, No. 2, 5 May 1864; A. C. Marsh to James F. Dwight, 12 May 1864; Dwight to Marsh, 12 May 1864; John P. Sanderson to Rosecrans, 15 May 1864; and Frank Eno to Clinton B. Fisk, 18 May 1864, *Official Records,* series 1, vol. 34, part 2, 411–12, 555–56, and 567; and vol. 34, part 3, 463–65. James O. Broadhead to Edward Bates, 24 July 1862, Lincoln Papers.

CHAPTER TEN

1. Henry E. McCulloch to J. B. Magruder, 3 February 1864; McCulloch to E. Kirby Smith, 5 February 1864; James G. Blunt to Samuel R. Curtis, 21 March 1864; McCulloch to E. P. Turner, 6 April 1864; and E. B. Brown to O. D. Greene, 26 May 1864; Sterling Price to Thomas C. Reynolds, 9 June 1864; and B. P. Van Court to Sterling Price, 26 August 1864, *The War of the Rebellion: A Compilation of the Official Records of the Union and Confederate Armies,* 128 vols. (Washington D.C.: Government Printing Office, 1880–1902), series 1, vol. 34, part 2, 685, 941–43, and 945; vol. 34, part 3, 742–43; vol. 34, part 4, 51; vol. 41, part 2, 1085–86; and vol. 53, 999–1000. Albert Castel, *General Sterling Price and the Civil War in the West* (Baton Rouge: Louisiana State University Press, 1968), 197 and 199. Michael Fellman, *Inside War: The Guerrilla Conflict in Missouri During the American Civil War* (New York: Oxford University Press, 1989), 103–06.

2. Frank Eno to E. B. Brown, 22 February 1864, *Official Records,* series 1, vol. 34, part 2, 397. *United States v. Anna Reed,* microfilm reel no. 1205, Anna Reed file, Union Provost-Marshals' File of Papers Relating to Individual Citizens, 1861–1866, Record Group 109, National Archives and Records Administration, Washington D.C. Abraham Lincoln to William S. Rosecrans, 23 April 1864; and Rosecrans to Lincoln, 24 April 1864, Abraham Lincoln, *The Collected Works of Abraham Lincoln,* ed. Roy P. Basler (New Brunswick, NJ: Rutgers University Press, 1959), vol. 7, 310–11.

3. Charles B. Scott and John T. Enchburg to Rosecrans, 31 March 1864; O. D. Greene to Scott and Enchburg, 31 March 1864; General Orders, No. 50, 2 April 1864; Frank Bond to C. W. Marsh, 21 April 1864; O. P. Steele to John P. Sanderson, 13 May 1864; Marsh to Greene, 14 May 1864; Sanderson to Rosecrans, 19 May 1864; Frank Eno to Thomas Ewing Jr., 20 May 1864; Ewing to Rosecrans, 21 May 1864; and John B. Sanborn to Hugh Cameron, 23 and 30 July 1864, *Official Records,* series 1, vol. 34, part 2, 800; vol. 34, part 3, 21–22, 248, 572–74, and 593–94; and vol. 41, part 2, 361–62 and 478.

4. For the cases of average persons arrested for using "disloyal language," see summary of proceedings against Barney Arnold, James B. Neill, Oliver P. Butler, George W. Coonce, Patrick Lyons, Patrick Riley, R. C. York, James Sullivan, and Wesley Wadley, Missouri Adjutant General records, series: Court-Martial papers, Record Group 133, Missouri State Archives, Jefferson City, Missouri. Microfilm no. 1219, file of Barney Arnold; microfilm no. 1233, file of Jackson Boughton;

and microfilm no. 1239, file of William Clyce, Provost-Marshal Records. John F. Philips, "Administrations of Missouri Governors: Second Paper, Governor Willard Preble Hall," *Missouri Historical Review* 5, no. 2 (January 1911): 70 and 77. William F. Switzler, *Switzler's Illustrated History of Missouri from 1541 to 1877* (St. Louis: C. R. Barns, editor and publisher, 1879), 325 and 332.

5. Microfilm no. 1336, file of William A. Hall, Provost-Marshal Records. Clinton B. Fisk to J. F. Williams, 18 June 1864, *Official Records,* series 1, vol. 34, part 4, 447. Joseph T. Glatthaar, *Forged in Battle: The Civil War Alliance of Black Soldiers and White Officers* (New York: Free Press, 1990), 51.

6. O. D. Greene to James L. Fawcett, 17 February 1864; and General Orders, No. 38, 10 March 1864, *Official Records,* series 1, vol. 34, part 2, 355 and 550. Robert S. Harper, *Lincoln and the Press* (New York: McGraw-Hill, 1951), 143. Walter B. Stevens, *Missouri, the Central State, 1821–1915* (Chicago: S. J. Clarke Publishing, 1915), 399.

7. John P. Sanderson to J. Gray and W. P. Owens, 29 May 1864, *Official Records,* series 1, vol. 34, part 2, 777. John L. Bittinger to John B. S. Todd, 27 February 1864; John B. Henderson to Lincoln, 23 April 1864; Samuel T. Glover to Montgomery Blair, 27 May 1864; James O. Broadhead to Edward Bates, 24 July 1864; and Benjamin F. Loan, 8 September 1864, Abraham Lincoln Papers, Library of Congress, Washington D.C. Bates to Broadhead, 30 July and 13 August 1864, James O. Broadhead Papers, Missouri Historical Society, St. Louis, Missouri. Lincoln to Loan, 22 February 1864, Lincoln, *Collected Works,* vol. 7, 197.

8. Edward McPherson, *The Political History of the United States of America During the Great Rebellion* (Washington D.C.: James J. Chapman, 1882), 521.

9. Lincoln to Edwin M. Stanton, 11 February 1864; and Lincoln's note to John Hogan, 13 February 1864, Lincoln, *Collected Works,* vol. 7, 178–80 and 182–83. Circular, 12 February 1864; and Rosecrans to Stanton, 28 February 1864, *Official Records,* series 1, vol. 34, part 2, 331 and 452–53. E. D. Townsend to Rosecrans, 13 February 1864, William S. Rosecrans Papers, Collection 663, Huntington Library, University of California, Los Angeles. William M. Leftwich, *Martyrdom in Missouri: A History of Religious Proscription, the Seizure of Churches, and the Persecution of Ministers of the Gospel, in the State of Missouri During the Late Civil War and under the "Test Oath" of the New Constitution,* vol. 1 (St. Louis: Southwestern Book and Publishing Company, 1870), 263–65 and 275–77.

10. O. D. Greene to John P. Sanderson, 5 March 1864, *Official Records,* series 1, vol. 34, part 2, 506. Leftwich, vol. 2, *Martyrdom in Missouri,* 64–71.

11. A. P. Forman to Edward Bates, 15 March 1864; and Lincoln to Rosecrans, 4 April 1864, Lincoln Papers. Rosecrans to J. P. Findley, 29 April 1864, *Official Records,* series 1, vol. 34, part 3, 348–50.

12. General Orders, No. 135, 14 November 1863; E. B. Brown to O. D. Greene, 22 January and 19 March 1864; A. Kempinsky to Marsh, 7 February 1864; S. S. Burdett to Kempinsky, 7 February 1864; and memorandum of Judge-Advocate James F. Dwight, 3 June 1864, *Official Records,* series 1, vol. 34, part 2, 660–6l; vol. 34, part 4, 130, 268, and 191–93; and series 3, vol. 3, 1034–36.

13. H. H. Hine file, file LL 2648, Judge-Advocate Papers, Record Group 153, National Archives, Washington D.C. General Orders, No. 35, 1 March 1864; *Official Records,* series 1, vol. 34, part 2, 477.

14. William Whiting, *War Powers under the Constitution of the United States: Military Arrests, Reconstruction, and Military Government. Also now First Published, War Claims of Aliens, with*

Notes on the Acts of the Executive and Legislative Departments During Our Civil War and a Collection of Cases Decided in the National Courts, 43d ed. (Boston: Lee and Shepard Publishers; New York: Lee, Shepard and Dillingham, 1871), 371–73. General Orders, No. 135, 14 November 1863, *Official Records,* series 3, vol. 3, 1034–36. Glatthaar, *Forged in Battle,* 61–80.

15. Microfilm no. 1412, file of John Watson, Provost-Marshal Records. William F. Switzler to Rosecrans, 30 March 1864; A. A. Rice to John P. Sanderson, 31 March 1864; Sanderson to Rosecrans, 31 March 1864; W. E. Fowkes to Clinton B. Fisk, 14 April 1864; *Official Records,* series 1, vol. 34, part 2, 787, 799–800; and vol. 34, part 3, 157–58.

16. Odon Guitar to O. D. Greene, 10 March 1864; A. Jacobson to Rosecrans, 14 March 1864; *Official Records,* series 1, vol. 34, part 2, 551–53. Microfilm no. 1415, file of Curtis F. Wells; microfilm no. 1412, file of Washington Watts, Provost-Marshal Records. Lincoln to Rosecrans, 4 April 1864, Lincoln Papers. Jo Davis to James O. Broadhead, 10 May 1864, Broadhead Papers. Joseph Holt to Stanton, 5 August 1864, *Official Records,* series 3, vol. 3, 577–79.

17. Military commission trial of Rachel Haynie, June 1864, Series: Court-Martial Papers, Missouri Adjutant General Papers. Clinton B. Fisk to Daniel M. Draper, 18 April 1864; Fisk to J. T. K. Hayward, 18 April 1864; T. A. Switzler to J. H. Steger, 21 May 1864; Steger to John F. Philips, 21 May 1864; Lucius Salisbury to Rosecrans, 5 June 1864; Frank Eno to John P. Sanderson, 9 June 1864; Sanderson to Rosecrans, 12 June 1864; Joseph Holt to Stanton, 31 July 1864, *Official Records,* series 1, vol. 34, part 3, 216 and 708; vol. 34, part 4, 233–34; and vol. 39, part 2, 212–15.

18. Clinton B. Fisk to A. C. Marsh, 28 May 1864; O. D. Greene to Fisk, 29 July and 1 August 1864; and Joseph Holt to Stanton, 5 August 1864, *Official Records,* series 1, vol. 34, part 4, 96; vol. 41, part 1, 56–59; vol. 41, part 2, 459; and series 3, vol. 3, 577–79. Bazel F. Lazear to his wife, 11 August and 13 September 1864, Bazel F. Lazear Papers, Western Historical Manuscript Collections, State Historical Society of Missouri, Columbia, Missouri. Amos J. Harding to Lucien Eaton, 5 August, 10 and 22 September 1864, Lucien Eaton Papers, Missouri Historical Society, St. Louis, Missouri. Cases of Thomas Lewis, Joseph Russell, James R. Crosswhite, James P. Griffin, John Forbis, James Lovell, Charles White, David T. Hampton, Ann Fickle, James M. Lafoon, Rebecca Romonoska, Pleasant McDonald, James Jeffries, Peter Stacy, and William J. Cole, Series: Court-Martial Papers, Missouri Adjutant General Records.

19. Charles L. Bernays to Lincoln, 2 May 1864; Edwin Weston to Lincoln, 2 May 1864; and General Orders, No. 107, 28 June 1864, Lincoln Papers. General Orders, No. 65, 29 April 1864; General Orders, No. 114, 11 July 1864; General Orders, No. 116, 12 July 1864; General Orders, No. 119, 15 July 1864; J. H. Baker to O. D. Greene, 18 July 1864; General Orders, No. 165, 9 September 1864; report of Rosecrans, 7 December 1864, *Official Records,* series 1, vol. 34, part 3, 345–46; vol. 41, part 1, 307; vol. 41, part 2, 128, 147, 199–200, and 236; and vol. 41, part 3, 118. Castel, *Price,* 199.

20. Castel, *Price,* 132–33, 135–36, 191–96, and 199–200. John H. Taylor to the OAK in Missouri, 1 October 1864, *Official Records,* series 1, vol. 41, part 3, 975–76.

21. Rosecrans to Lincoln, 2, 8, and 14 June 1864, Lincoln Papers. Lincoln to Rosecrans, 7, 8, and 10 June 1864, *Collected Works,* vol. 7, 379 and 386. William M. Lamers, *The Edge of Glory: A Biography of General William S. Rosecrans, U.S.A.* (New York: Harcourt, Brace and World, 1961), 420–21. Michael Burlingame and John R. Turner Ettlinger, eds., *Inside Lincoln's White House: The Complete Civil War Diary of John Hay* (Carbondale: Southern Illinois University Press, 1997), 200–08.

22. John P. Sanderson to Rosecrans, 27 June 1864; J. B. Devoe to Rosecrans, 28 and 29 June 1864, Rosecrans Papers. Joseph Holt to Edwin M. Stanton, 5 August 1864, *Official Records*, series 3, vol. 4, 577–79. Burlingame and Ettlinger, *Diary of John Hay*, 207. The standard account of Sanderson's investigation of the OAK too strongly dismisses the importance of what he discovered. It is noteworthy that Hay believed Sanderson had uncovered an important plot, especially as it regarded Price's raid. Nevertheless, Lincoln was correct in his judgment that the OAK conspiracy did not pose any great threat to the republic as Sanderson and Rosecrans believed. See Frank L. Klement, *Dark Lanterns: Secret Political Societies, Conspiracies, and Treason Trials in the Civil War* (Baton Rouge: Louisiana State University Press, 1984), 82–87.

23. William A. Hall to Rosecrans, 12 June 1864; O. D. Greene to Clinton B. Fisk, 14 June 1864; Fisk to Greene, 14 June 1864; E. J. Crandall to Fisk, 14 June 1864; Fisk to Crandall, 14 June 1864; and Grenville M. Dodge to John Pope, 4 June 1865, *Official Records*, series 1, vol. 34, part 4, 324–25 and 372–74; and vol. 48, part 2, 773–74. John G. Nicolay to John Hay, 29 June 1864, Lincoln Papers. Larry Wood, "Harry Truman: Federal Bushwacker," *Missouri Historical Review* 98, no. 3 (April 2004): 201–22.

24. Castel, *Price*, 199. William F. Switzler to Clinton B. Fisk, 1 August 1864; William McIlwrath to J. H. Shanklin, 11 August 1864; and report of General William S. Rosecrans, 7 December 1864, *Official Records*, series 1, vol. 41, part 1, 308–09; vol. 41, part 2, 510 and 668–70.

25. J. H. Steger to Milton Burris, 16 August 1864; O. D. Greene to Clinton B. Fisk, 19 August 1864; General Orders, No. 159, 1 September 1864; Mel. U. Foster to J. N. Pennock, 11 September 1864; report of General William S. Rosecrans, 7 December 1864; and report of General Samuel R. Curtis, January 1865, *Official Records*, series 1, vol. 41, part 1, 308–09, 311, 484–91, and 736; vol. 41, part 2, 730 and 773–74; and vol. 41, part 3, 8. Castel, *Price*, 222–25 and 238–47. William E. Parrish, *A History of Missouri: 1860 to 1875*, vol. 3 (Columbia: University of Missouri Press, 1973), 111–14.

26. Castel, *Price*, 226–27. S. P. Cox to General Craig, 27 October 1864; report of General Rosecrans, 7 December 1864; *Official Records*, series 1, vol. 41, part 1, 309 and 442. Fellman, *Inside War*, 110–12.

27. Special Orders, No. 5, 27 September 1864, *Official Records*, series 1, vol. 41, part 3, 424–25. Enoch Mather Marvin, *The Life of Rev. William Goff Caples of the Missouri Conference of the Methodist Episcopal Church South* (St. Louis: Southwestern Book and Publishing Company, 1870), 362–76.

28. Special Orders, No. 145, 22 September 1864; General Orders, No. 35, 27 September 1864; Clinton B. Fisk to Rosecrans, 27 September 1864; General Orders, No. 179, 27 September 1864; Dan M. Draper to Fisk, 29 September 1864; John V. Du Bois to Alfred Pleasonton, 21 October 1864; Special Orders, No. 290, 31 October 1864; report of John F. Philips, 7 November 1864; and Thomas Ewing Jr. to Maupin, 8 November 1864, *Official Records*, series 1, vol. 41, part 1, 350–54; vol. 41, part 3, 306, 406, 414–15, 417, and 440–41; and vol. 41, part 4, 158–59, 352–53, and 491.

29. Special Orders, No. 141, 1 July 1864; Isaac Gannett to John P. Sanderson, 24, 25, and 26 July 1864; and Sanderson to Gannett, 26 July 1864, *Official Records*, series 1, vol. 41, part 2, 8–9, 375–76, 395, and 412. Bazel F. Lazear to his wife, 11 August 1864, Lazear Papers.

30. Special Orders, No. 277, 6 October 1864; Ewing to Rosecrans, 17 October 1864; Joseph Darr Jr. to John V. Du Bois, 25 and 29 October 1864; Ewing to Du Bois, 25 October 1864; General Orders, No. 51, 26 October 1864; H. M. Matthews and others, 28 October 1864; and Du Bois, 29 October 1864,

Official Records, series 1, vol. 41, part 3, 657–58; vol. 41, part 4, 35, 236, 251, 299, 310, and 316. Amos W. Maupin testimony, 28 October 1864; James M. Kitchen testimony, 28 October 1864; and Michael Zwicky testimony, 29 October 1864; Contemporary newspaper clipping, undated; and Special Orders, No. 287, 7 November 1864, James Wilson Papers, Western Historical Manuscript Collections, State Historical Society of Missouri, Columbia, Missouri. *St. Louis Missouri Democrat,* 6 November 1864. John F. Frazer to Lincoln, 3 November 1864; Zadok Street to Lincoln, 9 November 1864; Barton Able and P. L. Terry, 10 November 1864; Rosecrans to Lincoln, 11 November 1864; Lincoln to Rosecrans, 19 November 1864; and Grenville M. Dodge to Lincoln, 19 January 1865, Lincoln Papers. Lincoln to Rosecrans, 10 November 1864, *Collected Works,* vol. 8, 102.

31. John L. Bittinger to John B. S. Todd, 27 February 1864; Lincoln to Rosecrans, 26 September 1864; Rosecrans to Lincoln, 3 and 4 October 1864, Lincoln Papers.

32. Samuel T. Glover to Montgomery Blair, 27 May 1864; Smith O. Scofield to Lincoln, June 1864; John G. Nicolay to John Hay, 29 June 1864; Charles D. Drake to Lincoln, 16 July 1864; Benjamin Loan to Lincoln, 8 September 1864; Carl Schurz to Lincoln, 1 and 19 October 1864; James B. Wright to Lincoln, 5 October 1864; Nicolay to Lincoln, 10, 12, and 18 October 1864; William L. Avery to Lincoln, 2 November 1864; and Rosecrans to Lincoln, 15 November 1864, Lincoln Papers. William McIlwrath to J. H. Shanklin, 11 August 1864, *Official Records,* series 1, vol. 41, part 2, 668–70. W. R. Singleton to John F. Williams, 16 March 1864; Williams to John B. Gray, 17 March 1864; and E. H. Kenner to Rosecrans, 29 July 1864, Missouri Adjutant General records, series: Enrolled Missouri Militia series and Provisional Companies of the Enrolled Missouri Militia series, Missouri Adjutant General Records, Record Group 133, Missouri State Archives, Jefferson City, Missouri.

33. Microfilm no. 1465, M. J. Payne file, Union Provost Marshal Records.

34. Charles C. Whittelsey to Rosecrans, 16 and 17 September 1864; General Orders, No. 11, 21 September 1864; and J. H. Baker to O. D. Greene, 25 September 1864, *Official Records,* series 1, vol. 41, part 3, 224–29.

35. Charles D. Drake to Lincoln, 5 October 1864; and D. W. Moore to Lincoln, 5 October 1864, Lincoln Papers. General Orders, No. 195, 12 October 1864; Bond to James Craig, 4 November 1864; Fisk to Harding, 5 November 1864; and Fisk to Du Bois, 12 November 1864, *Official Records,* series 1, vol. 41, part 3, 804–09; and vol. 41, part 4, 432, 444, and 548. A. J. Harding to Lucien Eaton, 1 and 7 November 1864; Circular, undated; Fisk to Eaton, 12 November 1864, Lucien Eaton Papers.

36. Fisk to John V. Du Bois, 12 November 1864, *Official Records,* series 1, vol. 41, part 4, 548. Fisk to J. H. Shanklin, 1864, Missouri Adjutant General records, series: Enrolled Missouri Militia, Record Group 133, Missouri State Archives, Jefferson City, Missouri. Parrish, *History of Missouri,* 114–15.

CHAPTER ELEVEN

1. Ulysses S. Grant, *Personal Memoirs of U. S. Grant* (New York: Library of America, 1990), 278–81 and 404–10.

2. William M. Lamers, *The Edge of Glory: A Biography of General William S. Rosecrans, U.S.A.* (New York: Harcourt, Brace, and World, 1961), 433–40. Grant, *Memoirs,* "Report of Lieutenant-General U. S. Grant, of the United States Armies–1864–1865," 813–14. Report of

Lieutenant George T. Robinson, 10 November 1864; Curtis to Halleck, 3 December 1864; and Halleck to Grant, 11 December 1864, *The War of the Rebellion: A Compilation of the Official Records of the Union and Confederate Armies,* 128 vols. (Washington D.C.: Government Printing Office, 1880–1902), series 1, vol. 41, part 1, 546–50.

3. Jacob R. Perkins, *Trails, Rails and War: The Life of General G. M. Dodge* (New York: Arno Press, 1981), 78–82, 151, 155, and 159–61. Grant, *Memoirs,* 423–24 and 637. William T. Sherman, *Memoirs of General W. T. Sherman* (New York: Library of America, 1990), 385. Report of General Grenville M. Dodge, 18 July 1865, *Official Records,* series 1, vol. 48, part 1, 329–35.

4. Proceedings against Simon Hausman, Henry Mason, and Kate Beattie, Missouri Adjutant General Records, Series: Court-Martial Papers, Record Group 133, Missouri State Archives, Jefferson City, Missouri. Microfilm no. 1283, file of Ruth Briscoe, Union Provost-Marshals' File of Papers Relating to Individual Citizens, 1861–1866, Record Group 109, National Archives and Records Administration, Washington D.C.

5. Dodge to Halleck, 21 December 1864; Clinton B. Fisk to Stephen Blanchard, 5 January 1865; and General Orders, No. 7, 8 January 1865, *Official Records,* series 1, vol. 41, part 4, 905–06; and vol. 48, part 1, 425 and 458–59. James M. McPherson, *Battle Cry of Freedom: The Civil War Era,* vol. 4 of *The Oxford History of the United States,* ed. C. Vann Woodward (New York: Oxford University Press, 1988), 596–99.

6. Fisk to J. B. Douglas, 10 January 1865, *Official Records,* series 1, vol. 48, part 1, 482–83. Microfilm no. 1242, file of Hosea R. C. Cowden; see also the account of Mary A. Bivens, microfilm no. 1138, Provost-Marshal Records. Perkins, *Dodge,* 168–69.

7. Lincoln to Rosecrans, 26 November 1864; Lincoln to Dodge, 13 December 1864 and 19 and 24 January 1865; and Lincoln to Henry T. Blow, 13 March 1865, Abraham Lincoln, *The Collected Works of Abraham Lincoln,* ed. Roy P. Basler (New Brunswick, NJ: Rutgers University Press, 1959), vol. 8, 122, 166, 223, 234, and 351. Rosecrans to Lincoln, 30 November 1864; Dodge to Lincoln, 26 January 1865; Austin A. King to Lincoln, 11 February 1865; and Henry T. Blow to Lincoln, 15 March 1865, Abraham Lincoln Papers, Library of Congress, Washington D.C. Microfilm nos. 1211 and 1219, files of Nancy Thompson and Elizabeth Arnold, Provost-Marshal Records. Lincoln to John Pope, 12 February 1865, *Official Records,* series 1, vol. 48, part 1, 828.

8. Lincoln to Dodge, 15 January 1865, *Collected Works,* vol. 8, 217. Dodge to Thomas C. Fletcher, 7, 15, and 23 January 1865; Fletcher to Dodge, 16 January 1865; E. M. Samuel et al. to Dodge, 16 January 1865; and state constitutional convention to Dodge, 17 January 1865, *Official Records,* series 1, vol. 48, part 1, 449, 535, 547–48, 564–66, and 620. Dodge to Lincoln, 16 January 1865; and William A. Hall to Lincoln, 19 January 1865, Lincoln Papers.

9. H. Hilliard to Clinton B. Fisk, 30 November 1864; Grenville M. Dodge to Thomas C. Fletcher, 15 January 1865; Fletcher to Dodge, 16 January 1865, *Official Records,* series 1, vol. 41, part 4, 725–26; and series 1, vol. 48, part 1, 535 and 547. Lincoln to Dodge, 15 January 1865, *Collected Works,* vol. 8, 217. Missouri General Assembly to Lincoln, December 1864; and Dodge to Lincoln, 16 January 1865, Lincoln Papers.

10. Lincoln to Fletcher, 20 February 1865; and Fletcher to Lincoln, 27 February 1865, Lincoln Papers. Perkins, *Dodge,* 163. Fletcher to Dodge, 27 February 1865, *Official Records,* series 1, vol. 48, part 1, 997.

11. Peter Cozzens, *General John Pope: A Life for the Nation* (Urbana: University of Illinois Press, 2000), 243–46. Perkins, *Dodge,* 171–77.

12. Lincoln to Pope, 12 February 1865; and Pope to Lincoln, 13 February 1865, *Official Records,* series 1, vol. 48, part 1, 828 and 834.

13. John B. Henderson et al. to Lincoln, 13 February 1865; and Henry T. Blow to Lincoln, 14 February 1865, Lincoln Papers. Lincoln to John Pope, 14 February 1865; and Dodge to J. McC. Bell, 24 February 1865, *Official Records,* series 1, vol. 48, part 1, 848–49 and 966. In 1861 McLaren helped to establish the minutemen, a Secessionist paramilitary group in St. Louis. See James Peckham, *Gen. Nathaniel Lyon and Missouri in 1861: A Monograph of the Great Rebellion* (New York: American News Company, 1866), 41 and 45; and Thomas L. Snead, *The Fight for Missouri: From the Election of Lincoln to the Death of Lyon* (New York: Charles Scribner's Sons, 1886), 136–37.

14. Pope to Fletcher, 3 March 1865, *Official Records,* series 1, vol. 48, part 1, 1070–77.

15. Ibid. and Cozzens, *Pope,* 247–48.

16. Proclamation of Governor Fletcher, 7 March 1865; and Pope to Lincoln, 8 March 1865, *Official Records,* series 1, vol. 48, part 1, 1115 and 1122–24.

17. Special Orders, No. 15, 17 March 1865; and Pope to Lincoln, 17 March 1865, *Official Records,* series 1, vol. 48, part 1, 1202–03. Peter Cozzens and Robert I. Girardi, eds., *The Military Memoirs of General John Pope* (Chapel Hill: University of North Carolina Press, 1998), 24. Lincoln to Pope, 19 March 1865, *Collected Works,* vol. 8, 365.

18. Clinton B. Fisk to J. B. Douglas, 10 January 1865; Grenville M. Dodge to Thomas C. Fletcher, 7 and 23 January and 11 March 1865; Pope to Lincoln, 8 March 1865; Fletcher to Dodge, 11 March 1865; John McNeil to Dodge, 15 March 1865; Fisk to Fletcher, 20 March 1865; Fisk to Arnold Krekel, 20 March 1865; and Dodge report, 18 July 1865, *Official Records,* series 1, vol. 48, part 1, 329–35, 449, 482–83, 620, 1122–24, 1152, 1183–84, and 1222. Fletcher to Lincoln, 27 February 1865, Lincoln Papers.

19. Fisk to Dodge, 3 and 5 April 1865; and Fisk to R. A. De Bolt, 3 April 1865, *Official Records,* series 1, vol. 48, part 2, 22, 22–24, and 33–35.

20. General Orders, No. 88, 31 March 1865; John Pope to Thomas C. Fletcher, 12 April 1865; Fletcher to Pope, 14 and 19 April 1865; Pope to Grant, 19 April 1865; and Pope to Dodge, 22 and 24 April 1865, *Official Records,* series 1, vol. 48, part 1, 1304; and vol. 48, part 2, 80–81, 98–99, 132–33, and 159.

21. John T. Sprague to Dodge, 25 March 1865; Pope to Dodge, 24 April 1865; and Pope to Edwin M. Stanton, 10 May 1865, *Official Records,* series 1, vol. 48, part 1, 1255; vol. 48, part 2, 179–80 and 395–97.

22. C. E. Rogers to Chester Harding Jr., 12 May 1865; Harding to Rogers, 12 May 1865; Harding to L. Martin, 13 May 1865; General Orders, No. 128, 18 May 1865; L. Bulkley to J. H. Baker, 24 May 1865, Baker to Bulkley, 24 May 1865; and report of General Grenville M. Dodge, 18 July 1865, *Official Records,* series 1, vol. 48, part 1, 329–35; and vol. 48, part 2, 421–22, 431–32, 496, and 585. Proclamation of Amnesty and Reconstruction, 8 December 1863, *Collected Works,* vol. 7, 53–56.

23. William E. Parrish, *A History of Missouri: 1860 to 1875,* vol. 3 (Columbia: University of Missouri Press, 1973), 139–40.

24. Bazel F. Lazear, 11 August 1864, Bazel F. Lazear Papers, Western Historical Manuscripts Collection, State Historical Society of Missouri, Columbia, Missouri. Arnold Krekel to Lincoln, 11 January 1865, Lincoln Papers. Parrish, *History of Missouri*, 116–17, 144, and 150–69. F. T. Russell to Clinton B. Fisk, 21 February 1865; H. N. Cook to W. T. Clarke, 28 February 1865; and General Orders, No. 150, 17 June 1865, *Official Records*, series 1, vol. 48, part 1, 934–36; and vol. 48, part 2, 913. Microfilm no. 1237, William Q. Kitridge file, Provost Marshal Records.

25. Indeed, Governor Hamilton R. Gamble and Inspector General of the Army R. B. Marcy both suggested that even guerrillas caught red-handed should be tried. See *Journal of the Missouri State Convention held in Jefferson City, June 1863* (St. Louis: George Knapp and Co., 1863), 9–10, and R. B. Marcy to O. D. Greene, 29 March 1864, *Official Records*, series 1, vol. 34, part 2, 775–77.

26. In this, I have in mind Lincoln's Executive Order No. 1 of 14 February 1862 and his proposal to Curtis and Dodge to end the provost-marshal system as detailed in chapter 6 and this chapter. See *Official Records*, series 2, vol. 2, 221–23. James G. Randall noted that the president similarly sought to minimize military interference in Kentucky. See James G. Randall, *Constitutional Problems under Lincoln*, rev. ed. (Urbana: University of Illinois Press, 1964), 172–73.

Bibliography

PRIMARY SOURCES

Alvord Collection. Western Historical Manuscripts Collection, State Historical Society of Missouri. Columbia, Missouri.

Annual Report of the Adjutant General of the State of Missouri for the Year 1863. St. Louis: n.p., 1864.

Barnes, Robert A. Papers. Missouri Historical Society. St. Louis, Missouri.

Bartlett, David W. *Cases of Contested Elections in Congress from 1834 to 1865 Inclusive.* Washington D.C.: Government Printing Office, 1865.

Bates, Edward. Unpublished diary. Bates family papers. Missouri Historical Society. St. Louis, Missouri.

Beale, Howard K., ed. *The Diary of Edward Bates, 1859–1866.* Washington D.C.: Government Printing Office, 1933.

Binney, Horace. *The Privilege of the Writ of Habeas Corpus under the Constitution.* Part one. Philadelphia: C. Sherman and Sons, Printers, 1862.

Blair, Frank P., Jr. *Confiscation, Emancipation, and Colonization "Indemnity for the Past and Security for the Future": Speech of Hon. F. P. Blair Jr. of Missouri in the House of Representatives, May 23, 1862.* n.p., 1862.

———. *Speech of Hon. F. P. Blair Jr. of Missouri on the Policy of the President for the Restoration of the Union and Establishment of Peace delivered in the House of Representatives, April 11, 1862.* New York: Baker and Godwin, 1862.

Blair v. Ridgely, 41 Missouri 63 (1866).

Broadhead, James O. Papers. Missouri Historical Society, St. Louis, Missouri.

Bryan, P. Taylor. Papers. Missouri Historical Society, St. Louis, Missouri.

Calder v. Bull, 3 U.S. 386 (1798).

Carpenter v. Pennsylvania, 58 U.S. 456 (1855).

Clark, William A. v. Dick, Franklin A., The American Law Register 18, no. 12, new series 9 (December 1870): 739–45.

Constitution of the United States.

Cook, John C. v. Crampton, Thomas. Probate Court of Macon County, Missouri.

Cummings v. the State of Missouri, 71 U.S. 277 (1867).

Decker, John v. Blair, Francis P. Jr. et al. St. Louis Court of Appeals.

Dennett, Tyler, ed. *Lincoln and the Civil War in the Diaries and Letters of John Hay*, with a foreword by Henry S. Commager. New York: Da Capo Press, 1988.

Drake, Charles D. Autobiography. Western Historical Manuscripts Collection, State Historical Society of Missouri, Columbia, Missouri.

Eaton, Lucien. Papers. Missouri Historical Society. St. Louis, Missouri.

Eliot, William G. Papers. Missouri Historical Society. St. Louis, Missouri.

Engler, Samuel v. Halleck, Henry W. et al. St. Louis Court of Common Pleas.

Ex parte McKee, 18 Mo. Rep. 599–603.

Ex parte Milligan, 71 U.S. 2 (1866).

Gamble, Hamilton Rowan. Papers. Missouri Historical Society. St. Louis, Missouri.

Gibson, Charles. Papers. Missouri Historical Society, St. Louis, Missouri.

Guitar, Odon. Papers. Western Historical Manuscripts Collection, State Historical Society of Missouri. Columbia, Missouri.

Halleck, Henry W. Papers. Missouri Historical Society, St. Louis, Missouri.

Henderson, John B. *Speech of Hon. J. B. Henderson of Missouri on the Abolition of Slavery delivered in the Senate of the United States, March 27, 1862*. Washington D.C.: L. Towers and Co., 1862.

Houston v. Moore, 18 U.S. 1 (1820).

Journal and Proceedings of the Missouri State Convention Held at Jefferson City and St. Louis March 1861. St. Louis: George Knapp and Co., 1861.

Journal of the Missouri State Convention Held at the City of St. Louis, October 1861. St. Louis: George Knapp and Co., 1861.

Journal of the Missouri State Convention, Held at Jefferson City, July 1861. St. Louis: George Knapp and Co., 1861.

Journal of the Missouri State Convention, Held in Jefferson City, June 1862. St. Louis: George Knapp and Co., 1862.

Journal of the Missouri State Convention, Held in Jefferson City, June 1863. St. Louis: George Knapp and Co., 1863.

Judge-Advocate papers. Record Group 153. National Archives. Washington D.C.

Krekel, Arnold. Papers. Missouri Historical Society, St. Louis, Missouri.

Lafayette County. Proceedings of the County Board, 2 October 1862. Western Historical Manuscripts Collection, State Historical Society of Missouri. Columbia, Missouri.

Lazear, Bazel F. Papers. Western Historical Manuscripts Collection, State Historical Society of Missouri. Columbia, Missouri.

Leighton, George E. Papers. Missouri Historical Society. St. Louis, Missouri.

Leopard, Buel, and Floyd C. Shoemaker, eds. *The Messages and Proclamations of the Governors of the State of Missouri*. Columbia: State Historical Society of Missouri, 1922.

Liberty Weekly Tribune, 1849 and 1861–1862.

Lieber, Francis. "Instructions for the Government of Armies of the United States in the Field." General Orders No. 100. Washington D.C.: Adjutant General's Office, Government Printing Office, 1898.

Lincoln, Abraham. *The Collected Works of Abraham Lincoln*, ed. Roy P. Basler. New Brunswick, NJ: Rutgers University Press, 1959.

———. Papers. Library of Congress, Washington D.C.

MacDonald, William. *Select Statutes and other Documents Illustrative of the History of the United States, 1861–1898*. New York: Macmillan, 1903.

McMahan, Robert T. Papers. Western Historical Manuscripts Collection, State Historical Society of Missouri. Columbia, Missouri.

Memphis, Tennessee, *Daily Appeal*, 1862.

Missouri Adjutant General records, series: Court-Martial papers, Record Group 133. Missouri State Archives. Jefferson City, Missouri.

Missouri Adjutant General records, series: Enrolled Missouri Militia, Record Group 133. Missouri State Archives. Jefferson City, Missouri.

Missouri Adjutant General records, series: General Orders Book, Record Group 133. Missouri State Archives. Jefferson City, Missouri.

Missouri Adjutant General records, series: Military Organization, Record Group 133. Missouri State Archives. Jefferson City, Missouri.

Missouri Adjutant General records, series: Second Missouri State Militia, Record Group 133. Missouri State Archives. Jefferson City, Missouri.

Missouri Militia Records. Duke University Library. Durham, North Carolina.

Mitchell v. Clark, 110 U.S. 633–51 (1884).

Monroe County, Provost Marshal papers. Western Historical Manuscripts Collection, State Historical Society of Missouri. Columbia, Missouri.

Moyer v. Peabody, 212 U.S. 78–86 (1909).

Munger Family Civil War Letters Collection. Butler Center for Arkansas Studies, Central Arkansas Library System. Little Rock, Arkansas.

Napton, William B. Papers. Missouri Historical Society. St. Louis, Missouri.

New York Times, 1862.

Norton, E. H. *Speech of Hon. E. H. Norton of Missouri on Confiscation and Emancipation delivered in the House of Representatives, April 24, 1862*. Washington D.C.: n.p., 1862.

Palmyra Courier, 1862.

Pease, Theodore C., and James G. Randall, eds. *The Diary of Orville Hickman Browning*. 2 vols. Springfield: Illinois State Historical Library, 1925–1933.

Phelps, John S. *Confiscation of Property and Emancipation of Slaves: Speech of Hon. John S. Phelps of Missouri in the House of Representatives, May 22, 1862*. Washington: n.p., 1862.

Phillips, Christopher, and Jason L. Pendleton, eds. *The Union on Trial: The Political Journals of Judge William Barclay Napton, 1829–1883*. Columbia: University of Missouri Press, 2005.

Proceedings of the Missouri State Convention Held at the City of Jefferson, July 1861. St. Louis: George Knapp and Co., 1861.

Proceedings of the Missouri State Convention Held at the City of St. Louis, October 1861. St. Louis: George Knapp and Co., 1861.

Proceedings of the Missouri State Convention Held in Jefferson City, June 1862. St. Louis: George Knapp and Co., 1862.

Proceedings of the Missouri State Convention Held in Jefferson City, June 1863. St. Louis: George Knapp and Co., 1863.

Record book of the St. Louis Criminal Court, vols. 11 and 12. 17 and 24 July 1861. St. Louis, Missouri.

Report of the Committee of the House of Representatives of the Twenty-Second General Assembly of the State of Missouri appointed to Investigate the Conduct and Management of the Militia: Majority and Minority Reports. Jefferson City: W. A. Curry, public printer, 1864.

Richmond, Virginia, *Daily Dispatch*, 1862.

Rolla Express, 1862.

Rosecrans, William S. Papers. Collection 663. Huntington Library, University of California. Los Angeles, California.

St. Louis Anzeiger des Westons, 1862.

St. Louis Christian Advocate, 1861–1862.

St. Louis Evening News, 1861.

St. Louis Missouri Democrat, 1861–1865.

St. Louis Missouri Republican, 1861–1865.

St. Louis Neue Zeit, 1863.

St. Louis Observer, 1861–1865.

St. Louis State Journal, 1861.

St. Louis Westliche Post, 1862–1863.

Sanderson, John P. Journal. Ohio Historical Society. Columbus, Ohio.

Sawyer, Orlando and Amanda v. The Hannibal and St. Joseph Railroad Company. Buchanan County Court and Supreme Court of Missouri. Missouri State Archives. Jefferson City, Missouri.

Sears, Stephen W., ed. *The Civil War Papers of George B. McClellan: Selected Correspondence, 1860–1865*. New York: Ticknor and Fields, 1989; reprint, Da Capo Press, 1992.

Shaler, James R. v. Lyon, Nathaniel et al. St. Louis Court of Common Pleas.

Siddali, Silvana, ed. *Missouri's War: The Civil War in Documents*. The Civil War in the Great Interior. Athens: Ohio University Press, 2009.

Taney, Roger B. *Reports of Cases at Law and Equity and in the Admiralty Determined in the Circuit Court of the United States for the District of Maryland*. Philadelphia: Kay and Brothers, 1871.

Tinker, Orwin C. Record of Service Card, Civil War, 1861–1865. Missouri State Archives. Jefferson City, Missouri.

Treat, Samuel. *The Supremacy of the Law in Missouri: Charge to the United States Grand Jury of the Western District of Missouri Given at the March Term 1865, Proclamation of Governor Fletcher, Letter of Major General Pope, Together with Instructions of the Attorney General of Missouri and Appendix Containing Forms, etc.* Jefferson City: W. A. Curry, public printer, 1865.

Union Provost-Marshals' File of Papers Relating to Individual Citizens, 1861–1866, Record Group 109, National Archives and Records Administration, Washington D.C., microfilm reel nos. 1158, 1185, 1189, 1190, 1203, 1205, 1206, 1217, 1218, 1219, 1233, 1237, 1238, 1239, 1242, 1244, 1246, 1276, 1277, 1285, 1289, 1292, 1293, 1297, 1305, 1311, 1312, 1315, 1322, 1330, 1336, 1339, 1348, 1349, 1350, 1351, 1366, 1400, 1408, 1409, 1412, 1415, 1462, 1465, 1468, 1471, 1475, and 1477. Missouri State Archives. Jefferson City, Missouri.

War Department Collection of Confederate Records, National Archives and Records Administration, Washington D.C.

The War of the Rebellion: A Compilation of the Official Records of the Union and Confederate Armies (OR). 128 volumes. Washington D.C.: Government Printing Office, 1880–1902.

Washington, D.C., Daily National Intelligencer, 1861.

Welles, Gideon. *Diary of Gideon Welles: Secretary of the Navy Under Lincoln and Johnson.* With an introduction by John T. Morse Jr., vol. 1: 1861–March 30, 1864. Boston and New York: Houghton, Mifflin, the Riverside Press Cambridge, 1911.

Whiting, William. *War Powers under the Constitution of the United States: Military Arrests, Reconstruction, and Military Government. Also now First Published, War Claims of Aliens, with Notes on the Acts of the Executive and Legislative Departments During Our Civil War and a Collection of Cases Decided in the National Courts,* Forty-third ed. Boston: Lee and Shepard Publishers; New York: Lee, Shepard and Dillingham, 1871.

Wilson, James. Papers. Western Historical Manuscripts Collections, State Historical Society of Missouri. Columbia, Missouri.

SECONDARY SOURCES

Articles

Barry, Peter J. "'I'll Keep Them in Prison Awhile . . .': Abraham Lincoln and David Davis on Civil Liberties in Wartime." *Journal of the Abraham Lincoln Association* 28 (Winter 2008): 20–29.

Belz, Herman. "Abraham Lincoln and American Constitutionalism." *The Review of American Politics* 50, no. 2 (spring 1988): 169–97.

———. "Lincoln's Construction of the Executive Power in the Secession Crisis." *Journal of the Abraham Lincoln Association* 27, no. 1 (2006): 13–38.

———. "Protection of Personal Liberty in Republican Emancipation Legislation of 1862." *The Journal of Southern History,* vol. 42, no. 3 (August 1976): 385–400.

Bestor, Arthur. "The American Civil War as a Constitutional Crisis." *The American Historical Review* 69, no. 2 (January 1964): 327–52.

Beth, Loren P. "The Case for Judicial Protection of Civil Liberties." *The Journal of Politics* 17, no. 1 (February 1955): 100–12.

Bickers, John M. "Military Commissions Are Constitutionally Sound: A Response to Professors Katyal and Tribe." *Texas Tech Law Review* 34 (2003): 899–932.

Blum, Virgil C. "The Political and Military Activities of the German Element in St. Louis, 1859–1861." *Missouri Historical Review* 42 (January 1948): 103–29.

Boman, Dennis K. "Conduct and Revolt in the Twenty-fifth Ohio Battery: An Insider's Account." *Ohio History* 104 (Summer–Autumn 1995): 163–83.

Cain, Marvin R. "Edward Bates and Hamilton R. Gamble: A Wartime Partnership." *Missouri Historical Review* 56 (January 1962): 146–55.

Carnahan, Burrus M. "Lincoln, Lieber and the Laws of War: The Origins and the Limits of the Principle of Military Necessity." *The American Journal of International Law* 92, no. 2 (April 1998): 213–31.

Castel, Albert. "Order No. 11 and the Civil War on the Border." *Missouri Historical Review* 57 (July 1963): 357–68.

Covington, James W. "The Camp Jackson Affair." *Missouri Historical Review* 55 (April 1961): 197–212.

Dennison, George M. "Martial Law: The Development of a Theory of Emergency Powers, 1776–1861." *The American Journal of Legal History* 18, no. 1 (January 1974): 52–79.

Dirck, Brian R. "Posterity's Blush: Civil Liberties, Property Rights, and Property Confiscation in the Confederacy." *Civil War History* 48, no. 3 (2002): 237–56.

Dorpalen, Andreas. "The German Element and the Issues of the Civil War." *The Mississippi Valley Historical Review* 29, no. 1 (June 1942): 55–76.

Dueholm, James A. "Lincoln's Suspension of the Writ of Habeas Corpus: An Historical and Constitutional Analysis." *Journal of the Abraham Lincoln Association* 29, no. 2 (Summer 2008): 47–66.

Farber, Daniel A. "Completing the Work of the Framers: Lincoln's Constitutional Legacy." *Journal of Abraham Lincoln Association* 27, no. 1 (2006): 1–12.

Finkelman, Paul. "Civil Liberties and Civil War: The Great Emancipator as Civil Libertarian." *Michigan Law Review* 91, no. 6 (May 1993): 1353–81.

Fisher, Sydney G. "The Suspension of Habeas Corpus During the War of the Rebellion." *Political Science Quarterly* 3, no. 3 (September 1888): 454–88.

Fitzharris, Joseph C. "Field Officer Courts and U.S. Civil War Military Justice." *The Journal of Military History* 68, no. 1 (January 2004): 47–72.

Freidel, Frank. "General Orders 100 and Military Government." *The Mississippi Valley Historical Review* 32, no. 4 (March 1946): 541–56.

Garner, Captain James G. "General Order 100 Revisited." *Military Law Review* 27 (January 1965): 1–48.

Gerteis, Louis S. "'A Friend of the Enemy': Federal Efforts to Suppress Disloyalty in St. Louis During the Civil War." *Missouri Historical Review* 96, no. 3 (April 2002): 165–87.

———. "'An Outrage on Humanity': Martial Law and Military Prisons in St. Louis During the Civil War." *Missouri Historical Review* 96, no. 4 (July 2002): 302–22.

Gienapp, William E. "Abraham Lincoln and the Border States." *Journal of the Abraham Lincoln Association* 13 (1992): 13–46.

Girard, Robert. "The Constitution and Court-Martial of Civilians Accompanying the Armed Forces: A Preliminary Analysis." *Stanford Law Review* 13, no. 3 (May 1961): 461–521.

Goff, John S. "The Civil War Confiscation Cases in Arizona Territory." *The American Journal of Legal History* 14, no. 4 (October 1970): 349–54.

Guelzo, Allen C. "Defending Emancipation: Abraham Lincoln and the Conkling Letter, 1863." *Civil War History* 48, no. 4 (2002): 313–37.

Halleck, Henry W. "Military Tribunals and their Jurisdiction." *The American Journal of International Law* 5, no. 4 (October 1911): 958–67.

Haney, C., W. C. Banks, and P. G. Zimbardo. "A Study of Prisoners and Guards in a Simulated Prison." *Naval Research Review* 30 (1973): 4–17.

Kaplan, Harold L. "Constitutional Limitations on Trials by Military Commissions." *University of Pennsylvania Law Review and American Law Register* 92, no. 2 (December 1943): 119–49.

Kirkpatrick, Arthur Roy. "Missouri on the Eve of the Civil War." *Missouri Historical Review* 55 (January 1961): 98–108.

———. "Missouri in the Early Months of the Civil War." *Missouri Historical Review* 55 (April 1961): 235–66.

Kleinerman, Benjamin A. "Lincoln's Example: Executive Power and the Survival of Constitutionalism." *Perspectives on Politics* 3, no. 4 (December 2005): 801–16.

Lanni, Adriaan. "The Laws of War in Ancient Greece." *Law and History Review* 26, no. 3 (Fall 2008): 469–89.

McPherson, James M. "Who Freed the Slaves?" *Proceedings of the American Philosophical Society,* vol. 139, no. 1 (March 1995): 1–10.

Mink, Charles R. "General Orders, No. 11: The Forced Evacuation of Civilians During the Civil War." *Military Affairs* 34 (December 1970): 132–36.

Nelson, Earl J. "Missouri Slavery, 1861–1865." *Missouri Historical Review* 28 (July 1934): 260–74.

Niepman, Ann Davis. "General Orders No. 11 and Border Warfare During the Civil War." *Missouri Historical Review* 66 (January 1972): 185–210.

Oaks, Dallin H. "Habeas Corpus in the States: 1776–1865." *The University of Chicago Law Review* 32, no. 2 (winter 1965): 243–88.

Philips, John F. "Administrations of Missouri Governors: Second Paper, Governor Willard Preble Hall." *Missouri Historical Review* 5, no. 2 (January 1911): 69–82.

———. "Hamilton Rowan Gamble and the Provisional Government of Missouri." *Missouri Historical Review* 5 (October 1910): 1–6.

Purifoy, Lewis M. "The Southern Methodist Church and the Proslavery Argument." *The Journal of Southern History* 32, no. 3 (August 1966): 325–41.

Randall, James G. "Some Legal Aspects of the Confiscation Acts of the Civil War." *The American Historical Review* 18, no. 1 (October 1912): 79–96.

———. "The Newspaper Problem in Its Bearing Upon Military Secrecy During the Civil War." *The American Historical Review* 23, no. 2 (January 1918): 303–23.

Siddali, Silvana R. "'The Sport of Folly and the Prize of Treason': Confederate Property Seizures and the Northern Home Front in the Secession Crisis." *Civil War History* 47, no. 4 (2001): 310–33.

Smith, W. Wayne. "An Experiment in Counterinsurgency: The Assessment of Confederate Sympathizers in Missouri." *Journal of Southern History* 35 (August 1969): 361–80.

Southall, Eugene Portlette. "The Attitude of the Methodist Episcopal Church, South, Toward the Negro from 1844 to 1870." *The Journal of Negro History* 16, no. 4 (October 1931): 359–70.

Stith, Matthew M. "At the Heart of Total War: Guerrillas, Civilians, and the Union Response in Jasper County, Missouri, 1861–1865." *Military History of the West* 38 (2008): 1–27.

Surrency, Erwin C. "The Legal Effects of the Civil War." *The American Journal of Legal History* 5, no. 2 (April 1961): 145–65.

Sutherland, Donald E. "Abraham Lincoln, John Pope, and the Origins of Total War." *The Journal of Military History,* vol. 56, no. 4 (October 1994): 567–86.

Sweet, William W. "Methodist Church Influence in Southern Politics." *The Mississippi Valley Historical Review* 1, no. 4 (March 1915): 546–60.

Tarrant, Catherine M. "To 'Insure Domestic Tranquility': Congress and the Law of Seditious Conspiracy, 1859–1861." *The American Journal of Legal History* 15, no. 2 (April 1971): 107–23.

Thomas, Raymond D. "A Study in Missouri Politics, 1840–1870." *Missouri Historical Review* 21 (January 1927): 166–84.

Towne, Stephen E. "Killing the Serpent Speedily: Governor Morton, General Hascall, and the Suppression of the Democratic Press in Indiana, 1863." *Civil War History* 52, no. 1 (2006): 41–65.

Turkoly-Joczik, Robert L. "Frémont and the Western Department." *Missouri Historical Review* 82, no. 4 (1988): 363–85.

Williams, Frank J. "Civil Liberties v. National Security: The Long Shadow of the Civil War." *Civil War Times* 46, no. 4 (2007): 24–29.

Williams, T. Harry. "Frémont and the Politicians." *The Journal of the American Military History Foundation* 2 (Winter 1938): 178–91.

Wood, Larry. "Harry Truman: Federal Bushwacker." *Missouri Historical Review* 98, no. 3 (April 2004): 201–22.

Books and Dissertations

Anderson, Galusha. *The Story of a Border City During the Civil War.* Boston: Little, Brown, 1908.

Astor, Aaron. "Belated Confederates: Black Politics, Guerrilla Violence, and the Collapse of Conservative Unionism in Kentucky and Missouri, 1860–1872." Ph.D. diss., Northwestern University, 2006.

Bay, William Van Ness. *Reminiscences of the Bench and Bar in Missouri.* St. Louis: F. H. Thomas and Company, 1878.

Beckenbaugh, Terry Lee. "The War of Politics: Samuel Ryan Curtis, Race and the Political/Military Establishment." Ph.D. diss., University of Arkansas, 2001.

Belz, Herman. *Abraham Lincoln, Constitutionalism, and Equal Rights in the Civil War Era.* New York: Fordham University Press, 1998.

———. "A New Birth of Freedom: The Republican Party and Freedmen's Rights, 1861 to 1866." In *Contributions in American History* no. 52. Westport: Greenwood Press, 1976.

Boman, Dennis K. *Abiel Leonard, Yankee Slaveholder, Eminent Jurist, and Passionate Unionist. Studies in American History,* vol. 38. Lewiston: Edwin Mellen Press, 2002.

———. *Lincoln's Resolute Unionist: Hamilton Gamble, Dred Scott Dissenter and Missouri's Civil War Governor.* Baton Rouge: Louisiana State University Press, 2006.

———. "All Politics Are Local: Emancipation in Missouri." In Brian R. Dirck, ed, *Lincoln Emancipated: The President and the Politics of Race.* DeKalb: Northern Illinois University Press, 2007.

Burlingame, Michael, and John R. Turner Ettlinger, eds. *Inside Lincoln's White House: The Complete Civil War Diary of John Hay.* Carbondale: Southern Illinois University Press, 1997.

Castel, Albert. *General Sterling Price and the Civil War in the West.* Baton Rouge: Louisiana State University Press, 1968.

Catton, Bruce. *Grant Moves South.* New York: Little, Brown, 1960; reprint, Edison, NJ: Castle Books, 2000.

Chafee, Zechariah Jr. *Free Speech in the United States.* Cambridge: Harvard University Press, 1942.

Cozzens, Peter. *General John Pope, A Life for the Nation.* Champaign: University of Illinois Press, 2000.

Cozzens, Peter, and Robert I. Girardi, eds. *The Military Memoirs of General John Pope.* Chapel Hill: University of North Carolina Press, 1998.

Curtis, Michael Kent. *Free Speech, "The People's Darling Privilege": Struggles for Freedom of Expression in American History.* Durham, NC: Duke University Press, 2000.

Dew, Charles B. *Apostles of Disunion: Southern Secession Commissioners and the Causes of the Civil War.* Charlottesville: University of Virginia Press, 2001.

DiLorenzo, Thomas J. *The Real Lincoln: A New Look at Abraham Lincoln, His Agenda, and an Unnecessary War.* New York: Crown Publishing, 2002.

Donald, David Herbert. *Lincoln.* New York: Simon and Schuster, 1995.

Donan, Peter. *Memoir of Jacob Creath Jr.* Cincinnati: R. W. Carroll and Co., 1872.

Duffus, Gerald R. "A Study of the Military Career of Samuel R. Curtis: 1861–1865." Master's thesis, Drake University.

Dyer, Frederick H. *A Compendium of the War of the Rebellion: Compiled and Arranged from Official Records of the Federal and Confederate Armies, Reports of the Adjutant Generals of the Several States, the Army Registers, and Other Reliable Documents and Sources,* part 3. Des Moines, Iowa: Dyer Publishing Company, 1908.

Eddy, T. M. *The Patriotism of Illinois: A Record of the Civil and Military History of the State in the War for the Union,* vol. 2. Chicago: Clark and Co., 1866.

Eliot, Charlotte C. *William Greenleaf Eliot: Minister, Educator, Philanthropist,* with an introduction by James K. Hosmer. Boston: Houghton, Mifflin, 1904.

Elliott, Charles. *Southwestern Methodism: A History of the M. E. Church in the Southwest from 1844 to 1864, comprising the Martyrdom of Bewley and Others; Persecutions of the M. E. Church and its Reorganization,* edited and revised by Leroy M. Vernon. Cincinnati: Poe and Hitchcock, 1868.

Farber, Daniel. *Lincoln's Constitution.* Chicago: University of Chicago Press, 2003.

Fehrenbacher, Don E. *Lincoln in Text and Context: Collected Essays.* Palo Alto: Stanford University Press, 1987.

———. *Prelude to Greatness: Lincoln in the 1850s.* Palo Alto: Stanford University Press, 1962.

Fellman, Michael. "At the Nihilist Edge: Reflections on Guerrilla Warfare During the American Civil War." In *On the Road to Total War: The American Civil War and the German Wars of Unification, 1861–1871,* ed. Stig Forster and Jorg Nagler. New York: Cambridge University Press, 1997.

———. "Inside Wars: The Cultural Crisis of Warfare and the Values of Ordinary People." In *Guerrillas, Unionists, and Violence on the Confederate Homefront,* ed. Daniel E. Sutherland. Fayetteville: University of Arkansas Press, 1999.

———. *Inside War: The Guerrilla Conflict in Missouri During the American Civil War.* New York: Oxford University Press, 1989.

Finkelman, Paul. *An Imperfect Union: Slavery, Federalism, and Comity.* Chapel Hill: University of North Carolina Press, 1981.

Finney, Thomas M. *The Life and Labors of Enoch Mather Marvin, Late Bishop of the Methodist Episcopal Church, South.* St. Louis: James H. Chambers, 1880.

Forman, Jacob G. *The Western Sanitary Commission: A Sketch of its Origin, History, Labors for the Sick and Wounded of the Western Armies and Aid Given to Freedmen and Union Refugees with Incidents of Hospital Life.* St. Louis: R. P. Studley and Co., 1864.

Freidel, Frank. *Francis Lieber: Nineteenth-Century Liberal.* Baton Rouge: Louisiana State University Press, 1947.

Fremont, John C. "In Command in Missouri." *Battles and Leaders of the Civil War,* ed. Robert Underwood Johnson and Clarence Clough Buel, 4 vols. Vol. 1. New York: Century Company, 1887; reprint, Secaucus, NJ: Castle, n.d.

Gerteis, Louis S. *Civil War St. Louis.* Lawrence: University Press of Kansas, 2004.

Glatthaar, Joseph T. *Forged in Battle: The Civil War Alliance of Black Soldiers and White Officers.* New York: Free Press, 1990.

Goodrich, Thomas. *Black Flag: Guerilla Warfare on the Western Border, 1861–1865.* Bloomington: University of Indiana Press, 1999.

Gorham, George C. *Life and Public Services of Edwin M. Stanton,* vol. 2. Boston: Houghton, Mifflin, the Riverside Press Cambridge, 1899.

Grant, Ulysses S. *Personal Memoirs of U. S. Grant Selected Letters, 1839–1865.* New York: Literary Classics of the United States, 1990.

Grasty, Rev. John S. *Memoir of Rev. Samuel B. McPheeters, D.D., with an introduction by Rev. Stuart Robinson.* Saint Louis: Southwestern Book and Publishing Company, and Louisville: Davidson Brothers and Company, 1871.

Grimsley, Mark. *The Hard Hand of War: Union Military Policy toward Southern Civilians, 1861–1865.* New York: Cambridge University Press, 1995.

Grotius, Hugo. *The Rights of War and Peace Including the Law of Nature and of Nations,* with an introduction by David J. Hill. Boston: Adamant Media Corporation, 2003.

Halleck, Henry W. *Halleck's International Law or Rules Regulating the Intercourse of States in Peace and War,* revised by Sir G. Sherston Baker and Maurice N. Drucquer. London: Kegan Paul, Trench, Trubner and Co., 1908.

Harley, Lewis R. *Francis Lieber: His Life and Political Philosophy.* New York: Columbia University Press, 1899.

Harper, Robert S. *Lincoln and the Press.* New York: McGraw-Hill, 1951.

Harris, William C. *With Charity for All: Lincoln and the Restoration of the Union.* Lexington: University Press of Kentucky, 1997.

Hartigan, Richard Shelly. *Lieber's Code and the Law of War.* Chicago: Precedent Publishing, 1983.

Hesseltine, William B., ed. *Civil War Prisons.* Kent, Ohio: Kent State University Press, 1972.

———. *Lincoln and the War Governors.* New York: Alfred A. Knopf, 1948.

Hubble, Martin J. *Personal Reminiscences and Fragments of the Early History of Spring-field and Greene County, Missouri.* Springfield: Inland Printing, 1914.

Hummel, Jeffrey Rogers. *Emancipating Slaves, Enslaving Free Men: A History of the American Civil War.* Chicago and La Salle: Open Court, 1996.

Hyman, Harold M. *Era of the Oath: Northern Loyalty Tests During the Civil War and Reconstruction.* New York: Octagon Books, 1978.

———. *A More Perfect Union: The Impact of the Civil War and Reconstruction on the Constitution.* New York: Knopf, 1975.

Hyman, Harold M., and William M. Wiecek. *Equal Justice under the Law: Constitutional Development, 1835–1875.* New York: Harper and Row, 1982.

Jaffa, Harry V. *Crisis of the House Divided: An Interpretation of the Issues in the Lincoln-Douglas Debates,* with a new preface. Chicago: University of Chicago Press, 1982.

Johnson, Michael P., ed. *Abraham Lincoln, Slavery, and the Civil War: Selected Writings and Speeches.* Bedford Series in History and Culture. Boston: Bedford/St. Martin's Press, 2001.

Klement, Frank L. *Dark Lanterns: Secret Political Societies, Conspiracies, and Treason Trials in the Civil War.* Baton Rouge: Louisiana State University Press, 1984.

Lamers, William M. *The Edge of Glory: A Biography of General William S. Rosecrans, U.S.A.* New York: Harcourt, Brace, and World, 1961.

Leftwich, William M. *Martyrdom in Missouri: A History of Religious Proscription, the Seizure of Churches, and the Persecution of Ministers of the Gospel, in the State of Missouri During the Late Civil War and under the "Test Oath" of the New Constitution.* St. Louis: Southwestern Book and Publishing, 1870.

Lewis, William Henry. *The History of Methodism in Missouri for a Decade of Years from 1860 to 1870,* vol. 3. Nashville: Barbee and Smith, 1890.

"Lincoln's First Inaugural Address." In *Documents of American History,* ed. Henry Steele Commager. New York: Appleton-Century-Crofts, 1949.

Marszalek, John F. *Commander of All Lincoln's Armies: A Life of General Henry W. Halleck.* Cambridge: Belknap Press of Harvard University Press, 2004.

Marvin, Enoch Mather. *The Life of Rev. William Goff Caples of the Missouri Conference of the Methodist Episcopal Church South.* St. Louis: Southwestern Book and Publishing Company, 1870.

McDonough, James L. *Schofield: Union General in the Civil War and Reconstruction.* Tallahassee: Florida State University Press, 1972.

McPherson, Edward. *The Political History of the United States of America During the Great Rebellion.* Washington D.C.: James J. Chapman, 1882.

McPherson, James M. *Battle Cry of Freedom: The Civil War Era.* In *The Oxford History of the United States,* vol. 6, ed. C. Vann Woodward. New York: Oxford University Press, 1988.

————. *Tried by War: Abraham Lincoln as Commander in Chief.* New York: Penguin, 2008.

Monaghan, Jay. *Civil War on the Western Border, 1854–1865.* Lincoln: University of Nebraska Press, 1955.

Neely, Jeremy. *The Border Between Them: Violence and Reconciliation on the Kansas-Missouri Line.* Columbia and London: University of Missouri Press, 2007.

Neely, Mark E., Jr. *The Fate of Liberty: Abraham Lincoln and Civil Liberties.* New York: Oxford University Press, 1991.

Parrish, William E. *Frank Blair: Lincoln's Conservative.* Columbia: University of Missouri Press, 1998.

————. *A History of Missouri: 1860 to 1875,* vol. 3. Columbia: University of Missouri Press, 1973.

————. *Turbulent Partnership: Missouri and the Union, 1861–1865.* Columbia: University of Missouri Press, 1963.

Peckham, James. *Gen. Nathaniel Lyon and Missouri in 1861: A Monograph of the Great Rebellion.* New York: American News Company, 1866.

Perkins, Jacob R. *Trails, Rails and War: The Life of General G. M. Dodge.* New York: Arno Press, 1981.

Perret, Geoffrey. *Lincoln's War: the Untold Story of America's Greatest President as Commander in Chief.* New York: Random House, 2004.

Peterson, Norman L. *Freedom and Franchise: The Political Career of B. Gratz Brown.* Columbia: University of Missouri Press, 1965.

Phillips, Christopher. *Damned Yankee: The Life of General Nathaniel Lyon.* Columbia: University of Missouri Press, 1990.

————. *Missouri's Confederate: Claiborne Fox Jackson and the Creation of Southern Identity in the Border West.* Columbia: University of Missouri Press, 2000.

Polenberg, Richard. *Fighting Faiths: The Abrams Case, the Supreme Court, and Free Speech.* Ithaca: Cornell University Press, 1999.

Pollard, Edward A. *Southern History of the War: The Second Year of the War.* New York: Charles B. Richardson, 1864.

Potter, David M. *The Impending Crisis: 1848–1861.* Completed and edited by Don E. Fehrenbacher, the New American Nation Series, ed. Henry Steele Commager and Richard B. Morris. New York: Harper and Row, 1976.

Primm, James Neal. *Lion of the Valley: St. Louis, Missouri.* Boulder, CO: Pruett, 1981.

Randall, James G. *Constitutional Problems under Lincoln.* Urbana: University of Illinois Press, 1951; rev. ed., 1964.

Raymond, Henry J. *The Life and Public Services of Abraham Lincoln, Sixteenth President of the United States, Together with his State Papers,* etc. New York: Derby and Miller, Publishers, 1865.

Rehnquist, William H. *All the Laws but One: Civil Liberties in Wartime.* New York: Alfred A. Knopf, 1998.

Reid, John Phillip; Michael Les Benedict, Don E. Fehrenbacher, James M. McPherson, Harry N. Scheiber, Stanley I. Kutler. *Essays in the History of Liberty: Seaver Institute Lectures at the Huntington Library.* San Marino, CA: Huntington Library and Art Gallery, 1988.

Rosin, Wilbert Henry. "Hamilton Rowan Gamble: Missouri's Civil War Governor." Ph.D. diss., University of Missouri, 1960.

Ryle, Walter H. *Missouri: Union or Secession.* Nashville: George Peabody College for Teachers, 1931.

Sanders, Charles W., Jr. *While in the Hands of the Enemy: Military Prisons of the Civil War.* Baton Rouge: Louisiana State University Press, 2005.

Schofield, John M. *Forty-six Years in the Army,* with a foreword by William M. Ferraro. New York: Century Co., 1897; reprint, Norman: University of Oklahoma Press, 1998.

Schurz, Carl. *The Reminiscences of Carl Schurz.* Vol. 3, with a sketch of his life and public services from 1869 to 1906 by Frederic Bancroft and William A. Dunning. New York: McClure Company, 1908.

Shalhope, Robert E. *Sterling Price: Portrait of a Southerner.* Columbia: University of Missouri Press, 1971.

Sherman, William T. *Memoirs of General W. T. Sherman.* New York: Library of America, 1990.

Sinisi, Kyle S. *Sacred Debts: State Civil War Claims and American Federalism, 1861–1880.* New York: Fordham University Press, 2003.

Snead, Thomas L. *The Fight for Missouri: From the Election of Lincoln to the Death of Lyon.* New York: Charles Scribner's Sons, 1886.

———. "The First Year of the War in Missouri." *Battles and Leaders of the Civil War,* ed. Robert Underwood Johnson and Clarence Clough Buel, 4 vols. Vol. 1. Secaucus, NJ: Castle, n.d.

Sprague, Dean. *Freedom under Lincoln.* Boston: Riverside Press Cambridge, 1965.

Stevens, Walter B. *Missouri, the Central State, 1821–1915.* Chicago and St. Louis: S. J. Clarke Publishing, 1915.

Stillwell, Leander. *The Story of a Common Soldier of Army Life in the Civil War, 1861–1865.* 2d ed. Kansas City, MO: Franklin Hudson, 1920.

Stuart, Captain A. A. *Iowa Colonels and Regiments: Being a History of Iowa Regiments in the War of the Rebellion and Containing a Description of the Battles in Which They Have Fought.* Des Moines: Mills and Company, 1865.

Switzler, William F. *Switzler's Illustrated History of Missouri from 1541 to 1877.* St. Louis: C. R. Barns, editor and publisher, 1879.

Tap, Bruce. *Over Lincoln's Shoulder: The Committee on the Conduct of the War.* Lawrence: University Press of Kansas, 1998.

Valentine, Mary T. *The Biography of Ephraim McDowell, M.D.: "The Father of Ovariotomy."* Second edition. Philadelphia: by the author, 1894.

Vander Velde, Lewis G. *The Presbyterian Churches and the Federal Union: 1861–1869.* Cambridge: Harvard University Press, and London: Humphrey Milford, Oxford University Press, 1932.

Vattel, Emmerich de. *The Law of Nations: or Principles of the Laws of Nature applied to the Conduct and Affairs of Nations and Sovereigns.* Trans. Joseph Chitty and with additional notes and references by Edward D. Ingraham. Philadelphia: T. and J. W. Johnson and Company, Law Booksellers, 1883.

Williams, Frank J. "Abraham Lincoln and Civil Liberties: Then and Now." In *Lincoln Revisited: New Insights from the Lincoln Forum,* ed. John Y. Simon, Harold Holzer, and Dawn Vogel. New York: Fordham University Press, 2007.

Wilson, Jerry E. "Willard Preble Hall (1820–1882)," *Dictionary of Missouri Biography,* ed. Lawrence O. Christensen, William E. Foley, Gary R. Kremer, and Kenneth H. Winn. Columbia: University of Missouri Press, 1999.

Winter, William C. *The Civil War in St. Louis.* St. Louis: Missouri Historical Society Press, 1994, reprint 1995.

Woolsey, Theodore Dwight. *Introduction to the Study of International Law Designed as an Aid in Teaching and in Historical Studies.* Revised and enlarged by Theodore Salisbury Woolsey. New York: Charles Scribner's Sons, 1871; 6th ed, 1892.

Young, John Russell. *Around the World with General Grant: A Narrative of the Visit of General U. S. Grant, Ex-president of the United States, to Various Countries in Europe, Asia, and Africa in 1877, 1878, 1879 to Which Are Added Certain Conversations with General Grant on Questions Connected with American Politics and History.* Vol. 2: New York: Subscription Book Department, the American News Company, 1879.

Index